# Lecture Notes in Computer Science 13219

More information about this series at https://link.springer.com/bookseries/558

Upinder Dhar · Jigyasu Dubey ·
Vinod Dumblekar · Sebastiaan Meijer ·
Heide Lukosch (Eds.)

# Gaming, Simulation and Innovations

## Challenges and Opportunities

52nd International Simulation
and Gaming Association Conference, ISAGA 2021
Indore, India, September 6–10, 2021
Revised Selected Papers

 Springer

*Editors*
Upinder Dhar ⓘ
Shri Vaishnav Vidyapeeth Vishwavidyalaya
Indore, Madhya Pradesh, India

Jigyasu Dubey ⓘ
Shri Vaishnav Vidyapeeth Vishwavidyalaya
Indore, India

Vinod Dumblekar ⓘ
Mantis
New Delhi, Delhi, India

Sebastiaan Meijer ⓘ
KTH Royal Institute of Technology
Stockholm, Stockholms Län, Sweden

Heide Lukosch ⓘ
University of Canterbury
Christchurch, New Zealand

ISSN 0302-9743        ISSN 1611-3349 (electronic)
Lecture Notes in Computer Science
ISBN 978-3-031-09958-8        ISBN 978-3-031-09959-5 (eBook)
https://doi.org/10.1007/978-3-031-09959-5

This Springer imprint is published by the registered company Springer Nature Switzerland AG
The registered company address is: Gewerbestrasse 11, 6330 Cham, Switzerland

# Preface

This collection of selected articles is the culmination of our long journey that began in August 2019 in Warsaw, Poland, when the International Simulation and Gaming Association (ISAGA) assigned us the responsibility of organizing the international conference in 2020 at Shri Vaishnav Vidyapeeth Vishwavidyalaya (SVVV), Indore, India. In early 2020, the COVID-19 pandemic stopped us in our tracks. By the time we had agreed to a hybrid conference, the pandemic had grown faster and more severe, preventing us from a hosting the conference that year.

Both SVVV and ISAGA are grateful that the collaboration continued, allowing us to hold the conference the next year, i.e., 2021. Taking into account the lockdown on international travel and other pandemic restrictions, we organized ISAGA 2021 at SVVV in online mode. We had expert speakers, research papers, workshops, poster presentations, and a round table discussion. Every day of the conference was flush with keynote speakers who covered a specialist theme in simulations and games (S&G). ISAGA 2021 was a product of less-than-ideal circumstances, but our speakers and other contributors made it a memorable experience for the participants.

S&G entertains and enables participants to test theories, create policies, make decisions, and draw conclusions from interactions and other experiences. S&G covers more content in less time, thus helping the participants to learn much faster than other learning practices. S&G offers challenges, mysteries, and problems that produce high levels of satisfaction and engagement in the participants. You will find such themes in this collection of articles that were presented by the authors at ISAGA 2021.

The articles have been collated into four sections, each of six chapters, for the convenience of the readers. The section on Gaming in Education has chapters on pedagogy, sustainability, and bio-safety. The section on Player Experience in Simulations has chapters on player satisfaction, learning style, and changing moods. The section on Policy Formulation and Serious Games has chapters on natural resources, urban resilience, and waste reduction. Finally, the section on Game Design and Facilitation has chapters on structured instruction, professional training, and mediated environments.

The tasks of review, assessment, timely communication, and other parts of the article publication process have been stupendous. We are grateful to the anonymous reviewers of the manuscripts whose work ensured the high quality of this post-proceedings. We thank the authors not only for their contributions to ISAGA 2021 but also for making the speedy changes to their manuscripts. We wish to thank our publisher, Springer, who has produced compilations of earlier ISAGA post-proceedings under their Lecture Notes in Computer Science (LNCS) series and is doing so again for ISAGA 2021.

This compilation contains the global expertise, considered opinions, and wisdom of the best thinkers, researchers, and practitioners in S&G. I am sure the contents will be useful to you and will provoke further thoughts, discussion, and action.

May 2022

Upinder  Dhar
Jigyasu  Dubey
Vinod  Dumblekar
Sebastiaan  Meijer
Heide  Lukosch

# Organization

## Conference Chair

Upinder Dhar                          SVVV, India

## Conference Coordinators

Jigyasu Dubey                         SVVV, India
Vinod Dumblekar                       MANTIS, India

## ISAGA Chairs

Heide Lukosch                         University of Canterbury, New Zealand
Sebastiaan Meijer                     KTH Royal Institute of Technology, Sweden

## Technical Support

Anand Rajavat                         SVVV, India

## Program Committee

Upinder Dhar                          SVVV, India
Vinod Dumblekar                       MANTIS, India
Heide Lukosch                         University of Canterbury, New Zealand
Sebastiaan Meijer                     KTH Royal Institute of Technology, Stockholm,
                                          Sweden
Elyssebeth Leigh                      FuTureSearch, Australia
Ivo Wenzler                           NHL Stenden University of Applied Sciences,
                                          The Netherlands
Toshiko Kikkawa                       Keio University, Japan
Yusuke Toyoda                         Ritsumeikan University, Japan
Ramesh Sharma                         Ambedkar University Delhi, India
J. Tuomas Harviainen                  Tampere University, Finland
Elena Likhacheva                      M.V. Lomonosov Moscow State University,
                                          Russia
Pieter van der Hijden                 Sofos Consultancy, The Netherlands
Pongchai Dumrongrojwatthana           Chulalongkorn University, Thailand
Marcus Watson                         University of Queensland, The Queensland
Hidehiko Kanegae                      Ritsumeikan University, Japan

Sandeep Athavale            TCS, India
David Wortley                360in360 Immersive Experiences/Independent
                             Consultant, UK

## Local Organizing Committee

Upinder Dhar            SVVV, India
Jigyasu Dubey           SVVV, India
Santosh Dhar            SVVV, India
Rajeev Shukla           SVVV, India
Anand Rajavat           SVVV, India
Tushar Kanti Mandal     SVVV, India
Namit Gupta             SVVV, India
K. N. Guruprasad        SVVV, India
Vinod Dhar              SVVV, India
Uttam Sharma            SVVV, India
Kavita Sharma           SVVV, India

# Contents

# Game Design and Facilitation

# Bring Joy to Gamers: Adding Renewable Energy Alternative through Sustainable Development Indicators

Shoeib Faraji Abdolmaleki(✉) ⓘ, Yesodharan Vaisakh,
and Pastora Maria Bello Bugallo ⓘ

TECH-NASE Research Group, School of Engineering (ETSE), Universidade de Santiago de Compostela Avda. Lope Gomez de Marzoa s/n 15782, Santiago de Compostela, Spain
shoeib.faraji@rai.usc.es

**Abstract.** This study aims to identify the indicators with the potential to be used in video games by using the concept of sustainable development through Renewable Energy (RE) sustainability assessment. A systematic review performs to gather the key indicators. Also, this study seeks to increase players' awareness about the role of RE in real life and expands the game appealing to sustainability. In this study, the game named TOWNSHIP™ is employed to evaluate if we can include RE and sustainability assessment concepts to use as a tool for sustainable development consciousness to the public. The work evaluates the availability of environmental, economic, social, technical, and governmental indicators in the game (capacity, aptitudes, and attractive options). First, from an existing inventory of sustainable indicators, more compatible ones for RE are selected. Second, with the help of expert viewpoints, potential indicators are picked for the game. Finally, from the analysis of the game structure, some scenarios were constructed, and the game run in an assumption atmosphere. The study concludes the video game's potential for sustainable development indicators in RE and advances recommendations for improving the game's attractiveness through updated options.

**Keywords:** Video game · Renewable energy · Sustainable development · Sustainability indicators · Gaming

## 1 Introduction

Today, to develop a video game in addition to the graphic quality that requires a high level of distinctive processor systems and platforms, creating content in games is also of particular importance. In the world of video games, developers try to measure the players' interest by using polls in the databases and platforms (e.g., Play Store which makes these games available for everyone), so they can make positive changes in these games by reviewing different feedbacks. A quick look at the participation of players and gamers in the polls can show how much the audience cares about the quality of the products they receive.

© Springer Nature Switzerland AG 2022
U. Dhar et al. (Eds.): ISAGA 2021, LNCS 13219, pp. 3–14, 2022.
https://doi.org/10.1007/978-3-031-09959-5_1

The necessity to create a game could be fueled by a variety of backgrounds. For example, a game can be developed for the sole purpose of entertainment, education (e.g., [1, 2]), understanding a process (e.g., [3, 4]), motivational issues, or considering all of these parameters (e.g., [5]). Meanwhile, games that have been produced for educational purposes to raise the awareness of the audience with concepts that are substantial such as energy transition, climate change, engineering process, etc., are in the stage of growth and development [6–10] (e.g., using RE as a game concept). A review of the existing literature shows that despite many efforts, the amount of games produced in this field is growing and the use of basic concepts, frameworks, and ultimately the target audience is in its infancy.

RE considers a solution and a concept for sustainable development [11], and its role has rarely been seen in video games. In addition to a small number of video games (based on Scopus and Web of Science platforms investigation) in which RE is part of the overall game process (e.g., [1, 8], and [12]), there are several simulations game (e.g., [6]) and serious games (e.g., [13]). Therefore, it needs to investigate the role of RE in a video game by designing a valid route, considering diverse terms and options. Then, we can expect that involving this notion in games will assist in boosting not only people's understanding but also the enjoyment of the game.

Therefore, this study examines the potential of sustainable development indicators (as options and terms) in RE in the form of video games. Also, it considers a type of video game that has a high quality, which gives some suggestions on creating game attractiveness based on enhanced options.

## 2 Indicators and Frameworks

Since RE is perceived as a crucial pathway to Sustainable Development (SD), its assessment is critical for SD Goals (SDGs). Some SDGs have an excellent connection with RE. For instance, SDG-7 (refer to ensuring access to affordable, reliable, sustainable, and modern energy for all) and SDG-13 (refer to taking urgent action to combat climate change and its impacts) are some examples [14]. As a result, successful implementation of a RE system can affect these SDGs outlines. In achieving SDGs, more effort than current policies and approaches is required. It is especially true in the energy sector, as energy is a necessary component of all development operations.

Many efforts have done to shape this idea to analyze the long-term development of a system. Sustainability assessments are conducted by SD frameworks, which is one of the essential factors. It is a logical design on which the indicators are based [15]. A framework is a high-level, direct reference to SD principles [16]. Many national and international legal frameworks have been created around the idea of designating energy sources such as renewable or non-renewable, and RE has become a dominating concept in energy policies. RE is designed to be firmly associated with the sustainability and successful mitigation of climate change in public discourse [17].

Besides, analysts and decision-makers at the local, national, and international levels can use indicators to gain a deeper understanding of the SD circumstances and trends, the effects of policies, as well as the long-term consequences of policy changes [18]. Indicators can provide a numerical value for the sustainability level and highlight all dimensions so that the users can compare the sustainability of different systems and select the most appropriate one with the lowest costs. The users also must determine if the benefit of a RE system exceeds its costs if it is more attractive than other systems, and a numerical value helps simplify their assessment and decision-making [19]. Furthermore, it provides a broad picture of whether governments have made sufficient progress toward SD plans and goals [20].

Indicator selection is vital to recognizing SD dimensions. In addition to the three main pillars of SD (environment, economic, and social), this study investigates the government's role and technical properties (i.e. by considering governmental and technical indicators in the RE sector). The study of ref [21] was followed to collect SD indicators for RE's evaluation, in which environmental, economic, social, governmental, and technological indicators were found by comprehensive literature analysis. The authors in ref [21] used the high-frequency indicators found in the RE and SD literature to choose the most important indicators in each dimension. Table 1 gathered up a list of indicators in each dimension.

**Table 1.** The most important indicators for RE sustainability assessment [21]

| Dimension | Indicators |
|---|---|
| Environmental | $CO_2$ emission, land use, impact on ecosystem, $NO_x$, and $SO_x$ emission, GHG emission reduction, particle emission, noise, need for waste disposal, and emission generally. |
| Economic | Investment cost, operation and maintenance cost, energy cost, fuel cost, payback period, net present value, service life, cost of capital, generation cost per unit, GDP, and employment rate |
| Social | social acceptability, job creation, social benefit, impact on health, compatibility with political and legislative situation international obligation, public awareness and willingness, availability, R&D, government support |
| Technical | Efficiency, reliability, resource availability, maturity, safety, primary energy ratio, feasibility, continuity and predictability of performance, capacity factor, and innovativeness |
| Governmental | Legal regulation of activity, government support, political stability, absence of violence/terrorism, control of corruption, the efficiency of subsidy for the feed-in tariff, compliance with international obligations, and influence on sustainable development of energy |

# 3 Material and Methods

## 3.1 Introducing a Capable Video Game

This study uses a game as an example to better comprehend the use of indicators. TOWN-SHIP™ is a free-to-play city-building game developed by "Playrix" that is accessible on various platforms. In this game, players can design their fantasy city according to their preferences using the game's choices. Building infrastructure, harvesting crops, mining, and trading are some of the game's most well-known elements. This game gives a core natural environment that players can personalize to their liking. The game's architecture allows players to develop cause-and-effect links with basic life ideas such as environmental awareness, economic relations, and social understanding, all while having fun with the game's options.

### 3.2 Hypothesizing and Assumptions

Using an existing video game provides the necessary foundations (e.g., a huge animation base, a high-performance technical staff to support new game options, a large fan number, etc.) to add new concepts and to realize whether players can get satisfied with the new features through online polls. However, this is an intellectual test to expand the concept of SD and the use of RE. Also to use a video game, this study follows the results of some scientific works. For two decades, scholars find out that video games bring happiness to players. For example, Przybylski et al. (2010) investigated that "video games have the potential to enhance intrinsic motivation and short-term well-being insofar as they provide players with experiences that satisfy universal psychological needs" [22]. Johnson et al. (2013) reviewed the role of video games and well-being. Their findings indicate a variety of advantages to playing video games, regardless of their substance. Then, playing video games can lead to improvements in mood, stress reduction, and emotions of competence and autonomy, among other things [23].

To engage the RE with this game, if we apply the concept of energy (energy transition) and sustainable development to the structure of this game, then we can use the capacity of indicators in this game as smart options. This study also omits the various perspectives on sustainable development (such as the triple button line) because it simply wants to discuss the role of indicators as in-game options.

Moreover, it is assumed that Table 1 provides a sufficient number of appropriate indicators for this study. This study assumes that all indicators are on an equal footing in the game to make it easy to use them.

Furthermore, like other features of this game, the RE has equal wealth. For example, just as a dairy factory, poultry, and other industries are essential for a city and a community, RE is also required. By following this supposition, the game forces players to follow sustainable development solutions for the energy supply of the city as well as utilizing RE.

### 3.3 Framework of the Study

This study presents a direction regarding the indicators selection and implementation through a game with excellent graphical quality and basic potential to add RE and SD definitions to utilize indicators in this game and evaluate the game's enjoyment.

Five experts were invited to create the game's key performance indicators, ensuring that they were well-versed in RE, SD, and sustainability indicators. They are also the ones who have played the game and are familiar with the gam's atmosphere. As a result, a questionnaire was created based on the data in Table 1 and the question of which indicators may be used in the game was posed. They then answered by evaluating two conditions: 1) what are the most essential indications, and 2) which indicators can be more consistent with the game's framework.

The essential information for the initial selection of indicators was acquired based on the opinions of five specialists (Fig. 1).

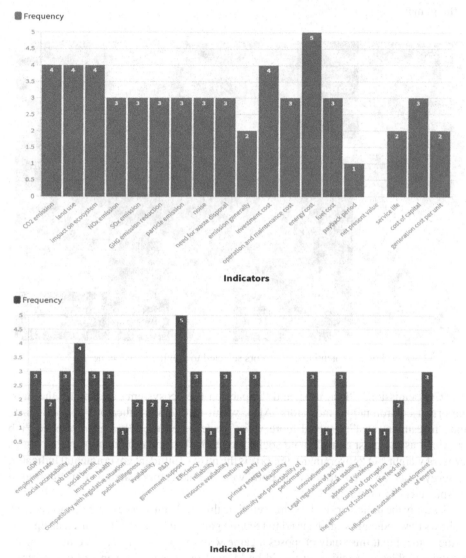

**Fig. 1.** Considering expert viewpoints regarding selecting indicators for the game (top and down)

According to this, they determined that 43 of the 48 accessible indicators possessed the necessary capacities. The next stage was to construct a condition so that a more appropriate set of indicators could be selected for use in the game with higher confidence in all opinions to achieve common ground amongst expert perspectives. As a result, indicators were chosen on which at least 60% of experts agreed. In other words, at least three of them must agree on a particular indicator. Finally, a total of 26 indicators were discovered. A hierarchical diagram of the selected indicators is shown in Fig. 2. Regarding this, nine environmental indicators, six economic indicators, four social indicators, four technical indicators, and three government indicators were finalized to use in the game.

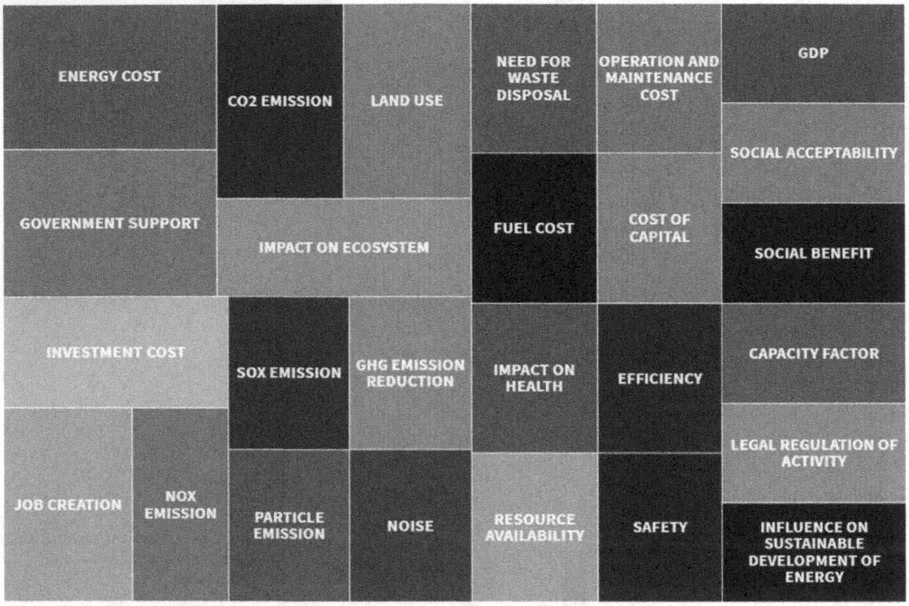

**Fig. 2.** Potentiated indicators selected to employ in the game

"CO$_2$ emission," "land use," and "impact on the ecosystem" are among the most important environmental indicators. Also, within economic indicators, "energy cost" and "investment cost" received more votes. Experts, on the other hand, ranked "job creation" as the most considerable social indicator. Technical indicators are on par in terms of weight, but "government support" is the most significant governmental indicator. "Energy costs" and "government support" were the indicators that drew the attention of all specialists (5 out of 5).

To apply the indicators in the game ventricle this study introduces a flowchart (Fig. 3). It shows how indicators can be used to feed the game and how they'll be used as options in the game. First, this study proposes a game with the possibility of selecting environmental variables (e.g., this city would be located on which continent) to demonstrate how a city's sustainability differs from one location to another. The level of sustainability for this hypothetical city gauges all the time in step 2 using the various terms and conditions that this game can add to its framework. For example, the game can assess the city's sustainability using SD criteria (environmental, social, economic, and so on) and approaches based on Multi-Criteria-Decision-Making (MCDM) to measure the sustainability level. The game then proposes a form of RE as a solution to the sustainability challenge in the issue of energy generation (wind, solar, bioenergy, hydropower, etc.). There is a range of terms that it is possible to employ to demonstrate how the game can provide some form of RE (step 3). For example, the amount of money (a player has earned while playing the game), the levels of the game, etc. The game will begin the RE sustainability evaluation after a player selected RE type(s) in step 4 (with the conditions in step 2). The game will check again if there is non-compliance with the utilization of RE and SD. If it was not sustainable at that time, the game refers to step 2 for further investigation. If the condition was sustainable, the game considers more indicators in each dimension to offer more RE options during the time-play and game stages.

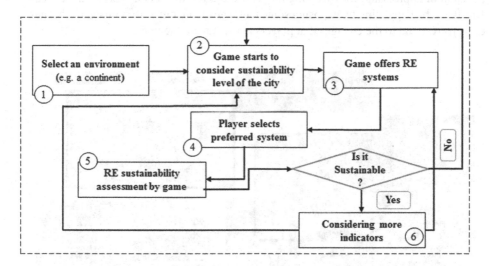

**Fig. 3.** SD indicators selection and implementation for the video game

### 3.4  Scenarios for Indicator Selection Within the Game

While renewables are very environmentally sound, the use of land (onshore or off-shore) for establishing a renewable structure can be a negative factor. Players can choose the RE option to secure the city's energy if the game offers several RE types to supply energy for manufacturing, housing, transportation, and other sectors related to the game's environment. However, players need to be careful about their budget, the size of RE (i.e., land use for renewable system implementation), and $CO_2$ emissions. Besides, the measure of power plant effect on surroundings, visual impact, manufacturing waste recycling, and primary greenhouse gas emission can represent other beneficial environmental indicators (Fig. 4).

Instead of sending messages to show players what they need and what the condition is, the government in this game (which is defined to control the game as an intelligent element) can support the idea of RE implementation and examine whether players are eligible to apply a type of RE. Therefore, the indicators introduced in Fig. 4 (government role) can be used in this game.

In this game, the criteria that affect the city's energy supply, such as the efficiency of a RE system, capacity, resource availability, and feasibility, can be realized as technical indicator possibilities. Technical indicators provide gamers with alternatives for determining which RE system is best to use throughout game stages. Players will be considered as decision-makers in RE system selection because this game has a dynamic concept.

People in each community affect government and vice versa. Therefore, society can ask about what they want. Then, they should be satisfied whit the RE type installed while it brings them benefits like job creation. The social indicators in Fig. 4 can aid in the decision of appropriate RE by taking into consideration the social aspects that concern RE. It can be happening by exposing some messages from citizens in this game because citizens respond to the changes that players apply during the game.

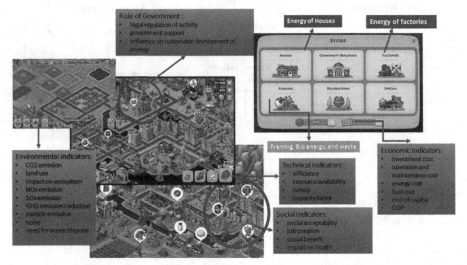

**Fig. 4.** Implementing selected indicators for the video game[1]

Finally, the economic situation of the game (i.e., the amount of money that players earn through each economic activity like selling products and mining) can control most of the activities that are happening in the game. Investment cost, as an economic indicator, includes all types of expenses. Hence, players can choose the appropriate RE type for their budget over time based on their financial resources. In the same way, for other economic indicators, we can make different scenarios to consider the sustainability of RE while gaming.

---

[1] In this study, a few snapshots were taken of the game (from Playrix-TOWNSHIP™: https://www.playrix.com/games/township) so that to present the game space and deal with some options in the form of indicators.

# 4 Results and Discussion

One of the goals of any game development company can be to create popular and enjoyable games. This study introduces how the scientific definition of RE can contribute to a video game. Therefore, a game is selected to see which interconnections exist between sustainability indicators and game options. After identifying the indicators of sustainable development in RE, the structure of the game will be assessed for SD and RE with available sustainable indicators.

Video games have the potential to be an extremely effective tool for telling stories. Furthermore, gamers have a pivotal role in the video game storyline as they are required to make decisions that affect the game route and atmosphere [22]. In this study, gamers are encouraged to not only have fun while playing, but also to learn about the game's possibilities through trial and error, paying fees, and completing RE tasks freely. Also, they serve as a process designer by providing crucial concepts (i.e., SD and RE).

Nowadays, a significant shift toward more sustainable energy systems is required. So, it needs both the utilization of renewable energy sources and comprehensive approaches that take into account cost reductions, energy efficiency, and institutional innovation [24]. This game is assumed to provide a geographical area for the game world and use environmental, economic, social, technical, and governmental indicators to select a renewable power plant. In this way, after playing a few times, the player realizes the importance of the indicators and can try to make the fitting choice, which is done in the real world using complex mathematical algorithms and methods such as MCDM. Citizens who have a minimum awareness of RE sources are more effective partners in increasingly complicated power economies and political decisions in general [1].

Developing various scientific strategies and scenarios can boost the attraction option of the game and player awareness. In this regard, Magnussen et al. in 2013 studied scientific discovery games for authentic science education. This study aimed to investigate how a scientific game concept can strengthen authentic experimental practice and create new science, education, and the elements that play a central role in such a game. They discovered that by collaborating with academics and participants in the research (where both are highly motivating features), games are commonly utilized in education to drive students to engage in instructional activities [25]. For instance, by increasing the level of knowledge (by designing a school and a university in TOWNSHIP™) and boosting the research level and development (R&D) as an indicator (Table 1), it is possible to create updates in renewable power plants while playing. It requires incorporating a component within the game, such as a university, which will display messages on the screen to assist players in determining whether or not to play the game depending on RE choices and energy conditions. Therefore, they can expect the amount of energy produced to increase the financial benefit of gameplay. Also, players are highly motivated by scientific discovery games and the fact that they allow them to participate in scientific investigations [25]. The video gaming industry is expanding at a breakneck pace, attracting the attention of gamers of all ages. Thanks to advanced graphics processors and innovations in software programming and computing platforms, modern games provide appealing and often odd worlds to explore, escape from, and enjoy. As a result, the majority of individuals spend a good deal of time engrossed in the gaming world. Furthermore, many people will devote a significant amount of time to perfecting their gaming abilities, learning the gaming environment, and inventing tools to aid them in their game success ([26] and [27]).

There is a vast literature to argue about the enjoyment of a video game. Some of the critical enjoyment attributes, this research concludes game world, storyline, characters, music, quality assurance, challenge, competition, art design, and graphics (e.g., [28–32]). Hence, if we add a new definition to an existing game, we can anticipate that new challenges added to the game. Therefore, players will face circumstances to solve the requirement by their decisions. So that is true if we apply SD and RE to the structure of a high-quality game. The concept of SD and RE should be a concern for the people while they are living in an era in which problems like climate change, natural security, energy production-transition, and economy are human being significant affairs. As a result, subjoining SD indicators to RE can convey some of the enjoyment features of video games. The game environment, for example, must provide space, or at least a perception of space, that encourages the player to explore. Therefore, including such a unique idea can enjoy the game and acquaint the audience with vital concepts. Also, each game must target a range of abilities, so the combination of experiences required to solve a game problem must progress incrementally [33]. It is envisaged that players get involved with the new idea deeply. Besides, incentives must be adequate for the mix of abilities and skill levels required to complete a gaming problem or challenge, which TOWNSHIP™ already uses this system of rewarding.

Thus, as can be seen from the examples, this study aims to increase the excitement by considering new ideas and capabilities of a game. However, it remains a profound investigation of other enjoyment factors; the emotion of joy, for instance, is out of this study's scope.

This study believes that the collaboration between academic and game companies can bring new ideas for games features. Also, it suggests that the conceptual frameworks in sustainability assessments should examine to create different scenarios. Therefore, various updates, different versions, and more attractive options can be provided for the future of this type of game.

## 5   Conclusion

This study provides a quick assessment of the potentiated sustainability indicators toward RE to investigate the hypothetic options that increase video game attraction. Considering environmental, economic, social, technical, and government drivers, this study came up with attractive proposals that create the right atmosphere for players. The relationship between the indicators and RE has examined as well as the creation of appropriate items to increase the status of the game. The results demonstrate that including a new impression in the game with sustainability ideas can level up the novel challenges. In this regard, some assumptions include assessing the ability of the game to adopt the innovative implication. Enjoyment factors consider both the game's structure (e.g., high graphic base) and new concept's capacity (e.g., bringing new challenges). Hence, it supposes that the pleasure of playing will increase due to these prospects, and players will be more associated with the concepts of sustainable development and RE after repeating this game. Despite the lack of high-quality video games focusing on RE, this study recommends using games that can combine this content. Also, to find the best scenarios in this game and better influence the game structure, it is necessary to evaluate sustainability frameworks.

# References

1. Cohen, M.A., Niemeyer, G.O., Callaway, D.S.: Griddle: video gaming for power system education. IEEE Trans. Power Syst. **32**(4), 3069–3077 (2017). https://doi.org/10.1109/TPWRS.2016.2618887
2. Li, H., Chabay, I., Renn, O., Weber, A., Mbungu, G.: Exploring smart grids with simulations in a mobile science exhibition. Energy, Sustainability and Society **5**(1), 1–8 (2015). https://doi.org/10.1186/s13705-015-0066-4
3. Robledo, J., Leloux, J., Lorenzo, E., Gueymard, C.A.: From video games to solar energy: 3D shading simulation for PV using GPU. Sol. Energy **193**(March), 962–980 (2019). https://doi.org/10.1016/j.solener.2019.09.041
4. Schauppenlehner, T., Graf, C., Latosinska, B., Roth, M.: Entwicklung einer neuen Schnittstelle für Mensch- Maschinen-Interaktion im Kontext raumbezogener partizipativer Prozesse, pp. 13–22 (2020). https://doi.org/10.14627/537698002.Dieser
5. Prilenska, V.: Serious game for modelling neighbourhood energy supply scenarios. IOP Conf. Ser. Earth Environ. Sci. **410**(1) (2020). https://doi.org/10.1088/1755-1315/410/1/012091
6. Ouariachi, T., Elving, W.: Accelerating the energy transition through serious gaming: testing effects on awareness, knowledge and efficacy beliefs. Electron. J. e-Learning **18**(5), 410–420 (2020). https://doi.org/10.34190/JEL.18.5.004
7. Dresner, M.: Changing energy end-use patterns as a means of reducing global-warming trends. J. Environ. Educ. **21**(2), 41–46 (1990). https://doi.org/10.1080/00958964.1990.9941930
8. Ouariachi, T., Elving, W., Pierie, F.: Playing for a Sustainable Future: The Case of We Energy Game as an Educational Practice. Sustainability **10**(10), 3639 (2018). https://doi.org/10.3390/su10103639. Oct.
9. Street, G.: Serious Games for Eco-Effective Transformations. In: Thirty Eighth International Conference on Information Systems. South Korea (2017). no. December
10. Gerber, A., Ulrich, M., Wäger, P.: Review of Haptic and Computerized (Simulation) Games on Climate Change. In: Wardaszko, Marcin, Meijer, Sebastiaan, Lukosch, Heide, Kanegae, Hidehiko, Kriz, Willy Christian, Grzybowska-Brzezińska, Mariola (eds.) ISAGA 2019. LNCS, vol. 11988, pp. 275–289. Springer, Cham (2021). https://doi.org/10.1007/978-3-030-72132-9_24
11. Wang, Y., Zhang, D., Ji, Q., Shi, X.: Regional renewable energy development in China: A multidimensional assessment. Renew. Sustain. Energy Rev. **124** (May 2020). https://doi.org/10.1016/j.rser.2020.109797
12. Khatib, T., et al.: Development of DAYSAM: An educational smartphone game for preschoolers to increase awareness of renewable energy. Sustain. **13**(1), 1–23 (2021). https://doi.org/10.3390/su13010433
13. Ouariachi, T.: Understanding the urgency and complexities of the energy transition through serious gaming. In: 18th European Conference on e-Learning, pp. 461–466 (2019). https://doi.org/10.34190/EEL.19.002
14. European Commission: Communication from the commission to the European parliament, the council, the European economic and social committee and the committee of the regions, Next steps for a sustainable European future, European action for sustainability (2016). [Online]. Available: https://eur-lex.europa.eu/legal-content/EN/ALL/?uri=CELEX%3A52012DC0673

15. Kristle Nathan, H.S., Sudhakara Reddy, B.: A conceptual framework for development of sustainable development indicators. Mumbai (2008). [Online]. Available: http://www.igidr. ac.in/pdf/publication/WP-2008-003.pdf
16. Pintér, L., Hardi, P., Bartelmus, P.: Sustainable development indicators: proposals for the way forward. Int. Inst. Sustain. Dev. New York, USA, pp. 1–35 (2005). [Online]. Available: https:// www.iisd.org/system/files/publications/measure_indicators_sd_way_forward.pd
17. Harjanne, A., Korhonen, J.M.: Abandoning the concept of renewable energy. Energy Policy **127**, 330–340 (2019). https://doi.org/10.1016/j.enpol.2018.12.029. Apr.
18. Anna, B.: Classification of the European Union member states according to the relative level of sustainable development. Qual. Quant. **50**(6), 2591–2605 (2016). https://doi.org/10.1007/ s11135-015-0278-x. Nov.
19. Liu, G.: Development of a general sustainability indicator for renewable energy systems: A review. Renewable and Sustainable Energy Reviews. Elsevier Ltd. **31**, 611–621 (2014). https://doi.org/10.1016/j.rser.2013.12.038
20. Unander, F.: Energy indicators and sustainable development: the international energy agency approach. Nat. Resour. Forum **29**(4), 377–391 (2005). https://doi.org/10.1111/j.1477-8947. 2005.00148.x
21. Abdolmaleki, S.F., Bello Bugallo, P.M.: Evaluation of renewable energy system for sustainable development. presented in World Renewable Energy Congress (2021)
22. Przybylski, A.K., Rigby, C.S., Ryan, R.M.: A motivational model of video game engagement. Rev. Gen. Psychol. **14**(2), 154–166 (2010). https://doi.org/10.1037/a0019440
23. Johnson, D., Scholes, L., Carras, M.C.: Videogames and wellbeing: a comprehensive review. CRC Young and Well and PAX Australia (2013)
24. Duke, R., Geurts, J.L.: Policy Games for Strategic Management: Pathways into the Unknown. Dutch University Press, Amsterdam, p. 54 (2004)
25. Magnussen, R., Sidse Damgaard, H., Planke, T.: Scientific Discovery Games for Authentic Science Education. In: 7th European Conference on Games Based Learning, pp. 344–351 (2013)
26. Arrasmith, W.W.: Video game knowledge modules for higher education and technology learning, assessment, and certification. In: 5th international technology, education and development conference, pp. 4195–4204 (2011)
27. Wells, D., Fotaris, P.: Game-based learning in schools: trainee teacher perceptions in implementing gamified approaches. In: European conference on games based learning (ECGBL), pp. 754–762 (2017)
28. Wirth, W., Ryffel, F., von Pape, T., Karnowski, V.: The development of video game enjoyment in a role playing game, Cyberpsychology. Behav. Soc. Netw. **16**(4), 260–264 (2013). https:// doi.org/10.1089/cyber.2012.0159. Apr.
29. Halbrook, Y.J., O'Donnell, A.T., Msetfi, R.M.: When and how video games can be good: a review of the positive effects of video games on well-being. Perspect. Psychol. Sci. **14**(6), 1096–1104 (2019). https://doi.org/10.1177/1745691619863807. Nov.
30. Klimmt, C., Blake, C., Hefner, D., Vorderer, P., Roth, C.: Player Performance, Satisfaction, and Video Game Enjoyment. In: Natkin, Stéphane., Dupire, Jérôme. (eds.) ICEC 2009. LNCS, vol. 5709, pp. 1–12. Springer, Heidelberg (2009). https://doi.org/10.1007/978-3-642-04052-8_1
31. Vorderer, P., Hartmann, T., Klimmt, C.: Explaining the enjoyment of playing video games: the role of competition. In: second international conference on Entertainment computing, pp. 1–9 (2003)
32. Klimmen, C.: Dimensions and determinants of the enjoyment of playing digital games: A three-level model. Faculty of Arts, Utrecht University, Utrecht, p. 257 (2003)
33. Kadle, A.: 9 Essential Elements for Fun in Games. UPSID learning (2011). https://www.ups idelearning.com/blog/2011/01/31/9-essential-elements-for-fun-in-games/

# The Effects of Structured Instruction on Team Performance

Mieko Nakamura[✉]

Ryutsu Keizai University, Ryugasaki 3018555, Ibaraki, Japan
mnakamura@rku.ac.jp

**Abstract.** Unpacking is one way to reduce bias in team planning. In a simulation game, a facilitator can ask a few questions before the game. Unpacking is occasionally a facilitator's role, although it does not necessarily enhance team performance. This study adds a thought-provoking question that requests participants to disclose the reasoning behind the estimation. Such structured instructions generate serious discussion in a team. Individual levels of understanding and outcome prediction were examined and the effect of the structured instruction about the process of the participants' estimations was analysed. To disclose the reasoning, participants needed to search for related information and perform calculations. This deepened their level of understanding, made their predictions reasonable and improved their team profit.

**Keywords:** Facilitator's role · Production management game · Structured instruction · Team planning · Unpacking

## 1 Introduction

### 1.1 General Review

At the beginning of simulation & gaming (S&G), instructions with information about rules, roles, alternatives, among others, are given to participants. One of the facilitator's roles is to help participants navigate this plethora of information and be ready for action. When participants work as a team for performing tasks, it should be noted that team planning tends to be optimistically biased where 'predictions generated through group discussion were more optimistic than those generated individually' [1]. Unpacking is expected to reduce optimistic bias in team planning. 'Unpacking will contribute to reducing inaccurate estimations, but accuracy of estimation will not automatically lead to a positive result in the actual game run' [2].

This study examines the effect of structured instructions in the form of questions prepared by a facilitator. Unpacking and planning fallacy are explained and the pressure of reaching a consensus in group discussions is described. The relationship between the depth of understanding and outcome profits is examined and the effect of structured instructions that inquire about the process of the participants' estimations is analysed.

© Springer Nature Switzerland AG 2022
U. Dhar et al. (Eds.): ISAGA 2021, LNCS 13219, pp. 15–27, 2022.
https://doi.org/10.1007/978-3-031-09959-5_2

## 1.2  Unpacking and Planning Fallacy

Planning fallacy is a phenomenon shown in individual predictions regarding time and is 'the tendency to underestimate the duration that is needed to complete a task' [3–6]. It occurs as people make plans by focusing on a project's specific aspect [3]. People usually fail to consider the situation from outside perspectives and become narrow-minded. 'People tend to generate their predictions by considering the unique features of the task at hand and constructing a scenario of their future progress on that task' [4]. The act of scenario construction may lead people to exaggerate the likelihood of the scenario taking place.

Unpacking a task improves the quality of judgment as it is 'to consider each of the subcomponents of the task' [5]. When participants were asked to predict how long it would take them to complete the task, the answer became 1.6 times longer after they were asked to list each specific step that would be needed to complete the task. Similar results were obtained when making a holiday gift shopping plan, cooking a meal, and dressing for a date. Unpacking was effective in reducing underestimation [5].

The task of document formatting was modified with two conditions of perceived time consumption: the atypical short component condition which introduces italics and boldface and atypical long component condition which adds special phonetic characters [5, 7]. The task duration estimates were assumed to increase only when the unpacked components are perceived as time consuming. If the unpacking of atypical components takes a short time to complete, the estimates decrease, but unpacking longer components increases the estimates.

In a production management game, informative questions were prepared to unpack the process of achieving the goals of the game [2]. Those who were not asked informative questions prior to the game were more optimistic when estimating net profits than those who were asked questions beforehand. Unpacking improved the quality of estimation, although its accuracy did not automatically lead to a positive result of net profit gain as an example of how unpacking reduces planning fallacy in S&G settings [2].

## 1.3  Pressure of Reaching Consensus

Unstructured discussion in the face of a consensus requirement may often fail as a means of combining unique informational resources [8]. People feel obligated to reach a consensus when they make decisions as a group. If their pressure of reaching a consensus can be released in some way, they can pay more attention to unique informational resources during a discussion. The expectation of the existence of a correct solution would shift the focus of discussion toward the critical clues [9]. If they expect the existence of a correct solution, they may discuss unshared critical information. In a production management game, the best strategy exists and participants would pursue a solution through discussions instead of caring about reaching a consensus.

A series of quantitative estimation questions, such as the coldest temperature ever recorded in Alabama, examined the factors affected group accuracy [10, 11]. Instructional interventions seem to contribute to structuring group discussion and better decision-making. Strategic suggestions could have beneficial effects on group performance either because they identify a practical strategy or permit groups to make comparisons [10]. In a group, people try to be courteous to each other and behave in a respectful manner. This atmosphere may hinder serious discussion. However, if people are presented with a cogent reason for a serious discussion, they are likely to participate without fear of being perceived as rude. In S&G, a facilitator can prepare a structured explanation for participants and ask thought-provoking questions to lead to productive discussions.

If participants get concrete instructions that shift their focus, they may be able to have fruitful discussions [12]. Additional strategic instructions would allow them to change their mindset and spark a serious conversation, resulting in their search for information regardless of whether it is shared by the majority. In a production management game, informative questions succeed in unpacking the critical path and reduce planning fallacy, but do not necessarily increase performance [2]. Participants should be asked a more powerful question so that they may have a deep discussion without being overly concerned about reaching a consensus.

### 1.4 Purpose of the Study

This study examines whether structured instructions enable participants to understand the meaning of critical information. The structured instructions consist of informative questions and an additional thought-provoking question. By being asked to disclose the reasoning behind their estimation, participants are expected to understand the meaning of the critical information deeply and discuss in a team. The purpose of this study is to examine how structured instructions affect team performance in the setting of S&G.

## 2 Method

### 2.1 An OPT Scheduling Game

The game is based on a concept outlined in *The Goal* and was designed to simulate a mechanism of optimized production technology called the OPT Scheduling Game [13, 14]. This study used a Japanese version of the game [15].

In the game, participants work in teams of about 10 people each with tasks (Table 1). The goal of the game is to generate profit by producing airplanes with A4 paper.

**Table 1.** OPT scheduling game: tasks and contents

| Task | Content |
| --- | --- |
| Draw lines | Draw two straight lines with a pencil and scale ruler on a sheet of A4 paper to trisect the length of the paper |
| Cut | Cut the sheet of paper with a pair of scissors into three pieces along the two straight lines |
| Fold wings | Fold a strip and make a pair of wings |

(*continued*)

Table 1. (*continued*)

| Task | Content |
| --- | --- |
| Write on the wings | Write 'OPT' on each wing |
| Fold fuselages | Fold a strip and make a fuselage |
| Write on the fuselages | Write the name of a company, such as 'RYUTSU KEIZAI UNIVERSITY,' and three words, 'TRY,' 'OUT,' and 'OPT,' on each side of the fuselage with two different colors |
| Combine wings with fuselages | Combine a pair of wings with a fuselage into the shape of an airplane by stapling the two parts |
| Transport materials | Transport materials between members who are allocated different tasks at different places. The materials include A4 plain paper, strips of paper, and the work-in-progress |

This game's total running time was 900 s. The process bottlenecked at the 'write on the fuselage' step which takes about 30 s to finish. The initial cost was ¥200,000 and the cost of a sheet of A4 plain paper was ¥3,000 (Table 2). As options, additional staff assignment cost ¥500,000, changing the location cost ¥200,000, and process improvement cost ¥50,000. In terms of profit, one airplane created ¥20,000, one pair of wings created ¥5,000 and one fuselage created ¥10,000. To recoup the initial cost, at least 10 airplanes needed to be produced. Making a profit was numerically possible since producing 10 airplanes takes about 350 s, which is much less than the 900-s running time. To solve the bottleneck, assigning the task of 'writing on the fuselage' to another person would be a possible alternative but should be avoided considering the cost of ¥500,000.

Table 2. OPT scheduling game: cost and profit

| Items | Cost | Items | Profit |
| --- | --- | --- | --- |
| Initial cost | ¥200,000 | Airplane | ¥20,000 |
| A4 plain paper | ¥3,000/sheet | A pair of wings | ¥5,000 |
| Additional staff assignment | ¥500,000/staff | A fuselage | ¥10,000 |
| Changing the location | ¥200,000/location | | |
| Process improvement | ¥50,000/improvement | | |

## 2.2 Participants and Procedures

Participants were students of a project management course for the first grade first semester in 2019 and 2020. In 2019, the class was held once a week for 15 weeks in the first semester. In 2020, the class was held once a week for 13 weeks and was postponed until the second semester due to COVID-19. The participants' age ranged from 18 to 22 years. The male students comprised 80%. During the semester, students experienced several types of simulation and gaming on subjects including information sharing, leadership, social dilemmas and team building before participating in the game. The game was run for two consecutive class sessions, with sessions 1 and 2 in June and July 2019 and in December 2020 (Table 3).

**Table 3.** OPT scheduling game: participants and sessions

| Year | Session 1 | Session 2 | Common members | teams |
|------|-----------|-----------|----------------|-------|
| 2019 | 105 participants | 103 participants | 99 participants | 11 teams |
| 2020 | 116 participants | 119 participants | 116 participants | 12 teams |

Session 1 was dedicated to preparation: understanding the game rules and procedures, organizing teams, making plans, allocating tasks to each member and rehearsing the process with the whole group. The participants made their own teams of about 10 members each in 2019. In 2020, teams were organized as an aggregation of small groups of a few close friends.

Session 2 was dedicated to the game itself: checking the plans and executing them. Some students were absent for the first session but attended the second session. Others attended session 1 but were absent from session 2. At the beginning of session 2, each team was checked for the presence of all members; teams were rearranged so that they were approximately the same size. In 2019, four teams had 10 members and seven teams had 9 members. Most teams had a few new members with little knowledge of the game or its procedures. In 2020, all teams but one had 10 members, while one team had 9 members. The first topic for all teams in session 2 was to review their previous plans within the team. This helped new members understand the team's plan and refreshed old members' memories.

## 2.3 Questionnaires

Data sets are obtained from 2019 and 2020. In each year, two questionnaires were prepared: before the game run and after the game run. Participants were asked four informative questions per year and an additional thought-provoking question only in 2020. The questionnaire after the game run was the same in both the years, where participants were asked four questions about attitudes. Thus, two sets of data are examined from the following angles:

1. The individual depth of understanding prior to the game run
2. The individual estimations prior to the game run and the team's profit
3. The individual attitudes subsequent to the game run

Participants answered questionnaires before and after the game run. A pre-game questionnaire was prepared to examine the depth of their understanding of related information and to express their estimations of their team's profit. A post-game questionnaire was used to assess their attitudes toward such factors as the process.

**Questionnaire Before the Game Run.**  At the end of session 1, after the group meeting, each participant answered four questions in 2019 and five questions in 2020 on the class website as shown below:

*Questionnaire*

Q1  Do you understand that the initial cost is ¥200,000?
Q2  Can you correctly estimate the minimum number of airplanes required to recoup the initial cost?
Q3  Which task do you think is the hardest? Please choose one from the following alternatives:

Draw lines; Cut; Fold wings; Write on the wings; Fold fuselages;
Write on the fuselages; Combine wings with fuselages; Transport materials

Q4  Please estimate the net profit gain (sales minus costs) of your team.
Q5  Please explain how you calculated the net profit gain. (only in 2020)

Participants answered questions Q1 and Q2 by choosing from among four options: 'Yes, I do/can,' 'Now I understand/can,' 'Neither yes nor no,' and 'I have no idea.' Participants answered question Q3 by choosing from among eight options. Questions Q4 and Q5 called for a free description.

**Questionnaire After the Game Run.**  At the end of session 2, after the game run, a questionnaire was distributed to each participant in 2019 and the questionnaire was on the website in 2020 as shown below:

*Questionnaire*

Q1    Please give us your feedback on this game run in two lines.
Q2-1  How much did you understand of the process of producing the airplane?
Q2-2  Which task looked the hardest?
Q3-1  How well did you understand your team's plan?
Q3-2  Please explain your team's plan.
Q4-1  Did you predict your team would end up with this result?
Q4-2  What result did you predict?
Q5-1  How satisfied are you with the result of this game?
Q5-2  Why do you think so?

Q6    What do you think should have been done better?

Participants answered questions Q2–1, Q3–1, Q4–1, and Q5–1 on a 6-point scale ranging from 1 (never) to 6 (fully) and then described the details in a few lines to the questions Q2–2, Q3–2, Q4–2, and Q5–2. Questions Q1 and Q6 called for free description.

## 2.4 Hypothesis

Answers to the questionnaire prior to the game run were to determine the index of how each participant understood the situation. Question 5 was added in 2020 prior to the game run to help participants understand the meaning of related information. This small difference would promote the depth of understanding in individual levels, generate serious discussions in a team, and enhance team performance. The greater the depth of understanding, the greater would be the team profit.

# 3   Results

## 3.1   Depth of Understanding Prior to the Game Run

Tables 4 and 5 show the depth of the participants' understanding before the game run in 2019 and 2020, respectively. Concerning the initial cost (Q1), 59 out of 99 understood the game in 2019 and 96 out of 116 did so in 2020. Concerning the minimum number of airplanes required to recoup the initial cost (Q2), 53 out of 99 understood it in 2019 and 82 out of 116 did so in 2020. The writing on the fuselages was the hardest task of the production process (Q3) and the bottleneck in the OPT scheduling game; it was chosen by 43 out of 99 in 2019 and 36 out of 116 in 2020. Instead of writing on the fuselages, transporting materials was chosen by more than half in 2020. This is because the size of the classroom was much larger in 2020 than in 2019 to maintain social distancing. Two columns on the extreme right in Tables 4 and 5 are indexes of the depth of understanding. Index 1 shows the ratio of participants who understood the situation. Index 2 shows the additional ratio which added the number of people who chose transporting materials to those who chose writing on the fuselages.

**Table 4.** Depth of understanding prior to the game run in 2019

| Team | 'Yes' in Q1 (a) | 'Yes' in Q2 (b) | 'Write on the fuselages' in Q3 (c) | 'Transport materials' in Q3 (d) | Number of answers (e) | Index 1: $(a + b + c)/(3*e)$ | Index 2: $(a + b + c + d)/(3*e)$ |
|---|---|---|---|---|---|---|---|
| A | 3 | 5 | 2 | 6 | 9 | 37% | 59% |
| B | 6 | 6 | 8 | 1 | 9 | 74% | 78% |

*(continued)*

**Table 4.** (*continued*)

| Team | 'Yes' in Q1 (a) | 'Yes' in Q2 (b) | 'Write on the fuselages' in Q3 (c) | 'Transport materials' in Q3 (d) | Number of answers (e) | Index 1: (a + b + c)/(3*e) | Index 2: (a + b + c + d)/(3*e) |
|------|------|------|------|------|------|------|------|
| C | 7 | 7 | 2 | 4 | 9 | 59% | 74% |
| D | 8 | 7 | 7 | 0 | 10 | 73% | 73% |
| E | 9 | 10 | 5 | 5 | 10 | 80% | 97% |
| F | 2 | 1 | 5 | 2 | 8 | 33% | 42% |
| G | 8 | 6 | 4 | 3 | 8 | 75% | 88% |
| H | 4 | 2 | 2 | 5 | 9 | 30% | 48% |
| I | 5 | 2 | 1 | 4 | 9 | 30% | 44% |
| J | 5 | 6 | 6 | 2 | 9 | 63% | 70% |
| K | 2 | 1 | 1 | 6 | 9 | 15% | 37% |
| Total | 59 | 53 | 43 | 38 | 99 | | |

**Table 5.** Depth of understanding prior to the game run in 2020

| Team | 'Yes' in Q1 (a) | 'Yes' in Q2 (b) | 'Write on the fuselages' in Q3 (c) | 'Transport materials' in Q3 (d) | Number of answers (e) | Index 1: (a + b + c)/(3*e) | Index 2: (a + b + c + d)/(3*e) |
|------|------|------|------|------|------|------|------|
| A | 8 | 6 | 2 | 6 | 10 | 53% | 73% |
| B | 9 | 10 | 8 | 0 | 10 | 90% | 90% |
| C | 7 | 5 | 2 | 5 | 10 | 47% | 63% |
| D | 7 | 5 | 4 | 5 | 10 | 53% | 70% |
| E | 9 | 8 | 5 | 1 | 9 | 81% | 85% |
| F | 7 | 7 | 3 | 6 | 9 | 63% | 85% |
| G | 10 | 8 | 3 | 7 | 10 | 70% | 93% |
| H | 7 | 7 | 1 | 8 | 9 | 56% | 85% |
| I | 7 | 6 | 1 | 8 | 9 | 52% | 81% |
| J | 7 | 3 | 4 | 6 | 10 | 47% | 67% |
| K | 9 | 8 | 1 | 9 | 10 | 60% | 90% |
| L | 9 | 9 | 2 | 7 | 10 | 67% | 90% |
| Total | 96 | 82 | 36 | 68 | 116 | | |

Figures 1 and 2 show the frequency distribution charts for indexes 1 and 2, respectively. Indexes in 2020 are higher than those in 2019. Participants in 2020 understood the meaning of given information better than those in 2019.

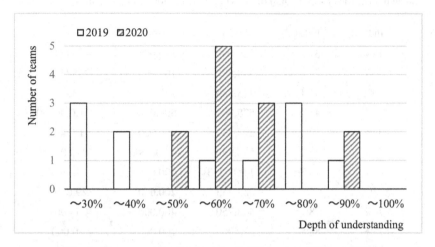

**Fig. 1.** Frequency distribution chart of index 1 in 2019 and 2020

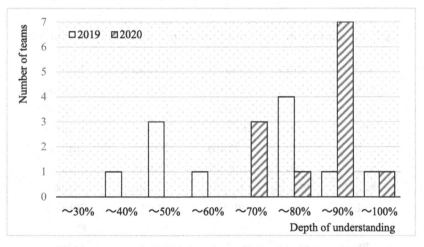

**Fig. 2.** Frequency distribution chart of index 2 in 2019 and 2020

### 3.2  Individual Estimations Prior to the Game Run and Teams' Profit

Tables 6 and 7 show the mean and median of individual estimations on their team's profit prior to the game run and the team's actual profit in 2019 and 2020, respectively. The Figures are in ascending order of index 1, showing the ratio of participants who understood the situation. In Table 6, we see that the profits of the upper half of the teams are negative, and in Table 7, the profits of the top two teams are negative. When the depth of understanding is low, a team profit is low.

**Table 6.** The mean and median of individual estimations and team profit in 2019

| Team | Index 1 | Index 2 | Mean (¥) | Median (¥) | Team profit (¥) |
|------|---------|---------|----------|------------|-----------------|
| K | 15% | 37% | 329,000 | 150,000 | −30,000 |
| H | 30% | 48% | 378,889 | 100,000 | −157,000 |
| I | 30% | 44% | 448,889 | 100,000 | −93,000 |
| F | 33% | 42% | 525,000 | 500,000 | −1,038,000 |
| A | 37% | 59% | 208,333 | 200,000 | −15,000 |
| C | 59% | 74% | 548,889 | 1,000,000 | 132,000 |
| J | 63% | 70% | 1,003,333 | 200,000 | −64,000 |
| D | 73% | 73% | 763,333 | 200,000 | 329,000 |
| B | 74% | 78% | 448,750 | 400,000 | 303,000 |
| G | 75% | 88% | 67,500 | 100,000 | −50,000 |
| E | 80% | 97% | 228,000 | 200,000 | 284,000 |
| Average | 52% | 65% | 449,992 | 286,364 | −36,273 |

**Table 7.** The mean and median of individual estimations and team profit in 2020

| Team | Index 1 | Index 2 | Mean (¥) | Median (¥) | Team profit (¥) |
|------|---------|---------|----------|------------|-----------------|
| C | 47% | 63% | 147,400 | 50,000 | −51,000 |
| J | 47% | 67% | 20,000 | 0 | −320,000 |
| I | 52% | 81% | 61,111 | 50,000 | 135,000 |
| A | 53% | 73% | 192,400 | 200,000 | 161,000 |
| D | 53% | 70% | 208,600 | 250,000 | 132,000 |
| H | 56% | 85% | 99,000 | 110,000 | 65,000 |
| K | 60% | 90% | 39,600 | 44,000 | 208,000 |
| F | 63% | 85% | 0 | 0 | 88,000 |
| L | 67% | 90% | 83,400 | 100,000 | 14,000 |
| G | 70% | 93% | 1,180,000 | 200,000 | 178,000 |
| E | 81% | 85% | 300,000 | 300,000 | −190,000 |
| B | 90% | 90% | 98,889 | 100,000 | 328,000 |
| Average | 62% | 81% | 202,533 | 117,000 | 62,333 |

Figure 3 presents the average of the mean and median of individual estimations and each team profit in 2019 and 2020. Comparing the averages for 2019 and 2020, we see that the mean and median of the individual estimations were higher in 2019 than in 2020, and the team profits were lower in 2019 than in 2020. Participants in 2020 predicted their team profit better than those in 2019, on average.

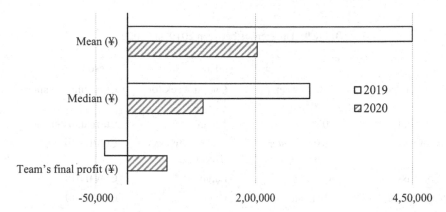

**Fig. 3.** The average of the mean and median of individual estimations in teams and team profit in 2019 and 2020

### 3.3 Answers to the Questionnaire After the Game Run

Table 8 presents the averages of individual answers to the questionnaire. Q2–1 indicates the level of understanding of the whole production process. There was a marginally significant increase in participants who understood the whole production process in 2020 than in 2019. Q3–1 indicates the level of understanding regarding the team's strategy. Participants in 2020 understood their team's strategy much more significantly than those in 2019. Q4–1 indicates the level of outcome prediction. The average scores on Q4–1 show no significant difference between 2019 and 2020. As shown in Fig. 3, participants in 2020 predicted their team profit more accurately than those in 2019 but those in 2020 did not believe that they did well. Q5–1 shows the level of satisfaction with the result. Participants in 2020 were significantly satisfied more than those in 2019.

**Table 8.** Answers to questionnaire and team profit in 2019 and 2020

| Year | Q2–1 | Q3–1 | Q4–1 | Q5–1 | Team's profit (¥) |
|------|------|------|------|------|-------------------|
| 2019 | 4.44 | 4.18 | 3.75 | 3.83 | −36,273 |
| 2020 | 4.75* | 5.09*** | 3.41 | 4.29** | 62,333 |

*: $p < .1$, **: $p < .05$, ***: $p < .01$s

Due to curriculum changes, the number of classes was reduced from 15 to 13 and the class period increased from 90 min to 120 min (Table 9). Consequently, participants could spend more time on planning and performing tasks. Another difference was the effect of COVID-19. Almost all classes were shifted online in the first semester of university education all over Japan in 2020. This course was postponed to the second semester for a larger classroom to avoid direct interaction among participants.

**Table 9.** Differences between 2019 and 2020

| Point | 2019 | 2020 | Reason |
|---|---|---|---|
| Number of classes | Once a week for 15 weeks | Once a week for 13 weeks | Curriculum change |
| Class period | 90 min | 120 min | Curriculum change |
| Time of year | First semester (June-July) | Second semester (December) | COVID-19 |
| Size of classroom | Medium | Large | COVID-19 |
| Motivation | Moderate | High | COVID-19 |
| Grouping | Autonomic | Half autonomic | COVID-19 |
| Additional question | No | Question 5 | Examination |

## 4   Discussion

This study examined how an additional thought-provoking question affected the depth of individual understanding and team performance. Question 5 was added prior to the game run only in 2020 about the process of the participants to estimate the net profit. It provided a good reason for them to search for related information thoroughly and encouraged them to exchange opinions actively in the team. They deepened their level of understanding to a greater degree in 2020. On an average, in 2020 they came to have reasonable estimations, reduced overestimation and succeeded in earning their team profit. They understood the production process and the team strategy better than in 2019 and were more satisfied with the result. In terms of outcome prediction, there was no significant difference between 2019 and 2020 in Table 8.

The structured instructions could shift the focus of discussion in S&G, with a few exceptions. Team G in Table 6 and Team E in Table 7 indicated very high understanding but resulted in negative profit. How did this happen? To understand possible causes of these results, further research would be needed.

In a game, rational estimation is expected to be organized through serious discussion. Participants in 2020 understood the meaning of the given information, estimated their team profit and performed well. This study demonstrated that structured instructions would contribute to bring about this result. Regarding the effect of unpacking and structured instructions, the additional question should have helped participants to understand the situation.

# References

1. Buehler, R., Messervey, D., Griffin, D.: Collaborative planning and prediction: does group discussion affect optimistic biases in time estimation? Organ. Behav. Hum. Decis. Process. **97**(1), 47–63 (2005). https://doi.org/10.1016/j.obhdp.2005.02.004
2. Nakamura, M.: Unpacking and Overconfidence in a Production Management Game. In: Wardaszko, M., Meijer, S., Lukosch, H., Kanegae, H., Kriz, W.C., Grzybowska-Brzezińska, M. (eds.) ISAGA 2019. LNCS, vol. 11988, pp. 306–319. Springer, Cham (2021). https://doi.org/10.1007/978-3-030-72132-9_26
3. Kahneman, D., Tversky, A.: Intuitive prediction: Biases and corrective procedures. Technical report. Decision Research/A Branch of Perceptronics Inc., Oregon (1977) https://apps.dtic.mil/dtic/tr/fulltext/u2/a047747.pdf. last accessed 19 Sep 2021
4. Buehler, R., Griffin, D., Ross, M.: It's about time: Optimistic predictions in work and love. Eur. Rev. Soc. Psychol. **6**(1), 1–32 (1995). https://doi.org/10.1080/14792779343000112,lastaccessed2021/9/19
5. Kruger, J., Evans, M.: If you don't want to be late, enumerate: Unpacking reduces the planning fallacy. J. Exp. Psychol. **40**(5), 586–598 (2004). https://doi.org/10.1016/j.jesp.2003.11.001
6. Moss, S.: The planning fallacy. SICOTESTS. https://www.sicotests.com/psyarticle.asp?id=385. last accessed 19 Sep 2021
7. Hadjichristidis, C., Summers, B., Thomas, K.: Unpacking estimates of task duration: the role of typicality and temporality. J. Exp. Soc. Psychol. **51**, 45–50 (2014). https://doi.org/10.1016/j.jesp.2013.10.009
8. Stasser, G., Titus, W.: Pooling of unshared information in group decision making: biased information sampling during discussion. J. Pers. Soc. Psychol. **48**(6), 1467–1478 (1985). https://doi.org/10.1037/0022-3514.48.6.1467
9. Stasser, G., Stewart, D.: Discovery of hidden profiles by decision-making groups: Solving a problem versus making a judgment. J. Pers. Soc. Psychol. **63**(3), 426–434 (1992). https://doi.org/10.1037/0022-3514.63.3.426
10. Henry, R.: Improving group judgement accuracy: information sharing and determining the best member. Organ. Behav. Hum. Decis. Process. **62**(2), 190–197 (1995). https://doi.org/10.1006/obhd.1995.1042
11. Henry, R., Kmet, J., Desrosiers, E., Landa, A.: Examining the impact of interpersonal cohesiveness on group accuracy interventions: the importance of matching versus buffering. Organ. Behav. Hum. Decis. Process. **87**(1), 25–43 (2002). https://doi.org/10.1006/obhd.2000.2945
12. Nakamura, M.: How to utilize unshared knowledge in a group discussion?. In: Ma, M., Fletcher, B., Göbel, S., Baalsrud Hauge, J., Marsh, T. (eds.) Serious Games. JCSG 2020. Lecture Notes in Computer Science, vol. 12434, pp. 289–302. Springer, Cham (2020). https://doi.org/10.1007/978-3-030-61814-8_22
13. Legg, L.: Planes or bust: an OPT scheduling game. In: Armstrong, R., Percival, F., Saunders, D. (eds.) The Simulation and Gaming Yearbook Volume 2: Interactive Learning, pp. 209–219. Kogan Page, London (1994)
14. Goldratt, E.M., Fox, R.E.: The Goal: A Process of Ongoing Improvement Third, Revised North River Press, Great Barrington (2004)
15. Nakamura, M.: Japanese translation of Legg's 'Planes or bust: an OPT scheduling game.' The Journal of Ryutsu Keizai University **31**(1), 57–65 (1996). (In Japanese)

# Facilitated Tabletop Games in a Mediated Environment

Harmen aan het Rot[1], Rens Kortmann[1]([✉]) [iD], Alexander Verbraeck[1] [iD], Gerdien de Vries[1] [iD], May Kooreman[2], and Birgit de Bruin[1,2]

[1] Faculty of Technology, Policy, and Management, Department of Multi-Actor Systems, Delft University of Technology, Delft, The Netherlands
`l.j.kortmann@tudelft.nl`
[2] Stichting MaySways, Aerdenhout, The Netherlands

**Abstract.** Tabletop games that require the aid of a human facilitator are typically designed for a physical environment. However, during the COVID-19 pandemic, lockdown measures prevented people from gathering. Therefore, tabletop games were sometimes played and facilitated in a mediated environment using online communication tools instead. But this setting possibly deteriorates the players' game experience. To understand the effect of playing facilitated tabletop games in a mediated environment we measured the player experience of the game *Cue Kitchen* in a mixed-method study comparing physical and mediated game sessions. Forty-four players played eleven game sessions, three in a physical environment and eight in a mediated environment. Of all seven dimensions of game experience measured, only one differed significantly between the two experimental conditions: players in a mediated environment became significantly more tired than players in a physical environment. The qualitative results explained why: players in a physical setting can wander off, while players in an online setting have to stay focused on their screen and, therefore, grow more tired. The research results suggest that facilitated tabletop games may be played in a mediated environment instead of a physical environment, without significant loss of player experience.

**Keywords:** Tabletop games · Game experience · Mediated environment · Sense of presence · Zoom fatigue

## 1 Introduction

Playing a tabletop game such as a board game, card game or role-playing game can be a useful method for analysing and designing complex systems. As opposed to games played for fun, game technologies can be used for purposes beyond entertainment [1, 2]. In other words, players play a tabletop game with a serious purpose, while having a good experience (i.e., being entertained) [3]. A game may support multi-actor decision-making to create an experimental environment for stakeholders to 'play around' with different policies and technologies [4]. Games can also be used to raise awareness or educate people about complexities in socio-technical systems like energy or public transport systems.

© Springer Nature Switzerland AG 2022
U. Dhar et al. (Eds.): ISAGA 2021, LNCS 13219, pp. 28–41, 2022.
https://doi.org/10.1007/978-3-031-09959-5_3

In a tabletop game, players sit together around a table and make decisions based on the gameplay in front of them [5]. These games are usually played in a physical environment, not only because it is a physical game but also because it is intended to reflect reality [6, 7]. Players can look at each other to interpret mimics and gestures which can help them understand each other's actions, even without verbal communication [8–10]. In the social environment of the game, the players can share emotions, laugh together and confront each other. Tabletop games for purposes beyond entertainment usually require a facilitator for storytelling and making the game reactive to the decisions of the players [11, 12]. The consensus in the field of gaming and simulation is that these games should therefore be played in a physical environment, but this is not always possible.

During the coronavirus pandemic in 2020, it was not possible to play a (facilitated) tabletop game in a physical environment. The use of digital tools such as Teams, Zoom or Skype could enable a mediated environment for players to play a facilitated tabletop serious game. However, playing a game in a mediated way does not feel the same as playing the game in a physical environment. Players are not able to feel each other's presence, use non-verbal communication, convey emotions, or physically hold the cards, dies, coins or pawns. In other words, a mediated environment likely changes the game experience, which is not trivial, because experience is a reason for people to play a game [13]. To our knowledge, the current scientific literature does not give a clear answer how playing a (facilitated) tabletop game in a mediated environment changes the game experience.

The question that will therefore be answered in this paper is: *How does playing a facilitated tabletop game in a mediated environment affect the players' experience when compared to playing face to face* [14]?

## 2    Expected Effects of a Mediated Environment

It is possible to obtain insight into the expected effects of a mediated environment on game experience by combining different ideas emerging from literature on game session design and facilitation, Zoom fatigue, and mediated presence.

### 2.1   Game Session Design and Facilitation

Designing a game session is part of the game design process [5]. A wrong game session design could cause the game to not being played as intended and therefore, cause the game to fail to achieve its intended objective. Playing a game in a mediated environment (e.g., using a screen and audio connection) instead of playing face to face may affect the players' ability to share emotions in the right way, including facial expressions and posture. This can change the interpretation of these emotions, and therefore the player experience. This also relates to the key characteristics of tabletop games where players sit around a table and can see each other, allowing them to understand each other's actions, even without verbal communication [8–10, 15].

Yuan et al. observed that the lack of environmental perception and player awareness may cause frustration and conflict among the players [16]. They conducted a multi-method qualitative study to research design opportunities for a socially connected game experience for (social) tabletop games in light of the recent COVID-19 pandemic. As environmental perception and player awareness are crucial in tabletop games, their advice is to include cameras and other technologies in the remote tabletop gaming setup to increase social awareness and empathy. They conclude that future research may benefit from (existing) quantitative methods measuring the social connectedness as part of the players' experience, including relationship salience, relationship satisfaction, feeling of closeness, loneliness, and quality of life [16].

During a physical session, a facilitator has a physical overview of players around the table and the playing board or cards, which enable them to steer the game. In a mediated environment, the facilitator does not have a physical overview of the players and is also responsible for carrying out the gameplay and moderating the discussion. These limitations in facilitation can jeopardize the game experience [6].

## 2.2  Zoom Fatigue

During the COVID-19 pandemic in 2020, the term 'Zoom fatigue' was introduced to indicate tiredness when using video conferencing applications like Zoom. Grey literature such as traditional media and lifestyle websites were observing an increased level of tiredness during video calling [17, 18]. Large studies have been set up to investigate the psychological effect of video conferencing but results are not published yet. A recent article based on academic research and small experiments provides interesting arguments for the cause of Zoom fatigue [19]. People in an online video session look to be really close on a screen compared to someone who is 1–2 m away. In a physical meeting, a majority of the people in the room are not looking at the speaker and apart from people having sidebar conversations, people close to each other do not look at each other's eyes, where everyone seems to be looking directly at you in a virtual meeting.

## 2.3  Mediated Presence

*Sense of presence* is considered to be a part of game experience [20, 21]. The exact meaning of presence can be considered vague and hard to grasp, but it is related to our very own existence and perception of reality. Presence is closely linked to ontology, the study of being [22]. Schloerb defined presence as something physical: "[Presence] designates the existence of an object in some particular region of space and time" [23]. However, according to Mantovani and Riva "[…] the meaning of presence depends on the concept we have of reality and different ontological positions generate different definitions of presence" [22]. They argue that presence should not be defined as something physical but propose an alternative conception of presence: (social) presence is a social construct, as part of reality, including relationships between actors and their surroundings.

The second interpretation creates more possibilities to see presence than only in its physical form. In other words, to have a sense of presence, despite physical absence. This phenomenon can be described as *mediated presence* [24]. Other authors are using similar terms such as virtual (co)presence or telepresence. The difference between these terms is mainly a different emphasis of context: 'tele' as in presence at or over a distance, virtual as in presence using software, and mediated as in using a medium. These terms have a similar notion of presence that is not physical; using a (digital) tool to make the communication and interconnection possible to experience presence over a distance. Through immersive, interactive and perceptually realistic media, people can have a similar experience of social presence to those in non-mediated environments [25]. People playing a facilitated tabletop game in a mediated environment could have a similar game experience as playing face to face, at least regarding their sense of presence.

To summarize, the game experience may be negatively affected by the choice of the environment since a mediated environment changes the ability of players to interact and recognize emotions. A mediated environment can limit facilitation and might jeopardize the outcome of the game. A mediated session may cause players to be more tired, similar to Zoom fatigue. However, it should also be possible to have some similarities between the game experience of players in both environments, when a *mediated presence* is created.

## 3  Method

To answer the question *'How does playing a facilitated tabletop game in a mediated environment affect the players' game experience when compared to playing face to face'*, an experiment was conducted where the players' game experience in a mediated environment was compared to playing face to face.

### 3.1  Design of the Study

The research question focuses on comparing the game experience between a physical and mediated environment and on finding an explanation for a possible difference. Therefore, a mixed-methods research methodology has been used, combining a qualitative and quantitative perspective. This method is not limited or constrained by the characteristics of typical quantitative or qualitative research such as a focus on deduction, confirmation and prediction from a quantitative perspective and focus on discovery, exploration, and induction from a qualitative perspective [26]. Instead, it offers the opportunity to collect, analyse and integrate both quantitative and qualitative data in a single study [27, 28]. The qualitative and quantitative data have been integrated following an explanatory design: the observations during the game sessions can give context and explanation to the measured game experience.

### 3.2  Experimental Setup

The game in this study was *Cue Kitchen*, a game developed in 2019, which aims to create awareness about the invisible symptoms of Parkinson's Disease (PD) in the social environment of people with PD [29]. *Cue Kitchen* is a cooperative tabletop card game in which four players have the objective to run a successful service in a professional kitchen by using ingredient cards to cook dishes. While playing, each player has an invisible symptom, something that limits the player in its play. Others need to guess this symptom and by providing the right cue, players can help each other to overcome this symptom. While the game is fun to play, the player can experience what it is to have an invisible symptom and needing a cue from others that relates to Parkinson's disease. During the debriefing, the players reflect on this. With the help of the facilitator, the players relate their experience in the game to the invisible PD symptoms and to the importance of cues that can help people with PD. A game session consists of two games of *Cue Kitchen* followed by a debriefing. Each game play takes 30–40 min and the debriefing takes about 30 min.

**Fig. 1.** Screenshot of the playing table          **Fig. 2.** Experimental setup

In a mediated session, all players can see the playing field of the game on their screen (Fig. 1), including the playing cards. By giving the facilitator directions for their desired actions, they participate in the gameplay. To achieve this, the software of Big Blue Button has been used. This is an open-source web conferencing software, similar to Zoom, specially set up for TU Delft for educational purposes[1]. To make a mediated environment possible, no professional tools have been used, but only day-to-day objects that are available to everyone. The playing table was filmed using a smartphone and a construction made of kitchen stairs, some books, rope, tape, and a bookshelf (Fig. 2).

### 3.3 Participants

The participants in the study were persons with PD and people in their social network like family, friends, colleagues or health-care providers. Participants (with PD) were recruited using the channels of the MaySways foundation[2] (e.g., the newsletter) and via a social media call from the Dutch Parkinson Association. Registered participants did not receive any compensation for their participation. Every participant was at least 18 years old. The research setup was officially approved by the TU Delft HREC.

---

[1] See https://bigbluebutton.org/ for more information.
[2] The MaySways foundation is committed to creating awareness of invisible symptoms of persons with PD by artfully expressing their invisible thought and emotional world.

## 3.4  Procedure

The first step was to contact a participant with PD who selected three or four players in their social environment. Participants from the same household were allowed to play the game face to face, while the other participants played the game in a mediated environment. After the selection of participants, the players were asked to fill in an online informed consent form, using the Qualtrics platform. A video tutorial explaining the game was shared beforehand, except for the first session.

The game was played twice, the first time without invisible symptoms so that the players could get used to the gameplay, and the second time with invisible symptoms. Each gameplay took about 30–40 min to complete. The debriefing started with a reflection on the game, followed by a conversation about the personal situation of the person with PD.

One to three days after the game session, players were emailed a questionnaire on the Qualtrics platform. Completing the questionnaire took about 10–15 min.

## 3.5  Data Collection

**Quantitative Data.** Game experience has been measured using a questionnaire based on the Game Experience Questionnaire (GEQ) [21], measuring game experience with 12 variables in three different modules. Each variable is an average, constructed out of two to six items using a five-point Likert-scale (from 0 = totally disagree to 4 = totally agree). The GEQ Core Module measures seven *in-game experience* variables: Competence, Sensory and Imaginative Immersion, Flow, Tension/Annoyance, Challenge, Negative affect and Positive affect. The GEQ Social Presence Module measures *sense of presence* using three variables: Behavioural Involvement, Psychological Involvement (Empathy) and Psychological Involvement (Negative Feelings). The GEQ Post-game Module measures how players felt *after* they had stopped playing, in contrast to the Core Module which is based on the experience *during* the game. The four variables measuring the post-game experience are Positive experience, Negative experience, Tiredness and Returning to reality.

**Qualitative Data.** By observing the game sessions, qualitative data has been collected on how a playing environment affects the game session. Most of the sessions have been recorded (with informed consent of the players) to make it possible to re-watch the session and describe the events in the session as specific as possible. In some cases, the session was not recorded, but notes were taken during the sessions. The observations are extensively described in game session reports focusing on 1) how the quality of the game was affected by the player environment, 2) how the playing environment affected the gameplay and 3) how the playing environment affected the debriefing.

## 3.6  Data Analysis

The data has been analysed using SPSS, with playing environment as the independent variable (physical vs. mediated) and the constructed game experience variables as dependent variables. A Mann-Whitney test has been used to determine the differences between the independent variables. This non-parametric test is an alternative for an independent samples t-test. A Mann-Whitney test is suitable for small and non-normally distributed outcome variables in small and uneven samples, and suitable for analysing variables that are not continuous but ordinal. When reporting the results of a Mann-Whitney test, the median (Mdn) is used as the measure of central tendency.

## 4  Results

In this research, 11 sessions have been played. Table 1 gives an overview of the number of sessions and the number of completed questionnaires per playing environment.

**Table 1.** Experimental conditions

| Environment | # sessions | # completed questionnaires |
|---|---|---|
| Physical | 3 | 13 |
| Mediated | 8 | 31 |
| *Total* | *11* | *44* |

### 4.1  Quantitative Results

Participants in a mediated environment were more tired (Mdn = 1) than participants playing face to face (Mdn = 0) which was confirmed with a Mann-Whitney test ($U = 91.5, z = -2.915, p = .003$). The *Tiredness* construct was found to be highly reliable (2 items; $\alpha = .839$).

In Fig. 3, the difference in the experience of *Tiredness* between the two environments is clearly visible. In a physical environment, all players disagreed or totally disagreed with the statements 'I felt exhausted' and 'I felt weary'. In a mediated environment, participants responded in a wider range, sometimes totally agreeing with this statement. This result indicates that participants in a mediated environment are more tired after having played the game.

The other game experience variables do not show any significant differences in the (ranked) scores between a physical and mediated environment (Fig. 3). These results indicate that, apart from tiredness, the playing environment does not affect the player experience in a significant way. The feeling of presence without the other players physically present was not significantly different from playing face to face.

### 4.2  Qualitative Results

Our observations related to the playing environment were not unambiguous and consistent. Some mediated sessions went very well with only a few problems and resulted in enthusiasm among the players. Some other mediated sessions had several problems, taking a long time to be remedied. We observed that most players in a physical environment had more social interactions with each other than players in the mediated sessions. Some players were quite comfortable in the mediated environment.

When playing face to face, players were able to have many fast and one-on-one interactions while interrupting each other. This does not necessarily mean that these sessions were more chaotic. Instead, a physical player was able to have a quick conversation with another player without bothering other players. During some physical sessions, non-active players (i.e., it was not their turn) were able to tune out for a moment. The opposite was true for players in a mediated environment, where players had to stay focused on their screen to follow the gameplay. Some of these players indicated that this was quite intense. Participants in a mediated environment showed more symptoms of fatigue than participants in a physical session. In many cases, we observed a decreased concentration during the second game as well as during the debriefing. In some sessions, there were connection issues that needed to be restored causing the game to start later or to interrupt the session. These observations were incidental and not consistent over all sessions. In some cases, the players seemed to be more focused after a short break, whether or not this was caused by a technical problem.

Clear differences between the facilitation in both environments were visible. In the physical sessions, the facilitator has a supportive role, only intervening in the game as needed. During one session, with the facilitator physically present, the debriefing became a little uncomfortable when discussing the personal situation of the person with PD. The facilitator had to ask questions which were answered by the participant, but almost without a conversation between the participants. During two physical sessions with the facilitator present through a video connection, an intimate atmosphere was created in which the conversation became more personal. During the mediated sessions, the role of the facilitator was much greater, because he controlled the playing table and acted as a moderator during the debriefing. The advantage of a mediated environment is that everyone takes turns speaking and allows others to speak.

During some mediated sessions, several people were in the same room. In these sessions, we observed increased interactions between the physical players but also significant noise. As a result, comments from the other players could not be heard and the interactions with and between these players were reduced.

# 5 Discussion

In this experiment, no significant difference between the game experience in a physical and mediated environment was found. From the literature, it could be expected that reduced non-verbal communication or the inability to convey emotions in a mediated environment would have affected the game experience. Although some difference has been observed in this study, these observations were not significant.

Although presence could be defined as something physical [23], the literature also suggested a feeling of presence could be established without a physical presence [22, 24, 25]. No difference was found in the feeling of presence between a physical and mediated environment, so it seems the latter is true.

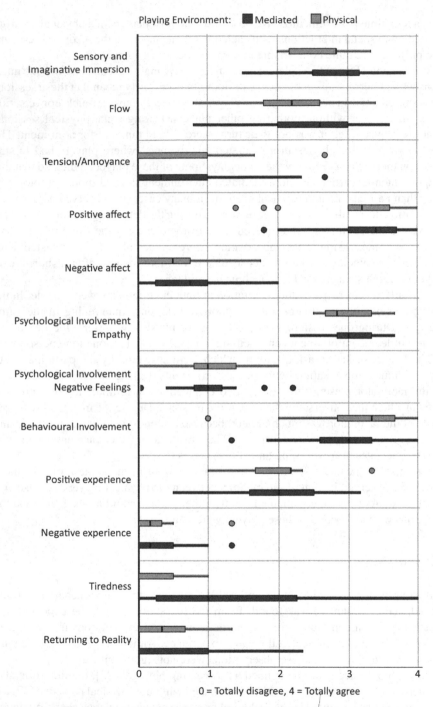

**Fig. 3.** Game experience in a physical and mediated environment

## 5.1 Tiredness and Zoom Fatigue

Participants in a mediated environment are significantly more tired than in a physical session. A decreased concentration during the second game and the debriefing was observed. In several cases where fatigue was higher than average, connection issues needed to be restored, causing the game to start later or resulting in interruption of the session. Although some sessions were longer for these reasons, no significant correlation was found between session duration and tiredness.

The result that mediated sessions cause more tiredness is supported by scientific literature that a mediated setting can be indeed more tiresome than a physical meeting and causing so-called 'Zoom fatigue' [19]. People have to stay focused on a screen up close, looking the other players in the eye, while players in a physical meeting can stare into the distance. It was observed that non-active players (i.e., it was not their turn) in a physical setting were able to 'tune out' for a moment, while players in a mediated environment had to stay focused. This possibility of being able to have a moment without concentration could contribute to the players being more energetic at the end of the game.

## 5.2 Differences Between Physical and Mediated Environment

The difference between a physical and mediated environment becomes clear in the quantitative results where no significant differences were established in the outcome variables except for tiredness. A clear dividing line could not be drawn between the performance of a physical and a mediated session for three reasons.

First, the outcome and game experience are highly dependent on the quality of each session. A mediated session can have no or only a few (technical) problems, resulting in a successful session. But if things go wrong and it takes a long time for a problem to be remedied, the outcome is visibly less good, as can be seen from the quantitative results. In mediated sessions, the dependence on digital technology increases the likelihood that something may go wrong, resulting in fatigue and a less positive experience.

Second, both physical and mediated sessions have advantages and disadvantages concerning facilitation. In a physical session, the facilitator plays a supportive role and can easily adjust intervention in the game as needed. However, the physical presence of the facilitator can also create an uncomfortable situation because the players play the game and do the debriefing under the 'watchful eye' of the facilitator. During a mediated session, the facilitator must be more active in guiding the conversation, with greater risks of making mistakes. On the other hand, a mediated environment makes the facilitator's role as a mediator easier because everyone takes turns speaking and allows each other to speak.

Finally, mediated sessions are sometimes not fully mediated. In several cases in this study, some mediated players were physically in the same room or even behind the same screen while the other players were present in a fully mediated way. This is clearly reflected in the behaviour of the players. The interaction between the physical players increased because they communicated back and forth faster. This caused significant noise in the session, where some comments were missed by the players. It also reduced the interaction with and between the mediated players.

## 5.3 Limitations

The test setup of this study has been quite austere. Although many players responded positively to the way the mediated environment had been designed, some testing sessions might have benefited from the use of more professional tools.

This study has small and uneven samples: 13 participants in a physical environment vs. 31 in a mediated environment. Corresponding statistical tests were used but these tests have less power, increasing the chance of a Type II error. Finding reliable and significant differences between both conditions is more difficult with these small samples, because the quality of a game session plays an important role and is very different per session.

This game was designed for and played by a very specific player group, people with PD and their relatives. Therefore, the results may not be generalized to other players of facilitated tabletop games. For example, people with PD can become tired more quickly [30]. Still, in this study, no significant difference has been found in the game experience between participants with PD and other players, except for 'Returning to reality', where players with PD seemed to have more difficulty returning to reality than those without $(U = 73.5, z = -2.87, p = 0.003)$ [14]. Future research should compare our results with those of different player groups.

Twelve statistical tests were performed to determine the differences between the game experiences in both conditions in this study, which increases the risk of a Type I error. Because of the use of the mixed-method approach that integrates both quantitative and qualitative data, this risk is reduced as the focus is on the relevance of significant relationships and differences. Only one significant statistical difference was found, the difference in tiredness between the two conditions, which was fully supported by the qualitative data and findings in the literature.

## 6 Conclusion

This article answers the question, *'How does playing a facilitated tabletop game in a mediated environment affect the players' game experience when compared to playing face to face?'* The players' game experience in a mediated environment is remarkably similar to the experience when playing face to face. The only significant difference we found between the two conditions was the degree of tiredness after the game session showing that playing a game in a mediated session makes players feel more tired than playing face to face.

Therefore, playing in a mediated environment does not have a significant effect on game experience compared to playing face to face. Apart from tiredness, no significant difference between the two conditions on all variables measuring game experience was found. This confirms the literature suggesting that it is possible to create a sense of presence without actually being present. To make this confirmation stronger, more research with a larger sample and statistical power, is needed.

Compared to players in a physical environment, players in a mediated environment had a more active posture at the beginning but were tired in the second part of a session. This was especially noticeable if the game had to start later or was interrupted due to video or audio problems.

All in all, the most striking result is that the game experiences in a mediated setting are so similar to those in a physical setting.

## 6.1 Recommendations for Future Research

This article fills the gap in scientific knowledge about playing facilitated tabletop games in a mediated environment instead of playing face to face. Some recommendations for future research are made below.

The effect of a mediated environment on the outcome of a game can be studied more extensively. Future research should include more participants and test sessions, evenly distributed between a physical and mediated environment, to measure the effect of mediated versus physical presence instead of being influenced by the quality of individual games. This research should also focus on other types of games and player groups.

Players in a mediated environment are more tired while other outcome variables are not significantly different. With working from home and meeting online being more common because of the coronavirus disease pandemic, it is important to study the effects of a mediated environment on people beyond gaming, such as psychological effects or health-related issues [19].

Finally, more scientific research needs to be done on how games can be played in a mediated way. Future studies can include more professional tools such as VR/AR 3D or holographic experiences. The effect of a fully digital game instead of a mediated tabletop game can be studied. There is much more to discover when researchers from several scientific disciplines (e.g., behavioural sciences, computer sciences and systems engineering) coordinate their academic efforts.

## References

1. Sawyer, B.: Serious games: broadening games impact beyond entertainment. Computer Graphics Forum **26**(3), xviii (2007). https://doi.org/10.1111/j.1467-8659.2007.01044.x
2. Michael, D., Chen, S.: Serious games: games that educate, train, and inform. Thomson Course Technology. Muska & Lipman/Premier-Trade (2006)
3. Ritterfeld, U., Cody, M., Vorderer, P.: Serious games: Mechanisms and effects. Taylor & Francis Group, London (2009). https://doi.org/10.4324/9780203891650
4. Mayer, I.S.: The gaming of policy and the politics of gaming: A review. Simul. Gaming **40**(6), 825–862 (2009). https://doi.org/10.1177/1046878109346456
5. Lukosch, H.K., Bekebrede, G., Kurapati, S., Lukosch, S.G.: A scientific foundation of simulation games for the analysis and design of complex systems. Simul. Gaming **49**(3), 279–314 (2018). https://doi.org/10.1177/1046878118768858
6. Hofstede, G.J., de Caluwé, L., Peters, V.: Why simulation games work-in search of the active substance: A synthesis. Simul. Gaming **41**(6), 824–843 (2010). https://doi.org/10.1177/104 6878110375596
7. Klabbers, J.H.: The Magic Circle: Principles of Gaming & Simulation (2009). https://doi.org/10.1163/9789087903107
8. Magerkurth, C., Memisoglu, M., Engelke, T., Streitz, N.: Towards the next generation of tabletop gaming experiences. In: Proceedings - Graphics Interface. pp. 73–80 (2004)
9. Freeth, M., Foulsham, T., Kingstone, A.: What Affects Social Attention? Social Presence, Eye Contact and Autistic Traits. PLoS ONE **8**(1) (2013). https://doi.org/10.1371/journal.pone.005 3286

10. Xu, Y., Barba, E., Radu, I., Gandy, M., MacIntyre, B.: Chores are fun: understanding social play in board games for digital tabletop game design. In: Proceedings of DiGRA 2011 Conference: Think Design Play (2011)
11. Tychsen, A., Hitchens, M., Brolund, T., Kavakli, M.: The game master. In: Proceedings of the second Australasian conference on Interactive entertainment (November), pp. 215–222 (2005)
12. Kortmann, R., Peters, V.: Becoming the unseen helmsman - game facilitator competencies for novice, experienced, and non-game facilitators. Simul. Gaming **52**(3), 255–272 (2021). https://doi.org/10.1177/10468781211020792
13. Huizinga, J.: Homo ludens: a study of the play-element in culture. Homo Ludens: A Study of the Play-Element in Culture (1949). https://doi.org/10.4324/9781315824161
14. Aan het Rot, H.: The effect of a mediated environment on the outcome of a facilitated tabletop game. MSc Thesis, Delft University of Technology, Delft (2021). Retrieved from: http://res olver.tudelft.nl/uuid:6a0c9260-711c-4678-be87-3c11921560af
15. Adams, R.B., Albohn, D.N., Kveraga, K.: Social vision: applying a social-functional approach to face and expression perception. Curr. Dir. Psychol. Sci. **26**(3), 243–248 (2017). https://doi. org/10.1177/0963721417706392
16. Yuan, Y., Cao, J., Wang, R., Yarosh, S.: Tabletop games in the age of remote collaboration: design opportunities for a socially connected game experience. Proceedings of Conference on Human Factors in Computing Systems (2021). https://doi.org/10.1145/3411764.3445512
17. Morris, B.: Why Does Zoom Exhaust You? Science Has an Answer. Published in: Wall Street Journal (May 28 2020)
18. Wiederhold, B.K.: Connecting through technology during the coronavirus disease 2019 pandemic: avoiding "Zoom Fatigue." Cyberpsychol. Behav. Soc. Netw. **23**(7), 437–438 (2020). https://doi.org/10.1089/cyber.2020.29188.bkw
19. Bailenson, J.N.: Nonverbal overload: a theoretical argument for the causes of Zoom fatigue. Technology, Mind, and Behavior **2**(1) (2021). https://doi.org/10.1037/tmb0000030
20. Mayer, I.S., et al.: The research and evaluation of serious games: toward a comprehensive methodology. Br. J. Edu. Technol. **45**(3), 502–527 (2014). https://doi.org/10.1111/bjet.12067
21. IJsselsteijn, W.A., de Kort, Y., Poels, K.: The Game Experience Questionnaire. Tech. rep. Eindhoven University of Technology, Eindhoven (2013). Retrieved from: https://research. tue.nl/en/publications/the-game-experience-questionnaire
22. Mantovani, G., Riva, G.: "Real" presence: how different ontologies generate different criteria for presence, telepresence, and virtual presence. Presence: Teleoperators and Virtual Environments **8**(5), 540–550 (1999). https://doi.org/10.1162/105474699566459
23. Schloerb, D.W.: A quantitative measure of telepresence. Presence: Teleoperators and Virtual Environments **4**(1), 64–80 (1995). https://doi.org/10.1162/pres.1995.4.1.64
24. Bourdon, J.: From correspondence to computers: a theory of mediated presence in history. Commun. Theory **30**(1), 64–83 (2020). https://doi.org/10.1093/ct/qtz020
25. IJsselsteijn, W.A., Harper, B.: Virtually there? a vision on presence research. Presence- IST 2000–31014 (December) (2001). ftp://ftp.cordis.lu/pub/ist/docs/fet/fetpr-4.pdf
26. Johnson, R.B., Onwuegbuzie, A.J.: Mixed methods research: a research paradigm whose time has come. Educ. Res. **33**(7), 14–26 (2004). https://doi.org/10.3102/0013189X033007014
27. Cresswell, J., Plano-Clark, V., Gutmann, M., Hanson, W.: Advanced mixed methods research designs. In: Tashakkori, A., Teddlie, C. (eds.) Handbook of Mixed Methods in Social and Behavioral Research, pp. 209–240. Sage, Thousand Oaks, CA (2003)
28. Creswell, J.W., Plano Clark, V.: Designing and Conducting Mixed Methods Research. No. 4, 2nd edn. Sage, Los Angeles (2011). https://doi.org/10.1111/j.1753-6405.2007.00096.x

29. Aan het Rot, H., De Planque, D., Hermias, J., Jansen, C., Kulkarni, S.: Love is a Cueing Game: Cue Kitchen - Game Design Report. Unpublished student report., Delft University of Technology, Delft (2019). Retrieved from: http://resolver.tudelft.nl/uuid:893ae907-bbcc-4ec8-bd93-aef3f12eae23

30. van Laar, T.: Extrapiramidale ziekten. In: Kuks, J., Snoek, J. (eds.) Klinische neurologie, chap. 26, 17 edn, pp. 377–396. Bohn Safleu van Loghum, Houten (2012). in Dutch

# Facilitating Training Simulations for Health Emergency

Heini Utunen[1,2(✉)] ⓘ, J. Tuomas Harviainen[1] ⓘ, and Gaya M. Gamhewage[2] ⓘ

[1] Tampere University, Tampere, Finland
heini.utunen@gmail.com
[2] Learning and Capacity Development Unit, Health Emergencies Program, World Health
Organization, Geneva, Switzerland

**Abstract.** The World Health Organization's (WHO) training simulation exercises (SimEx) are immersive activities that capacitate their audiences by enabling them to practice and perform various functions in an emergency response. This paper discusses four tools used in SimEx to maximize the facilitators' technical experience to meet the overall learning outcomes and objectives. The findings have been collected from 12 exercises through feedback sessions and debriefings with facilitators, written feedback and exercise management observations. They show that facilitation methods and their usability vary depending on the scope of the exercise and the facilitators' experience. Exercise planning needs to fully align the SimEx activities with their learning objectives for optimal outcomes.

**Keywords:** Competency-based assessment · Feedback mechanisms · Learning outcome · Role play · Technical work

## 1 Introduction

The World Health Organization (WHO) sets out the organization's strategic priorities [1]. For the five-year period 2019–2023, health emergencies are the focus of one of the ambitious triple billion goals setting a target of 1 billion more people better protected from health emergencies. To achieve this, a prepared and well-trained health workforce is needed. Against this backdrop, the WHO Health Emergencies Programme (WHE) launched a Learning Strategy [2] that provides an overarching framework for all learning and training activities of the health emergencies workforce to create a workforce of excellence across the globe.

Training simulation exercises (SimEx) for the WHE are designed as immersion exercises to capacitate training audiences by enabling them to practice and perform various functions in emergency response. WHE training events with simulation exercises aim to provide continued learning for professionals already working in health emergencies. WHE trainings draw from workforce learning needs and bring the necessary learning for critical roles and to support within the curriculum development for learning interventions. During a training programme, the participants can select problems from work,

© Springer Nature Switzerland AG 2022
U. Dhar et al. (Eds.): ISAGA 2021, LNCS 13219, pp. 42–52, 2022.
https://doi.org/10.1007/978-3-031-09959-5_4

reflect on them and then present and apply skills and concepts presented in the course to these problems and report back to the group.

Use of simulations in training has proven to be effective for positioning experts in a safe environment in which operational work can be tested. Evidence from public health emergency preparedness exercises based on realistic scenarios and specific outcome measures helped to clarify roles and responsibilities of public health workers. Such exercises are also useful for knowledge transfer among workers and for identifying distinct public health structural challenges. The workforce is likely to gain in knowledge and confidence in capabilities that are tested in exercises [3, 4].

A typical WHE SimEx training simulation is an immersion exercise with functional elements that lasts about 48 h and takes place physically. These trainings and training related exercises are developed to simulate working environments in WHE deployments such as Incident Manager of a response. It is designed to create a safe and realistic environment for participants to apply existing and newly acquired knowledge for working in a health emergency. It creates the pressure and urgency of an emergency response and participants can see how they manage to deliver on individual and team assignments under pressure. According to the WHE Learning Strategy, trainer capacity should be created, established and maintained to support a culture of excellence in learning [2]. WHE trainers and facilitators should have the capacity to:

- describe how adult learning theories can be applied to design high-impact training sessions;
- customize training materials to suit the assessed learning needs of a specific audience;
- apply facilitation skills in a range of participatory training activities and learning reinforcement techniques including training SimExes and
- exchange constructive feedback with peers and course participants as a means for refining the content and methodology of a training intervention.

The Strategy specifies the delivery of high-quality products that meet training objectives. The expectation involves facilitating face-to-face WHE trainings, including SimExes, and incorporating subject-matter expertise into the learning events. The WHE minimum standards for facilitators are to:

- respond to the particular needs of a local delivery context by adjusting the training design accordingly and
- engage the trainees in a learner-centred approach to ensure joint ownership of successful training outcomes.

This paper focuses on the facilitation of training SimExes in face-to-face trainings. A typical event would contain online learning before and after the face-to-face event including an intense 2-day simulation.

## 2  Intervention

Facilitators are often experienced professionals in health emergencies who join the training activity for a short period of time. The first author managed and designed health emergency training SimExes and presents various tools to help expedite facilitators' integration into the SimExes and functions in the simulation. The competency framework is a larger initiative by the Learning and Capacity Development Team of WHE. General SimEx planning is conducted in line with the WHO Simulation Exercise Manual [5].

The SimEx goal is to build on and exercise professional, personal and interpersonal skills critical to effective emergency response by reinforcing good practices learned during the training course prior to the SimEx, demonstrating knowledge of the WHO Emergency response Framework, Humanitarian Programme Cycle and working with the WHO Incident Management System (IMS). It also includes the special interventions required for response to both humanitarian crises and disease outbreaks and exercising field skills with emphasis on teamwork, self and stress management, working under pressure, understanding of the code of conduct and ethics, learning how to handle diverging views, positions, interests and values, networking techniques and negotiating skills.

## 3    Methods

This paper presents four different facilitator tools that relate to a facilitator's ability to provide professional inputs and transfer their expertise to the simulation exercise in a health emergency training context.

The research questions are:

1. How can we align the exercise facilitation with the achievement of the desired learning objectives and outcomes and present it simply for the facilitators?
2. How can experts transfer their expertise through role play?
3. What are the steps to perform a competency-based assessment (CBA) during the exercise?
4. How do we choose from and utilize a variety of feedback mechanisms during and after the exercise?

The findings have been collected from 12 exercises during 2015–2019. All exercises are similar, with humanitarian settings and health emergency events, such as outbreaks. SimExes have lasted the same time, 48 h each and have been performed through team-based activities. The assessments of the tools' usability are based on facilitator feedback and observations. These have been collected through debriefing sessions with facilitators, written and oral feedback, and exercise management observations. In total, more than 150 facilitators attended, 145 attended the debriefings, 15 facilitators provided written feedback, and 12 were interviewed.

Each exercise has given evidence and elements for further refinement of the tools and the improvements have been reflected and put in use in the next exercise. This development process has produced the tools to the stage in which they are presented here. The first author was the exercise manager, led the exercise controls, developed the tools for practical testing and contributed to the wider Learning and Capacity Development Unit which designed the CBA [6] for the WHO Health Emergencies Programme during 2018–2019.

# 4 Applications

## 4.1 Exercise Planning and Integration of the Learning Outcomes

Facilitators receive in advance a package on the whole training and SimEx planning and objectives, including a detailed Master Event List, scenarios, and a planning over- view. This documentation has been refined in detail to give the necessary at-ease use overview to manage the complex multi-activity exercise with live elements.

## 4.2 Knowledge and Skills Transfer Through Role Play

Facilitators perform various role plays during the SimEx to help create a realistic envi- ronment for the simulation. Through role play, they convey field realities and points of learning for the participants and collect assessment and feedback elements on the par- ticipants' performance. Exercise control provides a role play training spot objective to align with overall learning objectives and competency framework. Facilitators receive a role play sheet with the scenario elements and are asked to review it for suitability and adjust according to the field realities they have experienced.

## 4.3 Competency-Based Assessment (CBA) Framework

In training events supported by the Learning and Capacity Development unit (LCD), WHE regularly conducts assessments of its six Core Competencies (Fig. 1) through an established mechanism (Fig. 2) based on WHO corporate competencies. The behav- ioral indicators of the WHE CBA are designed for the health emergency personnel to demonstrate [7].

Competency-based learning consists of identifying the knowledge, skills and atti- tudes required by staff to fulfil their roles in the Organization's response and training to the identified competencies. The training event with SimEx included a process of assessment, interviews and briefings and was implemented in four training activities with more than 100 participants. The training activities each 5–6 days long comprised a mix of classroom sessions, tabletop exercises, group work and 2-day long simulation exercises. Prior to the training event, using the assessment process requires all facilita- tors to be trained just-in-time on how to conduct the observations and scoring during the SimEx, and for them to observe trainees throughout the course of the activity.

During SimEx, the training cohort was divided into teams; separate assessment sheets were made available for each team and team participant. Close involvement with partic- ipant team-based activities was required from the facilitators and observations had to be recorded immediately after each training activity. Exercise control compiled all obser- vations into two products: 1) Consolidated confidential reports summarizing feedback for each individual participant to be briefed only with the participants in question, and 2) Consolidated anonymized reports on the trends identified through facilitator feedback that can be part of a training outcomes report and can be used to identify learning needs for individuals and the workforce as a whole.

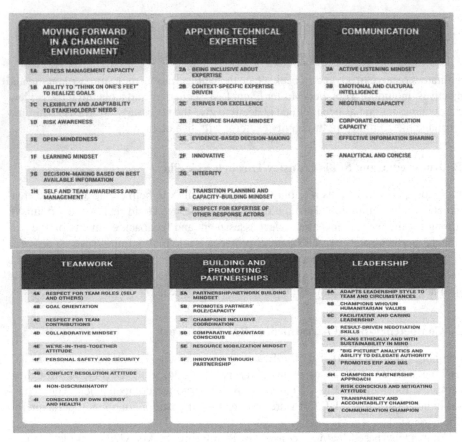

**Fig. 1.** WHE's 6 core competencies.

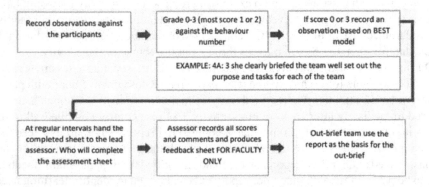

**Fig. 2.** Competency-based assessment process during training simulation exercise

## 4.4   Feedback

Feedback interventions developed for SimExes and lead by facilitators to enhance self-reflection, peer-to- peer feedback, team debriefs and individual in and out briefings. A set of feedback tools was developed for this purpose and refined over each exercise. People gain new skills in situations that include all four stages of the learning process: 1) gain knowledge 2) practice by applying that knowledge 3) get feedback and 4) reflect on what has been learned. The feed- back mechanisms of the SimExes address all the aspects of this learning loop.

# 5   Results

The facilitation methods are differently suited, depending on the scope of exercise and the facilitators' experience. Less experienced facilitators required more written and verbal instructions as well as access to more experienced facilitators throughout the process. More experienced facilitators tended to improvise when they were uncertain, but they too benefitted from regular debriefing to ensure that they kept the learning objectives in view at all times. The four tools and their uses are inter-linked and form a set of interventions that facilitators implement during the SimExes.

## 5.1   Exercise Planning Driven by Learning Objectives

Exercise planning needs to fully align the SimEx activities with the learning objectives for optimal outcomes and the planning aid documents need to be easily accessible and comprehensible at one view. The exercise elements need to be divided into sections that contribute to the simulation flow and completion of the learning objectives and competency assessments.

A major problem to be solved was to make available at-ease and at-a-glance types of simple planning documents that fully align each SimEx activity with the larger learning objectives for optimal outcomes. The overall objectives of a standard training SimEx for the participants are:

1. Apply existing and newly acquired knowledge and skills in a near-realistic simulated outbreak response
2. Demonstrate ability to work under pressure and as part of teams
3. Assess own learning gaps and develop a learning plan

These learning objectives guide the planning of the more detailed exercise activities, with simple handouts for the facilitators who might join before the start of the SimEx without any preparation. While facilitators receive a briefing on the exercise scenario – the learning objectives for each training spot, competency assessments and feedback mechanisms – some tools and ease-of-use handouts are needed to perform a facilitation that is aligned and produces desired outcomes during different SimEx activities.

The simulations often run in remote sites, army barracks or mountains for the optimal environment. Several times during activities, facilitators move swiftly from role players to assessors and technical feedback contributors. The most important planning documents need to be at hand for each facilitator. The facilitators must link the activities with a larger scope of learning outcomes. As well as the event updates, the planning documents should be easy to carry during the exercise, to follow the necessary sections and to arrange the competency-based assessment and feedback sessions.

## 5.2 Making Most Out of the Role Play with Scripting Support

Role play is at the most productive and targeted level, and meeting the learning objectives when pre-fabricated, standardized role-play scripts are offered. The script quality and scope should be reviewed, improved and reflected upon in the field and professional experience of the facilitators. Such scripts are further revised after the role play spot based on the training spot completion.

Role play scripts provide the foundation for the facilitators' contributions during the live elements in the SimExes. The SimEx Exercise Control (ExCon) suggests the basic role play script ahead of the events aligned with the exercise planning and outcomes. Facilitators with field experience can help review, proof and improve the scope, and ensure that the technical expertise and field realities are incorporated in the role play script. They are encouraged to incorporate their specific topical and contextual experience but stay in the SimEx scenario. Most of the training scripts are revised after a first run in the training spot. If the SimEx scenario changes, experienced facilitators improvise a role and then write the role play script afterwards. They can live scribe, adjust and improvise their role play.

If the role play cannot convey all the planned inputs, ExCon can inject them as news or events in other formats, or through other channels of information dissemination during an exercise, as role play also conveys scenario related information.

## 5.3 Competency-Based Assessments (CBA)

CBA with behavioural indicator observation, scoring and individual briefing and debriefing discussions require significant planning, staffing and focus. Training to perform the assessments is necessary as is seamless collaboration of the whole facilitator group. The aim and scope of the exercise and the facilitators' profiles determine the type of feedback mechanism and its utilization during the exercise. Experience and learning mindsets stipulate the scope and depth of the facilitator inputs.

The exercise preparatory planning work before each SimEx reflects and pre-defines behaviours to be observed and maps them based on the Core Competencies and SimEx planning. The aim of the CBA is to identify the critical knowledge, skills and attitudes that are required for success for all individuals working in WHO emergency operations. CBA is conducted through behavioural indicator observation, scoring and individual in-briefing and out-briefing discussions and requires significant planning effort, staffing and focus, including training to perform the assessments. In return, they yield meaningful results in the form of detailed participant assessments. CBA can provide, at best, individualized feedback on competency framework-based observations and help formulate learning objectives and pathways for participants and inform them of future deployment decisions. The CBA evidence provides information on training design and assessment of the learning outcomes.

In two SimExes, the full range of behaviours was observed. In another two SimExes, the number of behaviours observed was reduced to concentrate on the competencies expected of those participants. Where participants were observed against all behaviours throughout the entire training period, the assessment provided an indication of strengths and areas for development which were agreed with by participants. Where the number of behaviours observed was reduced, the assessment provided less indication and was less helpful in guiding briefing conversations with participants. A greater number of facilitators conducting observations improved the feedback as their observations of events and understanding of behaviours can vary.

It was beneficial to train and brief the observers in the use of the assessment to reduce the incidences of scores of 0 or 3. High numbers of the extreme scores made debriefing participants more difficult because justification for those scores was either not provided or contained insufficient detail to provide evidence for the score. Scores for all participants of a training activity were also aggregated to give an indication of areas of strength and weakness for the entire cohort.

From a learning perspective, providing constructive and accurate feedback to participants is a key part of the learning process and facilitators play a key role in the feedback process which goes hand-in-hand with assessments. Facilitators who had coaching skills tended to be more skilled at providing feedback and were able to link the feedback to the development of a future learning pathway.

## 5.4  Feedback Mechanisms

The experience over a dozen exercises has resulted in an array of optional methods to be used in the training simulation exercises. Training faculty and facilitators can also choose from the options and utilize a variety of feedback mechanisms before, during and after the exercise. SimEx facilitators are encouraged to work consciously on the feedback, including listing instances when feedback is required. They must immerse in self-reflection, peer-to-peer feedback and debriefing. They must characterize good feedback and the learning and development mindset to give or receive feedback. A set of tools and their suitability for the SimEx sequences is suggested (See Table 1).

In and out briefings provide an opportunity for participants and facilitators to discuss and shape participant learning based on the competency assessment. The information from these meetings can be used to assess the value and retention of learning including gaps and needs met. The briefings should ideally take place with three facilitators, at least one of whom is a learning expert or has coaching experience. This improves the opportunity for the meaningful feedback due to higher likelihood of having observed the participant during the training. The briefings should be semi-structured with clear points for discussion.

The feedback is most hectic where the most learning happens, according to both the participants and facilitators. Some SimEx events are followed by feedback sessions for technical work outside the roles, individually or in a team. They can be guided by detailed feedback instructions that follow the overall planning of the SimEx. Both individual and team feedback can be situational, based on self-reflection or any exchange with

**Table 1.** SimEx feedback tools

Feedback methods in different stages of the SimEx

| Feedback type | Method | Before SimEx | During SimEx | After SimEx |
|---|---|---|---|---|
| Individual in-briefing | Discussion | X | | |
| Individual feedback | Discussion | X | X | X |
| Individual self -reflection | Encouragement to reflection | X | X | X |
| Team feedback | Group discussion | | X | X |
| Feedback in role play role | Role-player reaction | | X | |
| Expert feedback outside the role play | Written, face-to-face | | X | X |
| Individual debriefing / Out-briefing | Structured discussion based on CBA | | | X |
| Team debriefing | Team discussion | | | X |

a meaningful approach to learning. As the teams produce content during the exercise, such as situation reports, communication across different levels, coordination meetings, planning and funding documents, there are many documents for facilitators to review and assess. These information products are collected centrally by the Exercise Control and reviewed by the facilitators who are technical experts in the domains. After the simulation, time is set aside at the final debrief to provide detailed feedback to the team on all information products.

Team debriefing has proven to be effective when conducted in an informal and egalitarian manner like sitting in a circle without desks. The facilitator can outline the questions and participants can take a moment to reply. Facilitators need to manage the conversation to ensure that each person is able to speak. Topics can include discussion such as the plan, the results, the differences, or what went well (list three things), what did not go well (list three things), and what one thing needs to change if this is done again.

Self-reflection should be encouraged in all training contexts. SimEx participants are asked to think about the simulation activity that took place, consider what they did well, what they did not do well and what they would do differently if they encountered the same situation again. Aids to self-reflection are observations, giving feedback to other participants, quiet thinking time and completing learning logs or diaries [8].

## 6  Discussion

An appropriate set of facilitator tools can help improve the experience and skill transfer from facilitators to learners and make the most out of the experts' time. The mix of these facilitation methods can also help build an immersive learning experience in a training simulation. Adequate and thought-out facilitator methods and tools assist in realizing a successful exercise for both facilitators and learners. Facilitators need a system of briefing, debriefing, coaching and support to help them complete the complex tasks in SimEx.

The facilitators and SimEx participants start with realistic and comprehensible learning objectives and out-comes. When the overall planning is easily understood, the pieces of the exercise puzzle are easy to absorb and implement. Various planning documents were tested both in print and electronic format but finally the two text documents were adequate for the facilitators. Participants have expressed things differently in the evaluations, placing the learning objectives in the live play training spots. This works well if the scenario allows you to anticipate the context and events. On the other hand, setting the expectations upfront deviates the attention from the simulation performance and puts unnecessary attention on the desired learning points only, while many learning objectives can be achieved in each training spot.

The educational content is present at all times due to the facilitator who ensure that the participants stay motivated and take part in the right activities by following the planning guidance [9]. Early work on the efficiency of educational role-playing games suggests that the effectiveness of role play within a simulation depends on the degree of congruence between the individuals and their roles [10]. Accordingly, the individual in the simulation and the role will determine knowledge, emotion and performance that are interdependent.

In transformative role-playing simulation, participants are involved through four levels of reality: a character, a player, a person and a human being that can be associated with four dimensions of learning: knowing, doing, being and relating [11]. This unveils the personal learning and paths towards personal development which is also a goal at the WHO health emergency training simulations. Researchers have emphasized the role of briefing and especially debriefing for accomplishing that purpose [12].

These elements make up the entire facilitator loop in the training exercises. In WHE contexts, the tool for assessing core competencies has provided a way for facilitators to develop meaningful feedback for learners about their demonstration of core competencies. The process is labour-intensive and requires a collection of multiple observations from all facilitators to be most effective. The assessment tool has allowed for constructive and critical feedback to be acknowledged by participants. Training and simulations following a CBA must consider different ways to provide feedback.

If feedback on core competencies is purely subjective, it risks a conscious or unconscious bias on behalf of the observer. The more feedback there is from different facilitators, the less the subjectivity. Each SimEx involved between 3,000 and 5,000 pieces of feedback from facilitators for an average group of 20–25 participants. Closing the loop, the analysis of the feedback corresponded with the participant's own self-assessment during the briefing. This further underscored the utility and accuracy of the CBA used. Providing objective, accurate and constructive feedback on behaviours can help a person identify and reflect on their strengths and areas for development which is a key part of the professional and function-specific learning process. Competencies must be understood by the staff and personnel supporting a learning programme and they need to be trained in their use for designing, delivering and assessment of learning and training activities. Feedback contributes to the training evaluation and improvement. It is essential to take the time and effort spent on training to take stock, which leads to improved outcomes over time.

# 7 Conclusion

This work discusses the training exercises and presents four tools for the facilitators. Simulation exercises are intensive and powerful tools for learning. They impose uncertainty on both participants and facilitators and require full engagement. To make the best of the experience, adequate planning for the simulation exercise facilitation is necessary. The time, resources and effort invested will be the best utility when the simulation has clear objectives and outcomes for learning.

As experienced in the training exercises of WHO's health emergencies, several tools are suited for making meaningful exercise facilitations with each having different strengths and limitations. The tools presented for different purposes are all interlinked and interdependent. Role play, assessments and feedback form a continuum in which all parts need to align for the best outputs. The exercise control plays an important role in selecting the appropriate methods for different exercises and facilitators. It requires professional grounding in both learning and operations domains to get all pieces playing together, smoothly and successfully.

# References

1. World Health Organization's Health Emergencies Programme: WHO Health Emer- gencies Programme's learning strategy (2018). https://www.who.int/emergencies/publicationre-sources/training/tools/whe-learning-strategy.pdf. last accessed 27 July 2021
2. Utunen, H., Black, A., Stucke, O., Attias, M., Gamhewage, G.M.: Identifying and assessing competencies for staff working in public health emergencies. Studies in Health Technology and Informatics **270**, 1311–1312 (2020)
3. Biddinger, P.D., et al.: Public health emergency preparedness exercises: lessons learned. Public Health Rep. **125**(Suppl 5), 100–106 (2010)
4. Emonts, M., et al.: Integration of social simulations into a task-based blended training curriculum. In: Pro- ceedings of the 2012 Land Warfare conference. DSTO, Canberra (2012). https://www.alelo.com/wp-content/up-loads/2014/06/Alelo_LWC2012_paper_Emonts_Row_Johnson_et_al_v2.pdf. last accessed 27 July 2021
5. Landers, R.N.: Developing a theory of gamified learning: linking serious games and gamification of learning. Simulation & Gaming **45**(6), 752–768 (2014)
6. World Health Organization: WHO Simulation exercise manual (2017). https://www.who.int/ihr/publications/WHO-WHE-CPI-2017.10/en/. last accessed 27 May 2021
7. World Health Organization: Introduction to competency-based assessments. Online learning resource. https://openwho.org/courses/intro-competency. last accessed 27 May 2021
8. Goosen, K.R., Jensen, R., Wells, R.: Purpose and learning benefits of simulations: a design and development perspective. Simulation & Gaming **32**(1), 21–39 (2001)
9. Kolb, A., Kolb, D.: Experiential learning theory: a dynamic, holistic approach to management learning, education and development. In: Armstrong, S.J., Fukami, C.V. (eds.) The SAGE handbook of management learning, education and development, pp. 42–68. Sage, London (2009)
10. Crookall, D., Oxford, R.L., Saunders, D.: Towards a reconceptualisation of simulation: from representation to reality. Simulation & Games for Learning **17**(4), 147–171 (1987)
11. Daniau, S.: The transformative potential of role-playing games: from play skills to human skills. Simul. Gaming **47**(4), 423–444 (2016)
12. Crookall, D.: Serious games, debriefing, and simulation/gaming as a discipline. Simul. Gaming **41**(6), 898–920 (2010)

# Factors and Attributes of Team Players: A Study of Engineering Students in India

Santosh Dhar[✉] [ID], Upinder Dhar[ID], and Anand Rajavat[ID]

SVIIT, Shri Vaishnav Vidyapeeth Vishwavidyalaya, Indore, India
santosh_dhar@hotmail.com

**Abstract.** Members of teams collaborate on tasks to achieve objectives. Each member is responsible for contributing to the team which is responsible for team success. In a game, its players contribute toward the goal of winning a game by collaborating on activities with defined outcomes. Each member's influence on team decisions is critical for overall team performance because mutual influence and members' ideas are integrated into decision making and implemented through team actions. Research has revealed that some universal and specific team actions exert a positive influence on outcomes. Members mostly highlight teamwork, decision-making, information processing, reaching agreements and dealing with uncertainty as the most relevant contributions towards their outcomes. The challenge for a team is to create enjoyment and engagement, relevant and personalized game experiences for its players which lead to outcomes of the game. The study is an attempt to understand the perception of engineering students about the factors and attributes of players and to see the impact of gender on their perception.

**Keywords:** Ability to collaborate · Ability to enjoy · Enjoyment · Functional conflict · Social interaction

## 1 Introduction

### 1.1 Conceptual Framework

The importance of teams has stimulated considerable interest in recent years. Effective teamwork is a major contributor for better outcomes in a game, an organization or a project. The attributes of an effective team are a shared vision, an informal atmosphere, participation of each team member, effective listening, functional conflict, consensus for important decisions, open communication, clarity of role, shared leadership and diversity of team-player styles. A high level of participation of every member is usually considered an effective characteristic but over involvement can at times lead to little or no progress towards achieving the team's goals and hence, calls for introspection. A new structure as a team is not enough. Members in the gaming team need to understand the key elements of what it means to be in a team and require direction and facilitation for team dynamics.

When equipped with the appropriate tactics and resources, team members can make their teams successful. The major differences between a team and a traditional work

U. Dhar et al. (Eds.): ISAGA 2021, LNCS 13219, pp. 53–60, 2022.
https://doi.org/10.1007/978-3-031-09959-5_5

group are the interdependent nature of the members' work and their joint accountability. There is a need to adjust some of the processes to ensure overall alignment with the team structure. For example, joint accountability runs counter to the individual player's performance rewards and incentives that many teams favour. Team members must understand the responsibilities accompanying team membership. Individual influence refers to the altering of others' thoughts, feelings and behaviours [1]. Each member's influence on team decisions is critical for overall team performance because it is only through mutual influence and the members' ideas which are integrated into decision making of the team and implemented through team actions [2].

There are various types of teams and the basic elements of participation are common in most of them. To become an effective team player, members must be active. Passive membership in no way can contribute to the team's successful performance. Gaming teams realize performance benefits that can be the integration of diverse perspectives due to the players' heterogeneous backgrounds [3]. Individual characteristics such as task competence and behaviours could influence the team's tactics [1]. Earning trust is a central footing for teams because without a trusting environment, members cannot accomplish their goals. In a game, team members cannot be jointly accountable in an environment that lacks trust.

It is the responsibility of all the players to create and foster a trusting environment. Effective team players first give trust to get trust. Too often, players set the entire team up for loss when they do not trust their fellow members and are not trustworthy themselves. Nurturing a trusting environment in a game requires opening up and becoming susceptible to accept each other. It is easier to play well when team members know that their fellow members are with them. Players may face insecure situations while playing a new game. They often seek relationships with members who can mentor and help them to be ready for the surprises they could face in the new context [4].

Social interaction becomes important because of the role played by team members in shaping identities of the new members [5]. Identification indicates how strongly (or not) the newcomer has accepted the goals and values of the team and the intent to become a full member of the team [6]. This process of identification not only supports the ability of newcomers to perform in the new team but also positively affects how existing members respond to them [7]. Members performing together in teams require effective communication. This is not simply the words that are spoken but non-verbal communication and listening too.

Members must be aware of how they communicate including the words they choose, the channel selected to convey the message and the use of feedback. Too often, people simply assume that others understand what they are saying and they understand what others are saying. Both of these assumptions are risky while playing a game together. Research has revealed that some universal and specific team skills exert a positive influence on outcomes. Members mostly highlight teamwork, decision-making, information processing, reaching agreements and dealing with uncertainty as the most relevant contributions towards their outcomes. These results have instructional implications for determining the best way to enhance team players' motivation and learning outcomes.

Functional conflict is essential for effectively playing the team games. While many believe that conflict should be avoided, functional conflict helps a team to mature and perform at optimal levels as against dysfunctional conflict. After resolving key issues, those teams that have a tentative peace or harmony are usually hesitant to take challenges. This can stall a team at an immature (and poor performing) stage. Teams that are more mature encourage their members to articulate their differences and conflict while playing the game. In any game, three faces of knowledge appear together in the form of action, the transaction of knowledge and in the performance of the players. Systemic interdependence arises by virtue of the constraints that these three aspects impose on each other in the context of every particular application [8].

During game play, specific local circumstances determine how the mutual influences between the faces of knowledge are affected. Players draw upon rules and resources and thereby, reproduce them in the course of the game. Especially in free play, the players have self-organizing transformative power. Games provide an opportunity to analyze the behavior of individual players within the social network of the team. Varied situations and broader contextual variables may moderate the effectiveness of a team. For instance, shared perceptions within the team about procedures followed may moderate the effectiveness of the team in terms of its members putting more efforts to be effective performers.

## 1.2  Rationale

The challenge for a team is to leverage the learning and skills required to play the game, create enjoying and engaging, relevant and personalized game experiences for all players which can be reflected in the outcome of the game. Team players could benefit from the sense of accomplishment during the gaming process and consequently, benefit from teamwork. The nature of games as interactive systems and playful activities help in explaining, analyzing and communicating amongst the team members. The perception of team players about the fellow members enriches the experience of playing team based games. Educational games usually offer nothing more than systems designed for repetitive exercises which do not take long to bore the players. Similarly, poorly designed educational games are unable to guide learners towards gradual learning to ensure the desired results. Developers must design the games keeping in view the perceived attributes of team players to enhance involvement, enjoyment and commitment of the members.

## 1.3  Objectives

The present study was undertaken with the following objectives:

- to understand the perception of engineering students about constituent factors and attributes of team players.
- to understand the difference in the perception of male and female engineering students about constituent factors and attributes of team players.

# 2  Method

## 2.1  The Study

It is an exploratory study focused at identifying the factors and attributes of team players. The convergence of attributes is intended to bring in more clarity about how team players are perceived by the youth.

## 2.2  The Design

The study is having multi stage randomized design starting from identification of the attributes of team players on the basis of review of literature. The attributes are presented in the form of statements to test the perception of engineering students. The data collected from students was analyzed for the next stage of the design by applying exploratory factor analysis to highlight the constituent factors of team players as perceived by the budding professionals.

## 2.3  The Sample

The sample was collected online through Google forms. A final sample of 650 engineering students studying in bachelor of technology course was drawn from the initial total sample of 720 respondents after purification of data, i.e., 70 incomplete, doubtful or erroneous forms were rejected. The extraneous variables were, thus, controlled by randomization and elimination. The respondents were in the age group of 18–23 years with an average age of 22 years. Further distribution of the sample was in terms of males and females.

## 2.4  The Tool for Data Collection

Based on review of literature, a tool for data collection was developed on five point Likert scale. The tool consisted of 28 items with five possible choices as strongly agree, agree, not sure, disagree and strongly disagree.

## 2.5  The Tool for Data Analysis

Simple correlation, factor analysis and Z-test were used for data analysis as per need of the multi-stage design of the study.

# 3   Results and Discussion

After running factor analysis on the data, two factors were identified: Ability to collaborate and ability to enjoy with an Eigen value of 13.05 and 1.96, respectively.

**Ability to Collaborate.** This factor is constituted of item 4: collaborative relationship (.79); item 14: thinking and feeling about the role (.74); item 8: willing to provide the support (.74); item 2: contributes as an active member (.72); item15: true gamer hits harder (.71); item 26: mind and body perform together (.71); item 7: competent and committed (.71); item 5: influence on the dynamics of team (.71); item 16: optimistic (.70); item 13: right frame of mind (.70); item 3: participation in important decisions (.65); item 11: adds value (.65); item 1: specific expectations related to roles (.64); item 9: flexible (.63); item 17: self–reassessment (.62); item 10: diversity of opinions leading to optimal solutions (.59); item 18: altering everything when nothing seems to work (.58); item 25: games are just fun (.57); item 12: different roles while game progresses (.54); item 6: responsible for outcome(.53) and item 24: new form of the game a priority (.52) with a total factor load of 13.75 and 35.16% of variance.

Collaboration is defined in many contexts. In the organizational context, it means working together for mutual benefits like exchange of resources, knowledge sharing, technological know-how, capacity for innovation and diffusion of technology, strengthening of purchasing power and capacity to exert a higher pressure on the market [9]. Collaboration for teamwork can be argued as seeking to share better results and benefits by establishing a relationship. Thus, what seems difficult for individuals to achieve individually can be achieved with relationships and generating strength through collaboration. The collaborative advantage is more than an inter-team competitive advantage generated by joint value creation mechanisms by which members of a team obtain strategic benefits.

The belief is that players act in their best interests in relationships while performing based on what was agreed. They work together to achieve joint benefits, a feature that affects collaboration [10]. The trust influences the interaction among the members of a team. It contributes to collective actions and common goals that reduce opportunistic behaviours. At a relationship level, trust depicts a direct positive effect on the performance. The development of trust arises from the connectivity established between companies often derived from informal linkages [11]. Trust alleviates exchange ratios and is based on relationships that members of the team establish over time. Intense relationship contributes to reputation of the team which is extremely an important feature to build trust between members.

**Ability to Enjoy.** This factor is constituted of item 28: games are just fun (.75); item 22: empathy has intended effects (.68); item 19: fastest route to victory (.68); item 27: players have fun (.67); item 20: risk is too great if it means avoiding defeat (.64); item 21: able to place soul within the body of the opponent (.60) and item 23: fresh game is engaging (.59) with a total factor load of 4.61 and 18.45% variance.

Emotional demonstrations are not always vibrant for they alter with time with some emotional instances more significant than others. Some emotional exhibits may influence players more while playing the game. The distinct emotion of happiness is the most needed form of positive emotions which are important for building relationships in interpersonal contexts [12]. Since a game is played for a prolonged period, the displayed emotions can vacillate. Exhibited delight at its peak moment plays a critical role in influencing the level of backing support received from the audience.

Gestalt theory maintains that peak is one of the few salient stimuli that are most memorable to and thus encoded by people, therefore showing a unique effect on people's summary assessment beyond the average or general state of all stimuli [13]. Visual selective attention theory also suggests that people pay the most attention to the stimuli that are the most vivid and expressive, such as peak moments; greater attention in turn leads to better memory [14]. Since displayed joy at its peak moment is particularly noticeable and salient, it has a distinct influence on the response of audience who may feel more joyful when they sees highest displayed joy by the team players.

This can happen through emotional contagion, a situation wherein an observer, while observing emotional expressions of another person, mechanically imitates the expressions and starts to feel the same emotion [15]. Emotional contagion is strong when the emotions are at their peak and are highly expressive [16]. The joyful feeling of the audience can become meaningful moments in a player's experience and evaluation of the game. Earlier studies have shown that positive emotions can reduce debate in decision-making and lead one to cultivate favorable decisions [17].

Escape smartphone gaming is linked to boredom proneness and gaming related problems [18]. People who experience intense boredom frequently in everyday life play smartphone games to escape or alleviate the feeling of boredom and end up with the problems of excessive game play like addiction to game play for longer periods with loss of awareness of time and space. The urge is more to escape boredom rather than to have fun or enjoyment. The game has to be played for fun rather than to escape the boredom. The joyful experience leads to positive emotions.

To find the difference in the perception of male and female students on the constituent factors of the team players, Z-test was applied. It was found insignificant on both the factors showing that there is no significant difference in the perception of male and female students on the factors, ability to collaborate and ability to enjoy. Both male and female students share similar perception on the factors and attributes of team players. This can be ascribed to the fact that these days, gender has lost its impact on the perception of male and female students about the attributes of team players due to digitization, exposure to social media and electronic media, equal opportunity to technical education, and games and sports.

It is well known that the ability to collaborate is essentially a part of teamwork but it is interesting to note that students perceive fun in terms of ability to enjoy as a constituent factor of the attributes of team players. Thus, the element of enjoying a game is seen to be essentially visible in team players and keeps teammates together while setting a goal to win. The common perception of students is reflected by having no impact of gender on the perception about the factors and attributes of team players. The study has, thus, revealed a two tier model in this regard (Fig. 1).

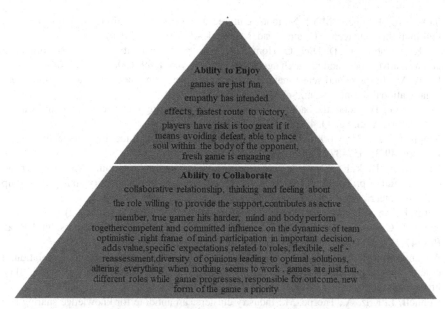

**Fig. 1.** Diagram: two tier model of attributes of team players

## 4   Conclusion

Games have the potential to mix positive experiences. They enhance the opportunities for players to engage in meaningful discourse, actively construct and reformulate their knowledge, and to practice scientific reasoning and argumentation. These practices allow players to enhance their cognitive and metacognitive abilities. The results of the study have implications for game designers who should consider the scope for collaboration and fun while designing a new game. Game administrators can also encourage team players to collaborate and enjoy the game for superior and satisfying outcome.

It needs to be further studied why 21 items converged into a single factor i.e., ability to collaborate, whereas only seven items converged into the other factor, ability to enjoy. A comprehensive study needs to be designed to clarify whether the findings of this study indicate that cognitive elements have an edge over affective elements in a team-based game. The endorsement of the results may show that a team game is perceived by students as an opportunity to learn while having fun. Enjoyment acts a bond to continue playing the game. The implications for researchers are to explore the perception in different age groups, study the perception of non-technical students in the same age group and compare the impact of culture on the perception of students.

## References

1. Anderson, C., Kilduff, G.J.: Why do dominant personalities attain influence in face-to-face groups? The competence-signaling effects of trait dominance. J. Pers. Soc. Psychol. **96**, 491–503 (2009)

2. Salk, J.E., Brannen, M.Y.: National culture, networks, and individual influence in a multinational management team. Acad. Manag. J. **43**, 191–202 (2000)
3. van Knippenberg, D., De Dreu, C., Homan, A.: Work group diversity and group performance: an integrative model and research agenda. J. Appl. Psychol. **89**, 1008–1022 (2004)
4. Louis, M.: Surprise and sense making: what newcomers experience in entering unfamiliar organizational settings. Adm. Sci. Q.. **25**, 226–251 (1980)
5. Pratt, M.G.: The good, the bad, and the ambivalent: managing identification among Amway distributors. Adm. Sci. Q. **45**(3), 456–493 (2000)
6. Knippenberg, D.V.: Work motivation and performance: a social identity perspective. Appl. Psychol. **49**(3), 357–371 (2001)
7. Kane, A.A., Rink, F.: When and how groups utilize dissenting newcomer knowledge: newcomers' future prospects condition the effect of language-based identity strategies. Group Process. Intergr. Relat. **19**, 591–607 (2016)
8. Barth, F.: An anthropology of knowledge. Curr. Anthropol. **43**(1), 1–18 (2002)
9. Rosas, J., Camarinha-Matos, L.M.: An approach to assess collaboration readiness. Int. J. Prod. Res. **47**(17), 4711–4735 (2009). https://doi.org/10.1080/00207540902847298
10. Anbanandam, R., Banwet, D.K., Shankar, R.: Evaluation of supply chain collaboration: a case of apparel retail industry India. Int. J. Product. Perform. Manag. **60**(2), 82–98 (2011). https://doi.org/10.1108/17410401111101449
11. Connell, J., Kriz, A., Thorpe, M.: Industry clusters: an antidote for knowledge sharing and collaborative innovation. J. Knowl. Manag. **18**(1), 137–151 (2014). https://doi.org/10.1108/jkm-08-2013-0312
12. Staw, B.M., Sutton, R.I., Pelled, L.H.: Employee positive emotion and favorable outcomes at the workplace. Organ. Sci. **5**, 51–71 (1994)
13. Ariely, D., Carmon, Z.: Gestalt characteristics of experiences: the defining features of summarized events. J. Behav. Decis. Mak. **13**, 191–201 (2000)
14. Treue, S.: Visual attention: the where, what, how and why of saliency. Curr. Opin. Neurobiol. **13**, 428–432 (2003)
15. Flack, W.: Peripheral feedback effects of facial expressions, bodily postures, and vocal expressions on feelings. Cogn. Emot. **20**, 177–195 (2006)
16. Sullins, E.S.: Emotional contagion revisited: Effects of social comparison and expressive style on mood convergence. Pers. Soc. Psychol. Bull. **17**, 166–174 (1991)
17. Sinclair, R.C., Mark, M.M.: The effects of mood state on judgemental accuracy: processing strategy as a mechanism. Cogn. Emot. **9**, 417–438 (2008)
18. Larche, C.J., Dixon, M.J.: Winning isn't everything: the impact of optimally challenging smartphone games on flow, game preference and individuals gaming to escape aversive bored states. Comput. Hum. Behav. **123**, 106857 (2021)

# Intercultural Dialogue Through Simulation and Virtual Exchange in Education

M. Laura Angelini[✉] and Rut Muñíz

Universidad Católica de Valencia 'San Vicente Mártir', 46110 Valencia, Spain
{marialaura.angelini,rut.muniz}@ucv.es

**Abstract.** The study presents partial results of the project Simulation+Virtual Exchange 2021 (Sim+VE 2021). This project successfully brought together students from a course on teacher training from the Catholic University of Valencia (UCV) in Spain with student teachers, in-service teachers and academicians from various universities in Spain, Tunisia, Austria, Romania, USA, Argentina, Canada, Netherlands and UK. The simulation 'The School of Valtance' was carried out for eight weeks by synchronous and asynchronous virtual exchanges. Using simulation as a methodological strategy, high quality education was continued through virtual exchanges and the application of simulation in a digital environment. Thus, this paper is a study of the school environments, doing thorough research and building intercultural dialogue between the professional agents participating in education. The positive results of the experience suggest that initiatives using simulation may challenge the policy-makers who perceive teacher education as a fairly closed experience of professional formation, rather than as global collaborative and lifelong learning.

**Keywords:** Simulation · Active listening · Intercultural dialogue · Classroom management · Cultural diversity · Educational challenges

## 1 Introduction

The study presented here gathers the most relevant insights of the academicians participating in the project Simulation+Virtual Exchange 2021 (Sim+VE 2021). Participants involved in education worked collaboratively in mixed international teams to solve some educational challenges collected in the simulation scenario, 'The School of Valtance' version 2. Pre-service teachers were given opportunities to develop and practice professional skills (assuming role profiles such as parents, special needs teacher, head of the school, language teacher and other colleagues) in a safe simulated environment [1]. This initiative makes perfect sense in teacher training since mistakes committed in a real-life environment are difficult to revert, most of the times. Through simulated environments in which reflective dialogue takes place (reflection-on-action), pre-service teachers have an opportunity to analyse their performance [2–5]. 'This kind of repeated practice is not only possible but encouraged and can be accomplished without any harm to real adults or children' [6].

U. Dhar et al. (Eds.): ISAGA 2021, LNCS 13219, pp. 61–70, 2022.
https://doi.org/10.1007/978-3-031-09959-5_6

The present project aligns with the International Higher Education Teaching and Learning Association, among others, to identify and reflect on the strengths and weaknesses of dialogue within the framework of simulation (https://www.hetl.org/). In times of pandemic, we have attempted to extend this dialogue to other professionals abroad through virtual exchange as we have had to adapt to an online mode of teaching unexpectedly. Originally consisted of face-to-face dialogue practice and a more traditional classroom simulation, our course had no option but to be adapted entirely to a virtual mode [7]. It was the leading coordinators' initiative to enhance intercultural dialogue in teacher training through the transformation of this project into a large-scale simulation.

## 1.1 Intercultural Dialogue Through Simulation

In the face of the increasing diversity of society and multicultural classrooms, the White Paper on intercultural dialogue, 'Living together as equals in dignity' defines intercultural dialogue as:

> a process that comprises an open and respectful exchange of views between individuals and groups with different ethnic, cultural, religious and linguistic backgrounds and heritage, on the basis of mutual understanding and respect. It requires the freedom and ability to express oneself, as well as the willingness and capacity to listen to the views of others. Intercultural dialogue contributes to political, social, cultural and economic integration and the cohesion of culturally diverse societies. It fosters equality, human dignity and a sense of common purpose. It aims to develop a deeper understanding of diverse world views and practices, to increase co-operation and participation (or the freedom to make choices), to allow personal growth and transformation, and to promote tolerance and respect for the other [8].

The document argues that coexisting with dignity will depend on our ability to promote mutual understanding for managing cultural diversity. Dialogue should be conceived as a collaborative process in which participants search for understanding rather than confronting [9, 10]. Dialogue involves active listening and the exercise of critical thinking and can reveal assumptions and biases for re-examination [11–14].

In Sim+VE 2021, intercultural dialogue has proved to be central to embrace educational issues from different contexts, personal experiences and realities. Testimonies from all the participants reveal the significance and impact of the learning about other educational systems, the way students learn better, strengths and limitations in each place. Training teachers for the future should comprise understanding and reflection from other educational realities as classrooms tend to be more and more multicultural.

Sim+VE 2021 addressed the communicative and international components in active dialogic interactions with agents of education worldwide in an effort to emulate a realistic school setting. In the proposed simulation, participants were actively involved to find solutions to certain educational problems or situations described in the scenario. They were exposed to reading material, audio-visual resources and recent online news to familiarise themselves with educational issues. They did research and proposed thorough ideas during the virtual exchanges.

## 1.2 Virtual Exchange

Broadly speaking, virtual exchange refers to online interactions comprising groups of learners/participants from other cultural contexts or geographical locations who carry out specific tasks as an integrated part of their educational programmes [13–15]. Through virtual exchange, people from diverse contexts are brought together in significant cross-cultural experiences. Due to the pandemic, many students were not able to have their international experience abroad. Therefore, in Sim+VE 2021, students from teaching degrees were offered an international experience by participating in an intercultural simulation through virtual exchange. The added value of the project was the voluntary participation of professionals from other levels of the educational strata such as school teachers and teacher trainers from universities. This collaborative intercultural dialogue facilitated by simulation and virtual exchange became an ideal pedagogical cluster in times of pandemic [7, 16, 17].

# 2 Method

The participants and the instruments to collect data in 'The School of Valtance' Version 2 are described below.

## 2.1 'The School of Valtance' Version 2

'The School of Valtance' Version 2 is a revised version of 'The National School of Valtance' which describes a school environment and tackles educational issues that coincide with the participants' professional expertise and training for the project [7]. Thus, this version addressed the following educational challenges for secondary education:

- Teaching methodologies in English as a Second Language (ESL): language teaching skills
- Classroom management
- Shared teaching through lesson study
- Literature, storytelling and drama in English
- Multiple modalities in teaching & assessing
- Crisis management: coping with crisis, online teaching (COVID19, …)

The scenario fully describes the school project and the educational challenges to be worked on.

## 2.2 Participants

Mixed teams [n = 16] of 6–8 participants each of in-service teachers, academicians and pre-service teachers from faculties of education of Spain, Tunisia, Austria, Romania, USA, Argentina, Canada, Netherlands and UK were created. All of them volunteered to participate in the project. An international certification was offered to each in recognition of their participation.

## 2.3 Procedure

Data was collected through:

1. Microsoft Teams for recorded synchronous sessions
2. Linkr Education for asynchronous conversations per team
3. Dedoose 9.0 for the qualitative study

The procedure consisted of preparing mixed teams to participate in all the phases of simulation: briefing, simulation and debriefing (Table 1). The leading university (Catholic University of Valencia) was in charge of making the teams with the three figures represented in each: pre-service teachers, academicians and in-service teachers. Profile roles were assigned to the participants such as Head of the School, the Valtance English Department (ValED), the Valtance Pedagogical Advisory Board (ValPE), Service learning (SerVal), the Valtance Special Education (SpEd) and the Valtance Parent Association (ValPAR).

The leading university (Catholic University of Valencia) contacted other professionals from the above-mentioned universities to coordinate the briefing phase and find in-service teachers and pre-service teachers from abroad as volunteers to participate in Sim+VE 2021(Fig. 1).

Research, team-making and simulation briefing constitute the initial phase. As in every simulation, participants not knowing the simulation scenario received guidance (instruction on simulation procedure, discussions on some educational topics) from their local university academicians. They did research on current educational topics such as teaching English as a second language, classroom management, lesson study, special needs in education, family and education and service learning. These discussions held at each place helped sharpen the simulation scenario 'The School of Valtance' Version 2.

The simulation phase comprised synchronous and asynchronous sessions. For the synchronous sessions, one session was formally scheduled every week in which teams got together via Microsoft Teams. Participants carried out the simulation by analysing the educational challenges in the scenario and discussing possible solutions. These sessions were recorded. For the asynchronous sessions, participants mostly used Linkr Education to post their views of some topics and share some reading or visual material with their team. Asynchronous sessions were agreed internally in each team though it was compulsory to participate at least twice a week. Some participants opted to use alternative tools such as Google Drive or OneDrive.

The simulation and debriefing phases were coordinated by the leading university in Spain (Table 2).

The preparation phase (finding participants, discussing educational issues and depicting educational challenges) was conducted from week 1 to week 4. This gave the academicians enough time to prepare the simulation scenario incorporating the suggestions after the discussions held at each place.

Week 5 to week 8 were devoted to the briefing, simulation and debriefing of the scenario. A qualitative analysis of the experts' perceptions was conducted. The debriefing session in Week 8 was recorded in order to recall the scholars' comments and transcribe

**Table 1.**  Some teams in Sim+VE 2021.

| PARTICIPANTS' NAMES & POSITION | CITY | E-MAIL | PROFILE | |
|---|---|---|---|---|
| Pre-service teacher | Valencia | | 1. Head of the School | **TEAM** |
| Pre-service teacher | Valencia | | 4. ValED, the Valtance English Department | |
| Academic | Tunis | | 2. ValPE, the Valtance Pedagogical Advisory Board | **1** |
| In-service teacher | Tunis | | 4. ValED, the Valtance English Department | |
| Academic | Lancaster | | 4. ValED, the Valtance English Department | |
| In-service teacher | Cluj-Napoca | | 5. SerVal: Service learning | |
| Pre-service teacher | Chicago, IL | | 6. SpEd: the Valtance Special Education | |
| Academic | Netherlands | | 3. ValPAR, the Valtance Parent Association | |
| Pre-service teacher | Valencia | | 1. Head of the School | |
| Pre-service teacher | Valencia | | 4. ValED, the Valtance English Department | **TEAM** |
| Academic | Tunis | | 2. ValPE, the Valtance Pedagogical Advisory Board | |
| In-service teacher | Tunis | | 3. ValPAR, the Valtance Parent Association | **2** |
| In-service teacher | London | | 4. ValED, the Valtance English Department | |
| Academic | Cluj-Napoca | | 5. SerVal: Service learning | |
| Pre-service teacher | Valencia | | 1. Head of the School | |
| Academic | Valencia | | 4. ValED, the Valtance English Department | **TEAM** |
| Pre-service teacher | Tunis | | 3. ValPAR, the Valtance Parent Association | |
| In-service teacher | Tunis | | 4. ValED, the Valtance English Department | **3** |
| In-service teacher | Argentina | | 5. SerVal: Service learning | |
| Pre-service teacher | Cluj-Napoca | | 2. ValPE, the Valtance Pedagogical Advisory Board | |

*Details of participants have been omitted for anonymity.

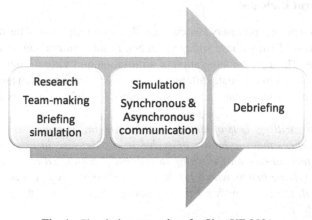

**Fig. 1.**  Simulation procedure for Sim+VE 2021

**Table 2.** Sessions organization

| Dates | Tasks |
|---|---|
| Week 1 to Week 3 (February 10th –24th) | Specialized literature analysis, discussion and exemplification |
| Week 4 March 3rd | Virtual Exchange 1. Synchronous Meeting only with academicians: Simulation scenario discussion and adaptations<br>Mixed Teams making |
| Week 5 March 10th | Virtual Exchange 2. Synchronous Meeting: Briefing+Getting to know each other |
| Week 6 March 17th | Scenario analysis Profiles assignation<br>Virtual Exchange 3. Synchronous Meeting: Simulation 'The National School of Valtance' |
| Week 7 March 24th | Virtual Exchange 4. Synchronous Meeting: Simulation 'The National School of Valtance' |
| Week 8 March 31st | Virtual Exchange 5. Synchronous Meeting: Debriefing by experts. Recorded session. Transcription and analysis for the qualitative study |

them for the study. University teachers' feedback was first classified into initial categories and subcategories until saturation of the data. The main conceptual categories were defined and analysed with the software application Dedoose version 9.

## 3   Results

The qualitative study yielded two main conceptual categories: intercultural dialogue (sub-categories: cultural differences and language restraints); and simulation interaction (sub-categories: content-knowledge and anxiety).

### 3.1   Intercultural Dialogue

The success of the project is closely associated with the commitment of the academicians at each place, most of whom have wide experience in intercultural communication and virtual exchange. Through the integration of simulation and virtual exchange, the dialogue was rich enough to elucidate different aspects of education which are conditioned by the participants' expertise and culture. Some participants' testimonies are:

– *I found it very thrilling. Lots of ideas about the simulation topics. There were some cultural differences that are harder to bridge in a short visit just as there would be if I, as an American educator teaching in a densely populated urban county would have if I was talking briefly with a teacher in a different city in another State in the US. But overall the issues with my European counterparts were the same dilemmas of practice. (A7)*

- *The simulation provided a great opportunity for all participants to share their concerns about their educational realities, and to build off of one another to provide adequate solutions. The variety of members in each team was especially interesting, as it allowed for a good range of discussion.* (A15)
- *I really liked the experience though in my team there was quite a lot of debate around, lesson study. Observers are allowed into the classroom in places such as Austria, UK, USA, etc. However, in some other countries, this is totally forbidden. A good discussion was held around the regulations in each country, the pros and cons of more conservative systems.* (A16)

This international dimension through simulation and virtual exchange has brought a unique value as it allowed participants to broaden their professional horizons without the need to travel while acquiring intercultural knowledge and communication skills. Participants highly valued the possibility to practice a second/foreign language as their feedback indicates:

- *Pre-service teachers in my team found some difficulties expressing their ideas, probably due to their level of English. However, they acted as true professionals, they participated in the discussions and used the chat and online translator when they occasionally got stuck with an idea. It did not affect the conversation.* (A2)
- *Dialogue was fluent and the level of English was fine, although I found most of the discussion based on opinions. I would have liked the participants to support their ideas more on the previous preparation they received or the specialized literature studied.* (A17)
- *The academicians had a very active role in my team. We had agreed on listening to the analysis of the different problems by the rest of participants, school teachers and practice teachers. We were surprised by the clear and sound understanding of the situations in spite of the lack of teaching experience of some of the participants.* (A9)

Two relevant aspects can be analysed from these testimonies. First, to be able to participate in a simulation or international event based on active communication, it is necessary to have a good command of the target language (English). This communication practice may stimulate participants to speak up their minds or may hinder them from collaborating with their opinions and knowledge simply because they lack a good command of the language. It is important to bear this in mind when making the teams. Initial interviews to detect participants' level of English should be conducted to properly make mixed-level teams and guarantee participation.

Second, to make the most out of the simulation experience, it is important to educate the ability to listen to each other. All participants should be taught multi-partiality to avoid mental triggers during the preparation and briefing phase. When triggered, participants have a hard time hearing what the person is actually trying to say because they may give more attention to those who speak more fluently or those they agree more with. In the study, academicians were more aware of this and acted as monitors, letting everyone participate and feel heard and represented.

### 3.2 Simulation Interaction

Most academicians highlighted the great value of simulations to tackle educational issues as their testimonies recall:

– *It was really beneficial to share different points of views about the educational delivery worldwide in order to try to improve it in the future.* (A3)
– *I am so happy to have such a chance and I definitely would do it again! All the participants are professional and confident and have a wonderful view on education!* (A6)
– *The simulation confirmed that all our student teachers struggle with similar issues on their journey to become teachers. All the teachers I participated with brought their full smart, empathetic, generous spirit to the dilemmas of practice. I appreciated their authentic, curious questions. Bravo to all of the teacher candidates that participated.* (A7)

The academicians observed that most participants found the simulation beneficial. The fact that they could speak with other professionals of education was something unique in itself. Most found an inner drive to perform their profile role very naturally. A few cases showed anxiety and nervousness. For most participants, the simulation was something new and was totally inexperienced. Yet, for a small group of participants, the simulation resulted in a problem more than an opportunity to share and learn. The schedule was tight and the preparation of the scenario may have demanded extensive research. As some scholars indicated, this anxiety was perceived during the first virtual exchanges (Weeks 4 and 5) and the synchronous session in the simulation (Week 6). After the participants got into the dynamics and trust was built among participants, the rest of the sessions ran smoothly for everyone.

## 4  Discussion

The integration of simulation and virtual exchange helped participants engage in intercultural dialogue conducive to learning. With this proposal, the strengths and weaknesses for an intercultural dialogue within the framework of simulation and virtual exchange were identified. An underpinning strength is the possibility offered to the participants, especially students from Spain, to successfully achieve the objectives of the Master Programme.

A true commitment of the academicians in each university made the experience possible and highly beneficial to all participants. As some recalled, they could practice English in a professional context. However, in such large scale projects, language restraints may hinder participants from achieving effective communication. In the case of Sim+VE 2021, only some participants found some limitations that could be solved with the assistance of other team members and technological tools (online translators). This should be taken into account when making teams in order to guarantee active participation. The difficulties expressing ideas may boost 'mental noise' or 'triggers' in some participants. In highly communicative-based activities, language problems may occur such as hearing what the person is actually trying to say or overly-active listening when someone plans a response without attention to the communications of other participants. It is important to teach and provide enough practice on how to listen and avoid mental triggers before the participants are engaged in the simulation. This could be a long process and the guarantee of success may rely on the effective guidance of the facilitators. This applies to anxiety management during the simulation. Anticipated practice and control over the content by thorough research should help participants better manage emotions during simulation interactions.

Finally, this collaborative intercultural experience enhanced by the integration of simulation and virtual exchange becomes an ideal strategy to foster interaction between students and educators worldwide and promote the internationalisation of higher education. Using simulation may well challenge the many policy-makers who still see teacher education as a closed experience of professional formation rather than as the starting point for global collaborative and lifelong learning which should characterize a twenty-first century teacher's career.

The results may be extrapolated to other fields in higher education. Faculties of Business Administration of Spain, Tunisia and Canada will carry out Virtual exchange + simulation in the course 2021–2022. Participants will work in international virtual teams in the identification of challenges that affect their different communities. Likewise, the faculties of law of Spain and Italy will work in international virtual teams comparing judicial systems and applying them through simulations.

# References

1. Darling-Hammond, L., Bransford, J. (eds.): Preparing Teachers for a Changing World: What Teachers Should Learn and Be Able to Do. John Wiley & Sons, California (2007)
2. Dawson, M.R., Lignugaris/Kraft, B.: Meaningful practice: generalizing foundation teaching skills from TLE TeachLivE™ to the classroom. Teach. Educ. Special Educ. **40**(1), 26–50 (2017)
3. Dieker, L.A., Rodriguez, J.A., Lignugaris/Kraft, B., Hynes, M.C., Hughes, C.E. The potential of simulated environments in teacher education: current and future possibilities. Teach. Educ. Special Educ. **37**(1), 21–33 (2014)
4. Leko, M.M., Brownell, M.T., Sindelar, P.T., Kiely, M.T.: Envisioning the future of special education personnel preparation in a standards-based era. Except. Child. **82**(1), 25–43 (2015)
5. Schön, D.A.: The Reflective Practitioner: How Professionals Think in Action. Routledge, London (2017)
6. Spencer, S., Drescher, T., Sears, J., Scruggs, A.F., Schreffler, J.: Comparing the efficacy of virtual simulation to traditional classroom role-play. J. Educ. Comput. Res. **57**(7), 1772–1785 (2019)
7. Angelini, M.L., Muñíz, R.: Simulation through virtual exchange in teacher training. Edutec. Revista Electrónica de Tecnología Educativa **75**, 65–89 (2021)
8. Council of Europe: White paper on intercultural dialogue. Living together as equals in dignity. Council of Europe, Strasbourg. http://www.coe.int/t/dg4/intercultural/source/white paper_final_revised_en.pdf (2008). Last accessed 4 Aug 2021
9. Helm, F.: A dialogic model for telecollaboration. Bellaterra J. Teach. Learn. Lang. Lit. **6**(2), 28–48 (2013)
10. Helm, F.: The practices and challenges of telecollaboration in higher education in Europe. Lang. Learn. Technol. **19**(2), 197–217 (2015)

11. De Benito, B., García, J.M., Moral, S.V.: Entornos tecnológicos en el codiseño de itinerarios personalizados de aprendizaje en la enseñanza superior. Edutec. Revista Electrónica De Tecnología Educativa **74**, 73–93 (2020). https://doi.org/10.21556/edutec.2020.74.1843

12. Gros, B., Durall, E.: Retos y oportunidades del diseño participativo en tecnología educativa. Edutec. Revista Electrónica De Tecnología Educativa **74**, 12–24 (2020). https://doi.org/10.21556/edutec.2020.74.1761

13. O'Dowd, R.: From telecollaboration to virtual exchange: state-of-the-art and the role of UNI-Collaboration in moving forward. J. Virtual Exch. **1**, 1–23 (2018). Research-publishing.net. https://doi.org/10.14705/rpnet.2018.jve.1

14. O'Dowd, R., Sauro, S., Spector-Cohen, E.: The role of pedagogical mentoring in virtual exchange. Tesol Q. **54**(1), 146–172 (2019). https://doi.org/10.1002/tesq.543

15. Erasmus+ Virtual Exchange: Erasmus+Virtual exchange. Intercultural learning experiences. https://europa.eu/youth/sites/default/files/eyp/eve/attachments/eve_brochure_2019.pdf. Last accessed 4 Aug 2021

16. Angelini, M.L.: Learning Through Simulations: Ideas for Educational Practitioners. Springer Nature, Switzerland (2021)

17. Angelini, M.L., Muñiz, R.: Simulation in Education. Towards a Collaborative Approach to Learning through Simulation and Virtual Exchange. Springer Nature, Switzerland (2022, in press)

# Gaming in Education

# The Co-design of Educational Video Games

Daniel Kleffmann$^{(\boxtimes)}$, Igor Mayer, and Thomas Buijtenweg

Breda University of Applied Sciences, Breda, The Netherlands
thekleffmann@gmail.com

**Abstract.** Co-design is a widely implemented practice in many areas of design and systematically incorporates the ideas, knowledge and interests of stakeholders into the design of an artefact. Literature gives insufficient insight into how the contemporary co-design practices in educational video games (EVG) are structured in the design process. This research aims to resolve that gap by answering the questions: (1) How are the co-design practices of EVG companies structured? (2) Who are the relevant stakeholders of EVG? (3) How are those stakeholders involved in the design process? (4) How do stakeholders influence game design elements (GDE) of EVG? Twelve educational game designers from international companies were asked to describe their co-design practices, define their stakeholders and explain how they are involved. They explored how stakeholders influence specific GDE that impacted game design. After systematically exploring the influence of the stakeholders, the data collected from the ranking and hierarchy exercises were aggregated and contrasted with the interviews for interpretation. The results show that most co-design practices are similarly structured but display varying degrees of stakeholder involvement. While stakeholders and their influence on GDE can vary across projects, some consistencies were found. Three co-design stages involving at least four of the five types of stakeholders were identified.

**Keywords:** Collaborative design · Content experts · Game design element · Pedagogy experts · Stakeholder involvement

## 1 Introduction

Educational Video Games (EVG) can be distinguished by their primary design purpose. Commercial off-the-shelf games may occasionally deliver educational content, but their design prioritizes fun over learning [1]. On the other hand, purely educational games prioritize learning over fun. Primary education is the most appropriate age to integrate EVG due to several reasons, primarily due to the positive attitude educators have towards games and the flexibility of their curricula [2]. Therefore, this study focuses on the co-design of purely educational games for children between 6 and 12 years in primary education.

The term co-design commonly conceptualizes collaborative design by involving parties from outside of a design and development team [3]. The needs and demands of students and educators should be met during the development of EVG which could transform serious games in education in innovation and acceptance [4]. Their involvement in the design process effectively makes them co-creators and stakeholders.

© Springer Nature Switzerland AG 2022
U. Dhar et al. (Eds.): ISAGA 2021, LNCS 13219, pp. 73–85, 2022.
https://doi.org/10.1007/978-3-031-09959-5_7

Previous studies navigate the discourse on the co-design of educational games, their application within an academic context and identify co-design challenges [5]. The extensive time investment required from stakeholders seems to be a recurring issue in practice. Co-design may be more efficient by involving stakeholders only when needed and relevant but where and when they should be included in the game's design process remains unclear.

It is necessary to review the applied methods to validate contemporary design practices and ensure the quality and positive impact of future EVG. While most serious EVG companies claim to co-design their games with stakeholders, they do not provide public documentation of their practices. No frameworks for co-design seem to be publicly available or exist in the context of EVG which is a gap in our knowledge. Examples of such frameworks can be taken from other industries' product design practices [6] and may guide the design of a context-specific co-design framework. The aforementioned gap thereby drives this research to explore the structure and stakeholders of contemporary co-design practices. The objective is to study the co-design practices of EVG companies to create a preliminary co-design framework.

## 2 Study Design

### 2.1 Research Questions

To close this knowledge gap, the following questions were designed to (1) understand the structure of co-design practices, (2) how stakeholders are being identified and (3) involved in the design process and (4) the influential game design elements within contemporary EVG companies.

- **RQ-1:** How are co-design practices structured?
- **RQ-2:** Who are the stakeholders of EVG?
- **RQ-3:** How are they being involved in their design process?

Through semi-structured interviews with open-ended questions, qualitative data is collected from educational game designers who define terms and processes of co-design or stakeholder involvement and explain how they are conceptualized and structured. Follow-up questions on specific aspects such as stakeholder prioritization or involvement methods are asked when more detail is needed.

The first research question gives an overview of their co-design practices and structure, the participants and their involvement. The second and third questions aim to provide insight into how stakeholders are identified. EVG are expected to be diverse in nature and purpose, leading them to require a specific cohort of stakeholders. In anticipation of this problem, a fourth question is asked to support the co-design process.

- **RQ-4: How do stakeholders influence game design elements (GDE)?**

Game Design Elements (GDE) are components or aspects of a game that can be conceptualized differently. Exploring how different stakeholders influence specific GDE during the collaboration appears not to have been done before and could highlight useful trends for a more generalized and structured co-design practice. This research uses GDE proposed by three different authors [2, 7, 8] to accommodate game designers with potentially different perspectives.

To explore how stakeholders influence GDE, a gamified exercise of custom de-sign was used to engage game designers during the online interviews. Participants were first asked to define and rank a maximum of five stakeholders how strongly they believed them to influence game design choices in a specific game. They often used examples of other games they had made to compare and exemplify their arguments. After defining stakeholders, participants built a six-piece pyramidal hierarchy of influence to illustrate how strongly a specific stakeholder influenced those GDE (Fig. 1). This exercise was systematically performed for all stakeholders in decreasing order of their ranking. The interviewer requested explanations to understand how stakeholders influenced the design process.

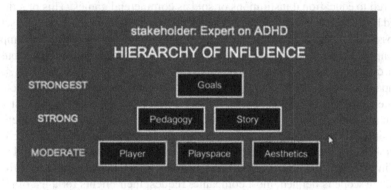

**Fig. 1.** Hierarchy of influence: example response from an interviewee.

This exercise provides qualitative data on how stakeholders influence the game design process while collecting quantitative data from their responses. Based on their placement within the hierarchies of influence, GDE are assigned values. If the quantitative and qualitative data coincide across interviewees, they may indicate relevant relationships to aid the design of a systematic approach for the stakeholder involvement process.

## 2.2 Data Collection

Twelve interviews were conducted with experienced educational game designers from eleven EVG companies from six countries (The Netherlands, Denmark, Portugal, Peru, Indonesia and United States of America). Enlisting these participants during COVID-19 pandemic was a challenge. Over 40 EVG were contacted over their websites, emails and social media. The majority of companies did not respond or declined. After almost four months, the twelve interviews were recorded.

Most companies within this sample are small; seven out of 12 companies had five or fewer employees of whom the game designer would also be the CEO, business developer, creative director, programmer, researcher or project manager. These interviews offered perspectives on their game design process, general company procedures and philosophies. The larger companies would have more specialized roles for their team members, leading to potential limitations in their knowledge. The different profiles within larger companies were interviewed to get sufficient insight into their co-design philosophies and procedures. Two interviewees were unfamiliar with the nuances of their companies' design practices and were not asked to answer the fourth question.

## 3    Results

### 3.1  Contemporary Co-design Practices

Interviews revealed that the co-design practices across companies were relatively similar in structure. Most EVG are commissioned by clients with specific goals. They occasionally also pitch projects to potential clients. In a few cases, EVG are developed first and then offered to educational institutions or sold as commercial games. This practice was described by interviewees as risky and unsustainable, with a limited impact on users and fewer possibilities of collaboration with stakeholders. From eight out of 11 companies of the sample worked for commission while the others were less committed to a business model or co-design process.

Companies working with clients always start with the scoping process which takes place once a project has been commissioned by a client. It is considered the first step in co-design and aims to define a set of parameters for the project. One company employs a questionnaire to establish parameters such as the target audience, context, goal and the desired change and measurement in behaviour. While larger companies tend to have systems in place for this process, smaller companies have a less structured approach.

Once the scope is defined, most companies request their clients for a list of relevant stakeholders for the project. Game designers engage these stakeholders in an iterative process of design and testing which are reported to overlap and intertwine until the game is complete. Only one large company profiled its stakeholders for a strategic approach while designers of other companies did not present a specific structure or a list of stakeholders for this iterative process.

### 3.2  Stakeholder Involvement

Game designers generally acknowledge the benefits of collaborating with stakeholders to design a game with a measurable impact. Interviews reveal mixed opinions on how extensively they like to involve stakeholders. Most companies do not like to interact with stakeholders. One interviewee explains how clients tend to be fixated on ideas or introduce biases which lead to difficult conversations that end in disappointment or frustration. Smaller companies tend to have fewer resources to manage these situations and prefer having more control over the creative design. They can cost time and negatively affect the relationship with their client and their reputation in the market. One of the smaller companies developed a gamified application that quantitatively samples their stakeholders' preferences on features for the project. They could quickly settle disputes and let the data guide their design process, reducing the need for recurring meetings with stakeholders.

Some designers also reported experiencing difficulties managing the expectations of multiple stakeholders with opposing opinions. Conflicts of interest among stakeholders, which the team was not equipped to handle, often created unexpected tension and, in one case, led to a situation where the client had to intervene and dictate the resolution. Companies that prefer more hands-on involvement from their stakeholders briefly mention the use of specialized workshops and brainstorming techniques that can last between 5–6 h and are said to enhance the team spirit. However, they require resources and time that not all companies, clients or stakeholders have or are willing to allocate.

As stakeholders, clients seem to be most involved at the beginning of the project during the scoping stage, after which their involvement declines. On the other hand, the other stakeholders are brought in soon after the scoping process, some for the design stage and others for the testing stage. Each stakeholder seems to have a place within the co-design process which varies based on their role and depends on the scope and context of the EVG. Different types of stakeholders were identified from interviewees but not all were considered relevant to all projects.

In the case of a mathematics or programming game, designers did not feel the need to involve content experts as some of their team members could fulfill that role. One of the interviewees was an instructional designer who may generally fulfill the role of a pedagogy expert. In other cases, many unexpected kinds of stakeholders for EVG emerged that were specific to a project, its learning objectives, context and the needs of their designers. Some examples were healthcare professionals who care for children with asthma and are familiar with their condition, psychology researchers who study how to improve children's performance with attention deficit disorders and where a client and a venue were presented as two different clients with different needs and interests.

To avoid the splintering of stakeholders, and to support the stakeholder involvement, emergent stakeholders were categorized into groups based on the roles they played. (1) *Content experts* include subject matter specialists, curriculum coordinators and researchers who provide knowledge on the subject and guide the content creation of the game while (2) *pedagogy experts* include freelance consultants, researchers, healthcare professionals and psychologists who would guide the pedagogical aspects of the game. Researchers could play either role depending on their expertise. Interviewees' explanations were essential to guide the interpretation of their roles within their specific contexts for the most appropriate categorization. This grouping is therefore contextual, non-exclusive and potentially biased by interpretation. Six stakeholder groups with forty-two stakeholders were identified across the ten game designers.

### 3.3 Stakeholder Prioritization

The quantitative data collected from the application shows the influence of stakeholders on GDE. Only two of the 10 interviewees defined five stakeholders, while all others defined four. The fifth stakeholder was discarded to homogenize the responses so that only four would be taken into account per participant. Higher ranking stakeholders are considered to have a higher priority in terms of influence in the game design process. The highest ranking would receive four points to numerically represent this, while the lowest would only receive one point. Each interviewee would thereby be assigned 10 points to different stakeholders, adding up to 100 points. Their rankings were added individually to quantify their accumulated weight within this sample, labeled as their prioritization values. All stakeholder groups are arranged in order of these values which coincide with their reoccurrence, showing how often they were included as stakeholders by game designers (Fig. 2). Only two stakeholders were discarded, leaving the total points in reoccurrence at 40.

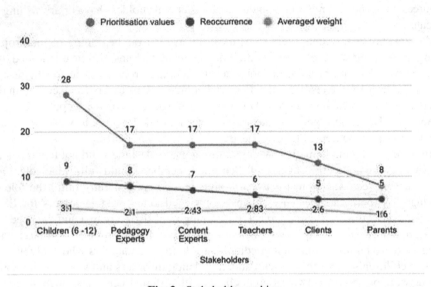

**Fig. 2.** Stakeholder ranking.

The mean average weight is calculated by dividing the prioritization values by their reoccurrence. It averages the influence of the stakeholders in co-design practices within this sample. Teachers, pedagogy experts and content experts have the same amount of prioritization points and explain why their average weight inversely mirrors the decrease in reoccurrence. Teachers are therefore more likely to influence design choices within a game than pedagogy experts. It is important to note that this can shift dramatically from project to project according to their context. For example, if the EVG were designed to be used outside a class, teachers may not be involved at all.

### 3.4 Stakeholder Influence

From the application data, it can be concluded that GDE are most likely influenced by stakeholders and are assigned a symbolic value based on their placement within the hierarchies of influence (Fig. 1). The top pyramid tier gives three points, then two points and finally one point. These accumulate over entries and show which GDE are most influenced by stakeholders. Multiplying them with the stakeholders' prioritization points from their corresponding hierarchy of influence allows their relative weight to be factored in for more distinctive results. The accumulated values for all GDE, normal and factored, and arranged by factored values reveal a relatively steady curve of decline which is mirrored by the normal values with very few discrepancies (Fig. 3).

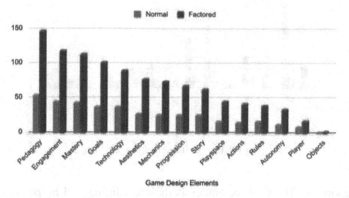

**Fig. 3.** Most influenced GDE

Stakeholders will be reviewed in descending order of reoccurrence to show how strongly the identified groups of stakeholders influence individual GDE. Due to the small sample size and exploratory nature of the quantitative data, these numbers have low reliability. Strong outliers are only considered indicative if the qualitative data supports them. Under these conditions, GDE may be potentially relevant in the context of a specific stakeholder.

**Children.** As stakeholders, children have the most substantial influence on the engagement, aesthetics and mechanics of EVG as distinctive quantitative outliers as confirmed by game designers during the interviews (Fig. 4). Aesthetics and mechanics seemed to create engagement. Some game designers mention their occasional reliance on mechanics as a method of keeping children engaged. Game mechanics seem to be a more intuitive and less challenging method of engagement unlike aesthetics.

One interviewee expressly focuses on their efforts of appealing to children and drawing their attention for engagement. During the design and testing stage, they *'[...] try to see whether this style of animation or this storyline is appealing for them and those are very iterative processes'*. Aesthetics are often portrayed as an efficient method of engaging children with the game but this is not an easy task and must be extensively iterated. Another game designer acknowledges the importance of aesthetics and elaborates on the challenges they encountered measuring the impact of aesthetics on children. *'[...] You can't ask them 'hey, do you like how this is drawn?'-They'll have an emotional connection with the picture, depending on what the picture depicts and not depending on the art style. [...] They could like a specific image with some art style, but then they would have preferred maybe the other art style if we'd continued with the other one. It's hard to measure'*. Many other game designers shared similar experiences and some report relying on parents or guardians to help children convey their feedback accurately.

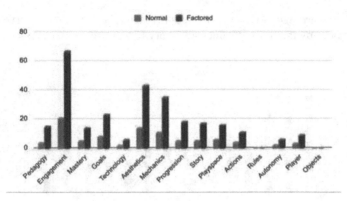

**Fig. 4.** GDE most influenced by children.

**Pedagogy Experts.** The GDE pedagogy is the most influenced by pedagogy experts (Fig. 5) who are only one point below children in reoccurrence. Outliers become more challenging to identify, for which the reliance on qualitative data becomes more important. Pedagogy is the main outlier and is supported by qualitative data. This stakeholder group is defined by its role in the pedagogical design of EVG. To be specific, one interviewee explains how they have *'[...] their own ways of teaching and we do not want to block that. [...] We want to enhance their ways and that's one of the most important things'*. This illustrates how strongly they can influence the pedagogical aspect of the game.

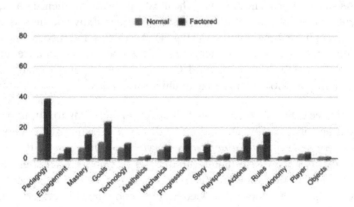

**Fig. 5.** GDE most influenced by pedagogy experts.

To a lesser degree, the mastery, goals and rules of GDE were often discussed in the context of learning objectives and pedagogy of a game. However, due to their more ambiguous result in the application, only goals will be considered a distinctive yet ambiguous GDE by pedagogy experts.

**Content Experts.** The influence of content experts is spread out across many GDE, resulting in a far too ambiguous graph that does not show distinctive outliers (Fig. 6). It is possible that the content of an EVG consistently influences most GDE or that the ambiguity could be resolved by analyzing examples by topic such as STEM, history and language.

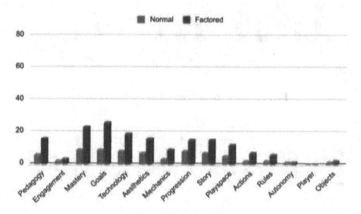

**Fig. 6.** Most influenced GDE by content experts.

**Teachers.** Similar to pedagogy experts, teachers have a strong influence on the pedagogical design of the game, almost exclusively when the EVG is being designed for a classroom (Fig. 7). Unlike pedagogy experts, teachers seem more influential due to their role as facilitators by using the game in a classroom. They may have a lower reoccurrence than pedagogy experts within the presented sample but rank higher, increasing their average weight of influence. They are effectively users and are therefore more influential than most stakeholders and often included in the game's design and testing stage.

Some game designers briefly referred to mastery, goals and progression as other GDE factors that teachers often want to influence. However, only mastery is quantitatively distinctive enough to be considered a potentially consistent GDE that teachers influence. Yet this is only true for games designed in the context of a class.

**Clients.** When included, clients tend to be influential in defining the technology and, to a lesser extent, pedagogy of a game. Their primary role seems to be to determine the general scope and context of the project. It reflects their distinctive influence on the technology for which the game needs to be developed, corresponding to its context (Fig. 8). According to game designers, the learning objectives tend to be defined by the clients who sometimes prefer to remain involved, although they are not necessarily pedagogy experts.

**Parents/guardians.** The stakeholder group is rarely involved and almost exclusively considered a facilitator for children who play EVG at home. With the lowest scores

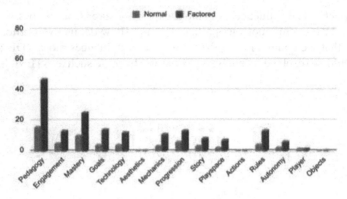

**Fig. 7.** Most influenced GDE by teachers.

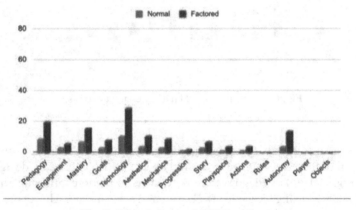

**Fig. 8.** Most influenced GDE by clients

on all accounts, parents have the most ambiguous result with engagement, mastery and technology as potential candidates, but the qualitative data is insufficient to support this (Fig. 9).

## 4  Discussion

### 4.1  Co-design

Most contemporary serious game companies that make EVG seem to follow similar co-design practices which can be divided into three stages; (1) the scoping process, where the purpose and context of the game are defined, (2) the co-design stage, where stakeholders are differently involved and the (3) testing stage, where users and facilitators test the prototypes until the product is ready for delivery. While the first and second stages are separate, the second and third stages initially overlap in an iterative cycle, as different

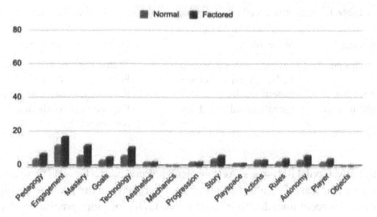

**Fig. 9.** Most influenced GDE by parents/guardians.

aspects of the game are adjusted. This structure may have evolved by mimicking the flexible and iterative nature of game design and is, therefore, appropriate.

According to experienced game designers, involving stakeholders is essential because it improves the effectiveness and quality of the content and its appeal and practical application within the intended context. This study did not identify any indicators to show that the process of extensive and hands-on collaborations was indispensable to achieve the results. The collaboration can be sufficient when the stakeholders are sampled for their input. Therefore, small companies should develop tools that aid them in their data collection from stakeholders and systematize their collaboration efforts. This can reduce the amount of time and resources needed. On the other hand, larger companies may choose to do the same or lead more hands-on collaborations.

### 4.2 Stakeholders

Stakeholder interaction starts with the clients who have been exclusively relied upon by the subsequent definition of stakeholders for their involvement in the co-design process. Four stakeholder roles, i.e., the clients, end-users, content experts and pedagogy experts have been consistent throughout the examined projects and would be required for co-design practices.

Occasionally, depending on the context, facilitators such as parents, guardians, teachers and healthcare practitioners may be included. Game designers may prioritize facilitators over other stakeholders. While teachers and pedagogy experts rank as influential, parents or guardians rank as the lowest. This preference is due to the relevance of the facilitator in the context of the game. More research would be required to understand this observation.

Table 1 presents a summary of the findings regarding stakeholder influence on GDE which have been arranged by their occurrence in co-design stages and effectively show stakeholder involvement. GDE written in italics are the more ambiguously influenced elements that are only slightly distinguished by quantitative and qualitative data.

**Table 1.** Most influenced GDE per stakeholder in each co-design stage.

| Co-design stage | Stakeholder | Game design elements |
| --- | --- | --- |
| Scoping/co-design | Clients | Technology, *pedagogy, mastery* |
| Co-design | Pedagogy experts content | Pedagogy, *goals Ambiguous* |
| Co-design/testing | experts teachers | Pedagogy, mastery *Ambiguous* |
| co-design/testing | Parents/guardians children | Engagement, aesthetics, mechanics |

Additionally, Goals, Playspace, Actions, Rules, Players and Objects were among the lowest ranking and least distinguished GDE who may have contributed to ambiguity in this research. It is recommended to include fewer GDE for more precise results. These findings may guide the design of a systematic stakeholder involvement method.

### 4.3  Limitations

This study is constrained by limitations that are intrinsic to qualitative studies such as the interpretation of statements and opinions. Interviewees' responses are limited to their perception of company processes and co-design practices and may not be entirely accurate. Cultural differences and ambiguity in expressions or terminology across our international sample of interviewees could also distort the data and influence the interpretation of qualitative data. The quantitative data collection method is exploratory, uses arbitrary values and has not been thoroughly tested to guarantee conclusive statistical data.

## 5  Conclusion

Co-design is being practiced by serious game companies that develop EVG because of the benefits. The involvement of stakeholders can improve games in terms of content quality, user engagement and their impact on their intended audience. The degree to which stakeholders are involved varies among companies. As long as they are thoroughly sampled for input and feedback, the benefits of their involvement should persist. Companies with fewer resources may systematize their co-design practices through custom applications and structured processes.

This study identified three stages of co-design and five types of stakeholders and stakeholders' involvement and influence on GDE in a diverse sample of EVG. While their influence on most GDE was inconclusive, indicators were found to support certain stakeholders consistently influencing specific GDE. A larger research sample may have been able to provide more reliable data and less ambiguous results. Most stakeholders can be related to a few specific GDE but provide a preliminary understanding of their influence over specific aspects of the game. Further research of stakeholder-GDE relationships could lead to more efficient, reliable and systematized methods to selectively involve stakeholders in the co-design process. This research focused on EVG for children of primary education but it would be worth exploring how co-design may differ when applied for other age ranges, specific cultural contexts or the delivery of specific content in STEM, history, language and other fields.

Developing data-driven systems and methodologies for the co-design of EVG could optimize the design process and improve the products themselves. EVG are used in many contexts from cultural and healthcare to formal education. Having well designed games could enhance their impact and the reliability of games as educational tools, providing a meaningful contribution to those contexts.

**Acknowledgments.** This research was conducted in fulfillment of the requirements of the first author's master thesis at Breda University of Applied Sciences Master in Game Technology (MGT). DK conceptualized, conducted the study and wrote this paper. IM and TB supervised and co-edited this paper. The authors declare no conflict of interest.

# References

1. Papadakis, S.: The use of computer game in classroom environment. Int. J. Teach. Case Stud. **9**(1), 1 (2018). https://doi.org/10.1504/IJTCS.2018.10011113
2. Manesis, D.: Digital games in primary education. In: Game Design and Intelligent Interaction 1st edn. IntechOpen, United Kingdom (2020). ISBN 9781838800109
3. Prahalad, C.K., Ramaswamy, V.: Co-creation experiences: the next practice in value creation. J. Interact. Mark. **18**(3), 5 (2004)
4. Sužnjević, M., Homen, M.: Use of cloud gaming in education. In: Game Design and Intelligent Interaction 1st edn. IntechOpen, United Kingdom (2020). ISBN 9781838800109
5. Bolstad, R., McDowall, S.: Games, Gamification, and Game Design for Learning: Innovative Practice and Possibilities in New Zealand Schools. New Zealand Council for Educational Research, New Zealand (2019). ISBN 978-1-98-854266-9
6. Webb, R., et al.: Sustainable urban systems: co-design and framing for transformation. Ambio **47**(1), 57–77 (2017)
7. Macklin, C., Sharp, J.: Games Design and Play: A Detailed Approach to Iterative Game De-sign, 1st edn. Addison-Wesley Professional, United States (2016)
8. Kalmpourtzis, G.: Educational Game Design Fundamentals: A Journey to Creating Intrinsically Motivating Learning Experiences. CRC Press, United States (2019)

# Reframing the Boundaries of Experiential Education Using Cynefin Domains

Elyssebeth Leigh[1](✉) and Laurie L. Levesque[2]

[1] University of Technology Sydney NSW, Sydney, Australia
elyssebeth.leigh@icloud.com
[2] Suffolk University, Boston, USA

**Abstract.** We explore ways in which managers' work environments differ from those in which business students are *learning* about management. The volatile, uncertain, complex, and ambiguous (VUCA) environments in which graduates will be *doing* management are unlike the stable, contained, familiar and well-defined classrooms that dominate institutions of higher education. We employ concepts including the Cynefin Domains of Knowledge (Snowden & Boone, 2009) to explore how available management education/learning techniques do - do not - replicate those complex/chaotic VUCA environments. The persistence of the gap between theory and practice in management education is examined. To reduce the gap, we propose greater use of experiential simulations and activities. Applying the concepts explored here may require a willingness to risk entering non-linear and unfamiliar learning experiences since an efficient transition from stable academic contexts to VUCA conditions is neither simple nor easily achieved.

**Keywords:** Cynefin domains of knowledge · Simulation-based learning · Systems thinking

## 1 Introduction

While higher education is intended to prepare students for success in contemporary workplaces[1], there is a wide and expanding gap between formal and orderly academic teaching contexts and the unorderly and ambiguous conditions of 21st century workplaces, [1, 2]. Since the nature of this gap and its effect on graduate success has been identified, our focus here is to propose actions educators can take to reduce its adverse impact on graduate preparedness for employment.

In the 1990's Peter Vaill described working conditions as 'permanent white water' characterised by continuing uncertainty, requiring different strategies to many of those popular at that time in management education [3]. Prior to his pronouncement the US Military had already coined the term VUCA - Volatile, Uncertain, Complex and Ambiguous - to describe the global conditions emerging in the late 1980s. By the early 21st

---

[1] Higher education has many goals including creating 'workplace ready' graduates. This paper is focusing on proposing ways to create a state of workplace readiness for students.

© Springer Nature Switzerland AG 2022
U. Dhar et al. (Eds.): ISAGA 2021, LNCS 13219, pp. 86–100, 2022.
https://doi.org/10.1007/978-3-031-09959-5_8

century this term was in extensive use to describe emerging business conditions [4]. Paradoxically, teaching and learning conditions remain largely unchanged.

Employment conditions for academic staff may have changed dramatically, but expectations about how classrooms should operate have largely not done so. However, since graduates will experience VUCA conditions almost anywhere, they will need to know how to become informed about situational characteristics and the constraints facing them. This awareness is enhanced by using the Cynefin Domains of Knowledge [5]. It is a deceptively simple and rational sense making framework (see Fig. 1) that helps clarify a decision-maker's context and provides heuristics about the knowledge needed to guide action in that context. However, this schema for considering knowledge as existing in quite distinct ways can be quite difficult to grasp when attempting to achieve desired outcomes, as that knowledge needs to be managed in qualitatively distinct ways.

In this article we are exploring realistic actions for use by individuals wanting to align academic analysis more closely to practical applications. Aligning learning experiences with reality provides students with skills and capabilities relevant to prospective workplaces. However, in attempting that, educators must deal with major barriers, not the least of which is the challenge of designing simulations and learning experiences to replicate aspects of complex environments so that students will gain insights that can be transferred to their future work situations. Additionally, faculty will face the potentially contradictory demands arising from meeting formal teaching and assessment requirements, which may have little direct connection with either knowledge acquisition or future workplace expectations. Attempts to recreate relevant aspects of VUCA environments, may cause students to resist unfamiliar and uncomfortable learning activities.

## 2   The Disconnect Dilemma

Quinn raised the issue of deeply engaging students by introducing the concept of 'hard fun', described as *"fun, in the sense that you're engaged … and you have the power to act; it's hard in that it's not trivial there is sufficient challenge to keep you on your toes"* [6]. To create such engaged learning Quinn maintains that the work of educators in the 21st century is not and cannot be … *about designing content … we are designing experiences* [and must be] *thinking not about creating content but about designing learner environments and architecting experiences* [6]. In effect, he was inviting educators to consider how to bring knowledge alive in ways that enable students to engage with theory and put it into practice in the moment. His own work [6] provides rich examples of how to do so, and clearly implements Dewey's advice from much earlier in the 20th century that *… rather than the child being a passive recipient of knowledge … children were better served if they took an active part in the process of their own learning.* [and place] *greater emphasis on the social context of learning* [which at] *the turn of the 20th-Century, were radical ideas* [7].

Higher education recognises that its students must become aware that after graduation they will be working in a world experiencing change at a rapid rate. As an example of efforts to address this need, healthcare education heavily relies on simulation to create a variety of teaching and learning environments that mirror the array of professional contexts where learning is a constant. Practice and drills rehearse behaviours needed to succeed in chaotic, complex, and complicated situations and simulations help health professionals assess their information needs and actions and assure effective transfer of learning [8, 9].

Business schools are expected to have a *future-oriented mindset, with an eye to the knowledge, skills, and abilities needed by both faculty and learners* and they will update *curriculum content and faculty skill sets where trends in business education, employer feedback, and best practices clearly emerge* according to AACSB, a prestigious international accreditor of business schools [10].

Despite this, there is still a significant disconnect between learning and doing in business education. Consider this example which highlights the ways in which course content may contradict, or at the very least inhibit, learning experiences. In the textbook Management: A Practical Introduction, [11], the authors propose that:

... *planning and strategic management can help people focus on the most critical problems, choices and opportunities. If a broad group of employees is involved in the process, that can foster teamwork, promote learning and build commitment.*

At face value this seems an unexceptional statement. Western societies with democratic tendencies widely acknowledge that involvement fosters commitment. However, academic classrooms are less often considered to be places where 'engagement' is engendered, thus ensuring that modelling of this management proposition seldom occurs. Indeed, students and administrators often share an expectation that the teacher will be 'doing' all the planning and strategic management of classroom, course content and teaching processes. Such expectations do not allow for involvement of students in any of these components. Which leads to the question of how students are supposed to learn '*to do*' such complex processes as earning staff commitment, or designing teamwork to engage, involve and grow commitment?

Business students do engage intellectually with VUCA when put into in the role of distal analysts applying concepts to cases written by third parties or to organizations in the news. This neutral and objective perspective provides a very different learning experience from an experientially based one where students are invited to develop those same diagnostic and information-seeking skills amid experiencing realistic situational pressures and ambiguities.

**'Being Told' Versus 'Doing'.** However, being *told about* the truth of a proposition gives no hint of the potential difficulties likely to arise when it needs to be implemented. Misalignment of message and process mean that students will learn (memorise) the message but not necessarily have any idea of how to enact it into practice, nor even recognise the need to think about the possibility of needing to know how to do so.

An example, common to organizational behavior courses occurs when an educator introduces 'Theory X and Theory Y' [12]. The information can be presented from a stance of being 'in charge' where the lecturer is, knowingly or otherwise, implicitly employing a Theory X mode of behavior, or they may utilize the precepts of Theory Y by running an activity allowing students to discover for themselves key aspects of this theory. If they take the latter path, they may be surprised to find themselves on the receiving end of complaints from students who believe they were *not* learning because they had not 'been told' what they think they are supposed to know. Looking ahead to the information about the Cynefin Domains we suggest that adverse reactions to experiential approaches to knowledge transmission may be the result of the educator moving students from the Complicated domain in which they know to rely on 'the teacher as expert'. Instead, students find themselves in the Complex domain where they are expected to demonstrate expertise by 'probing' for information to develop a reasonable outcome while simultaneously building their personal knowledge. Unaware of the change in context, students may remain stuck in the Complicated domain believing that *learning occurs when I am told what is important, by an expert, and I need to avoid deviations that may unnerve me because of the uncertainty.*

Vaill's precept of 'learning as a way of being' provides a way to address the kinds of complexities we are describing. Writing of his own experience as a managerial educator, Vaill identified a split *between the fairly well developed ideology of keeping theory and practice together in management education on the one hand and ... the.. increasingly obvious fact that the prevailing forms of education for managerial leadership did not seem to be contributing very much to the improvement of managerial practice,* [for] *individual learners or in the management profession at large.* His observation was that the challenges and puzzles facing managers are *potentially infinite in number and that there are thousands of cultures and sub-cultures to produce them.* Given the endless plethora of possible trials ahead for fledgling managers he concluded that organisations [including academic ones] have been slow to recognise the interconnectedness of everything [3].

**Management as Permanent White Water.** Vaill was adamant that management is 'permanent white water' Viewing it as such challenges systems and individuals adhering to positivist principles relying on the possibility (necessity) of finding and applying abstract and universal laws to the operative dynamics of the social universe. For positivist thinking 'orderliness' is an imperative and VUCA-infused complexity must be restrained and confined in every way possible. In formal educational contexts positivist approaches allow for neatly sequenced units of study for which individual students must find their own logic, i.e., their internal curriculum, which may or may not fit the intentions of certain curricula (see more on this below). Vaill's key component for addressing white water conditions is systems thinking which involves learners in understanding how to operate amid interconnectedness through (in part) learning to map relationships in ways extending far beyond more familiar dichotomies [13]. He did however, caution that *systems thinking can probably not be taught or learned effectively within a learning philosophy that is itself profoundly antisystemic* [3].

This warning has not stopped many educators from attempting to institute various forms of systems-thinking based teaching and learning strategies. Aware of his own location within such potentially anti-systemic contexts, he proposed a mix of self- directed learning, creativity learning, 'expressive learning' (*learn in and through expression, learn from expression and learn by expressing*) and feeling learning (*Facts do not speak for themselves ... Meanings, implications, significances, and portents are* wrested *from the flow of events* [by all those] *who have a* felt *stake in how things are unfolding* [3]. All four modes of learning are more relevant than ever in these socially tumultuous times when views on politics, race, and managing a pandemic are radically diverse and emotions are high.

Senge and Vail identified a systemic conflict characterised as based on the disconnect which occurs when *the types of behaviour rewarded are those which the rewarded is trying to discourage, while the behaviour desired is not being rewarded at all'* [14, 15]. Consider academic grades where students express interest in knowing what to do to get a 'good grade' and are only tangentially interested in the knowledge they might acquire. Consider this feedback from a first-year student in an Introduction to Management subject –

*All the assignments were given during the first day and the deadline was the last day of the course. I understand that it is a management course, and we should take initiative ourselves in doing work, but I've never done this before and all the assignments being given at once just made me anxious and unwilling to complete them. (anonymous student feedback 2020)*

Clearly the paradox in the message is not evident to the writer who knows what 'should' be the focus of attention, but seems mainly concerned to avoid anything likely to engender anxiety. It is important to note that interim submission milestones were notified as part of the learning process, and all tasks were designed to help students track their own learning journey. It seems, therefore, that this student is already – in the first year of university –entrained to expect clearly delineated step by step progress to a grade without concern for how the tasks themselves might help to acquire the *initiative* acknowledged as something *we should take.* How this will play out as s/he leaves the cosy academic environment for real world complexity is yet to be seen, although this comment indicates that a world of permanent whitewater might be a very difficult concept to entertain.

**A Knowledge Gap.** Thus, the gap between what novice managers expect to learn at university and how they will be expected to perform as managers has already begun to become real for this writer and will be reinforced for them and their peers by too many courses where passing exams is the goal and 'acquiring knowledge' is of peripheral interest. It is strange but true that this paradox may be visible to few of those involved in academic education, and only then because circumstances have in some way altered their awareness.

For example, much of the literature in management education is sourced from academic work, even though it has long been understood that "*Management writing has never shown a complete unity, and one of the main distinctions that can be drawn in the literature is that between books coming out of universities and books written by managers*". [16]. To help management educators understand the origins of familiar themes in management literature (drawing on UK and USA writers as far back as the mid-1800's) as well as helping them learn to identify implications for future research activity and educational directions [16]. In 2021 it is clear they identified a well-established trend, and the gaps between academic theory and managerial practice have continued to widen rather than close. Argyris alone and with Schön, Wills, Vaill, Rooke and Torbert, Wheatley, all in various ways conducted careful research to provide well-formed advice about linking research to workplace practices and academic classwork [3, 17–22]. While such authors work is *taught* as abstract concepts the precepts are rarely practiced; ensuring students 'know' concepts well enough to write essays or answer multiple choice questions but have had little chance to enact them. Yet skilled practice is what workplaces expect of them.

Workplace indicators suggest that graduates are too often deemed unable to fully contribute in the manner that employers were or are expecting [23–25]. While management theory and research have advanced and evolved concurrent with societal changes and business practices, higher education workplaces and expectations of (and about) professional educators and course design have not kept pace. Many academic contexts require appropriate adherence to 'accepted' teaching practices and established modes of learning assessment often align less with the conditions we must prepare our students to face and more with institutionalized expectations of the academic classroom and faculty course delivery. In effect this leads to a paradoxical requirement that we teach in the mode of *do as I say – not as I do*. When academic practices misalign message and intent, it seems that sensible actions are needed to match teaching practices to the workplace contexts in which the knowledge will be applied. However, doing so is inhibited by several factors, some of which are explored below.

## 3  Barriers to Use of Experiential Learning for Simulating Complex/Chaotic Conditions

Given that the work of educators like Dewey and research and applications following and paralleling it are widely acknowledged [26–29] why do we not see more direct engagement in experiential learning about these workplace conditions? Why are 'conventional forms' of teaching and assessing such as lectures, tutorials exams, essays still so prevalent in business education? Why do less conventional learning formats encounter resistance and generate controversy?

We focus on three possible barriers: i) lack of understanding that knowledge works differently in different contexts and the paucity of experiential activities to replicate VUCA conditions, ii) role-related expectations of faculty that limit their use of experiential learning to take students (however temporarily) out of their comfort zones, and iii) assumptions about curricula that prevent such radical experimentation.

**Understanding where Education Formats Fit in the Cynefin Domains.** Despite the barriers, we agree that many educators do still bring the conditions of VUCA in their classrooms to provide experiences of real workplaces. For those interested in expanding their teaching repertoire to better match workplace conditions, we propose that understanding the Cynefin Domains of Knowledge framework will help such adventurous educators to step into the (comparatively) unknown space of complexity to bridge theory and practice.

Cynefin conceptualises knowledge in a way that (eventually) aids understanding of how clashes and gaps may arise and appear irreconcilable. The framework emerged from research to *understand how informal networks and supporting technologies allow greater connectivity and more rapid association of unexpected ideas and capabilities than formal systems* and slowly morphed into one that challenges *the universality of three basic assumptions prevalent in organizational decision support and strategy* [viz] *assumptions of order, of rational choice, and of intent* [30, 31]. These assumptions underlie belief systems expressed in terms of dichotomies – right/wrong/ either/or etc. and can inhibit human ability to recognise or manage the impact of complex conditions that are *neither right/wrong* and may be *both/and*. Such assumptions prevent recognition of uncertainty, disorder and confusion as inevitable states of the human condition. To make such states visible, the Cynefin Domains provide heuristics for guiding processes of examination of conditions prior to making suitable decisions.

Despite its acceptance as a helpful framework for workplace applications, it is evident that workplace uptake is occurring well ahead of steps needed for academic knowledge to catch up. While academic contexts present themselves as being 'ahead of the curve' regarding such things as 'good' and 'best' practice, lived experience is highlighting problems with the capacity of academic contexts to address factors represented by the VUCA acronym and identified by the Cynefin framework.

As illustrated in Fig. 1 the Cynefin framework introduces five domains of knowledge each of which has its own features and processes for managing information. Together they are a framework for action through the means they provide for understanding how information and knowledge work in different contexts. In the centre is the tricky, puzzling (aporetic[2]) *Confusion* space into which almost any set of conditions can thrust us - momentarily or for long and anxious periods of time. The most helpful advice for extrication from Confusion is – *'first identify the Domain most likely to be the one you have been thrust into, employ the relevant heuristic and take action/make decisions as suggested'* [32]. While it is less obvious in the figure, it is an equally important component of the model. When individuals find themselves in a state of confusion, the goal is to assess the context quickly to determine which quadrant most closely maps onto it, and then use the correct heuristics for that domain to guide behavior.

The four sectors of Clear, Complicated, Complex and Chaos, surround Confusion. The right side of the model represents environments that are orderly and familiar. In the 'Clear' Domain occupants know what to do without effort. The heuristic calls for making sense of a context. Since it is familiar you know what to do and can act. Imagine yourself walking into a lecture theatre as a student – you know not to go to the podium, but to sit down facing the front of the room. In the 'Complicated' Domain, expertise is there to be relied on to provide guidance and direction. While conditions may not be readily familiar to new entrants, guidance is available from experts. The heuristics for this domain require making sense then analysing before responding.

In contrast to this orderliness, the left-hand side of the Cynefin framework reflects contexts that are uncomfortable, and disorderly. There is no known and familiar knowledge with which to address conditions in the Complex Domain. While guidance may be available, the heuristic indicates the need to probe for relevant information, often in unexpected places, delaying decisions until it is possible to make sense of what is found. Complexity requires problem-finding and exploring multiple options to create an appropriate means of addressing the situation.

Beyond that there is also acceptance that success or failure may not be evident until after the chosen option is implemented. In the 'Chaos' Domain, the injunction to take

---

[2] Aporetic refers to *involving doubt or puzzlement.*

**Fig. 1.** Cynefin domains of knowledge

action is paramount. The heuristic indicates that analysis and understanding can only happen long after the event and thus action precedes any form of analysis.

In Fig. 2 we have mapped categories of experiential activities onto the model. Most recognised educational formats reside in the two Orderly quadrants. However, it also indicates that few experiential exercises in collegiate business programs can replicate the conditions of the left hand (Complex and Chaos) quadrants – although these will be the ones where graduates will struggle to perform effectively as decision makers. For educators who truly want to enhance the transfer of learning by engaging their students in conditions replicating the demands of real-world contexts, this mapping emphasises the need to identify and/or develop experiential learning to mirror the conditions on the left side of the model.

**Expectations of the Faculty Role-Preventing Use Experiential Learning.** Academic educators are expected to always be the experts in the room, even when it may be more realistic for them to operate as guides, such as when materials are new, knowledge is emergent, and conditions are changing more rapidly than textbooks can match. Experts are supposed to know everything relevant and always lead the way. This image of the faculty role aligns with the complicated contexts, where students know their place and experts guide them to the discovery of preferred solutions for handling issues, thus providing security and intellectual guidance o novice learners.

If/when they abandon the stance of 'sage on the stage' to become a 'guide on the side' educators may be generating unnecessary discomfort. Faculty are not expected to create distress and anxiety nor emphasize that current comfort in academe is not only short lived, it is short-changing students by providing knowledge without applicable

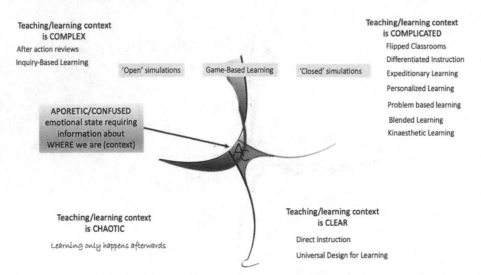

**Fig. 2.** Proposed mapping of educational strategies onto the cynefin domains of knowledge

skills. For students familiar with educational systems that do not 'throw them into deep water' to teach them to swim, experiential situations can appear to be chaotic, creating anxiety, as evidenced in the student's feedback comment previously quoted.

It is also true that learning processes intended to replicate Complex domains can unsettle an educator's own sense of balance. Thus, even if the value and validity of creating and using conditions to mirror the 'real life' beyond academia is accepted, it can be difficult to step beyond the comfort zone of the Clear and Complicated domains of knowledge. Such difficulties will keep faculty iterating course designs better suited to the right hand side of the Cynefin model and remaining well away from the messiness of workplace conditions. The Complicated domain can appear to provide enough learning challenges through expectations about content expertise to make it seem unnecessary to explore ways to align academic knowledge with workplace requirements and justify the avoidance of complex simulations with open-ended outcomes.

It therefore takes courage, and an assumption that teaching failures will occur sometimes, to step outside the role expectations associated with expertise in higher education. An evident paradox here concerns the use of learning designs requiring educators to step outside the role of 'expert' inviting students to become engaged with knowledge in practical ways. This is not how students expect 'to be taught' - yet enabling them to recognize and operate within complex systems requires accepting that teaching/learning experiences will not be fully predictable or controlled.

**Reframing 'Curricula' to Uncover Tacit Knowledge.** Wilson examined educational curricula in American contexts to uncover their varied origins and highlight the sources of influence exerted on expectations about teaching practices and learning experiences [33]. Her work underlines associated problems for academics choosing to operate beyond the implicit and tacit expectations of the various from of curriculum her work identifies.

She unveiled the complexity built into the apparently routine nature of curriculum development and identified 11 'sources' of curricula. In Table 1 we have arranged these into sub-groups based on their source. *Overt* curriculum documents are written by academic educators to accord with institutional guidelines, within a generalised understanding that these are, in turn, influenced by local, regional and national policymakers and administrators – i.e., the *Rhetorical* curriculum. These two originate from institutional sources and may be quite enough to cause strife if the institution and policymakers have different views of what is required. Yet they are so familiar as to easily overshadow any awareness of the remaining sources of curricula.

A teacher's personal *curriculum-in-use* is based on their belief in, and use of, educational principles which may or may not, accord with their institution's overt position. For example, an institution that espouses positivist educational concepts will not readily accept actions that cause student and/or administrative unease through, for example, an educator employing unfamiliar values (say, for example, constructivist principles). Torbert recorded his experiences of this clash of principles, describing the (eventual) failure of efforts to employ a curriculum intended to expose students to self-management and a 'liberating structure') which he termed *A Course to "Force Students to be Free"* [34]. Schor wrote of his battle with students to force them to face hidden power issues and differing aims separating their avoidance of engagement from faculty aspirations of students owning control within a higher education course [35].

These are extreme and well written examples of the progress and impact of such a clash of curriculum ideologies. Curricula from 'within students' are first, those things they interact with and take out of the classroom (materials, exam results, etc.) and second, the ways they integrate (or not) the content of those materials. Wilson emphasizes that educators have no control over this latter form of curriculum.

We consider the next four sources of curricula to be 'invisible' because their influences are generally unseen until/unless something happens to cause a reframing, such as happened when Jane Elliott created her 'brown eyes/blue eyes' experiments and subsequent educational work. As she noted recently, the hidden workings of discrimination are still very active, its 'hiddenness' only slowly becoming obvious [36]. Also, in this category is the 'null' curriculum which emerges as choices are made about what to include or exclude in *overt* curriculum documents. In his book on the Silk Roads, Frankopan vividly writes about history lessons where he was taught about Roman and British Empires, Nazi Germany, and western industrialisation [37]. He would then go home and look at a map of the world on his bedroom wall and see the huge *regions of the world that had been passed over in silence*. Equally well concealed, are the influences of the 'phantom' (e.g., media including advertising, and 'tops of the pops' programs) and 'electronic' curricula as shaped by various platforms and their algorithms, which may be noticeable but are seldom considered as contributors to learning.

Lastly, the *community* sources of curriculum content are familiar, but usually unrecognised as contributors shaping aspects of the overt and rhetorical sources. The fate of the educational program known as *Man a Course of Study* – MACOS [38] is a longstanding example of a curriculum that was demolished by community-based backlash [39]. Although reviewed positively, including by Time Magazine (1970), "*it was much criticized in the United States* [partly] *because of its emphasis upon questioning aspects*

**Table 1.** Types of curricula influencing learning (based on Wilson)

| (Source is) INSTITUTIONAL | |
|---|---|
| Overt, explicit, or written curriculum | Written /produced documents chosen to support an institution's intentional instructional agenda. |
| Rhetorical curriculum | Ideas offered by policymakers, school officials, administrators, or politicians. |
| **(Source is) - TEACHER** | |
| Curriculum-in-use | The actual curriculum as delivered and presented by each teacher |
| **(Source is) - STUDENT** | |
| Received curriculum | Those things that students actually take out of the classroom |
| Internal curriculum | Processes, content, knowledge combined with the experiences and realities of the learner to create new knowledge. Educators have little control over the internal curriculum since it is unique to each student. |
| **(Source is) - INVISIBLE** | |
| The hidden or covert curriculum | It may include both positive or negative messages, depending on models enacted and learner perspectives. ... *derived from the very nature and organizational design of the [institution], as well as behaviors and attitudes of teachers and administrators.* (Longstreet & Shane, 1993 p46) |
| The null curriculum | All that is *not* taught, thus conveying the message that these elements are not important in their educational experiences or in our society. *What students cannot consider ... they are unable to use, [which has] consequences for the kinds of lives they lead.* (Eisner 1993) |
| Phantom curriculum | The messages prevalent in and through exposure to any type of media can play a major part in enculturation of students into a predominant meta-culture, or narrower or generational subcultures. |
| The electronic curriculum | Those lessons learned through searching the Internet for information, or through using e-forms of communication |
| **(Source is) - COMMUNITY** | |
| Societal curriculum (or social curricula) | The *massive, ongoing, informal curriculum of family, peer groups, neighborhoods, churches, organizations, occupations, mass media, and other socializing forces that "educate" all of us throughout our lives* (Cortes, 1981 p24) |
| Concomitant curriculum | What is taught, or emphasized at home - may be received at church, in the context of religious expression, lessons on values, ethics or morals, etc. based on the family's preferences |

*of the American tradition, including Western paradigms of belief and morality"* [40]. Today much of its content and underlying precepts would be considered unremarkable, yet it is a lasting example of an educational experience where 'good practice' was gutted by community resistance.

Working through this list of influences on the design and enactment of education in university contexts, additional causes of complexity and uncertainties surrounding curriculum choices come into focus. Each source of curriculum materials and approaches has its own underlying values and beliefs, and none of them are likely to be fully in accord with all the others. The challenge of providing learning experiences that do align with the realities of volatile VUCA-affected workplaces, are significant when done within educational environments constrained by hidden or strongly controlled beliefs about what curriculum is, and how it should be offered.

We propose that the 21st century needs an approach that embraces the Cynefin Domains of Knowledge as a sensemaking framework to help learners become aware of how to identify situational characteristics and the types of knowledge needed to help them take informed action. In doing so, we believe they will engage more closely with knowledge as they move with greater awareness from familiarity to uncertainty within a flexible and supportive – although still challenging - manner. Indeed, the umbrella term *constructivist learning theory* already offers such a learner-centric framework in that the underlying belief of all its component theories holds learners to be the center of attention as builders (constructors) of their own knowledge. Shepherd devised an interactive tool for exploring some of the many variants of educational theory that aim to directly engage learners in forming and shaping their own learning experiences [41, 42]. Table 2 lists a selection of relevant educational theories which, taken in almost any order, can help academic educators explore and choose ways to shift their teaching from passive transmission of data to active engagement with information and knowledge.

**Table 2.** Educational concepts informing constructivist practices enabling learning to operate in complex and chaos domains of knowledge

| Educational theory | Indicative researchers | Core concepts |
|---|---|---|
| Adult learning theory (Andragogy) | John Dewey Malcolm Knowles | Adults are motivated to learn through needs and interests Learning is most effective when it is problem centered rather than content oriented |
| Self-determined learning (Heutagogy) | Stewart Hase Chris Kenyon | Learning is addressed as a learner-led and proactive approach with learners as the lead player in their own learning |
| Tacit knowledge | Michael Polyani Richard B. Gasaway | Learners bring to new learning context their prior educational, social and cultural knowledge. These will impact on new experiences. |
| Learning preferences | David Kolb Peter Honey & Alan Mumford | e term refers to the composite of factors that indicate how individuals perceive, interact with and respond to contexts |
| Experiential learning | Kurt Lewin Karl Rogers Jean Piaget | Learning is a contextualised process; learners benefit from immersion in situationally relevant experiences which trigger actions to acquire/refresh knowledge |
| Critical thinking/clinical reasoning/clinical judgment | Peter Facione Norene Facione Carol Giancarlo | A tool of inquiry generating cognitive skills important to purposeful learning |
| Reflective learner/guided reflection | Donald Schon Carol Rogers | A metacognitive process allowing learners to make sense of experiences and decide on actions. |
| Novice to Expert | Stuart Dreyfus Hubert Dreyfus Patricia Benner George Miller | Traces a continuum through five stages of development for aligning teaching practices with learner stages |
| Self-efficacy | Albert Bandura | Individual beliefs about personal capability influence responses to learning in new contexts |
| Deliberate practice and Acquisition of expert performance | K. Anders Ericsson | Deliberate practice (effortful activity) refers to the way that repetition - more than single experiences - leads to expertise |

One example of such an approach is that called Classroom as Organisation (CAO), a well-known format for active engagement of learners which creates, in effect, an array of complex factors that turn out to be replicas of VUCA conditions. Just as in real life it too can trigger responses ranging from total engagement to absolute rejection by students. And over time it has become clear that, for some learners, its complexity is too far from their perceptions of what it means to be 'a student' to allow them to participate in the working out of solutions to the kinds of real-life problems they will one day face in future workplaces.

## 4   Future Considerations

Through all this we have noted our awareness that not all students or administrators appreciate the paradoxes of the misalignments arising from use of teaching methods that do not align with the content of the message. In future, we will be considering how to provide students who are studying within traditional course offerings at universities with experiences of working within, and managing, complexity, given the constraints outlined. How can instructors simultaneously introduce theories and concepts for 'decoding' the paradox of clashing expectations while encouraging students to appropriately diagnose the situation and seek out the knowledge needed to accomplish sound decision making? We have not proposed a 'new' framework for choosing teaching/learning methods to approximate VUCA conditions and tactics enabling their application in specific educational contexts. Rather we have highlighted the nature of some of the barriers embedded in current systems inhibiting closer alignment while also noting that much research exists supporting the need to change.

Educators need guidance on how to craft learning experiences that replicate the dynamics and sensibilities of complex environments. This requires the support and resources of the institution to experiment and move in a direction that allows. The Cynefin Domains can help to choose and focus experiential learning activities – especially simulations that help learners to appreciate the difference between stable academic context and VUCA workplace ones. Cynefin can also assist in choosing learning processes for looking beyond the 'known' and 'safe' by providing a framework for mapping out the moves needed to step into the unfamiliar and even the entirely unknown – as workplaces will be initially.

Educators benefit from using Cynefin together with an understanding of Wilson's array of syllabus influencers to address student concerns when the 'expert faculty' role is abandoned in favour of a co-inquiry role. Student discomfort with the resulting ambiguity may be assuaged as they learn to apply the heuristics provided for each Complex domain.

Educators will also need support to become confident in making the switch, including acquiring new and unfamiliar facilitation skills for shifting to operating in classrooms replicating Complex environments (in whole or part). We propose that management educators need to reflect self-critically on the principles they espouse as they teach and, by doing so, find ways to make their medium fit their message.

We acknowledge that sometimes this will lead to failures – given the strength of habituated reliance on educational processes that nurture dependence and prefer passive reception of data. Our own teaching practice has certainly encountered barriers and challenges as we have worked to enact what we are espousing. However, our efforts are made worthwhile by results produced by students transitioning from dependent learners via independence to interdependence.

# References

1. Lachs, J.: Closing the skills gap: how educators and employers can work together inform ED. https://www.opencolleges.edu.au/informed/features/closing-the-skills-gap-how-educators-and-employers-can-work-together/ (2017). Accessed 16 Apr 2022
2. Morrison, N.: The gap between school and work is becoming a chasm. https://tinyurl.com/haumehuy (2015)
3. Vaill, P.: Learning as a Way of Being. Jossey Bass, San Francisco (1996)
4. Bennett, N., Lemoine, G.J.: What VUCA Really Means for You. Harvard Business Review Magazine, January–February (2014)
5. Snowden, D.J., Boone, M.E.: A Leader's Framework for Decision Making. Harvard Business Review (2007)
6. Quinn, C.N.: Engaging Learning: Designing e-Learning Simulation Games. John Wiley and Sons Inc, San Francisco, CA (2005)
7. Wheeler, S.: The Pedagogy Of John Dewey: A Summary. https://www.teachthought.com/learning/pedagogy-john-dewey-summary/ (2020). Accessed 16 Apr 2022
8. Gaba, D.M.: The future vision of simulation in health care Qual Safe. Health Care **13**(Suppl 1), i2–i10 (2004). https://doi.org/10.1136/qshc.2004.009878
9. Al-Elq, A.H.: Simulation-based medical teaching and learning. J. Fam. Community Med. **17**(1), 35 (2010). https://doi.org/10.4103/1319-1683.68787
10. AACSB: 2020 Guiding Principles and Standards for Business Accreditation. Effective Date: July 28, 2020. AACSB International, Tampa, FL (2020)
11. Kinicki, A., Williams, B.: Management a Practical Introduction. McGraw Hill, USA (2020)
12. McGregor, D.: The Human Side of Enterprise. McGraw-Hill, New York (1960)
13. Checkland, P.: Systems Thinking, Systems Practice. John Wiley and Sons, New York (1981)
14. Senge, P.: The Fifth Discipline. Doubleday, New York (1990)
15. Kerr, S.: On the folly of rewarding A, while hoping for B. Acad. Manag. Exec. **9**(1), 7–14 (1995)
16. Tillett, A., Kempner, T., Wills, G.: Management Thinkers. England: Pelican Books. Time. (1970). Education: Teaching Man to Children. Time Magazine. http://content.time.com/time/subscriber/article/0,33009,878677,00.html (1978). Accessed 16 Apr 2022
17. Argyris, C., Schön, D.: Theory in Practice: Increasing Professional Effectiveness. Jossey-Bass, San Francisco (1974)
18. Argyris, C., Schön, D.: Organizational Learning: a Theory of Action Perspective. McGraw-Hill, New York (1978)
19. Wills, G.: Business school graffiti: a decennial transcript. UK Emerald Publishing. In: Wilson, L.O. (ed.) (2020). Types of curriculum. https://tinyurl.com/xvefkcch (1978). Accessed 16 Apr 2022
20. Rooke, D., Torbert, W.R.: Seven transformations of leadership Harvard business review (April 2005). https://tinyurl.com/s3fyra5d (2005) Accessed 16 Apr 2022
21. Wheatley, M.: Leadership and the New Science: Discovering Order in a Chaotic World. Berrett-Koehler Publishers, Inc. (2006)
22. Senge, P., Kleiner, A., Roberts, C., Ross, R., Smith, B.: The Fifth Discipline Field book London. Nicholas Brealey Publishing, UK (1997)
23. Prikshat, V., Nankervis, A., Priyono, O., Salleh, N., Connell, J.A.: Graduate work- readiness in the Asia-Pacific region: perspectives from stakeholders and the role of HRM. Equality, Diversity and Inclusion: An International Journal **37**(4). https://tinyurl.com/p689n3hc (2018). Accessed 16 Apr 2022
24. Evolve: An Industry Survey and Comment on Preparedness of Science Graduates for Work. Mechanisms of Engaging with Universities and the Importance of Work Integrated Learning (WIL). https://tinyurl.com/yk966dej (2016). Accessed 16 Apr 2022

25. Grasgreen, A.: Preparedness Paradoxes. https://tinyurl.com/frx2tvuc (2014)
26. Kolb, D.: Experiential Learning: Experience as the Source of Learning and Development. Prentice Hall, New Jersey (1984)
27. Vygotsky, L.S.: Mind in Society: The Development of Higher Psychological Processes. USA Harvard University Press (1980)
28. Neil, A.S.: The Dominie Books of A. S. Neil. Hart Publishingv
29. Knowles, M.S.: The Adult Learner: A Neglected Species. Gulf Publishing Co, Houston (1990)
30. Snowden, D., Curry, A.: Complied edition of the origins of Cynefin by David Snowden. https://tinyurl.com/687tt4e8 (2007). Accessed 16 Apr 2022
31. Kurtz, C.F., Snowden, D.J.: The new dynamics of strategy: sense-making in a complex and complicated world. IBM Syst. J. **42**(3), 462–483 (2003). https://doi.org/10.1147/sj.423.0462
32. Sketching Maniacs: Cynefin Framework. https://tinyurl.com/2vkuy49c (2019)
33. Leslie Owen Wilson: Types of curriculum. https://thesecondprinciple.com/instructional-design/types-of-curriculum/ (2020)
34. Torbert, W.R.: The Power of Balance: Transforming Self, Society, and Scientific Inquiry. Sage, USA (1991)
35. Schor, I.: When Students Have Power: Negotiating Authority in a Critical Pedagogy. The University of Chicago Press, Chicago (1996)
36. Martin, R.:. We are repeating the discrimination experiment every day, says educator Jane Elliott. https://tinyurl.com/4v622x (2020). Accessed 16 Apr 2022
37. Frankopan, P.: The silk roads a new history of the world. Bloomsbury Paperbacks, UK (2015)
38. Link, F.R.: Man: a course of study: getting innovative curricula into the bloodstream of American education. Theory Pract. **10**(3), 178–184 (1971). https://doi.org/10.1080/004058 47109542325
39. EDC: Man a course of study. https://www.jstor.org/stable/1475911 (2020). Accessed 16 Apr 2022
40. Wikipedia: Man: a course of study. https://en.wikipedia.org/wiki/Man:_A_Course_of_Study (2020) Accessed 16 Apr 2022
41. Shepherd, I.: Interactive representations of a conceptual framework for simulation in healthcare education http://www.btwebz.com.au/simulation/framework.htm (2014)
42. Shepherd, I.: A conceptual framework for simulation in healthcare education. Victoria University, Victoria. https://tinyurl.com/9x6jefps (2017). Accessed 16 Apr 2022

# Experimental Research: Simulations and Serious Games for Sustainability

Uyen-Phuong Nguyen[1]([⊠]) and Philip Hallinger[1,2]

[1] College of Management, Mahidol University, Bangkok, Thailand
rachel.uyenphuong@gmail.com
[2] Department of Educational Leadership and Management, University of Johannesburg,
Johannesburg, South Africa

**Abstract.** A review of experimental studies accounts for the effectiveness of simulation-based learning in generating behavior and other variables towards sustainability. A set of 35 studies from 1997–2019 was derived from the bibliometric database on simulations and serious games (SSG) featuring education for sustainable development (ESD). Key findings highlighted the effects of SSG on sustainable variables. The SSG featured in experiments focused on either multiple or single dimensions of sustainability and appeared in academic, household and workplace settings. The experiments are overweighed with quasi-experimental designs, indicating the challenges to achieve random assignments. The majority of the simulation gaming interventions showed significant effects on knowledge, attitude and behavior towards sustainability. Interpreting the effects requires clear evidence, particularly when effect size indicators were likely to be ignored or skipped. Future researchers must use appropriate analytical tools and justify key results to achieve statistically significant effects of SSG on outcome variables.

**Keywords:** Simulation-based learning · Planned behavior · Quasi-experimental research · Triple-bottom line · Pretest-posttest design

## 1 Introduction

Simulations and serious games (SSG) have become significant pedagogical and training tools used to meet the demands of education for sustainable development (ESD) [1] [2]. However, the field lacks a critical review of methodologically rigorous studies and quantitative analysis that are capable of validating existing conclusions on the efficacy of simulation-based learning (SBL) in ESD [3, 4].

First, the question whether intention toward a sustainable behavior is desirable in SSG research remains unanswered [5, 6].

Second, the effectiveness of SSG is defined by the framework of knowledge-attitude-behavior [1, 7]. The unique role of knowledge in the empirical research needs more attention.

Third, the majority of reviews on SSG effectiveness featuring ESD seems to target SSG's design elements, formats or subjects rather than look at research designs [8, 9].

© Springer Nature Switzerland AG 2022
U. Dhar et al. (Eds.): ISAGA 2021, LNCS 13219, pp. 101–114, 2022.
https://doi.org/10.1007/978-3-031-09959-5_9

Fourth, scholars discussed whether SSG on ESD should equally or fully contribute to triple-bottom line of sustainability [4, 10, 11].

Fifth, experimental and quasi-experimental designs are considered to be most suited for assessing the effects of interventional treatments [7, 12]. Conceptual and commentary approaches are the most prevalent methods used in empirical studies representing a modest portion of research during the last two decades [4]. The examination of the whole subset of experimentation offers a unique opportunity to investigate methodological patterns in the empirical SSG research on ESD.

This study is the first attempt to review the effectiveness of SBL on sustainability by taking into account experimental research. The following questions guide the purpose of the review:

- What are the characteristics of experimental research featuring SSG in the domain of ESD?
- What can be concluded regarding the effectiveness of SSG from the findings of experimental research in ESD literature?

To explore the research questions, the authors used the secondary databases indexed by Scopus and Google Scholar between 1997 till 2019. The review began by delving into the nature of SSG incorporating ESD in experimentation. It examined outcome variables and analyzed research findings.

## 2 Method

### 2.1 Identification of Sources

The authors determined three criteria for inclusion in the analysis: (1) each study explored a simulation or a serious game used for ESD; (2) each study was empirical with experiments or quasi-experiments; (3) the work employed quantitative or mixed methods.

This review uses the existing bibliometric data to explore the effects of SBL on ESD which was not done in the original work [4]. Following PRISMA (Preferred Reporting Items for Systematic Reviews and Meta-Analyses) guidelines for the document identification (Fig. 1), three criteria resulted in the selection of 35 experimental and quasi-experimental studies [13].

### 2.2 Data Analysis

From 35 experimental studies, relevant data were extracted and aggregated in Excel. One full quasi-experiment was not available and its data were obtained from the abstract. Criteria were determined to meet the purpose of the review and recorded in Excel (i.e., research design, settings, mode of delivery, method, triple-bottom line dimension, gaming features, statistics, sample size, effect size, attitude, intention, sustainability-related behavior, other variables and key findings).

The data analysis primarily relied on the use of descriptive statistics and graphing of research trajectory (e.g., the growth of the behavioral studies) [4]. Comparable criteria were categorized to capture the findings and compare their variability.

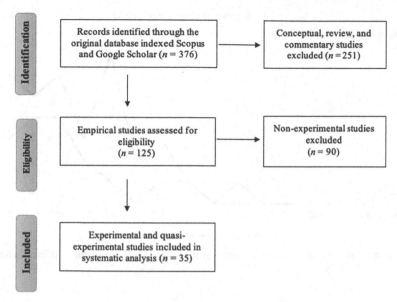

**Fig. 1.** The flow chart for identification of sources for the review

## 3   Results

### 3.1   Characteristics of Experimental Research Featuring SBL in the Domain of ESD

**Growth in SSG-ESD Research.** Although the original dataset including 376 studies was drawn from 1997 to the end of 2019; the first study in the field was uncovered in 2004 [4]. The experimental portion of SBL in ESD literature did not emerge until the last decade (2013–2019) and continues growing in the recent years (Fig. 2).

**Nature of SSG in Experimental Research in the Domain of ESD.** The settings of SSG in teaching and training sustainability were varied and distributed among higher education (32%), K-12 schools (26%), household and professional development contexts (29%) and even multiple settings (9%). Researchers and practitioners used different tools to deliver SSG in experimentation (Table 1). While computer-based simulations were preferably used, others used online modes, role-play games, board games and smartphone gamified apps. Some SSG were conducted in multiple forms of delivery accounting for 9% of the database.

Content analysis was used to examine the conceptualizations of environmental, economic and social dimensions of sustainability in the SSG studies (Table 2). The descriptive analysis shows that the environment-related contents account for the most prominent portion (32 studies), followed by social aspects (29 studies) and profitable issues (26 studies).

A majority of the studies incorporated three dimensions of triple-bottom line into their design conceptualization (59%) (Table 2). Some studies show only one or two of

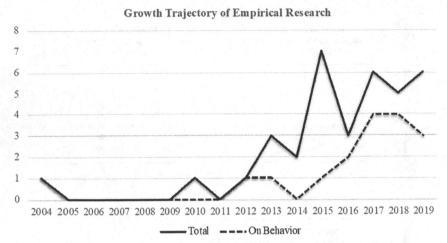

**Fig. 2.** Number of experimental articles per year in total and on sustainability-related behaviors

**Table 1.** Types and subjects of simulations and serious games used in educating for sustainable development (2004–2020)

| Mode of Delivery | Studies | Subjects and Articles (Examples) |
|---|---|---|
| Computer | 9 | Climate literacy (Harker-Schuch et al, 2020); water management (Khoury et al, 2018); climate change (Feldpausch-Parker, O'Byrne, Endres, & Peterson, 2013; Nussbaum et al., 2015); environmental impact (Schrier, 2015; Su, 2018); manufacture and production (Ordaz, Romero, Gorecky, & Siller, 2015); public-goods (Theodorou, Bandt-Law, & Bryson, 2019); multiple subjects (Weijs et al., 2016) |
| Online | 6 | Green construction (Ayer et al., 2016); corporate social responsibility (Maltseva et al., 2019); ocean literacy (Brennan et al., 2019); manufacture and production (Perini, Margoudi, Oliveira, & Taisch, 2017); climate change (Yang et al., 2012); natural resource (Doucet & Srinivasany, 2010) |
| Role-play Game | 7 | Waste management (Chow et al., 2017; Yeung et al., 2017); manufacture and production (Choomlucksana & Doolen, 2017); climate change (Jacquet et al., 2013); political responsibility (Lohmann, 2019); water management (Meinzen-Dick et al., 2018) |
| Board Game | 8 | Green construction (Juan & Chao, 2015); sustainable consumption (Bevilacqua, Ciarapica, Mazzuto, & Paciarotti, 2015); waste management (Hirose, Sugiura, & Shimomoto, 2004); climate change (Meya & Eisenack, 2018); green chemistry (Miller, Wentzel, Clark, & Hurst, 2019); lean production (Yukselen, Ahiska, & E.king, 2014) |
| Mobile App | 1 | Sustainable consumption (Mulcahy et al., 2020) |
| Multiple | 3 | Climate change (van Pelt et al., 2015); green construction (Dib & Adamo-Villani, 2014); multiple subjects (Rowe, Lobene, Mott, & Lester, 2014) |
| Undefined | 1 | Marine ecosystems (Mayer et al., 2013) |

**Table 2.** Dimensions of sustainability featured in simulations and serious games in empirical research (1997–2019).

| Dimension | Studies | % | Multiple Dimensions | Studies | % |
|---|---|---|---|---|---|
| Environmental | 32 | 94% | One | 1 | 3% |
| Social | 29 | 85% | Two | 13 | 38% |
| Economic | 26 | 76% | Three | 20 | 59% |

those three dimensions depending on contexts [14, 15]. The only simulation to feature one dimension explicitly explored a factory's economic performances "such as cycle times, clocks produced, orders shipped on time, orders shipped late and quality rates" [16].

**Methodological Characteristics of Experimental Research on SSG in ESD.**
Five methodological characteristics of research including research design, research methodology, statistical test, sample size, and effect size were described below.

*Research Design.* In 11 experimental designs (31.4%), researchers randomly assigned participants into either a treatment group where they had treatment featuring SBL, or a control group in which they did not receive the treatment or only received conventional interventions. Twenty four quasi-experimental studies (68.6%) did not provide evidence of random assignment (Table 3) [12].

The two designs found among 11 experimental studies were *pretest-posttest control group design* (five studies) and *posttest-only control group design* (six studies). The

**Table 3.** .

| Design Type | Studies | % |
|---|---|---|
| *Experimental Designs* | 11 | |
|    1.  Pretest-Posttest Control Group Design | 5 | 45% |
|    2.  Posttest-Only Control Group Design | 6 | 55% |
| *Quasi-Experimental Designs* | 24 | |
|    3.  Pretest-Posttest Design | 16 | 67% |
|    4.  Combination Designs | 7 | 29% |
|       4.1. Nonequivalent Groups Design & Pretest-Posttest Design | 3 | |
|       4.2. Nonequivalent Groups Design & Time Series Design | 4 | |
| **Total** | **34** | |

numbers imply that the database is quite limited to draw a concrete conclusion on whether the pretest-posttest control group design was the most strongly recommended design of SSG experimentation for ESD as expected [12].

Twenty-four quasi-experimental studies in which the random assignment was manipulated were classified as pretest-posttest design (16 studies) and combination design (seven studies). The outstanding number of quasi-experimental studies using pretest-posttest design indicates that they dominate in SSG efficacy research. The type of combination designs (29%) is normally better than a segregated quasi-experimental design [17–19].

A typical limitation in quasi-experiments is that it is hard to presume the improvements in dependent variables as the success of the SSG intervention over other methods [20]. Unless participants are truly randomly assigned to conditions, some important confounding variables may be neither put into account nor kept constant (i.e., students' GPA, learning motivation, teaching methods).

*Method.* Among 35 empirical studies, quantitative and mixed methods were both employed (57% and 43% respectively) of which the majority of quasi-experimental studies use only quantitative methods (61%), while experimental studies tend to employ equally quantitative and mixed methods. The use of qualitative methods to amplify or broaden quantitative results in those mixed methods studies seems popular [21, 22].

*Statistical Test.* The authors used the scheme including four analytical levels (Table 4) to describe statistical approaches [23]. Average statistical levels are dominant in those studies (43%). Specifically, the t-test seems to be the most common null hypothesis test to compare the difference between two means. A study ($N = 156$) was among the few to predict and explain the behavior based on the players' subjective norms, attitude, and intention by employing SEM [19].

**Table 4.** Sample sizes and levels of statistics in experimental and quasi-experiential studies featuring simulation-based learning for sustainability education (1997–2019)

| Sample | Studies | Percentage | Statistics | Studies | Percentage |
|---|---|---|---|---|---|
| Small (N <= 20) | 3 | 9% | Level 1 (Descriptive statistics) | 6 | 17% |
| Medium (N= 21-100) | 16 | 46% | Level 2 (Correlation and difference tests without control variables) | 15 | 43% |
| Large (N > 100) | 15 | 43% | Level 3 (Correlation and difference tests with a control variable) | 7 | 20% |
| | | | Level 4 (Multi-factor structure) | 7 | 20% |
| Total | 34 | 97% | | 35 | 100% |

The inferential analysis challenges readers to draw a complete conclusion how and whether the observed changes in the outcome variables were caused by chance or by a SBL intervention. A quasi-experiment ($N = 116$) reported the mean pre-game knowledge score was 6.86, while the mean post-game score was 8.45 with p-value was much lower ($p < 0.0001$) [24]. This implies that the significant difference in student knowledge is more meaningful and occurred as an effect of their gaming experience.

*Sample Size.* Most studies rank from medium to large sample sizes (e.g., 401 eligible respondents in one sample) [20]. However, sample size appeared to be explicitly problematic when reporting the effects. For example, a quasi-experiment showed differential correlational relationships among knowledge, attitude and behavior [1]. With an average sample ($N = 35$), caution must be applied when interpreting those relationships as the findings might not be generalized for the public.

*Effect Size.* Table 5 summarizes the interpretations of the effect size, a critical element of experimentation [25]. Fifty seven per cent of the studies did not report effect size. Only 39% of the studies provided a justification of effect size and 18% of the studies explained how discrepant the effect size when compared with p-value. For example, the multiple regression tests showed the impact of schools was not significant [20]. One school reported a significant difference in the post-test score compared to the mean score across all schools.

The articles using level-2 reported no effect size, whereas more complex models offer the higher percentage of effect size calculations at 64% by average. This finding seems inconsistent with prior research that effect size was more often explained in t-test and regression methods.

**Table 5.** Reporting effect size in experimental research ($N = 28$) ( adopted from Sun et al., 2010)

| Frequency of ES definition and justification | Studies | % |
|---|---|---|
| ES was reported | 12 | 43% |
| ES was justified | 11 | 39% |
| ES was explained with p-value | 5 | 18% |
| Frequency of ES reporting for different ES measures | | |
| Measures of mean differences* | 6 | |
| Measures of strength of relations** | 15 | |
| Levels of analytical testing methods | | |
| Level 2 | 0 | |
| Level 3 | 6 | |
| Level 4 | 6 | |

*i.e., *Cohen's d, f, h*
**i.e., *R squared, r, eta-squared, β*

The effect size measures of mean differences (i.e., Cohen's d, f, h) were less reported than those of strengths for relationships. This can be explained by the fact that the frequency of effect size reporting tends to depend on the statistical levels of testing, suggesting that more complex models offer the higher frequency of effect size calculations. This finding seems inconsistent with prior research that effect size was more often explained in t-test and regression methods. This may also imply that researchers in this simulation gaming field who use lower levels of analysis are likely to ignore or omit those important indicators while those using more advanced statistics may highlight the use of effect size in designing and explaining their quasi-experimental models.

**Effectiveness of SBL on Outcome Variables.** In general, 22 articles studied variables of knowledge, while 48% of the articles focused on behaviors. In total, 16 studies focused on variables of sustainability-related behavior in real, simulated, or gamified environments. Those variables of behavior were categorized into: (1) Actual behavior in game/in simulation; (2) Intended behavior in reality; (3) Actual behavior in reality (Fig. 3).

|  | PLANNED BEHAVIOR | |
|  | Intended | Actual |
|---|---|---|
| In-game/simulation | | Monitoring (Hirose, Sugiura, & Shimomoto, 2004) Adjusting/Reviewing information (Yang, Chien, & Liu, 2012) Cooperative/Defective decision-making (Meya & Eisenack, 2017) Cooling/Washing/Switching (Mulcahy, et al., 2018) Switching (Su 2018) Design fixation (Ayar et al., 2016) Dwelling (Rowe, Lobene, & Lester, 2017) Cooperating/Competing (Theodorou et al., 2019) Using water (Meinzen-Dick et al., 2018) |
| SIMULATION/GAMING | | |
| Actual | Waste Recycling (Yksung et al., 2017) Donation (Maltseva, et al., 2019) Collective pro-environmental behaviors (Brennan, Ashley, & Molloy, 2019; Chappin et al., 2017) | Energy-saving (Mulcahy, et al., 2018) Using fertilizers (Mose & Müllhoff, 2016) |

**Fig. 3.** Categorization of sustainability-related behaviors in experimental simulation gaming research

Another aspect showed that the variables standing for game features (e.g., fun, melodramatic frame, validity, visual elements and user interface) frequently appeared along with outcome variables. Twelve of the 34 studies assessed game features and six studies used quantitative methods to calculate the efficacy. Accordingly, presuming game features as either direct or indirect, predictors of SBL effects must be approached with some caution since researchers often use qualitative data to declare the impacts [24, 26].

**Research on the Effects of SSG on Learner Behaviors.** The analysis shows that simulation and serious game interventions yielded significant effects on behaviors in the majority of the studies. Eighty one per cent of studies reported positive effects of simulation-based learning on behaviors while 13% of studies showed no effects (two studies) and mixed effects with one study. The Sustainability Game facilitated cooperative behaviors among anonymous players (p = 0.004) and identifiable players (p = 0.076), both at small effect size ($\eta 2p > 0.1$) [27]. There exist statistically non-significant effects of those interventions on behavioral variables [15, 28].

More than half of the behavioral studies did not report effect size metrics, while seven of 16 studies testing sustainability-related behaviors as dependent variables showed large-sized effects. The only Cohen's d found in the database indicated the large-sized effect on users' behaviors [29]. The other effect size measures on behaviors were represented by R-squared and eta-squared, indicating strength for relationships with behaviors in treatments. The authors found a considerable difference between the effect size on in-game and actual behaviors. Particularly, using a gamified app significantly improved energy saving behaviors in the app with $R2 = .49$ (p < 0.001) and saving behaviors on energy bills with $R2 = .10$ (p < 0.05) [30]. Similarly, consistent results were found in another study ($R2 < .01$) in which game-based communities were significantly more likely to adopt water sustainability actions compared to those without the game interventions [31]. There would be more evidence in future research to consider if simulation gaming treatments can cause more effects on in-game behaviors than those in reality to benefit sustainability.

**Research on the Effects of SSG on Learner Knowledge.** Eighty two per cent of the measured sustainability knowledge variables indicated that the majority of simulation-based learning yielded significant effects on sustainability knowledge [20, 29, 32], 9% showed non-significant effects [1, 33] and 9% mixed-effects [16, 34].

The popularity of knowledge measures in simulation gaming empirical studies over other variables can be explained by the fact that 63% of the 35 articles described and explained knowledge variables, while 46% of the articles focused on behavioral variables. Only 32% of studies on sustainability knowledge reported effect size.

**Research on the Effects of SSG on Learner Attitudes.** Another frequently studied variable in simulation gaming research is associated with users' attitude although effect size reports on attitude towards sustainable development are limited. Six of the 9 articles reported significant effects [1, 19, 22, 29, 35]. At the same time, simulation and game-based interventions were shown to have no or mixed significant impacts on attitudinal variables [15, 28].

Attitudinal variables had lower studied rate compared with that of behavior or knowledge variables. The proportional gaps appear to be relevant to the claim that pro-environmental behaviors are mainly related with knowledge rather than attitudinal factors as usually asserted in planned behavior theory [36].

**Research on the Effects of SSG on Learner Intention.** A modest proportion of studies measures intentional factors through simulation-based settings (11%) which interestingly contradicts prior findings on green behaviors studied in general. Prior pro-environmental studies showed a particular preference on intention, rather than behaviors, with such explanations as it is not practical to measure behaviors or intention is a key to actual behavior [6, 37]. This is rather opposite in the simulation and gaming field. It looks like researchers have attempted to develop and understand pro-environmental behavioral developments by using simulations and serious games. Thus, it is not true to conclude that intention is more preferable than behavior particularly in simulation and gaming research.

# 4  Discussion

## 4.1  Limitations of Findings

First, this study was limited to experimental research on simulations and serious games in the domain of sustainability. Thus, the review neither covered the entire range of empirical research (quantitative and qualitative) on simulations and serious games in the domain of sustainability, nor did it examine experimental studies in simulations and serious games more broadly. The former objective was previously addressed to some extent in a prior study [4]. The latter objective is one that could be addressed in a future study. Nonetheless, the authors examined in detail an important subset of studies on the use of simulations and serious games for sustainability.

Second, insufficiency of evidence in the database prevents the authors to understand the causal relationships between sustainability-related behaviors and other outcome variables in general. In other words, the authors cannot conclude the power of planned behavior theory in explaining and predicting sustainability-related behavior from other variables in simulation gaming research. It is promising to explore different behavioral theories in the general sustainability field [38]. A wide variety of variables has been targeted in research to address the assumptions of simulation-based learning effectiveness. This should not be perceived necessarily as a disadvantage but rather as promising opportunity for future research on sustainability-featured simulations and serious games [11].

Third, unlike the majority of review studies on simulation- or game-based learning for ESD, this current study shifted the focus from the roles of design elements of a simulation or a serious game into features of experimental research design in order to encapsulate the essence of effectiveness [8, 9]. Although 35% of experiments mentioned game features, half of them used qualitative methods to deduce the effects of the interventions.

## 4.2  Interpretations and Suggestions for Future Research

Experimentation accounts for less than 10% of the available literature and did not evolve until the last decade. The observations in multiple settings indicate a growing demand of applying and advancing experimental designs into SSG research and understanding behavior towards sustainability [4, 30].

Diverse forms of SSG have been delivered in practice with various sustainability topics. Environmental contents are dominant while social and profitable aspects are expected to be more frequently targeted in empirical research. Researchers are likely to integrate three dimensions into their designs to address general sustainability issues.

The fundamental purpose of the study is to investigate the effectiveness of simulation-based learning from experimental research. The findings broadly support the work of other studies in this area linking the applications of simulations and games with learning for sustainability. Consistently using simulation-based learning can increase subjects' knowledge of sustainable development and develop their sustainability attitudes and behaviors [39]. Although there was a lack of compatibility between the essential features of studies, earlier researchers encouraged a clarification of the effectiveness of simulations and serious games [8, 11]. Based on the experimental analysis, it can be concluded that the current results suggest a positive effect from the impact of SSG on the sustainability knowledge, attitudes and behaviors of users while a few outliers reported non-significant effects. However, experimentation requires strict evidence and procedures to interpret the findings.

First, the experimentation segment was overweighed with quasi-experimental designs whereas experimental designs comprised half. Conducting random assignment may not be a feasible choice in SBL experimental settings. On the other hand, it might not be possible to conduct randomized controlled designs while introducing a new teaching tool or method [18]. Thus, it cannot be concluded that the use of quasi-experimental research designs is a flaw. In many research and development contexts, they may represent a justifiable compromise between the needs for stronger research designs and the constraints imposed by the teaching and learning contexts in which simulations and games are designed and used.

Second, while some researchers might agree that the pre-test did not necessarily matter whether SSG interventions worked or not, some others may not skip them in randomized trials. It is unquestionably simpler to carry out a quasi-experiment with pretest-posttest design. It is advised to combine different variants of quasi-experimental designs, such as nonequivalent groups or time series into a quasi-experiment [40].

Third, experiments with or without randomization might confront some statistical concerns in design procedures. It is necessary to plan the selection of acceptable statistical tests and the interpretation of predicted findings. When t-test is the most popular tool, the lack of advanced analysis makes it hard to conclude if significant changes are due to SSG treatments or by coincidence. This recognizes the critical role of reporting effect size in experimentation.

Although medium and large sample sizes were common, it appears inconceivable to recognize that 57% of the experimental research ignored or skipped effect size indicators. It is recommended that effect size measures need to be defined, justified and interpreted with p-values, research designs, sample size and analytical techniques. This ensures experimental findings are not only statistically significant but also practically meaningful on a certain size, especially for studies with small sample size.

Fourth, the heterogeneity of sustainability-related behavior implied that scientists like to create their own measures to operationally define variables. Thus, it is not totally true to claim that the lack of behavioral measurements disputes the understanding of behaviors for sustainability [37]. Behavioral measures in either natural or in-game settings can be intended or recorded tasks, timing or self-report questionnaires. Researchers must clarify the reliability and validity of consistent measures in SSG research.

Fifth, knowledge and behavior are among the most frequently studied constructs in trials to demonstrate the SSG efficacy, and have yielded the highest frequency of statistically significant effects alongside a few insignificant or mixed effects. The limited numbers of reported effect size indicators prevent further conclusions on the practical significance of experimental studies.

The intention is rarely targeted even if it is regarded as an important variable to directly affect behavior. The lack of conceptual definitions can lead to the ambiguity in developing and measuring some variables such as intention to act sustainably. It can be more complicated to conceptualize intention towards a sustainable behavior than behavior itself. The future researchers must explicitly define abstract and complex variables conceptually before measuring them.

In summary, the study demonstrated the diversity of the emerging experimental designs in SBL for sustainability in the recent decades. The effectiveness of an intervention using a simulation or serious game, regardless of design, depends on the choice of outcome constructs featuring sustainability, models of experimental design, analytical methods and key metrics. It is important that research design is clearly presented before collecting data and interpreting the results.

**Acknowledgement.** The study was supported by the ASEAN Center for Sustainable Development Studies and Dialogue, College of Management, Mahidol University, Bangkok, Thailand.

# References

1. Chappin, E.J., Bijvoet, X., Oei, A.: Teaching sustainability to a broad audience through an entertainment game–the effect of Catan: oil Springs. J. Clean. Prod. **156**, 556–568 (2017)
2. Gatti, L., Ulrich, M., Seele, P.: Education for sustainable development through business simulation games: an exploratory study of sustainability gamification and its effects on students' learning outcomes. J. Clean. Prod. **207**, 667–678 (2019)
3. Chen, J.C., Martin, A.R.: Role-play simulations as a transformative methodology in environmental education. J. Transform. Educ. **13**(1), 85–102 (2015)
4. Hallinger, P., Wang, R., Chatpinyakoop, C., Nguyen, V.T., Nguyen, U.P.: A bibliometric review of research on simulations and serious games used in educating for sustainability, 1997–2019. J. Clean. Prod. **256**, 120358 (2020)
5. Fishbein, M., Ajzen, I.: Prediction and Change of Behavior: The Reasoned Action Approach. Psychology Press, New York, NY (2010)
6. Wang, Z., Dong, X., Yin, J.: Antecedents of urban residents' separate collection intentions for household solid waste and their willingness to pay: evidence from China. J. Clean. Prod. **173**, 256–264 (2018)
7. Schrader, P.G., Lawless, K.A.: The knowledge, attitudes, & behaviors approach how to evaluate performance and learning in complex environments. Perform. Improv. **43**(9), 8–15 (2004)
8. Madani, K., Pierce, T.W., Mirchi, A.: Serious games on environmental management. Sustain. Cities Soc. **29**, 1–11 (2017)
9. Reckien, D., Eisenack, K.: Climate change gaming on board and screen: a review. Simul. Gaming **44**(2–3), 253–271 (2013)
10. Dos Santos, A.D., Strada, F., Bottino, A.: Approaching sustainability learning via digital serious games. IEEE Trans. Learn. Technol. **12**(3), 303–320 (2018)

11. Stanitsas, M., Kirytopoulos, K., Vareilles, E.: Facilitating sustainability transition through serious games: a systematic literature review. J. Clean. Prod. **208**, 924–936 (2019)
12. Campbell, D.T., Stanley, J.C.: Experimental and Quasi-Experimental Designs for Research. Ravenio Books.X, Chicago (2015)
13. Moher, D., Liberati, A., Tetzlaff, J., Altman, D.G., Prisma Group: Preferred reporting items for systematic reviews and meta-analyses: the PRISMA statement. PLoS Med. **6**(7), e1000097 (2009)
14. Lohmann, R.: Effects of simulation-based learning and one way to analyze them. J. Political Sci. Educ. **16**(4), 479–495 (2020)
15. Maltseva, K., Fieseler, C., Trittin-Ulbrich, H.: The challenges of gamifying CSR communication. Corp. Commun. Int. J. **24**(1), 44–62 (2019)
16. Choomlucksana, J., Doolen, T.L.: An exploratory investigation of teaching innovations and learning factors in a lean manufacturing system engineering course. Eur. J. Eng. Educ. **42**(6), 829–843 (2017)
17. Jhangiani, R.S., Chiang, I.C.A., Cuttler, C., Leighton, D.C.: Research Methods in Psychology. Kwantlen Polytechnic University, British Columbia (2019)
18. Thyer, B.A.: Quasi-Experimental Research Designs. Oxford University Press, NY (2012)
19. Su, C.H.: Exploring sustainability environment educational design and learning effect evaluation through migration theory: an example of environment educational serious games. Sustainability **10**(10), 3363 (2018)
20. Harker-Schuch, I.E., Mills, F.P., Lade, S.J., Colvin, R.M.: CO2peration–structuring a 3D interactive digital game to improve climate literacy in the 12–13-year-old age group. Comput. Educ. **144**, 103705 (2020)
21. Doucet, L., Srinivasan, V.:. Designing entertaining educational games using procedural rhetoric: a case study. In: Proceedings of the 5th ACM SIGGRAPH Symposium on Video Games, pp. 5–10 (2010)
22. Mayer, I., et al.: Integrated, ecosystem-based marine spatial planning: design and results of a game-based, quasi-experiment. Ocean Coast. Manag. **82**, 7–26 (2013)
23. Hallinger, P.: A conceptual framework for systematic reviews of research in educational leadership and management. J. Educ. Admin. **51**(2), 126–149 (2013)
24. Feldpausch-Parker, A.M., O'Byrne, M., Endres, D., Peterson, T.R.: The adventures of carbon bond: using a melodramatic game to explain CCS as a mitigation strategy for climate change. Greenh. Gases: Sci. Technol. **3**(1), 21–29 (2013)
25. Sun, S., Pan, W., Wang, L.L.: A comprehensive review of effect size reporting and interpreting practices in academic journals in education and psychology. J. Educ. Psychol. **102**(4), 989 (2010)
26. Nussbaum, E.M., et al.: Losing the lake: simulations to promote gains in student knowledge and interest about climate change. Int. J. Environ. Sci. Educ. **10**(6), 789–811 (2015)
27. Theodorou, A., Bandt-Law, B., Bryson, J.J.: The sustainability game: AI technology as an intervention for public understanding of cooperative investment. In: 2019 IEEE Conference on Games (CoG), pp. 1–4. IEEE (Aug 2019)
28. Chow, C.F., So, W.M.W., Cheung, T.Y., Yeung, S.K.D.: Plastic waste problem and education for plastic waste management. In: Emerging Practices in Scholarship of Learning and Teaching in a Digital Era, pp. 125–140. Springer, Singapore (2017)
29. Brennan, C., Ashley, M., Molloy, O.: A system dynamics approach to increasing ocean literacy. Front. Mar. Sci. **6**, 360 (2019)
30. Mulcahy, R., Russell-Bennett, R., Iacobucci, D.: Designing gamified apps for sustainable consumption: a field study. J. Bus. Res. **106**, 377–387 (2020)
31. Meinzen-Dick, R., Janssen, M.A., Kandikuppa, S., Chaturvedi, R., Rao, K., Theis, S.: Playing games to save water: COLLECTIVE action games for groundwater management in Andhra Pradesh, India. World Dev. **107**, 40–53 (2018)

32. Bevilacqua, M., Ciarapica, F.E., Mazzuto, G., Paciarotti, C.: "Cook and Teach": learning by playing. J. Clean. Prod. **106**, 259–271 (2015)
33. Weijs, R., Bekebrede, G., Nikolic, I.: Sustainable competence development of business students: effectiveness of using serious games. In: Bottino, R., Jeuring, J., Veltkamp, R.C. (eds.) GALA 2016. LNCS, vol. 10056, pp. 3–14. Springer, Cham (2016). https://doi.org/10.1007/978-3-319-50182-6_1
34. Dib, H., Adamo-Villani, N.: Serious sustainability challenge game to promote teaching and learning of building sustainability. J. Comput. Civ. Eng. **28**(5), A4014007 (2014)
35. Yeung, S.K., So, W.M.W., Cheng, N.Y.I., Cheung, T.Y., Chow, C.F.: Comparing pedagogies for plastic waste management at university level. Int. J. Sustain. High. Educ. **18**(7), 1039–1059 (2017)
36. Stern, P.C.: Toward a coherent theory of environmentally significant behavior. J. Soc. Issues **56**(3), 407–424 (2000)
37. Yuriev, A., Dahmen, M., Paillé, P., Boiral, O., Guillaumie, L.: Pro-environmental behaviors through the lens of the theory of planned behavior: a scoping review. Resour. Conserv. Recycl. **155**, 104660 (2020)
38. Ketprapakorn, N., Kantabutra, S.: Culture development for sustainable SMEs: toward a behavioral theory. Sustainability **11**(9), 2629 (2019)
39. Liarakou, G., Sakka, E., Gavrilakis, C., Tsolakidis, C.: Evaluation of serious games, as a tool for education for sustainable development. European Journal of Open, Distance and E-learning **15**(2) (2012)
40. Krishnan, P.: A review of the non-equivalent control group post-test-only design. Nurse Res. **29**(1) (2021)

# Frame Game as Teaching Methodology in Higher Education: The Case of RElastiCity

Geertje Bekebrede$^{(\boxtimes)}$ and Carissa Champlin

Delft University of Technology, P.O. Box 5015, Delft, The Netherlands
g.bekebrede@tudelft.nl

**Abstract.** The objective of the study is to illustrate the use of the frame game, *RElastiCity* as a framework to learn about the resilience of urban areas and the shocks and stresses in those areas. The question is if use of the frame game as a basis for game co-design is a useful approach to explore complex systems and its dynamics. This study covers the exploratory application of the approach in two university courses in the Netherlands. The results show divergent student experiences between the two courses. The main difference between the courses was the scope of the co-design assignment and the amount of time students had to complete the design process. It was found that using frame games as a framework for understanding complex systems is useful if students have sufficient time to investigate the topic, develop the game and playtest the game.

**Keywords:** Co-design · Complex systems · Frame game · Teaching method · Urban resilience

## 1 Introduction

By 2050, 80 percent of the world population will live in urbanized regions. Cities are incubators for innovation; yet their interconnected infrastructures are vulnerable to shocks, particularly in deltas. According to statements in a press release on April 16, 2013 from the European Union, more than 5.5 million people between 1980 and 2011 were affected by floods in Europe. The costs of not adapting are expected to rise to 250 billion Euros per year in 2050. The need to adopt a comprehensive strategy to make cities more resilient cannot be postponed [1].

With this comes the requirement to teach engineering students about urban resilience and make them aware of the impact of engineering solutions on the urban system. For this research, the following objectives for urban resilience are adopted: well-functioning cities that ensure the security and safety of people, property and infrastructure, provide basic services such as public health, water, sanitation and electricity and guarantee basic norms and rights [2]. Students of urban resilience must think in interdependencies between systems and the expected and unexpected (negative) consequences of interventions in preparing urban areas for shocks. Gaming is seen as one of the methods to experience such complex systems and their dynamics [3].

© Springer Nature Switzerland AG 2022
U. Dhar et al. (Eds.): ISAGA 2021, LNCS 13219, pp. 115–123, 2022.
https://doi.org/10.1007/978-3-031-09959-5_10

Many scholars use games as teaching methods in a variety of topics for knowledge, skills and changing attitudes. Besides using games, gamification or gamified approaches are used in classrooms to increase the motivation of learners. Another use of games in education is to design games to acquire skills like students' knowledge and skills in programming [4], to learn about mathematics [5] or teaching Human Computer Interaction Skills [6].

Research shows positive effects on learning skills and a positive attitude of students about the topic when using games in higher education. Some studies focussed on using game design to teach specific content-related topics such as in the field of construction and engineering [7]. By designing games, students improved their knowledge about the concepts and had a greater enjoyment because of the involvement of creativity and group work [7]. Game design in secondary education was used to teach students about informatics and society topics [8]. Using game design did not specifically lead to an increase in level of knowledge compared to not using game design, but that game design led to a higher degree of sensitisation although it took time to learn how to design games [8].

In professional settings, frame games have been shown to provide a combination of structure and flexibility that help practitioners to engage in shared learning about complex urban systems [9]. Game co-design has been used to gather knowledge about real-world issues for contextualization [10]. A frame game is a structured set of rules of a game into which different contents can be loaded, i.e. the frame contains the rules and procedures of the activity in which the desired information/knowledge to be transferred is placed [11]. The advantage of using a frame game is that students gain the creative and discursive aspect of game design by focusing on content and are not hindered by the lack of knowledge about the game design process.

The research question is: What can we learn about the use of frame games as teaching method to increase understandings of urban resilience? The research objective is to explore the use of a frame game as teaching method to teach urban resilience. An explorative approach is used to get a general understanding of the frame game as a conceptual model. *RElastiCity* is a game about urban resilience conducted in two different occasions in engineering courses in the Netherlands. At Delft University of Technology, a multi-session game was conducted where results and general observations of the co-design experience were collected. For the single-session game at the University of Twente, a short survey was used to collect data about the use of the frame game as a conceptual model. This paper begins with an explanation of frame games as conceptual models for simulating urban systems.

## 2 Frame Games as Conceptual Models

Simulation gaming can deal with complex, uncertain and unique issues and provides a language for combining the social-human with the physical, technological and economic knowledge domains and can represent socio-technical complex systems [12, 13]. Designing simulation games follows a generic design process: understanding the real world issue, developing a conceptual map of the situation, using that map for a conceptual game design, followed by the specification of the game and testing and application

[14]. The finished game can be used in classroom settings to learn about the behaviour of the real world dynamics and challenges (Fig. 1).

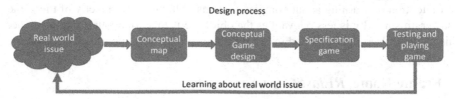

**Fig. 1.** Basic structure of developing simulation games and playing to understand the real world issue

Game design is a time consuming process and the designers need expertise. The use of a frame game makes it possible to easily adapt the content of the game to new issues or problem environment without changing the game mechanics and structure of the game [15]. This makes it possible to implement contextual variables of specific situations in an existing game environment. The design process of a frame game is slightly different in that the first design step uses the frame game as a structure for integrating real-world contextual issues (Fig. 2).

Starting with the conceptual game, the game elements have to be specified based on the real world issue. By putting all the elements together and after some tests, one gains a better understanding of the real-world situation from a system perspective, as the students define game elements and their relations with other elements. On a higher level of abstraction, students use higher order thinking specifically analyzing, evaluating [16] and creating to translate a complex real-world situation to this simplified representation.

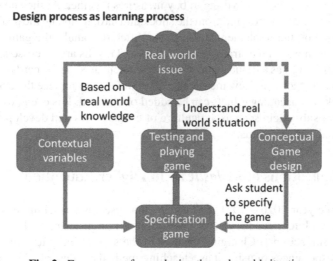

**Fig. 2.** Frame game for analysing the real world situation

The difference between using a frame game as teaching method in comparison to a game design assignment is that students are not distracted by the conceptual game design and the knowledge required for game design. Giving students a framework provides a low threshold to start the assignment and a high ceiling of challenges as all elements have to come together [8]. Working with this framework, therefore, allows them to focus their attention on learning about complex systems. Although the novelty of the games is lower, this novelty is less relevant as the objective is to learn about urban resilience. This model of learning is applied in two different settings with the use of *RElastiCity*.

## 3  Frame Game, *RElastiCity*

*RElastiCity* (combination of Resilience Engineering, Elasticity and City) is a game about urban resilience [17]. The objective of the game is to understand the effects of shocks (such as earthquakes, heat, dam breaks and power outages) on the urban area, the measures to make the urban areas more resilient and the consequences. One of the learning outcomes is that urban subsystems are connected and problems in one system cause cascading effects in other systems.

The game has a basic version simulating a generic Dutch urban area with four subsystems (transportation, energy, water and built environment). The game is played with four participants, each participant being responsible for one subsystem. A participant has to take measures (adaptive, mitigation and recovery) by playing cards that prepare the urban area to deal with shocks represented by cards and to improve the environmental, social and economic resilience of the area. After an introduction, the game is played in 10 rounds. Each round consists of rolling a dice to determine if a shock happens (the further in the game, the higher the probability of a shock occurring). In case of a shock, the players need to check if they are sufficiently prepared or if they have to recover within the turn. Next, players can discuss and decide which measures they want to buy and implement and if they are willing to buy measures together. At the end of the turn, the players check if they recovered from the shock and have to update the resilience level of the city based on the implemented measures. After 10 rounds, the game ends and a debriefing starts in which the strategies, decisions and results are discussed.

*RElastiCity* is built as a frame game where the content used on the cards can easily be replaced with other content. New measures can be added to or replace the existing cards and new shocks or cascading effects can be added or changed. It is even possible to add an entirely new subsystem such as agriculture or coastal areas and develop appropriate shock cards and measure cards.

## 4  Two Applications of *RElastiCity* in Higher Education

In the academic year 2020 – 2021, *RElastiCity* was used as a teaching method in two different courses, Integrated Project for Environmental Engineering in the first semester and Urban Resilience in A Changing Climate in the second semester. The way it was used and the experiences of using it as a teaching method are described below.

### 4.1 Integrated Project for Environmental Engineering

Integrated Project is a first-year Master course at Delft University of Technology about integrated engineering and students learn about problem structuring and project management. The course is given in two periods. In the first period, students selected an urban area and made an initial concept map, followed by an analysis of shocks and stresses in the urban area leading to different trend reports about a specific area. In the second period, the students developed a game based on *RElastiCity* by using the trend reports for defining the game elements and exploring the interaction of the different shocks and stresses analyzed in the first period. They developed 34 trend reports and 10 different games and presented the games at the JIRC conference in November 2020 [18].

Data of the experiences of the students was collected in feedback sessions and discussions with them and from the opinion of the course manager of the results. The students were asked about what they learned by using this frame game in their project.

Students used the elements of the game to search for specific information. A student group told us that they design stress cards based on actual journal articles; shock cards were based on news articles and measures based on policies of the municipality under study. This group found that this was a creative way to communicate and another group observed that the game opened the discussion about integrating other factors than the key performance indicators (KPIs) given in the format. A third group found that the game helped them to prepare for the worst. All groups learned about 'the complexity of urban resilience' and 'how integrated everything is' while designing the game.

The course coordinator observed that using a frame game stimulates students to think analytically as conceptualization and abstraction is required rather than merely listening to information which is a risk with writing reports. Students were more motivated to work on a game in comparison to writing a report. They have to place the information in context and consider the relationships and integration. Working in a group to design a game supports collaboration and communication. In many group work situations, students divide the work and the different outcomes are loosely coupled. In game design this does not work.

Although results are based on generic feedback sessions, we observed using the frame game gave a context for students to co-design and discuss the content. The frame serves as a framework for analyzing the system and as a starting point for discussion. These discussions were focused on the content and designing relations between elements of resilience challenge which is in line with our objectives and hardly on discussion and confusing about the game concepts.

### 4.2 Urban Resilience in a Changing Climate

The Urban Resilience course is an 8-week Master course at the University Twente in different topics such as conceptual modelling, measures and effects. One of the workshops in the course was 'Evaluating the Impact of Resilience Measures – a game design exercise' whose objective was resilience measures and to explore and discuss the impact of these measures.

*RElastiCity* was used as framework for the workshop which lasted two hours and was conducted online. The idea was that a group of students select a (published) trend report of the Integrated Project Course. With this information as starting point, students worked in groups to develop 'measure cards' for the game. This meant that they had to think about type of measures, costs and effects of these measures. Students discussed and developed a list of measures in Excel sheets about shocks, stresses and potential effects, but could not develop playing cards due to lack of time.

The survey instrument of 11 questions with a 7-point Likert scale (1 means totally agree, 7 means totally disagree) was completed by 13 students after the session. It had two ranking questions and one question of 10-point Likert scale (1 means totally agree, 10 means totally disagree). The objective of the workshop was to learn about shocks, measures and effects of measures on urban resilience. The students did not agree or disagree that they gained a deeper understanding of the measures or the impact of shocks on the system (Table 1). The students slightly agree that they could evaluate the impact of the measures from the indicators of economy, community and nature.

**Table 1.** Average score of learning effects

|  | N= | M= | SD= |
|---|---|---|---|
| Q2. I gained a deeper understanding of the measures for which I filled in game | 13 | 3.6 | 1.50 |
| Q3. While filling in the game cards, I gained a better understanding of the impact of the shocks I selected on a specific urban (sub) system: | 13 | 3.7 | 1.25 |
| Q4. The performance indicators (economy, community, nature) were an effective means of evaluating the impact of the measures: | 13 | 2.8 | 0.55 |

The second group of measures was about the use of the game as conceptual framework (Table 2). The students somewhat agreed that the assignment was useful and that filling in the cards was an engaging way to learn about measuring resilience. They somewhat disagreed that they had enough time. They said that it was difficult to fill in the excel sheet as more explanation was necessary and that they need more time to do the exercise. They assessed the exercise with 5.7 out of 10 and stated that the exercise was useful to learn to measure resilience in an integrated way. Taking a closer look at the individual answers, the average is highly influenced by one participant scoring extremely low and in complete disagreement with each statement.

The number of respondents of the survey has been limited, however based on the overall numbers, we conclude that in principle the idea of using this game as a frame to discuss urban resilience can work. However, we and the teachers experienced that time for doing the exercise in this workshop was too limited to dive into the topic completely.

**Table 2.** The game as conceptual frame-work

|  | N= | M= | SD= |
|---|---|---|---|
| Q9. I found the assignment useful for understanding the impact of measures on the resilience of an urban (sub) system: | 11 | 2.9 | 1.22 |
| Q10. I thought that creating the game cards was a fun way to learn about measuring resilience: | 11 | 3 | 1.95 |
| Q13. I had sufficient time to complete this in class assignment | 11 | 4.4 | 1.56 |
| Q14. How likely are you to recommend this assignment to other students or your friends? (10 point scale) | 11 | 5.7 | 2.02 |

For Q9, Q10, Q13 (7-point Likert scale) and Q14 (10-point scale)

## 5  Discussion

*RElastiCity* was used as a conceptual framework to analyze the resilience of an urban area with a focus on shocks and stresses. The game functioned as a starting point to explore measures and analyze their effects in an integrated way. This concept was studied in two different ways. In the first situation, the game gave structure to an extensive analysis and design process while in the second situation the game was used in a two-hour workshop.

One of the difficulties for students when they start a project or explore a complex system is to choose a focus when everything seems interesting. Students in a frame game are given an open framework within which to think and explore. Students apply it to a specific urban area and that provokes discussions on complexity of the topic and how to simplify that into a game. The openness of the game concept grants students the flexibility to explore topics of interest to them but also the structure to guide them in the translation of real-world issues into the game environment. The game opened discussions with conference participants about how to integrate social factors like health and well-being with engineered systems. This way of thinking demonstrated by the students shows the current resilience conversations within municipalities, representing an important link between their education as engineers and real-world impact. Social considerations of health, well-being and justice will be fundamental as cities are set to encounter increasing shocks and intensifying stresses in the decades to come.

Second, it is necessary to include the interdependencies and integration by developing a game. In the Integrated Project course, all elements had to be connected, and if not, students needed to discuss. In the second course, the effects of measures were discussed, although these were more per measure and not about the integration of the measures with the existing system.

Third, students can engage in game design without previous training or a specific skill set by using a simple game concept. Starting game design from scratch requires prerequisite knowledge, training and time to develop a concept. By excluding this step, students can focus on learning and communicating about interdependencies and dynamics of a complex system.

Big differences between the two setups were observed. In the Integrated project, the results were better and students were more engaged due to the time spent on this exercise. The students had the time to analyze a specific area and its urban resilience. They had sufficient time to translate this to the game elements, could playtest the game and reflect on the system analysis in the first part of the course. In the limited time of a two-hour workshop, this process was not possible. The proportion of time in a two-hour session to understand the teaching method is much greater than in a semester-long course where more time can be spent on experimentation and iterative learning. Although using a frame game as a framework can be time saving from a game co-design perspective, it takes time to engage in important processes of learning about the real-world issues, negotiating with group members to decide how to fill in the framework and playtesting to understand the interdependencies. This iterative process contributes to learning about complex urban systems.

## 6  Conclusion

Based on two instances of using *RElastiCity* as conceptual framework to study Urban Resilience, students could experience structured shared learning and communication about an urban area using a game concept as a starting point of a game design process. It supports setting boundaries which is always a challenge for students, enabling more attention to specific elements, while granting space to include other elements. All elements have to be integrated for playtesting and reflection by the students. This can be applied without detailed instructions about game design or a lot of time to create a conceptual game. Finally, in general students enjoy the game design process.

Students must have sufficient time to do the complete loop of analysis, design, play, reflect, redesign and replay, as this contributes to the learning process. In short sessions, the time to become acquainted with the conceptual game is relatively long because less focus can be given to the content and its discussion. Just as for other simulations and models, choices have been made about what to include and what to exclude which must be discussed in the debriefing of the exercise.

In conclusion, conceptual game customization is an engaging and fun alternative to more traditional modeling approaches. The level of engagement generated from students and the integral understanding of the interrelations shows that the frame game is well suited for learning about complex systems and their interdependencies.

## References

1. Moraci, F., et al.: Cities under pressure: strategies and tools to face climate change and pandemic. Sustainability **12**(18), 7743 (2020)
2. De Boer, J., Muggah, R., Patel, R.: Conceptualizing City Fragility and Resilience. United Nations University, Centre for Policy Research, Tokyo (2016)
3. Bekebrede, G.: Experiencing complexity. A gaming approach for understanding infrastructure systems. NGI, Delft (PhD thesis) (2010)
4. Seralidou, E., Douligeris. C.: Learning programming by creating games through the use of structured activities in secondary education in Greece. Educ. Inf. Technol. **26**(1) 859–898 (2021)

5. Gallear W., Lameras P., Stewart C.: Students' experiences of learning mathematics through games design. In: Auer, M.E., Tsiatsos T. (eds.) Internet of Things, Infrastructures and Mobile Applications. IMCL 2019. Advances in Intelligent Systems and Computing, vol. 1192. Springer, Cham (2021). https://doi.org/10.1007/978-3-030-49932-7_52
6. Santana-Mancilla, P.C., et al.: Teaching HCI skills in higher education through game design: a study of students' perceptions. Informatics 6(2) (2019)
7. Dancz, C.L.A., Parrish, K., Bilec, M.M., Landis, A.E.: Assessment of students' mastery of construction management and engineering concepts through board game design. J. Prof. Iss. Eng. Educ. Pract. 143(4) (2017)
8. Kayali, F., et al.: Using game design to teach informatics and society topics in secondary schools. Multimodal Technol. Interact. 2(4), 77 (2018)
9. Champlin, C.J.: Contextualizing planning support (Systems): co-designing to fit the dynamics of spatial strategy making (2019)
10. Champlin, C., Flacke, J., Dewulf, G.: A game co-design method to elicit knowledge for the contextualization of spatial models. Environment and Planning (B): Urban Analytics and City Science 0(0), 1–16 (2021). https://doi.org/10.1177/23998083211041372
11. Ballon, B., Silver, I.: Context is key: an interactive experiential and content frame game. Med. Teach. 26(6), 525–528 (2004)
12. Klabbers, J.H.G.: The Magic Circle: Principles of Gaming and Simulation. Sense Publishers, Rotterdam, The Netherlands (2006)
13. Lukosch, H.K., Bekebrede, G., Kurapati, S., Lukosch, S.G.: A scientific foundation of simulation games for the analysis and design of complex systems. Simulation and Gaming 49(3), 279–314 (2018)
14. Duke, R.D., Geurts, J.: Policy Games for Strategic Management. Rozenberg Publishers, Amsterdam, The Netherlands (2004)
15. Greenblat, C.S., Duke, R.D.: Game Generating Games: A Trilogy of Games for Community and Classroom (1979)
16. Forehand, M.: Bloom's taxonomy. Emerging Perspectives on Learning, Teaching, and Technology 41(4), 47–56 (2010)
17. RElastiCity: TUDelft. https://edusources.nl/materialen/503f546e-a3ce-47b9-aa61-188f59 080d40 (2021). Accessed 17 Aug 2021
18. Trend Reports: TU Delft. https://edusources.nl/materialen/2639fced-eb70-493e-8b0f-cb9af6 71703a. (2020). Accessed 17 Aug 2021

# "Risk Management Can Actually Be Fun" - Using the Serious Cards for Biosafety Game to Stimulate Proper Discussions About Biosafety

Maria Freese[✉], Simon Tiemersma, and Alexander Verbraeck

Faculty of Technology, Policy and Management, Delft University of Technology, Jaffalaan 5, 2628 BX Delft, The Netherlands
M.Freese@tudelft.nl

**Abstract.** As part of a Dutch Science Foundation project called T-TRIPP, the authors developed the serious game Cards for Biosafety. The aim of Cards for Biosafety is to let young biotechnology researchers learn more about biosafety. Analyses of workshops with researchers from the biotechnology domain as well as results of interviews with several biosafety officers clearly indicated the need for such a serious game with a focus on educational learning. Cards for Biosafety is a physical (also playable online on Tabletopia) round-based card game and playable with up to eight players. The game itself consists of scenario, risk and measure cards, and the task of the players is to choose risk and measure cards that fit the scenario explained by the facilitator at the beginning of each round. To test the efficiency of Cards for Biosafety as a learning tool, the authors conducted two online-workshops with twelve participants. The results of these sessions have not only shown that Cards for Biosafety is a well-designed game, but also a successful game to achieve the intended learning goal. In addition, the authors recognized that 'fun' is an important element in the game which leads to 'learning' in a very effective way. Future research should focus on the role of such positive states in serious games and their influence on learning outcomes.

**Keywords:** Biosafety · Biotechnology · Cards for Biosafety · Covid-19 · Game design · Learning goals · Self-reflection moments · Serious games

## 1 Introduction

The Dutch T-TRIPP (Tools for Translation of Risk Research into Policies and Practices) project is part of a National Biotechnology and Safety research programme, and it aims to design and develop interactive and innovative tools to give biotechnology stakeholders a platform to interact with each other. Serious games can be an important part of such a platform, because of advantages, such as providing a safe and interactive environment for the participants [1]. Therefore, the decision has been made to develop such a game. To identify the problem this game should address, the authors followed the IDEAS approach [2]. In general, IDEAS consists of four steps: interviews with subject-matter experts, discussion round(s) with experts, Moscow analysis [3], and participatory gamestorm

© Springer Nature Switzerland AG 2022
U. Dhar et al. (Eds.): ISAGA 2021, LNCS 13219, pp. 124–133, 2022.
https://doi.org/10.1007/978-3-031-09959-5_11

sessions. In a first step, all project partners of the T-TRIPP project conducted six inter-active and gamified (online) workshops (each with max. 4 participants) in June 2020 with researchers (Principal investigators, Postdocs and PhD's) from different projects of the Biotechnology and Safety programme to identify the major issues around biotech-nology and safety, to learn more about the current risk governance system and how people working in modern biotechnology view and experience this system. According to the issues and challenges mentioned by the workshop participants, these workshops were transcribed and analysed, and several clusters (groups of identified issues and chal-lenges) were derived according to the frequency of issues and challenges mentioned by the workshop participants. In a second step, the authors discussed these derived clus-ters with biotechnology experts, brainstormed some first game ideas, and conducted a Moscow analysis as a third step (see Fig. 1). In general, a Moscow analysis can help to prioritize game objectives and / or ideas by putting them into one of the following four categories: must-haves, could-haves, should-haves and won't haves (see Fig. 1).

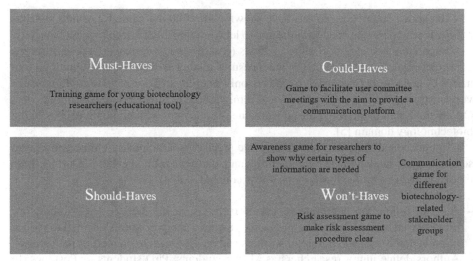

**Fig. 1.** Moscow analysis to prioritize derived game ideas as part of the IDEAS approach and with the aim to identify the problem the game should address.

As can be seen in Fig. 1 from the won't haves, the game will not address any of the following game objectives:

– Providing insight into risk assessment procedures (decisions, involved parties), because the risk assessment procedures in biotechnology are too complex to be covered by a serious game;
– Improving communication between different stakeholders, because the authors already developed the MachiaCelli game that can be used to focus on communication-related barriers [4];
– Increasing awareness of needs for certain types of information. Also here, the above mentioned MachiaCelli game be used as a game to address this topic.

The results of this Moscow analysis and the frequency of statements the authors got during the conducted workshops and interviews with biosafety officers included statements, such as:

- "It is difficult to explain the system/rules to a researcher"
- "For a researcher, publishing new innovative research is more important than safety"
- "[There are] differences in or lack of awareness amongst researchers"
- "Yeah, I'm not always following it [safety] because it depends on the workload I guess."
- "There is no clear definition of safety (what is safe?) and that is a problem in communication"
- "And it also means that everybody must be aware about the fact that safety is important, and that there's also kind of commitment to safety as being one of the primary values or norms [...]."
- "I'm not always thinking about the risks, and I don't think all scientists do".

The above-described analyses have shown that a training game for young biotechnology researchers is needed with the aim to let them think more deeply about biosafety. In comparison to standard training methods (e.g., bi-annual refresher courses), such a game can create awareness of risks and measures related to different biotechnology scenarios by actively discussing them (and not only listening to a person who communicates very abstract input in a passive way) and it might help to prevent desensitisation. Also, Orhan and Sahin highlighted the added value of innovative teaching approaches in the biotechnology domain [5].

To understand the aim of the game more precisely, participatory online gamestorm sessions were held with project partners and partners from the field. During these meetings and several feedback loops it was concluded that:

- Authors follow the definition of biosafety by Biosafety Europe [6]: "Laboratory biosafety embraces facilities, equipment, practices and procedures deemed to reduce or prevent the risk of exposure of workers and environment to dangerous pathogens".
- Authors define junior researchers as Master students, PhD students or Postdocs. In addition to this, the authors recommend to let the game be facilitated by a more experienced senior researcher or a biosafety officer.
- Authors structure their game according to biotechnology-related scenarios, risks and measures.

These decisions functioned as a solid base for the development of the interactive Cards for Biosafety game.

## 2 Cards for Biosafety

The aim of Cards for Biosafety is to let junior researchers in biotechnology think more deeply about biosafety. The game should be played with both junior and senior researchers and / or biosafety officers to enhance the learning potential. The game is flexible in terms of play time because it is possible to play as many rounds as you want. It is also easy to adjust the game for different scenarios or different biotechnology directions, because it follows a modular approach.

## 2.1 Game Play

Cards for Biosafety is a physical round-based card game and playable with up to eight players (up to five junior researchers, and up to three senior researchers or biosafety officers). Due to Covid-19 the game is also playable online on Tabletopia. The facilitator hosts the game and starts by choosing a predefined scenario or picking a random scenario and introducing it to the researchers. After this, every player will get five risk cards from which they must choose one card that represents the most appropriate or interesting risk for that scenario. The players also need to think about a good argumentation, presented as a short pitch, why they have chosen this card.

Depending on the general set-up, a first (in-between) debriefing can follow. Hereby, the discussion between the senior and junior researchers about the chosen risk cards including the players' argumentation, and also the connection with the real world is crucial. The senior researchers (who can take over the role of a facilitator) stimulate the other players in their discussion, argumentation and linkage with real life situations. Even if a player has chosen a card that is less suitable for the situation or contains some unrealistic elements, it is possible to convince the other players by appropriate argumentations and to discuss in exchange with the senior and more experienced scientists to what extent realistic elements are contained. More than 98% of all predefined risks and measures in the game can actually occur in reality and have been checked by experts from the biotechnology field.

Based on the chosen risk cards, a voting phase takes place, meaning that every player can vote for a risk card that represents the most appropriate risk for the chosen scenario in their opinion. Of course, this decision can be influenced by the short pitches and convincing arguments of the other players. Based on the scoring, the risk card with the most points will be the starting point for the next phase, namely the choice for an appropriate measure card. Every player will get five measure cards from which they must choose one card that represents the best measure for the previously chosen risk. After this, a second voting with regard of the best measure card takes place. A new round can be played after that, meaning that the facilitator can pick a new scenario, either randomly or from a predefined sequence of scenarios.

It takes approximately 20 min (1st and 2nd round) to get acquainted with the game plus 10 min (from the 3rd round onward) per round to play this game. This is excluding the final debriefing, which might take 15 to 30 min, or as long as the facilitator wants it to take. Quite some time of the 10 to 20 min per round is spent on the in-game debriefing between the different phases and different rounds.

To make a connection with the real working practices of the participants and with the aim to deepen the discussions about real-life (self-experienced) examples, the authors defined those in-game debriefing questions with regard to the choice of a risk card:

- Why did you choose this card?
- Do you have an idea about what a specific reason for the occurrence of such a risk could be?

- Have you (or a colleague) already experienced this or a similar situation?
- For the chosen scenario, what is the main risk you need to take into account when planning, preparing or doing research?

Possible in-game debriefing questions related to the choice of a measure card could be:

- Why did you choose this card?
- For the chosen scenario, what could be an appropriate measure to mitigate the corresponding risk?
- Do you see a connection between the information about the measure on the card and reality?
- How can you transfer such a measure to your everyday work and what is needed to do so?

## 2.2  Adjustments Due to Covid-19 Pandemic

To be able to test and play the Cards for Biosafety card game during the Covid-19 pandemic and its lockdowns, the authors published the game on the web-based board game simulator Tabletopia [7].

Tabletopia is a tool in which players can log in and play a board game in a 3D environment without automation. It is therefore a direct board game simulator which means that players need to move cards and pawns and roll dice themselves, just like playing a real board game. The authors chose to use Tabletopia because the platform is relatively easy to use, looks very realistic and has an easy to learn editor in which you can create your own board game. It does not take any programming experience and because it is such a direct copy of a real board game, the authors could design the game like a physical one.

To set up the game in Tabletopia, the authors needed to upload the art of the Cards for Biosafety cards (see Fig. 2) in the editor and place them on a virtual table, together with some pre-made tokens and coins. To play the game, one can create a virtual room that loads a pre-set of the game on a table and people can use a link to enter this room.

The system is quick in setup. However, some challenges in building and using the platform for playtests and sessions exists which the authors recognized during several prototyping sessions:

- The platform is still relatively limited in editing options and has some user interface issues. Cards for Biosafety is a simple game which did not limit the authors too much.
- Connection issues are a bigger challenge. In many cases players could not connect or needed to start in different browsers or on different computers.
- Using the 3D environment is difficult for some players. It is therefore important to provide a legend and do a tutorial or test round of five to ten minutes, so players can get familiar with the controls.
- You still need a secondary videoconferencing application to communicate.

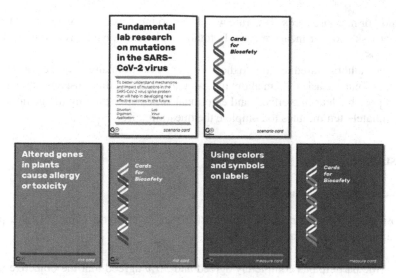

**Fig. 2.** Design of Cards for Biosafety game cards.

## 3 Experimental Set-Up

To test the efficiency of Cards for Biosafety as a learning tool – that has the aim to let participants learn more about biosafety aspects – the authors conducted two workshops with five participants (junior researchers) in the first, and seven participants (six junior researchers and one senior researcher) in the second workshop ($n = 12$, $w = 6$). Two participants were Bachelor and nine participants were Master students. The authors also asked them about their experience in the field. Ten participants answered zero to five years, one participant said six to 10 years, and one participant chose 11 to 20 years (senior researcher).

Due to the ongoing Covid-19 pandemic, the authors organized two online gaming sessions in which they used a combination of both a communication platform and Tabletopia as the gaming platform. The sessions consisted of several phases:

- First, they had an interactive introductory round in which the authors asked the participants to think about a board game that represents their personality best.
- Second, the authors introduced the general aim of the session as well as the T-TRIPP project.
- Third, the authors explained the main functions of Tabletopia and the participants had the chance to get to know this platform by practicing certain actions.
- Fourth, the authors shared the link to the pre-game questionnaire with the participants. This questionnaire included some demographic questions, questions about board and digital game play experience, questions about personality traits of the participants, and their emotional state. It took approximately ten minutes to complete this questionnaire.
- Fifth, the authors explained the game rules by letting players interactively play the first round of Cards for Biosafety. After finishing the first round, the authors continued with the second one and added a new rule to the game, namely the exchange of two

risk and / or measure cards. This rule was added to increase the probability of finding a proper risk and / or measure card. In total, all players played three rounds in both workshops.

- Sixth, the authors shared the link to the post-game questionnaire with the participants. This questionnaire asked them about the game itself, about their in-game strategies as well as possible learning effects and emotional states after playing the game. It took approximately ten minutes to complete the questionnaire.

## 4  Results

### 4.1  Feedback on the Game

In the post-game questionnaire, the authors asked the players about game-related aspects. From the survey data,

- 50% of the participants completely agreed and 50% agreed that the objective of the game was sufficiently clear;
- 50% of the participants completely agreed and 41.67% agreed (8.33% neutral) that they were engaged in the game play and
- 66.67% of the participants completely agreed and 33.33% agreed that it was easy to understand the rules of the game.

During the feedback round, participants shared that it was a fun game to play and that all of them could imagine to use the Cards for Biosafety game in an educational setting.

### 4.2  Learning Goal

With respect to the learning goal, the authors asked the participants what they learned. In Fig. 3, an overview of self-clustered learning experiences is depicted. These clusters were grouped by the authors.

Choosing the 'right' risk and measure card is one of the most important game mechanics of the Cards for Biosafety game. To find out more about the motivation of the participants, the authors asked them about the strategy they followed for choosing an appropiate (risk and / or measure) card. Three participants said that they made use of "[…] knowledge I have on risk and calamity management […]", "[…] protocols I have learned […]" and "Mostly from experience […]". Three participants focused on cards that "could have the greatest impact" and "the likelihood that it would really happen". One participant specified his / her answer a bit by saying that "it can happen to me when I am in lab […]". Other participants "tried to come up with realistic risks and measure cards […]" or they tried to choose the "most out of the box […]" card.

In addition to this, Fig. 4 compares the achieved learning goal between the two sessions. Particpants of the second session agreed more that they learned something about biosafety. This can be explained by the attendance of a senior resarcher during the second session who explained several things to the junior researchers, shared his experiences

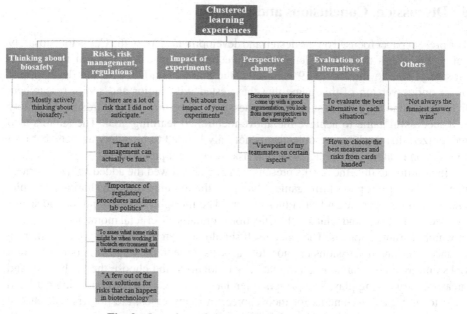

**Fig. 3.** Overview of clustered learning experiences.

with them and communicated interesting anecdotes. One participant mentioned that a senior or more experienced researcher is needed "to bring it [the game] to the next level". This shows that it is of utmost importance to include more experienced researchers in the game play.

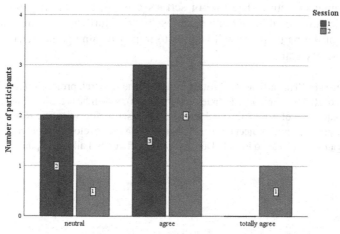

The game gave me an opportunity to learn more about biosafety aspects.

**Fig. 4.** Comparison of the two sessions with regard to learning outcome.

## 5  Discussion, Conclusions and Outlook

The present paper focused on the design and development steps of the Cards for Biosafety game which has the aim to let young biotechnology researchers learn more about biosafety. Due to the Covid-19 pandemic, the authors started with the development of an online-version of this game that they tested with junior and senior researchers from biotechnology. The results of these sessions have shown that Cards for Biosafety is a successful game to achieve the above-mentioned learning goal. The authors also recognized that the learning objective is not only limited to biosafety aspects, but also focused on related risk management and risk assessment procedures.

In addition to this, the results presented in Sect. 4 showed the added value of serious games. The serious part of this game is based on the learning through sharing principle, meaning that players learn from other players. The interplay between junior and senior experienced players and related self-reflection moments are crucial moments of the game in which learning happens. The game itself should be seen as a starting point for sharing of anecdotes and discussions on biosafety aspects. Due to the huge variety of different risks and measures cards, it is not that easy to identify and choose the 'right' risk and measure card during play. The players often have to pick the least non-fitting card and need to find good arguments for their choice. In many cases, the players will choose seemingly funny cards, but might defend their choice very interestingly or might cause other players to explain that their card is actually realistic and relevant. In this way 'fun' (e.g., "That risk management can actually be fun") leads to 'learning' in a very effective way. This 'Out-of-the-lab thinking' is what the authors want to support with this game, because it allows players to get to interesting anecdotes and lessons learned for the junior researchers. The seemingly funny cards might initiate the most interesting discussions and in addition to this, the players will be having fun doing so. Adding serious discussions as part of the debriefing closes the bridge between funny moments and the intended learning objective. The role of serious fun [8], related emotions, and their influence on learning could be an interesting subject of further research. Furthermore, the feedback of the participants will help us to improve some game mechanics of the Cards for Biosafety game.

**Acknowledgements.** This article was written as part of the research project T-TRIPP (Tools for the Translation of Risk research into Policies and Practices), which has received funding from the Technology Foundation of NWO, the Netherlands Organisation for Scientific Research (NWO). The authors are grateful to all project partners for supporting the development process of the Cards for Biosafety game as well as to the TU Delft biosafety officer and all participants for taking the time to test the game.

## References

1. Kriz, W.C.: Types of gaming simulation applications. Simul. Gaming **48**(1), 3–7 (2017). https://doi.org/10.1177/1046878117689860
2. Freese, M., Lukosch, H.K.: The Funnel of Game Design - Proposing a New Way to Address a Problem Definition Using the IDEAS Approach. In: Wardaszko, M., Meijer, S., Lukosch, H.,

Kanegae, H., Kriz, W.C., Grzybowska-Brzezińska, M. (eds.) ISAGA 2019. LNCS, vol. 11988, pp. 170–180. Springer, Cham (2021). https://doi.org/10.1007/978-3-030-72132-9_16

3. Clegg, D., Barker, R.: Case Method, Fast-Track: A RAD Approach. Addison-Wesley, Amsterdam (1994)

4. Freese, M., Lukosch, H.K., Tiemersma, S.: From Entertainment to Seriousness – How to Translate Entertainment Games into Simulation Games? ZMS-Schriftenreihe 12. Book on Demand GmbH, Norderstedt (2020)

5. Orhan, T.Y., Sahin, N.: The impact of innovative teaching approaches on biotechnology knowledge and laboratory experiences of science teachers. Education Sciences **8**(4), 213 (2018). https://doi.org/10.3390/educsci8040213

6. Biosafety Europe: Final Considerations: Coordination, harmonisation and exchange of biosafety and biosecurity practices within a pan-European network (2008). Retrieved from: https://www.sciprom.ch/resources/Print-Products/Booklets/Biosafety-europe.pdf 11 May 2021

7. https://tabletopia.com/

8. Lazzaro, N.: Why we play: affect and the fun of games. In: Sears, A., Jacko, J.A. (eds.), Human-Computer Interaction Designing for Diverse Users and Domains (chapter 10). CRC Press, USA (2009)

# Social Economy: A Simulation Game in Model Social Enterprises

Marcin Łączyński[✉] [iD]

Laboratory of Media Studies, Warsaw University, Warszawa, Poland
laczynski.marcin@gmail.com

**Abstract.** The social economy and social enterprises are a part of entrepreneurship, gaining more visibility in recent years, especially in the European Union. The unique characteristic of social enterprises and their complex relationship to the concept of profit pose significant challenges in designing educational tools for this sector. Accurate simulation of social enterprise must include elements of profit and loss analysis because those enterprises operate as usual market entities. It must highlight the importance of each social enterprise's social impact on its community. This paper presents the game mechanics, the simulation model of the social enterprise and the implementation of the educational game, Social Economy, designed for the Regional Center of Social Politics in Poland.

**Keywords:** Simulation board game · Social entrepreneurship · Social cooperative · Social indicators · Worker placement

## 1 Introduction

Social economy is understood as 'commercial and non-commercial activity largely in the hands of third-sector or community organizations that gives priority to meeting social and environmental needs before profit maximization' [1]. It is a concept not new to the economic theory and gained a lot of momentum after the 2008 financial crisis. The idea of economic activity that benefits the local community and stakeholders other than the owner of the enterprise or its shareholders is at the center of this concept and is fundamental to the Social Economy game presented in this paper. Promotion of the concept of social economy and education about its applications is an important element of the EU strategy of economic development. A decade ago, the development of the social economy sector was perceived as a means of recovery after the 2008 financial crisis and recession, which resulted in long-term unemployment in several EU countries [2, 3]. Recently, social entrepreneurship has been perceived more as an integral element of several strategic goals of EU economic development, mainly in the areas of youth employment, development of small and medium enterprises, the inclusion of people disconnected from the job market and creation of high-quality secure job positions with sustainable wages. This recent approach is well visible in the communication from European Commission to the European Parliament, the Council, the European and Social Committee and the Committee of the Regions titled 'A Strong Social Europe for

© Springer Nature Switzerland AG 2022
U. Dhar et al. (Eds.): ISAGA 2021, LNCS 13219, pp. 134–144, 2022.
https://doi.org/10.1007/978-3-031-09959-5_12

Just Transitions' (2020). In the contemporary Polish context, the central government document implicating the high role of social economy is the Strategy for Responsible Development (2014) and the area III of the National Program of Social Economy Development (first published in 2014, [4]. The Program's priority 2 highlights the importance of education and tools fostering cooperation and mutual understanding between social enterprises and business organizations. At the regional level, the guidelines for social economy development are included in the Regional Plans of Social Economy Development. The game Social Economy was funded as a part of such a program for Silesian voivodship.

## 2  Social Economy – Game Design

### 2.1  Game Concept

Social Economy is a simulation game developed in 2016 for the Regional Center of Social Politics (RCSP) in Katowice, capital of Polish Silesian voivodship. The game development team included the author of this paper and Katarzyna Kotarska from InteliGames company and was supervised by the project team from RCSP. It was created as an education tool for five types of model social enterprises specific to the Polish social economy sector that was considered as the new types of social enterprises as opposed to traditional, well-established forms like cooperatives [5]:

- Disabled cooperative
- Social cooperative
- Vocational Rehabilitation Facility
- Social Integration Centers
- Foundation

The game target groups were teenagers and young adults who didn't have any previous experience or knowledge about the social economy sector. The main educational goals of the game were:

- Teaching the basic concept of social economy
- Increasing the awareness of stakeholders surrounding the social enterprise
- Raising the awareness of types of activity (economic and organizational) conducted by the management team of social enterprise
- Improving the understanding of specific activities for different kinds of social enterprises
- Improving the understanding of the complexity of impact and the measure of success of a social enterprise.

### 2.2  Development Process

Social Economy was developed during the three months of 2016 which included a complete design process. It started with precise guidelines about the game goals pre- pared by the RCSP, brainstorming and prototyping, testing, production and finally delivering the game. It was play- tested over 50 times with internal testers, eight test groups of independent testers and assessors and finally reviewed by the RCSP team before running the final print. The RCSP had a significant impact upon the final shape of the game, consulting all the test results and delivering field-specific knowledge such as reports and articles about the social enterprises models.

## 2.3  Game Content and Setup

Players start the game by selecting one of the available types of social enterprise:

- Disabled cooperative
- Social cooperative
- Vocational Rehabilitation Facility
- Social Integration Centers
- Foundation

This decision impacts the initial social factors which represent the specialization of each type of enterprise. For example, the social cooperative begins with level 2 of job development and a low level of fixed costs, reflecting its focus on workforce activation and tendency to rely on low-cost or costless solutions such as work by volunteers. The game is played by a team of five players in a cooperative mode. Players discuss their preferences and then each player assumes one role from those below:

- Head of the organization
- Financier
- Marketing specialist
- Work coordinator
- HR Manager

Each player receives two special cards associated with his role, representing unique assets, contacts and knowledge that a management team member brings to the organization (Fig. 1). For example, the marketing specialist has two cards, Community Support and Community Project, which reflect the focus of social enterprise marketing on relation- building rather than on direct sales marketing.

The game board setup includes marking the starting level of social factors on three tracks in the lower part of the board (Fig. 2). The board itself comprises three main components:

- Available actions - in rectangle fields around the board, with the name of the action, places for pawns to activate each action, its requirements, and effects (costs and benefits for the organization).
- The impact made by the organization stakeholders and competition - in the central part of the board, each stakeholder can have a minor random effect described in the relevant field.

**Fig. 1.** Game board of social economy

- The tracks of social factors - three tracks that represent the level of each factor, which impacts the overall score and after moving through a certain threshold, unlocks additional actions that require a high level of each factor.

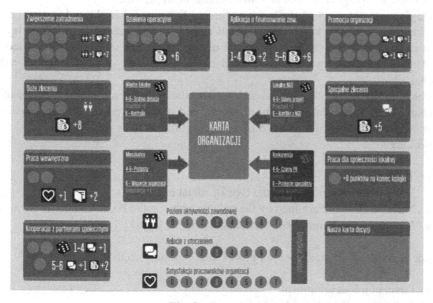

**Fig. 2.** Game board

## 2.4  Game Process

The game consists of three main stages:

- Selection of one social enterprise type which impacts the basic financial parameters of the simulation and the available special action card placed upon the board.
- Selection of a specific role for each player which is associated with a pawn representing the time one can allocate to enterprise management and two cards representing unique competencies or assets related to a particular position.
- Four decision-making rounds in which players conduct operational decisions for their enterprise.

The decision-making rounds in the central part of the game and each round is structured around four stages:

1. Dice roll to determine the small but sometimes significant impact of enterprise stake-holders or the market due to effects such as losing the most valuable employees to the competition, inspection from the local government agency or conflict with project partner. This stage is based on the roll of a simple dice but the event table is con-structed so that the long run effects of random events impact the result of the game minimally.
2. Group discussion and placing the player pawns on the selected action fields on the board give players some benefits of income or social impact having additional costs and requiring at least one pawn to be activated. This stage represents their internal discussion on organizational and time management priorities.
3. Playing particular action cards for additional benefits. Each player has two cards which can be played in each round. Thus eight out of 10 available cards are played in each game. Each card represents the unique skills or assets such as knowledge of additional funding possibility, extra business contacts or knowledge of each character.
4. The summary of profit and loss and social indicators of each round is made in a chart. The players summarize the economic and social effects of all their decisions in the profit and loss account (P&L) with categories such as
- P&L data

  - Total income
  - Fixed costs (determined by the type of social enterprise)
  - Variable costs (determined by the actions taken on the board and cards played)
  - Net income (difference between income and all costs)

- Social indicators typical for the Polish social economy sector:

  - Level of job development
  - Relations with stakeholders
  - Level of employee satisfaction

At the end of the last round, the final score is calculated as the sum of points after each round. This model promotes effective strategic planning throughout the game and reduces the risk of unrealistic decision making based on profit maximization to win the game in the last round. The game is played in the cooperative mode where all players around a single board work towards a common goal, but the inclusion of several teams in the classroom or the workshop adds an element of competition. Different simulated social enterprises may compare the results of their strategy and its impact on organization profitability and achieved social indicators in this mode.

## 2.5 Design Challenges

The project team faced several challenges in game development, symptomatic of the social economy sector. First, the business simulation games in entrepreneurship are a well-established genre of educational tools and their research is widely available and present in the scientific and professional discourse since at least the early '80s [6–10]. Yet, the literature and examples of business games aimed at the social economy sector and the promotion of social entrepreneurship are scarce. This challenge may be attributed to several factors.

Games simulating social economy are scarce and are a relative novelty in training social entrepreneurs [11]. They are hard to reach because most of them are funded as a part of educational projects for particular groups. Very few of them are published for a wider audience. Of the several titles useful for business education in the social economy sector, the only ones widely available are those simulating regular business organizations such as Simventure and The Startup Game [2].

The second challenge was to address the complexity of social enterprise business and social goals in the game narrative and simulation framework. Most early business simulations and some even now present the financial indicators as the only measure of success of the entrepreneur. In the social economy sector, profit is essential for the organization's sustainable growth but other impact areas such as the three sectors of the economy are as important [12]:

- The private sector, profit-driven and market-oriented
- The public sector, driven by the population needs and oriented towards providing centrally planned public services that fulfill those needs
- The social economy, which is partially market-based and based on multiple agents with- out central planning but oriented towards the needs and well-being of the local community

It is the role of the profit that distinguishes the three groups:

- The private sector: the profit is transferred to the shareholders and is essential for the enterprise continuity
- The public sector: the profit is absent by definition
- The social economy: the profit is present but consumed by the organization to secure its continuity

This specific situation required the reward structure in the game to be designed around the maximization of profit and the measurement of social impact. The business games in corporate social responsibility face similar problems as they mostly use social or environmental indicators to measure business success which varied from game to game [13–15].

After the discussion with the RCSP team, the final list of factors representing the impact of the social enterprise was found to be:

- Level of job development - most simulated organizations are aimed at social inclusion through work and returning people who had dropped out to the job market. The level of employment is their primary measure of success.
- Relations with stakeholders - all organizations in the game provide, to some extent, public services for the local community, complementary for the public sector. The level of satisfaction of local society was taken as a synthetic measure of organizational impact.
- Level of employee satisfaction - most social economy organizations in the game are team-oriented as employee engagement and teamwork are the factors that contribute significantly to their success. They are limited by the amount of financial motivation they can provide to their workers. The satisfaction was taken as a measure of the impact of organizational culture upon social enterprise members.

Those factors are present in the game in two forms. Firstly, they are the success indicators in the game and measure the quality of decisions made by the players. Secondly, they impact the course of the game so that, on high levels, they unlock specific additional actions and options and reward the organization's development and specialization during the game.

The third challenge of the design process was to include the classical board game mechanics of worker placement [16]. The simulation of the social enterprise is constructed on a high level of abstraction in the game. Worker placement was considered an efficient compromise between strategic challenge presented by the game, simulation accuracy and the cognitive load on the player. The underlying rhetoric of moving pawns on the board might be considered an example of instrumental treatment of enterprise employees. This meaning is often a problem in board game design because its elements such as color or shape of the components, a pattern of movement, types of decisions made by the player and the avatar may be discriminatory or evoke associations that may distract the players from the game [17]. This problem was managed through the game manual narrative where pawns are described as measuring the players' work time.

## 3   Game Reception and Evaluation

The data about game reception and evaluation is from three sources:

- Yearly reports about the development of the social economy in the Silesia region published by RCSP (published twice a year: mid-year and for the whole year)
- Evaluation made during the development phase including the pretest and post-test surveys with game testers (85 complete surveys from 17 recorded sessions)

• Interviews with 32 participants (teenagers and adults) conducted by the game development team independently

The game was delivered in November 2016 and came to public use in early 2017. At first, the RCSP employees used the game during the planned educational sessions in local schools (10 educational events for 2017 and 2018) and distributed it to local high schools for use during the classes on promoting the social economy. The recommendations from the 2017 mid-year report stated that the game has the potential for use in a more engaging tournament form [18].

In early 2017, the management of the game community was redirected from the RCSP team to the Fajna Social Cooperative which was assigned the task of preparing the game tournament and conducting additional promotional events. The game was presented during fairs and conferences dedicated to the social economy sector (the First Forum of Social and Solidary Economy held on 17 November 2017). Fifteen schools and 65 students participated in the first two-stage regional tournament.

Excellent reception of the game and higher than expected interest in the game distribution from the schools resulted in the second print of 300 copies in late 2018 and a recommendation for another tournament in 2019. This tournament included the eliminations in five cities of the region (Częstochowa, Bielsko-Biała, Dąbrowa Górnicza, Katowice and Rybnik) and the final on November 6 held in Katowice.

The project team also has access to the evaluation of the game from the final stage of the development phase which included 85 surveys as a pretest and post-test measurement of these variables:

• Assessment of overall game attractiveness (post-test only)
• Level of knowledge about social economy sector (pretest and post-test)
• Attitude towards social economy sector (pretest and post-test)

Game attractiveness was measured after the game on a five-point Likert scale. The overall attractiveness was high or very high (together 82% responses). There was no significant impact of demographic variables of gender and age on the level of perceived attractiveness.

The level of knowledge about social economy sector was measured from a test of ten questions about the definition of key terms in this field such as types of institutions, social factors and economic terms. It was measured on a 10- point scale as a number of correct answers. The post-test showed a significant increase of knowledge as predicted, since initial knowledge level was very low. The result of comparison (mean in pretest: 3.34, mean in post-test: 7.73, $t = -20.64$, $df = 129.63$, p-value $< .05$) was strong and statistically significant.

The attitude towards social economy sector was measured before and after the game on a five-point Likert scale. In this case, the difference was also statistically significant showing a better perception of social economy sector after the game session. The overall effect should be considered weak (mean in pretest: 3.32, mean in post-test: 3.79, $t = -3.36$, $df = 145.05$, p-value $< .001$).

In both cases of knowledge and attitude, there was no significant impact of demographic variables. In the qualitative reviews of the game, the school participants highlighted certain strong sides of the game:

- For most players, it was the only business simulation they ever played and for all of them, it was the only one focused on the social economy.
- The game mechanics of 'worker placement' was well received as an excellent way to provide strategic challenges during the game.
- The game allowed players to efficiently learn basic concepts of social economy such as types of institutions, types of projects and tasks in social enterprise, assets, and funding options which help the organization and the general issues of social economy sector. Most players could recall those concepts correctly in the interviews conducted two to eight months after the game.
- The game allowed several non-trivial strategies of play such as specialization, balanced development and focus on profit. Players could evaluate and figure out the optimal development pattern by themselves although the balanced development was optimal but hard to follow in the simulation model, which significantly increased their understanding of the difference between social economy and regular business.
- Although unintended for adults as a target group, the game worked out well during the workshops with them who received the P&L chart exceptionally well.

The interviewed players also stated some drawbacks of the game and the areas to improve:

- The cognitive load in the beginning of the game was declared as still high, even though its reduction was one of the primary project goals, especially when the game was played in school within a week.
- The game's replay value was limited to 4–8 plays. The most limiting factors were the number of various organizations in the game (five types) and possible winning strategies perceived by the players (3 to 4, dependent on the player).

## 4   Discussion

Social Economy is one of the most successful simulation games developed for the Polish social economy sector in terms of player frequency and range of the educational activities conducted with the game. The design was based on a high-level simulation combined with mechanics from entertainment board games and limited knowledge elements and critical concepts and processes. It resulted in a tool that is highly effective as an introduction to the field of social economy and is well received by its target group of high school students and adult players. Game evaluation shows that it was well received and significantly increased the understanding of basic concepts of social economy and players' attitude, although only the knowledge improvement effect could be considered large. This result was not surprising to the project team, as the social economy is a concept basically unknown by general audience. Presenting the students with new knowledge about its scope as an engaging simulation game could almost certainly improve their understanding.

The game implementation in partnership with the social cooperative as a project leader resulted in forming an active community of students playing the game. In addition to other benefits, it allowed two editions of the regional tournament. The biggest challenge in the game design was to obtain the correct balance between simulation accuracy, gameplay attractiveness and cognitive load for the players.

The Social Economy is well balanced in the first two areas although the simulation complexity is limited. The cognitive load required to play the game proved to be its most significant limitation. The most common game mode used in the schools was quite challenging to grasp for its youngest target group.

# References

1. Amin, A. (ed.): The Social Economy. Zed Books, The International Perspectives on Economic Solidar- ity (2009)
2. Padilla-Zea, N., Aceto, S., Burgos, D.: Social seducement: empowering social economy entrepreneurship. The training approach. Int. J. Interac. Multime. Artifi. Intelli. 5(7), 135–150 (2019). https://doi.org/10.9781/ijimai.2019.09.001
3. Monzon, J.L., Chaves-Avila, R.: The european social economy: concept and dimen- sions of the third sector. Annals of Public and Cooperative Economics 79(3–4), 549–577 (2008)
4. Report on the Condition of Social Economy in the Silesia Region: (2019). https://es.rops-katowice.pl/wp-content/uploads/2020/09/Raport_ES_2019_po_konsultacjach.pdf. last accessed 19 June 2021
5. Brandeleer, C.: Social Economy in Poland. Think tank européen Pour la Solidarité (2013)
6. Murff, E.J., Teach, R.: Entrepreneurship: a game of risk and reward phase i – the search for opportunity. Developments in Business Simulation and Experiential Learning 36, 183–189 (2009)
7. Schwartz, R.G., Teach, R.D.: Congruence II: a strategic business board game. Developments in Business Simulation and Experiential Learning 28, 221–224 (2001)
8. Pavett, C.M., Lau, A.W.: Managerial education and the real world: foundations for designing educational tools. Developments in Business Simulation & Experiential Exercises 11, 68–71 (1980)
9. Almeida, F.: Learning entrepreneurship with serious games—a classroom approach. Int. Educ. Appli. Sci. Res. J. 2(1), 1–4 (2017)
10. Wawer, M., Miłosz, M., Muryjas, P., Rzemieniak, M.: Business simulation games in forming of students' entrepreneurship. Int. J. Euro-Mediterranean Studies 3(1), 49–71 (2010)
11. Barçante, L.C., Norte, A., Nogueira, M.: Development and implementation of a business game for the training of social entrepreneurs in poor communities in brazil, 56 (2012)
12. Pearce, J.: Social economy: engaging as a third system? In: Amin, W.A. (ed.) The Social Econ- omy. The International Perspectives on Economic Solidarity, pp. 22–36. Zed Books (2009)
13. Gatti, L., Ulrich, M., Seele, P.: Education for sustainable development through business simu- lation games: an exploratory study of sustainability gamification and its effects on stu- dents' learning outcomes. J. Clean. Prod. 207, 667–678 (2019). https://doi.org/10.1016/j.jclepro.2018.09.130
14. Cannon, J.N., Cannon, H.M., Friesen, D.P., Feinstein, A.H.: Would you take a marketing man to a quick service restaurant? Modeling corporate social responsibility in a food service menu-management simulation. Developments in Business Simulation and Experiential Learning 38, 284–292 (2011)

15. Chisholm, J., Warman, G.: Experience CSR – a corporate social responsibility simulation. Developments in Business Simulation and Experiential Learning **32**, 97–100 (2005)
16. Engelstein, G., Shalev, I.: Buliding Blocks of Tabletop Game Design. CRC Press (2019)
17. Booth, P.: Board Game as Media. Bloomsbury Academic (2021)
18. http://gra.fajna.eu last accessed 19 June 2021

# Player Experience in Simulations

# Development of the Player Satisfaction Scale - A Factor Analytic Study

Vinod Dumblekar[1]($\boxtimes$) (iD), Jigyasu Dubey[2] (iD), and Upinder Dhar[2] (iD)

[1] MANTIS, New Delhi 110025, India
dumblekar@yahoo.com
[2] Shri Vaishnav Vidyapeeth Vishwavidyalaya, Indore 453111, India

**Abstract.** To develop a scale of player satisfaction in simulation and games, an instrument of 30 statements was first developed. The initial pool of 658 responses (undergraduate students and others) was purified by rejecting 61 duplicate and incorrect responses and two inappropriate statements. The data from the remaining 597 responses and 28 statements were processed for factor analysis. Five factors each of eigenvalue more than 1 were produced at high reliability of Cronbach α of .93. The factors were named excitement, challenge, learning experience, team victory and self-discovery to represent the statements that comprised the factors. The study found no impact of gender and category on player satisfaction. This paper discusses the nature of the factors of player satisfaction and their potential utility in further research and applications.

**Keywords:** Challenge · Excitement · Learning experience · Player satisfaction · Self-discovery · Team victory

## 1 Introduction

The success of some kinds of games depends on the satisfaction of the players. The satisfaction affects their emotional attachment to the game. It drives their repeated use of the product and encourages them to recommend it to others. Player satisfaction emerges from expectations of utility, value and quality of the product features and the game experience. Therefore, satisfaction is an important consideration in game design, development, use and sales. For video game players, satisfaction is 'the degree to which the player feels gratified with the experience while playing a video game' [1].

Playing games is attractive because it offers diverse experiences [2]. Some games offer a learning experience while others offer problems to solve. Some games offer an artificial scenario that could be engaging and far from reality, yet captivating its players. Because of the inherent entertainment in some games, the experience is a diversion for players. Generally, the player experience is comprised of their thoughts, feelings and interactions with other players which motivate and shape their gameplay.

The games and simulations have common characteristics of design and facilitation and similar objectives such as entertainment and learning. This study applies to both of them. Henceforth, the terms 'games' and 'simulations' will be used interchangeably in this paper.

© Springer Nature Switzerland AG 2022
U. Dhar et al. (Eds.): ISAGA 2021, LNCS 13219, pp. 147–160, 2022.
https://doi.org/10.1007/978-3-031-09959-5_13

## 1.1 Player Satisfaction is an Experience

The satisfaction of 140 students in an enterprise business management simulation game was influenced by their participation and grades from their relative overall performance (net profit) in the game [3]. In an online course, the students' satisfaction is due to their self-motivation, learning style and actions, the course structure and their interactions and their teachers' competence and behaviour [4]. These reasons may also be true for a serious game where the objective of play is only to learn.

Player satisfaction derives from the perceived benefits such as entertainment, pleasure, challenge, interest, ease of use such as conveniences of consistency, flexibility, navigation, documentation and authenticity from play [5]. The players' experience is affected by the suspense, narrative and competitiveness in the game [6]. Their self-efficacy in action, performance, convenience in play, control over game features and actions, and their fantasy-based relationship with the game characters enhance or reduce their satisfaction with the game. Their ease of use of the game features also drives their satisfaction. The learning satisfaction in a marketing simulation game can be a proxy for their learning effectiveness and outcome in the game [7].

Player satisfaction may be derived from clashing with opponents, overcoming difficult challenges, learning and practising new skills, achieving personal and team goals and winning competitions and battles [8]. The nature of games varies in terms of their artificial environment, the kind of problems posed to the players, their skills and actions, the nature of their social interactions with their team members and competitors, and the pace at which the challenges and stages maintain the players' interest in the games.

Player satisfaction is related to game complexity, expectations of success and players' performance in the games. It is an outcome of resolving problems or completing tasks and is reflected in the players' rising self-esteem. Players seek success through their gaming actions and choose challenges that are appropriate for them to address with their abilities and actions to win the game [9]. Both their expectations and actions are based on their evaluations and therefore, their satisfaction is an experience of fun, enjoyment and feelings of accomplishment.

Interactivity in play is one of the most powerful factors in player satisfaction, irrespective of any other form of motivation [10]. When the players' need for excitement and stimulation is high, their enjoyment is high, but only when their interactivity is high. When their need for interest and engagement is high, their enjoyment is high irrespective of the level of interactivity. Similarly, rising levels of interactivity address and satisfy their needs for competence (the feeling of capability) and autonomy (the freedom to behave independently) and thus, help them enjoy their game experience.

Player satisfaction develops from the feelings of mastery (ability to overcome challenges) and control (freedom to choose and act). Collecting points, deploying resources, defeating competitors and reaching tougher stages of the games are some tasks that arouse players' actions leading to their fun and enjoyment in games. Their actions in the game generate their self-efficacy experience which predicts and shapes their enjoyment [11].

## 1.2  Satisfaction in Online, Video and Other Electronic Games

The satisfaction of online game players is determined by the reliability, responsibility, assurance and empathy perceptions of the service quality of the game [12]. Touchscreen players are satisfied with their feelings of pleasure, achievement, involvement, game design elements of story and interactions and game process and delivery [13]. Their experience could be measured by their satisfaction, ease of task completion (movement or other actions within the game) and ease of controls, such as keyboard and other tools.

Video gamers are satisfied due to usability, playability, narratives, enjoyment, creative freedom, audio and visual aesthetics, personal gratification and social connectivity of the games [14]. While earlier research had found immersion, fun, aesthetics, motivation, engagement, presence, flow and enjoyment in games to be factors and facets of game satisfaction, some terms like immersion and engagement had multiple definitions and different meanings. Consumer videogame engagement was conceptualised as a state of interactions between the consumer and the product that produced cognitive, affective and behavioural types of consumer engagement [15]. Game engagement was found to be a composite of three constructs with two factors each, viz., cognitive engagement (absorption and conscious attention), affective engagement (dedication and enthusiasm) and behavioural engagement (interaction and social connection).

Satisfaction is derived from expectations of utility and value and quality of the product features and is a sign of the users' intention to buy and use the product again. Pokémon players' satisfaction was affected by their feelings of flow, such as challenge, control, curiosity and concentration and their expected service quality in terms of the immediacy of information and responsiveness of the entertainment services [16]. A study of 244,360 reviews from 6,170 video games in nine genres such as adventure, racing and strategy showed that satisfied gamers played the games repeatedly and recommended them to others [17].

A study of 353 video gamers using the game user experience satisfaction scale (GUESS) [15] found that their desire to play the game could be seen in their curiosity, eagerness to win, desire to experience a fantasy role or story in the game, solve a problem, use intellectual abilities and connect with others. Players with a need to compete, interact and imagine and like fancy worlds would be more satisfied than others. Those who experience high satisfaction may play the game more often. Some frameworks of game experience have components such as challenge, sensation, curiosity, absorption, concentration, motivation, arousal, fantasy, discovery and interaction [18].

From the review of literature, player satisfaction may be defined as a range of experiences that may include ease of use, freedoms and controls, participation, performance, competitiveness, interactions and learning. For online and related game players, the satisfaction may be affected by their engagement, narrative, discovery, fantasy, sensation, need to compete and win, immersion and game features and aesthetics. Thus, player satisfaction is a product of several forces such as the nature of the game, players' expectations, perceptions and behaviour and the learning, competition or other objectives of the game.

### 1.3 The Objectives of the Study

Much of the foregoing review of literature showed that no research attempted to develop a meaning of player satisfaction in games except in the domain of electronic games. Player satisfaction appears to be a multi-dimensional construct with many sources, explanations and perceptions. A deeper understanding of player satisfaction may guide the design and development of more satisfying games. Therefore, the objectives of the study are:

1. To develop a scale of player satisfaction in games
2. To identify the factors of player satisfaction
3. To study the effects of player gender and category on player satisfaction.

## 2 Method

### 2.1 The Instrument

From the review of literature, several feelings representing player satisfaction as experiences at the end of a game were identified and simplified. After a preliminary scrutiny, the feelings were converted into statements and were tested for ambiguity, simplicity, repetition and grammar. The new list of statements was then reviewed by other faculty for the statements' logical links to player satisfaction. After receiving the observations of players of some games, a few statements were combined, while some others of similar themes were restructured and relocated within the instrument. This pruned list had 30 statements which were finally reviewed by the authors in comparison to the objectives of the study. The statements were scored from 1 to 5 with 1 for 'least agreement' and 5 for 'highest agreement'; a 0 (zero) option was added for 'not applicable'.

To this list, cells to enter the respondent's name, gender, age and other demographics and names of games played by the respondent were added. Respondents were also invited to discuss their experiences with the authors. This instrument was then transcribed into the Google Forms page. It was again scrutinized by the authors till no further error was found.

### 2.2 The Respondents

The instrument for data collection was emailed to more than 1,550 students (undergoing graduation and post-graduation in engineering and management) and others who were not students. Students and others were treated as two separate categories for the study. Responses were received from 658 survey recipients (42.45%). After a visual examination of the data, 61 duplicate and incorrect records were rejected and 597 records were processed. The sample had a mean age of 20.57 years with a standard deviation (SD) of 5.03 years. The age of 549 students was in the range of 17–26 years while age of 48 others was in the range of 21–59 years (Fig. 1).

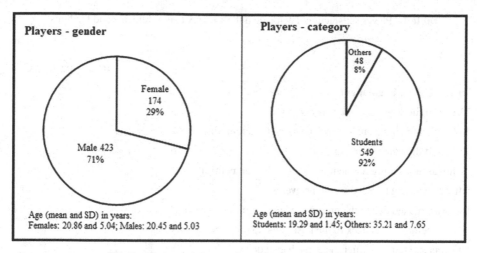

**Fig. 1.** Players: Age, gender and category distribution

## 2.3   The Procedure

The instrument was communicated to the prospective respondents in May and June 2021 along with an appeal for their cooperation. After a fortnight, the survey was closed and the data were processed using SPSS 21.0. To understand the players' responses to the instrument, the first author interviewed approximately 5 percent of the sample after the consents of the respondents were received. The respondents were asked to name their favourite games, to explain why they played games and to describe what they learnt from playing games.

## 3   Results

A reading of the completed forms showed that chess, ludo and sudoku were the most common indoor games, while rummy was the popular card game. Cricket was the leading outdoor game; Volleyball, football, badminton and basketball were also liked but less popular outdoor games. PUBG was their favourite mobile game. Athletics was also mentioned as a popular game by many respondents. Thus, the respondents had played a wide variety of games.

The statements #15 ('I felt sad when it ended') and #16 ('When I played alone, my confidence increased') were dropped because of their insignificant correlations with the total. The factor analysis processed the remaining 28 statements in the instrument and extracted five factors each of eigenvalue more than 1 that explained the variance of 53.53 percent. The KMO measure of sampling adequacy of .95 and Cronbach $\alpha$ of .93 of the results confirmed the reliability of the instrument. Bartlett's test of sphericity was highly significant ($\chi 2$ (378) = 6496.24, p < .000). The factors were named excitement, challenge, learning experience, team victory and self-discovery after considering the relative weights of the statements comprising each factor (Table 1).

**Table 1.** Player satisfaction: Factors and their respective statements and loadings

| | Loadings | | | | |
|---|---|---|---|---|---|
| | F1 | F2 | F3 | F4 | F5 |
| **Factor 1 (F1): Excitement** | | | | | |
| 23 I liked the way the game was organised | .65 | | | | |
| 24 I will cherish the outcome of the game for a long time | .62 | | | | |
| 25 I liked the game structure | .56 | | | | |
| 21 It was an exciting moment to conquer the competition | .55 | | | | |
| 5 It was exciting to recall the game events | .53 | | | | |
| 18 I was relaxed due to the presence of my team members | .52 | | | | |
| 26 My memory goes back to the post-game experience | .49 | | | | |
| 19 I was excited even after the game had ended | .48 | | | | |
| **Factor 2 (F2): Challenge** | | | | | |
| 17 I was happy that I will remember the game experience for a long time | | .28 | | | |
| 20 The game prepared me to face bigger problems in the real world | | .65 | | | |
| 8 I understood many things that I did not know before | | .63 | | | |
| 14 I am now ready to face new problems | | .62 | | | |
| 7 I discovered that I could overcome difficult problems | | .58 | | | |
| 22 I am glad that I know more after the end of the game | | .51 | | | |
| **Factor 3 (F3): Learning experience** | | | | | |
| 1 I felt elated | | | .69 | | |
| 2 I learnt how to confront problems | | | .56 | | |
| 3 As I played more games, my satisfaction increased | | | .53 | | |
| 6 The game experience was thrilling | | | .49 | | |
| 4 In team games, we talked a lot | | | .46 | | |
| 27 It is worth playing such games | | | .41 | | |
| **Factor 4 (F4): Team victory** | | | | | |
| 12 I wanted to win, and I did | | | | .73 | |
| 10 I am glad I won | | | | .73 | |
| 11 I learnt from other members in the team | | | | .57 | |
| 13 Everyone's communication had something valuable for me | | | | .50 | |

*(continued)*

**Table 1.** (*continued*)

|  | Loadings | | | | |
|---|---|---|---|---|---|
|  | F1 | F2 | F3 | F4 | F5 |
| 9 I am happy that I helped my fellow team members in the game |  |  |  | .48 |  |
| **Factor 5 (F5): Self-discovery** |  |  |  |  |  |
| 29 Every time I finished playing a game, I wanted to play it again |  |  |  |  | .71 |
| 30 Playing such games gave me recognition |  |  |  |  | .66 |
| 28 I discovered myself every time I played the game |  |  |  |  | .59 |
| Eigenvalues | 9.98 | 1.54 | 1.28 | 1.17 | 1.02 |
| Percent of variance explained | 14.80 | 10.36 | 10.14 | 9.34 | 8.89 |

The factors showed highly significant and positive correlations with each other (Table 2). The results suggest that player satisfaction is a multi-dimensional construct composed of factors closely associated with each other.

**Table 2.** Player satisfaction factors: Descriptives and correlations

|  | Mean | SD | F1 | F2 | F3 | F4 |
|---|---|---|---|---|---|---|
| F1 Excitement | 27.68 | 7.38 | 1 |  |  |  |
| F2 Challenge | 20.91 | 5.65 | .70 | 1 |  |  |
| F3 Learning experience | 20.35 | 5.54 | .70 | .66 | 1 |  |
| F4 Team victory | 18.41 | 4.74 | .64 | .62 | .63 | 1 |
| F5 Self-discovery | 10.27 | 3.33 | .62 | .58 | .51 | .48 |

All correlations are significant at the 0.01 level (2-tailed)

The sample groups were based on gender (female and male) and category (students and others); z tests were conducted to determine the differences within the groups. Player satisfaction did not significantly differ within the gender and the player category for the construct of player satisfaction and its factors.

### 3.1 Interview Results

Only 21 students, not the others, volunteered for the interview. Here are two responses (edited for brevity):

**Student 1.** *Plays only online games (3–4 h a day). Learning experience: playing within a team (PUBG), coordination, strategy, leadership, role, guiding others, patience, and how to deal with failure.*

**Student 2.** *Plays only online games (4–5 h a day). Likes simulations and plays for plea-sure and competition. Online games are better because time moves faster and learning is faster. One can learn from a chemistry simulation within hours as against a lab exer-cise that may take a week or more. Learning experience: strategy, repetition, failure, learning, making decisions, solving problems through trial and error, never give up, and learn and act under pressure. We need more S&G, and games must show reality more often.*

Twelve more respondents filled the instrument with their feedback, although they did not offer to be interviewed. Three observations (edited for brevity) are shown below:

**Student 3.** *Every game brings a chance to enhance skills and do well. Through watching scrims and all I come to learn that we can learn through seeing others the way they practice and exercise their skills and perform.*

**Student 4.** *When I play games it relieves tension, and there is a different kind of excite-ment. Especially, the Single-player computer games are really good. They have this cinematic experience, making use of all sorts of modern technology, and they are more immersive.*

**Student 5.** *After corona came in March 2020 and lockdown happened. Since then, I am here in my village and I am playing cricket for two hours daily for the last one and a half years. We play even when it is raining and I can proudly say that after every day's play, I feel absolutely energetic. Those two hours of play give me the strength to face the world (right now virtually) for the next 24 h, and it's not that we only play cricket, we talk a lot, we make fun of each other a lot and we enjoy every moment of the time that we play. The satisfaction which it gives to me, I cannot say it in words. Now, even after playing for this much time, every day I feel the same energy to go there and play. Even when I go out to the town to do some of the housework that my family gives me, I try my best to finish the tasks and come home before 16:30 so that I can play. And this also gives me the courage to overcome the negativity going around in this tough time. And lastly, I feel so much better mentally and physically.*

Out of the 33 interview and feedback respondents, 25 said that they played for the competition, excitement and relaxation without specifying any learning as a goal or an achievement.

## 4   Discussion

The study created, reviewed and administered an instrument of player satisfaction for over 1,550 potential respondents. From 597 valid responses and 28 valid statements, it achieved the first study objective by developing a scale of player satisfaction in games of adequate statistical reliability.

### 4.1   Factors of Player Satisfaction

The second objective was achieved when five factors were extracted from the respondent data and named as excitement, challenge, learning experience, team victory and self-discovery. For a better understanding of the results, these factors and their relevance to the study objectives are discussed below.

**Excitement.** Excitement could be measured to represent the changes in the expectation of victory during the game. Higher scoring rates, clashes between stronger teams, swings during the game and proximity to an expected win enhance the excitement in games such as soccer [19]. It may be seen as the probability of winning and could be codified and mathematically expressed as a formula for use in games such as tennis and golf [20]. The simulation is an active learning mechanism that engages students by evoking intrinsic interest, enjoyment, confidence, understanding, self-efficacy, enthusiasm and excitement for their course [21].

Excitement is an emotion that is characterised by feelings of elation, exhilaration and enthusiasm. Like any emotion, it influences decision making and communication and is an active and powerful ingredient in gamification [22]. Within groups, it is a product of interactions such as in games that may further enhance engagement and cohesion. Both hope and fear generate excitement in the form of uncertainty, pleasure, anxiety, suspense and nervousness during the game [23]. The results may produce other emotions such as annoyance, dissatisfaction, elation, relief, anguish and disappointment as different forms of excitement at the end of the game.

**Challenge.** A game is a set of problems that provokes players into action. Players may be more inclined to challenge and solve problems due to their experience in difficult situations, their conviction to solve problems, resilience, self-esteem, self-efficacy and determination to act. [9, 24]. A game evokes and retains the players' interest when it offers challenge, fantasy, control and curiosity. Game features include difficulty levels, points, badges and goals to challenge the players [25].

Successful problem solvers confront, learn from and enjoy challenges. They are extremely curious about new and difficult environments, ready to investigate problems from all angles, prepared to seek ideas and advice from others and eager to experiment for better results [26]. Problems can be solved effectively by using a broader lens for perception and understanding. One view of this lens may see problems as networks of people connected by trust, relationships and interactions. Another could be the evolution of groups of people, things and others connected by problems, decisions and behaviours. A systems view may see an information system of objects and resources connected by their features, flows, costs and applications. These views shape mindsets to choose one or more of these views to solve problems [27].

**Learning Experience.** Significant improvements in learning outcomes can be achieved even from small improvements like aesthetic features (such as graphics and music in a video game) in game design [28]. Quizzes and other gamification elements provide feedback that enhances engagement, learning outcome, motivation and subjective satisfaction [29]. Games that use different kinds of assignments and gamification markers such as badges and scorecards increase player motivation. Such actions would influence player performance to produce better learning and satisfaction.

The players are more engaged when they solve problems in the game because their actions enhance their learning and retention [30]. Learning is the product of interactions and experiences in a business simulation game where the players understand business goals and how to compete and collaborate and become aware of business and selling skills [7, 31]. This learning is possible due to the design of the game, the game documents, the facilitation during and after the game ends and the problems solved by the players during the game.

**Team Victory.** Group conditions such as size, heterogeneity, status, empowerment and climate and group interactions such as discussions and leadership affect the satisfaction of team members [32]. The players' task satisfaction would be affected by the team's levels of task satisfaction and vice versa.

Heterogeneous teams with members of diverse backgrounds and opinions perform better in a cohesive environment of psychological safety for their members [33]. In cohesive teams, their members are focused on and interact with each other towards the goal, share information and opinions with other members of the team without fear or embarrassment and trust, assist and depend on each other to resolve their problems [34]. Such teams are more likely to win competitions and therefore, have high levels of team satisfaction [35]. Satisfaction is an outcome when members share knowledge with others in the team and focus on the goal; both are facets of cohesiveness [36]. Therefore, satisfaction is a personal and team result of accomplishing team goals which translate to victories in competitive games.

**Self-discovery.** Self-examination leads to self-discovery which is the players' deter-mination that dictates and shapes intentions, decisions and behaviour and builds their self-mastery. Thus, their satisfaction arises because they recognize their own and others' strengths and weaknesses and manage them to seek mastery of their environments. Such understanding enables the players to make deliberate decisions and solve problems [37].

Players discover themselves most when they solve tough challenges using their superior skills. The discovery encourages them to learn more, use their capabilities again and attend to more problems to enhance their self-esteem. In this state of flow, the players would feel more active, alert, concentrated, happy, satisfied, creative and motivated [38]. Players discover what they can do when confronted with problems in social interactive environments. They learn to think flexibly by integrating their understanding with other domains under varied conditions. They develop learning and reasoning skills and the maturity for assessing their actions and results. In team games, they construct meaning and learn to communicate, negotiate and share ideas and assist one another [39].

## 5   Effects of Player Gender and Category on Player Satisfaction

**Gender and Category.** The absence of the effects of gender and category suggested that both genders and both categories of respondents had similar levels of satisfaction. Thus, no gender or category had more excitement and challenges, better learning experience and team victory, and more self-discovery than the other gender and category. Therefore, game features would not engage one gender or category more than the other.

The interviews and written observations of some students described and con-firmed the statistical findings that they played games mostly for excitement and social engagement.

## 5.1 Limitations

The instrument was administered during the covid19-related lockdown of 2021. Students who normally play outdoor games like cricket and football would not have played them for (perhaps) the previous two months or more. The reduced duration of their playing experiences may have diluted their responses to the instrument.

The study covered a variety of games where the fun, engagement, enjoyment and excitement experiences were generated from high levels of participation and interactivity. None of the respondents based their survey answers on any serious game. Therefore, the study did not cover serious games whose focus is on the learning of facts and events such as in historical simulations [40] and where the nature and factors of the player satisfaction may be vastly different from the findings of the study.

## 5.2 Conclusion

The authors developed a scale of player satisfaction based on many games. The scale was built from a survey of 658 respondents of indoor, outdoor, board, electronic and other games. The study extracted, named and discussed the factors of player satisfaction as *excitement, challenge, learning experience, team victory* and *self-discovery* and found that the gender and player category of the respondents did not affect player satisfaction.

## 5.3 Implications of the Study

The findings of this study may be valid for youth aged 18–21 years because the sample size (n = 549) of students was large and fairly homogeneous (mean = 19.29 years, SD = 1.45 years). The sample of others (n = 48) was relatively small and more heterogeneous (mean = 35.21 years, SD = 7.65 years) than the student sample; therefore, extending the findings to older others may not be suitable.

Researchers may study the nature of satisfaction and its antecedents throughout a game because the player's satisfaction would change during play. The findings may be useful and interesting to game developers so that they can add the appropriate features to generate satisfaction at desired stages in the game. An index of satisfaction may help to measure and understand it better than before as in the case of excitement [19].

Researchers must use measures, such as the number of times or hours that players played the most satisfying games as an objective and reliable assessment [20]. The study used players' self-reports as measures to assess their perspectives about their satisfaction. While it was convenient to capture their playing experience as perceptions, their subjective responses may not have been fully factual. Therefore, the frequency of play is a better pointer to satisfaction than self-reports [41].

Researchers must develop scales of player satisfaction for specific games like chess and football. Players would face different kinds and levels of engagements, emotions and satisfaction as experiences even if the games belong to the same genre [41]. Games within the same genre differ vastly in terms of competitive strategy, game modes, design and features.

Game designers and developers must embed the five factors as necessary elements into their games so that players play often and recommend the games to others. The objective of gamification to entice and keep customers engaged with the game can be served by using features like scoring, rewards and frequent communications. Satisfied customers would then be a sign of business capability to serve its customers and perform and survive in the future [42, 43].

A serious game is a teaching tool that promotes learning and behavioural change, unlike other games where the objective is to challenge and win against competitors. Serious game developers should include elements of challenge, recognition, problems to solve and social interactions in the games to enhance the players' excitement and their learning experience [44]. Serious games must capture and engage the players' attention with elements like fantasy, challenge and adventure to create an enjoyable learning experience [45].

# References

1. Patzer, B., Chaparro, B., Keebler, J.R.: Developing a model of video game play: motivations, satisfactions, and continuance intentions. Simul. Gaming **51**(3), 287–309 (2020)
2. Oksanen, K.: Subjective experience and sociability in a collaborative serious game. Simul. Gaming **44**(6), 767–793 (2013)
3. White, C.S.: A path analytic approach to some correlates of students' satisfaction with a computerized management simulation. Simul. Gaming **26**(1), 92–96 (1995)
4. Edom, S.B., Wen, H.J.: The determinants of students' perceived learning outcomes and satisfaction in university online education: an empirical investigation. Decis. Sci. J. Innov. Educ. **4**(2), 215–235 (2006)
5. Theng, Y.L., Wanzhen, L., Zhiqiang, L., Robert, C., Pallavi, R.: Investigation of the antecedents and consequences of player satisfaction: an individual perspective. ACM Computers in Entertainment **9**(3), 26 (2011). Article 15
6. Elson, M., Breuer, J., Quandt, T.: Know thy player: an integrated model of player experience for digital games research. Handbook of Digital Games. In: Marios, C. (eds.) Angelides and Harry Agius, pp. 362–387. John Wiley & Sons Inc. (2014)
7. Caruana, A., Rocca, A.L., Snehota, I.: Learner satisfaction in marketing simulation games: Antecedents and influencers. J. Mark. Educ. **38**(2), 107–118 (2016)
8. Sweetser, P., Wyeth, P.: GameFlow: a model for evaluating player enjoyment in games. ACM Computers in Entertainment **3**(3), 1–24 (2005)
9. Klimmt, C., Blake, C., Hefner, D., Vorderer, P., Roth, C.: Player performance, satisfaction, and video game enjoyment. In: Natkin, S., Dupire, J. (eds.) Eighth International Conference on Entertainment Computing 2009. Lecture Notes in Computer Science, vol. 5709, pp. 1–12. Springer, Berlin (2009)
10. Tamborini, R., Grizzard, M., Bowman, N.D., Reinecke, L., Lewis, R.J., Eden, A.: Media enjoyment as need satisfaction: the contribution of hedonic and nonhedonic needs. J. Commun. **61**, 1025–1042 (2011)
11. Trepte, S., Reinecke, L.: The pleasures of success: game-related efficacy experiences as a mediator between player performance and game enjoyment. Cyber Psychol. Behav. Soc. Netw. **14**(9), 555–557 (2011)
12. Yang, H.-E., Wu, C.-C., Wang, K.-C.: An empirical analysis of online game service satisfaction and loyalty. Expert Syst. Appl. **36**, 1816–1825 (2009)
13. Halloran, J., Minaeva, A.: Touch and play? Investigating the value of touchscreens for gamer experience. Entertainment Computing **32**, 1–16 (2019)
14. Phan, M.H., Keebler, J.R., Chaparro, B.S.: The development and validation of the game user experience satisfaction scale (GUESS). Hum. Factors **58**(8), 1217–1247 (2016)

15. Abbasi, A.Z., Ting, D.H., Hlavacs, H.: Engagement in games: developing an instrument to measure consumer videogame engagement and its validation. Int. J. Comp. Games Technol. **2017**, 85–100 (2017)
16. Lee, C.-H., Chiang, H.-S., Hsiao, K.L.: What drives stickiness in location-based AR games? an examination of flow and satisfaction. Telematics Inform. **35**, 1958–1970 (2018)
17. Heo, S., Park, J.: Are you satisfied or satiated by the games you play? An empirical study about game play and purchase patterns by genres. Telematics Inform. **59**, 101550 (2021)
18. Wang, X., Goh, D.H.-L.: Components of game experience: An automatic text analysis of online reviews. Entertainment Computing **33**, 1–7 (2020)
19. Vecer, J., Ichiba, T., Laudanovic, M.: On probabilistic excitement of sports games. J. Quanti. Analy. Sports **3**(3,6), 1–21 (2007)
20. Pollard, G.: Measuring excitement in sport. Journal of Sports Analytics **3**(1), 37–43 (2017)
21. Hendrickson, P.: Effect of active learning techniques on student excitement, interest, and self-efficacy. J. Politi. Sci. Edu. **17**(2), 311–325 (2019)
22. Kucher, K., Cernea, D., Kerren, A.: Visualizing excitement of individuals and groups. In: EmoVis on Emotion and Visualisation, Workshop proceedings, pp. 15–22 (2016)
23. Moulard, J.G., Kroff, M., Pounders, K., Ditt, C.: The role of suspense in gaming: inducing consumers' game enjoyment. J. Interact. Advert. **19**(3), 219–235 (2019)
24. Smith, M.S., Gray, S.W.: The courage to challenge: A new measure of hardiness in LGBT adults. J. Gay Lesbian Soc. Serv. **21**(1), 73–89 (2009)
25. Garone, P., Nesteriuk, S.: Gamification and Learning: A Comparative Study of Design Frameworks. In: Duffy, V.G. (ed.) HCII 2019. LNCS, vol. 11582, pp. 473–487. Springer, Cham (2019). https://doi.org/10.1007/978-3-030-22219-2_35
26. Conn, C., McLean, R.: Six problem-solving mindsets for very uncertain times, 1–7 (2020). https://www.mckinsey.com/business-functions/strategy-and-corporate-finance/our-insights/six-problem-solving-mindsets-for-very-uncertain-times. Retrieved 25 September 2021
27. Leclerc, O., Moldoveanu, M.: Five routes to more innovative problem solving, 1–11 (2013). https://www.mckinsey.com/business-functions/strategy-and-corporate-finance/our-insights/five-routes-to-more-innovative-problem-solving. Retrieved 25 September 2021
28. Martin, M.W., Shen, Y.: The effects of game design on learning outcomes. Computers in the Schools: Interdisciplinary Journal of Practice, Theory, and Applied Research **31**(1–2), 23–42 (2014)
29. Kim, E., Rothrock, L., Freivalds, A.: An empirical study on the impact of lab gamification on engineering students' satisfaction and learning. Int. J. Eng. Educ. **34**(1), 201–216 (2018)
30. Yu, Z., Gao, M., Wang, L.: The effect of educational games on learning outcomes, student motivation, engagement and satisfaction. J. Edu. Comp. Res. **59**(3), 522–546 (2021)
31. Dumblekar, V., Dhar, U.: Learning from a business simulation game: a factor-analytic study. In: Wardaszko, M., Meijer, S., Lukosch, H., Kanegae, H., Kriz, W. C., Grzybowska-Brzezińska, M. (eds.) Simulation Gaming Through Times And Disciplines. 50th International Simulation and Gaming Association Conference, LNCS, vol 11988, pp. 328–340. Springer Nature, Switzerland (2021)
32. Mason, C.M., Griffin, M.A.: Group task satisfaction: Applying the construct of job satisfaction to groups. Small Group Research **33**(3), 271–312 (2002)
33. Lavy, S., Bareli, Y., Ein-Dor, T.: The effects of attachment heterogeneity and team cohesion on team functioning. Small Group Research **46**(1), 27–49 (2015)
34. Dumblekar, V., Dhar, U.: Development and standardization of business simulation game team cohesion scale. AIMS Journal of Management **3**(1), 1–22 (2017)
35. Shang, I.-W., Ku, G.C.-M.: How youth athletes satisfy their team? Identifying significant predictors of perceived coach leadership and team cohesion, team commitment: A hierarchical regression analysis. Int. J. Sports Sci. Coach. **13**(6), 883–890 (2018)

36. Super, J.F., Betts, T.K., Keller, H., Humphreys, J.R.: A multilevel examination of knowledge sharing norms, transactive memory systems, and individual learning goal orientations. Simulation & Gaming 1–29 (2020)
37. Unah, J.I.: Self-discovery: Who am I? An ontologized ethics of self-mastery. Cultura, International Journal of Philosophy of Culture and Axiology **8**(1), 143–158 (2011)
38. Csikszentmihalyi, M., LeFevre, J.: Optimal experience in work and leisure. J. Pers. Soc. Psychol. **56**(5), 815–822 (1989)
39. Hmelo-Silver, C.E.: Problem-based learning: What and how do students learn? Educ. Psychol. Rev. **16**(3), 235–266 (2004)
40. Schrier, K.: Designing digital games to teach history and historical thinking. In: Schrier, K. (ed.) Learning, education and games, vol. 1: Curricular and design considerations. ETC Press/Carnegie Mellon, Pittsburgh, PA (2014)
41. Adinolf, S., Türkay, S.: Differences in player experiences of need satisfaction across four games. In: Proceedings of DiGRA International Conference: Game, Play and the Emerging Ludo-Mix. Digital Games Research Association, Kyoto, Japan (2019)
42. Johnson, M.D., Gustafsson, A.: Improving customer satisfaction, loyalty, and profit: An integrated measurement and management system. Jossey-Bass Inc, San Francisco, California (2000)
43. Fornell, C.: The Satisfied Customer – Winners and Losers in the Battle for Buyer Preference. Palgrave Macmillan, New York (2007)
44. Dimitriadou, A., Djafarova, N., Turetken, O., Verkuyl, M., Ferworn, A.: Challenges in serious game design and development: educators' experiences. Simul. Gaming **52**(2), 132–152 (2021)
45. Zin, N.A.M., Yue, W.S.: History educational games design. In: International Conference on Electrical Engineering and Informatics, pp. 269–275 (2009)

# Effect of Learning Styles on Learning Experience in Marketing Management Game

Rajeev K. Shukla[1]([✉]) and Monica Sainy[2]

[1] Indira Gandhi National Open University, New Delhi, India
rkshukla@ignou.ac.in
[2] Shri Vaishnav School of Management, SVVV, Indore, Madhya Pradesh, India

**Abstract.** The effect of the learning styles of management students on a learning experience in marketing management game was studied. The scales on learning experience and Kolb's learning styles inventory were administered on 120 students who played the game. The findings of the study revealed a significant effect of Concrete Experience (CE) and Abstract Conceptualization (AC) on the learning experience. The gender-wise significant difference was observed in the learning experience. Findings of the study revealed a significant interactive effect of gender and Reflective Observation style of learning on the learning experience in the marketing management game.

**Keywords:** Brainstorming · Concept development · Field exercises · Instructional games · Systematic planning

## 1 Introduction

The instructional games in the curriculum improve learning; therefore, the teaching fraternity has shown interest in using these games as one of the student learning styles [1]. Learning brings changes in the behavior of the students. It is the process through which knowledge is created through the transformation of experience [2] Learning style is the way an individual processes and retains new information and skills; hence, it plays an important role in the behavior of the students. No single approach provides the best learning for the students as every individual has different approaches in the learning process because of the different backgrounds, motivations, demographics, and their characteristics [3]. Better management games can be developed by understanding the learning styles and encouraging students' participation to develop better learning about the concepts. In complex disciplines such as management where the educators must link theory into practice, they take the help of in-class and out-of-class activities to make the learning more effective. Learning styles are measured by the Learning Scale Inventory (LSI) and generalized in four stages of the learning process [4].

### 1.1 Kolb's Learning Style

Simulations contribute to all phases of Kolb's (1984) learning cycle [5]. Experiential learning accommodates learners of all styles and described simulations as learning activities [6]. Students found games as fun and motivating [7]. Fun and humor elements also

© Springer Nature Switzerland AG 2022
U. Dhar et al. (Eds.): ISAGA 2021, LNCS 13219, pp. 161–170, 2022.
https://doi.org/10.1007/978-3-031-09959-5_14

facilitated creative problem solving [8]. Games lead to improved learning and academic performance [9].

Kolb's model of learning style was used to understand the effect of marketing management games on students learning experience. Games have been known to engage and interest people since their inception. Management games have found their use in different fields such as marketing, healthcare, business and education [10]. If implemented correctly, gamification can make a positive impact on students' learning, motivation and participation [11]. Students in the marketing stream are very diverse in nature and have learners of different styles [12] Therefore, for effective learning, the interesting marketing game would give the students a better learning experience.

Management games provide a real learning experience to the students and hence make the learning more effective. [9] The use of instructional games has grown in the past decade and students find the games full of fun and interesting but sometimes, do not constitute any learning [13]. These games are at least an inducement to learning and necessary preconditions for higher-order learning and self-learning [14]. Primary goals of experiential learning consider them to serve as reasonable substitutions for learning [15–19]. Another essential factor to consider is whether games should be fully incorporated or only partially integrated into the learning process. Games should be viewed as supplemental elements because complete integration necessitates high-quality mechanisms, student involvement and instructor support [20]. In other circumstances, the inclusion of games in the curriculum has been successful if the instructions provided to the students are effective.

Studies discussed the role of gender in simulation games and have suggested that women lack technological competence and want to adequately perform femininity; on the other hand, men are technologically proficient by virtue of their performance of masculinity [21] Games are often used in educational settings because they provide increased learner motivation. It is particularly important to use games that appeal to both genders to provide equal educational opportunities to all students. The present study uses the literature on Kolb's learning model, experiential learning, strategic business games, and learning styles.

## 2  Rationale of the Study

Different learning styles make the students learn in different ways. Management games play an important role to make learning more effective and provide a real learning experience to the students. Research suggested that around 2000 instructional games are available and faculty members are using these games to make the students more engaged in learning. Marketing is the area where the students must go in the field to understand the concepts practically. To provide real-time exposure to the marketing students, the marketing game was planned for experiential learning.

## 3  Objectives

1. To study the impact of learning style on the learning experience of marketing management games.

2. To study the effect of gender on the learning experience of marketing management games.
3. To study the interactive effect of gender and learning style on the learning experience.

## 4   Method

**Sampling Procedure:** Purposive sampling method was used.

**Sample size:** 120 students played marketing management game.

**Tools for Data Collection:** Students' learning experience was measured on a self-developed eight-item scale.

The Kolb's Learning Style Inventory was used to assess learning styles (Table 1). It has 12 items and is measured on a ranking scale. However, for the study, these items were measured on a five-point rating scale from 'strongly disagree' (1) to 'strongly agree' (5). The ranking format essentially forces the data to fit into two opposing dimensions and the rating format should allow a less biased test of the "polar opposite" prediction [22] Thomas (1978)]. Changing from a ranking format to a rating format increased the average reliability of the sub-scales from .48 to .57.

**Table 1.** Reliability coefficient of learning experience and LSI scales

|                                    | Cronbach's Alpha |
|------------------------------------|------------------|
| Learning Experience (LE)           | 0.82             |
| Concrete Experience (CE)           | 0.63             |
| Reflective Observation (RO)        | 0.68             |
| Abstract Conceptualization (AC)    | 0.76             |
| Active Experimentation (AE)        | 0.75             |

**Tools for Data analysis:** Regression analysis, independent sample T Test, and Two-way ANOVA were used as tools for data analysis.

**Hypotheses.** Following null hypotheses were formulated and tested at a 5 percent level of significance.

H01: There is no significant effect of Concrete Experience (CE) on the learning experience in the marketing management game.
H02: There is no significant effect of Reflective Observation (RO) on the learning experience in the marketing management game.
H03: There is no significant effect of Abstract Conceptualization (AC) on the learning experience in the marketing management game.

H04: There is no significant effect of Active Experimentation (AE) on the learning experience in the marketing management game.

H05: Gender-wise, there is no significant difference in the learning experience in the marketing management game.

H06: There is no interactive effect of gender and Concrete Experience (CE) on the learning experience in the marketing management game.

H07: There is no interactive effect of gender and Reflective Observation (RO) on the learning experience in the marketing management game.

H08: There is no interactive effect of gender and Abstract Conceptualization (AC) on the learning experience in the marketing management game.

$H_{09}$: There is no interactive effect of gender and Active Experimentation (AE) on the learning experience in the marketing management game.

**An Examination of Learning Experiences Toward Playing Marketing Games.** One hundred and twenty MBA students played a game as in-class and out-of-class exercises in two sections with the same faculty who administered the game. The students played in groups of six each; hence 20 teams.

### Description of the Game
The game consists of four customer segments and two different product categories of different features offered to the market. The industry in the game is the chocolate industry which needs to start its fresh operations in urban areas (Tier II city). One student in every team was appointed as a marketing manager to build a marketing mix to increase the profitability by 20 percent assuming that breakeven was achieved.

1. Every team consisted of six members having equal number of males and females.
2. A budget of 2 million was allocated to each team.
3. Every team decided the strategy for the first quarter of Jan-March.
4. Two varieties of chocolate products were manufactured and sold at their decided price.

Each group needed to frame a business model showing the price mix, promotion mix and distribution mix.

### Participants' Tasks

1. Every team decided the four customer segments.
2. The data of costing of the product was provided to every team.
3. They allocated the budget on the different heads – Research & Development promotion, pricing & distribution mix.

### Key Learning Areas
The game covered the basic understanding of the topics such as product mix, market segmentation and targeting, distribution channel investments, promotional budget allocation, pricing, market research, competitor's analysis and overall profitability.

**Data Analysis:** To test the hypotheses, regression analysis was used to study the effect of learning style on the learning experience in marketing management games.

The Table 2 shows the descriptive statistics of learning experience and learning styles of the sample.

Table 2. Descriptive statistics of the sample

|  | Mean | Std. Deviation | n |
|---|---|---|---|
| Learning Experience | 3.83 | .48 | 120 |
| Concrete Experience | 3.68 | .56 | 120 |
| Reflective Observation | 3.84 | .70 | 120 |
| Abstract Conceptualization | 3.89 | .74 | 120 |
| Active Experimentation | 3.30 | .84 | 120 |

The R-value of 0.62 indicates a moderate degree of regression (Table 3). The $R^2$ value of 0.38 indicates that learning styles contribute to only 38% variation in the learning experience. The Durbin Watson value is below 2 and indicates a positive autocorrelation.

Table 3. Model summary

| Model | R | R Square | Adjusted R Square | Std. Error of the Estimate | Durbin-Watson |
|---|---|---|---|---|---|
| 1 | .62 | .38 | .36 | .38 | 1.99 |

Predictors: (Constant), Active Experimentation, Abstract Conceptualization, Concrete Experience, Reflective Observation. Dependent Variable: Learning Experience.

The F ratio is 17.73 and the p-value is less than 0.05 (Table 4). Hence, the null hypotheses which suggest that there is no relationship between the learning style and learning experience in marketing management games stand rejected.

**Table 4.** Details of the analysis of variance

| | Model | Sum of Squares | Df | Mean Square | F | Sig |
|---|---|---|---|---|---|---|
| | Regression | 10.51 | 4 | 2.63 | 17.73 | .00* |
| 1 | Residual | 17.03 | 115 | .15 | | |
| | Total | 27.54 | 119 | | | |

*Dependent Variable: Learning Experience. Predictors: (Constant), Active Experimentation, Abstract Conceptualization, Concrete Experience, Reflective Observation*

The regression model for the learning styles and learning experience of the students in the marketing management games shows significant effects of Concrete Experience (CE) and Abstract Conceptualization (AC) on the learning experience (Table 5). Thus, hypotheses $H_{01}$ and $H_{03}$ were rejected. $H_{02}$ and $H_{04}$ hypotheses were accepted which showed that Reflective Observation and Active Experimentation have no significant effect on the learning experience in marketing management game.

**Table 5.** Regression model for the learning styles and learning experience

| Model | | Unstandardized Coefficients | | Standardized Coefficients | T | Sig. | Collinearity Statistics | |
|---|---|---|---|---|---|---|---|---|
| | | B | Std. Error | Beta | | | Tolerance | V I F |
| | (Constant) | 1.89 | .26 | | 7.33 | .00 | | |
| | Concrete Experience (CE) | .21 | .08 | .24 | 2.67 | .00* | .67 | 1.50 |
| | Reflective Observation (RO) | .14 | .074 | .20 | 1.89 | .06 | .47 | 2.12 |
| | Abstract Conceptualization (AC) | .21 | .07 | .32 | 2.92 | .00* | .46 | 2.16 |
| | Active Experimentation (AE) | -.04 | .05 | -.08 | -.96 | .34 | .85 | 1.17 |

*Dependent Variable: Learning Experience.*

The Independent-sample t-Test was used to compare means of male and female groups of students (Tables 6 and 7).

If the significance value for the Levene test is greater than 0.05, it satisfies the assumption of equal variances for both groups. The p-value (significance) for the t-test

**Table 6.** Gender-wise mean and standard deviation

|  | Gender | n | Mean | Std. Deviation |
|---|---|---|---|---|
| Learning Experience | Male | 50 | 3.94 | .52 |
|  | Female | 70 | 3.76 | .44 |

is less than 0.05, hence null hypothesis $H_{05}$ was rejected. It indicated that gender-wise there was a significant difference in the learning experience (Table 7).

**Table 7.** Gender-wise T-test

|  |  | Levene's Test for Equality of Variances | | | | |
|---|---|---|---|---|---|---|
|  |  | F | Sig. | t | df | Sig. (2-tailed) |
| Learning Experience | Equal variances assumed | .59 | .44 | 1.98 | 118 | .04* |

Gender and Reflective Observation have a significant interactive effect on learning experience as the p < .05 and hypothesis H07 was rejected (Table 8).

**Table 8.** Two way ANOVA to test the Hypotheses: H06-H09

|  | Source | Sum of Squares | df | Mean Square | F | Sig. |
|---|---|---|---|---|---|---|
| H06 | Gender * Concrete Experience | 1.51 | 6 | .25 | 1.54 | .17 |
| H07 | Gender * Reflective Observation | 4.12 | 8 | .52 | 4.53 | .00* |
| H08 | Gender * Abstract Conceptualization | 1.57 | 7 | .23 | 1.91 | .08 |
| H09 | Gender * Active Experimentation | 2.12 | 9 | .24 | 1.31 | .24 |

## 5  Discussion

Overall, the students have a very positive experience in this marketing management game and found the game very interesting and challenging. Results indicated that out of the four Kolb's learning styles, the Concrete Experience (CE) and Abstract conceptualization (AC) have shown a significant impact on the learning experience in the marketing management game. However, the effects of Reflective Observation (RO) and Active Experimentation (AE) style of learning were found to be insignificant on the learning experience. The findings of the present study were also supported by Kolb who had suggested that in Concrete Experience, the learning aspect covered intuition and special experiences and established a relationship with the people [23]. The activities included in the concrete experience were readings, field searches and simulations. The Abstract Conceptualization (AC) consists of learning by thinking, logical analysis of thoughts and systematic planning which included activities such as field exercises, simulation exercises and situation-based exercises. The games helped to build the concept development and learn to assess simulation effectiveness [24].

The findings of the study revealed the significant gender-wise difference in the learning experience. The probable reason could be that most females do not take up marketing as a specialization or field jobs. A similar result was observed that female enrollment in the marketing field was less, and they had not shown much interest in playing situation-based games [25]. Men generally prefer to play games that are active and competitive while women prefer logic, puzzles and skill training games and enjoy social interactions in games [26] These gender differences provide some unique challenges to game designers as they attempt to design games that appeal to as broad as of a game playing audience as possible.

Gender-wise learning differences were also observed in an empirical study with a small sample size supporting the finding that Gender and Reflective Observation (RO) have a significant interactive effect on the learning experience [27]. The Reflective Observations were measured with the help of brainstorming activities, discussions and thought-provoking questions and included learning through their senses and an attentive observation before deciding. The task of the students in the game was to take the decisions related to 4 P's (Product, Price, Promotion and Place) and the group consisted of both males and females. In a similar result, students had shown more interest when they performed the activities such as excursions, discussions, brainstorming and thought-provoking questions [28].

## 6 Conclusion

The Learning style plays an important role in creating a positive and unforgettable experience about the concepts of marketing. For the study, Kolb's Learning Style Inventory (LSI) was used and the effects of four learning styles on learning experience were studied. The findings revealed the significant effect of Concrete Experience (CE) and Abstract Conceptualization (AC) on the learning experience in the marketing management game. The gender-wise significant difference was observed in the learning experience. The findings showed the significant interactive effect of gender and Reflective Observation style of learning on the learning experience in the marketing management game.

## References

1. Kolb, A.Y., Kolb, D.A.: The learning way: meta cognitive aspects of experiential learning. Simul. Gaming **40**(3), 297–327 (2009)

2. Arthurs, J.B.: A juggling act in the classroom: managing different learning styles. Teach Learn Nur's. **2**(1), 2–7 and 3 (2007)
3. Brown, T., et al.: Are learning style preferences of health science students predictive of their attitudes towards e-learning? AJET **25**(4) (2009)
4. Kolb, D.A.: Experiential Learning. Prentice-Hall, Englewood Cliffs, NJ (1984)
5. McHaney, R., White, D., Heilman, G.E.: Simulation project success and failure: Survey findings. Simul. Gaming **33**(1), 49–66 (2002)
6. Vaidyanathan, R., Rochford, L.: An exploratory investigation of computer simulations, student preferences, and performance. Journal of Education for Business **73**(February), 144–149 (1998)
7. Fortmüller, R.: Learning through business games: acquiring competencies within virtual realities. Simul. Gaming **40**(1), 68–83 (2009)
8. Prouty, D.: Zip lines: the voice for adventure education. Creativity **40**, 9–11 (2000)
9. Wilson, K.A., et al.: Relationships between games attributes and learning outcomes: review and research proposals. Simul. Gaming **40**(2), 217–266 (2009)
10. Mason, C.H., Perreault, Jr., W.D.: The Marketing Game! 3d ed. Irwin, Chicago (2002)
11. Barata, G., Gama, S., Jorge, J., Gonçalves, D.: Improving Participation and Learning with Gamification. In: Proceedings of the First International Conference on Gameful Design, Research, and Applications, pp. 10–17. ACM, New York, NY, USA (2013). https://doi.org/10.1145/2583008.2583010
12. Frontczak, N.T., Rivale, G.J.: An empirical investigation of learning styles in marketing education. In: McKinnon, G., Kelley, C. (eds.) Proceedings of the Western Marketing Educators' Association, pp. 93–100. Western Marketing Educators' Association, San Diego, CA (1991)
13. Chin, J., Dukes, R., Gamson, W.: Assessment in simulation and gaming: a review of the last 40 Years. Simul. Gaming **40**(4), 553–568 (2009)
14. Bloom, B.S., Englehart, M.D., First, E.D., Hill, W.H., Krathwohl, D.R.: Taxonomy of Educational Objectives Book 1: Cognitive Domain. David McKay, New York (1956)
15. Boyatzis, R.E., Kolb, D.A.: Assessing individuality in learning: the learning skills profile. Educ. Psychol. **11**(3), 279–295 (1991)
16. Comer, L.B., Nicholls, J.A.F.: Simulation as an aid to learning: how does participation influence the process? Developments in Business Simulation & Experiential Exercises **23**, 8–14 (1996)
17. Hergert, M., Hergert, R.: "Factors affecting student perceptions of learning in a business policy game. Developments in Business Simulation & Experiential Exercises **17**, 92–96 (1990)
18. White, C.S., Dale Von Riesen, R.: Computer MANAGEMENT SIMULATIONS AND SOME CORRELATES OF STUDENTS' SATISFACTION. Developments in Business Simulation & Experiential Exercises **19**, 225 (1992)
19. Zalatan, K.A., Mayer, D.F.: Developing a learning culture: assessing changes in student performance and perception. Developments in Business Simulation & Experiential Exercises **26**, 45–51 (1999)
20. Sitzmann, T.: A meta-analytic examination of the instructional effectiveness of computer-based simulation games. Pers. Psychol. **64**(2), 489–528 (2011)
21. Jenson, J., Suzanne, C.: Gender, simulation, and gaming: research review and redirection. Simul. Gaming **41**(1), 51–71 (2010)
22. Thomas, L.R.: A psychometric analysis of Kolb's learning styles inventory. Exploring Experiential Learning: Simulations and Experiential Exercises **5**, 193–198 (1978)
23. Kolb, D.A.: Experiential Learning: Experience as a Source of Learning and Development. Prentice Hall, Englewood Cliffs, NJ (1984)
24. Washbush, J.B., Gosenpud, J.: Student Attitudes About Policy Course Simulations. Developments in Business Simulation & Experiential Exercises **18**, 105–110 (1991)

25. Kaenzig, R., Hyatt, E.M., Anderson, S.: Gender differences in college of business educational experiences. J. Edu. Bus. **83**(2), 95–100 (2007)
26. Slavin, R.: Enhancing Intergroup Relations in Schools: Cooperative Learning and Other Strategies. In: Hawley, W.D., Jackson, A.W. (eds.) Toward a Common Destiny: Improving Race and Ethnic Relations, pp. 291–314. Jossey Bass, San Francisco (1995)
27. Loo, R.: A meta-analytic examination of Kolb's learning style preferences among business majors. J. Edu. Bus. **77**(5), 252–256 (2002)
28. Celenk, S., Karakis, O.: The usage level of general learning strategies of students attending different faculties "The AIBU example. AIBU, Egitim Faculty of Dergisi. **7**(1), 26–46 (2007)

# The Impact of Changing Moods Based on Real-Time Biometric Measurements on Player Experience

Helena Polman[✉]

Breda University of Applied Sciences, Breda, The Netherlands
helenapolman@live.nl

**Abstract.** This paper focused on using mood changes created by biometric measurements to improve the player experience (PE). Currently, biometric measurements are being used in game experience research. Earlier studies focused on the possibilities of modifying the game experience with real-time biometric measurements. The biometric measurements were gathered from the Empatica E4 and used to apply the mood changes while questionnaires were used before and after the experience to gather data. For the adapted group, the weather effects increased when their arousal increased while it remained constant for the control group. The adapted group rated their emotions, the overall experience and game features lower than the control group, just as their arousal and valence. The player experience was not enhanced but reduced. There are many explanations for this finding such as the negative feedback loop and the negative connotations of rain. The emotions and the experience of the participants were negatively impacted by the heavy storm indicating that real-time biometric measurements could impact the PE which could be improved by a positive feedback loop.

**Keywords:** Emotional arousal · Feedback loop · Maze · Transitional music · Virtual reality

## 1 Introduction

A key component of games is the player experience (PE). When the PE is not enjoyable, it has an impact on the graphics and the gameplay [1]. The entertainment of the player, created by the interactivity of the game, is frequently seen as the definition of PE [2]. It is suggested that without players, games have little or no value [3]. PE testing is constantly evolving since the creative media industry is competitive. The use of biometric measurements in the gaming industry is one of these evolutions. Interest has been shown in implementing biometric measurement in the gaming industry [4]. The integration of physiological measurements is to evaluate the emotional engagement of the player and has been demonstrated as a suitable method using sensors for the game industry [4]. The measurements could be acceleration, eye tracking, heart rate, skin connectivity and skin temperature [5]. The gathered data could be analysed and combined to create datasets such as the arousal or valence of the player [6].

© Springer Nature Switzerland AG 2022
U. Dhar et al. (Eds.): ISAGA 2021, LNCS 13219, pp. 171–181, 2022.
https://doi.org/10.1007/978-3-031-09959-5_15

Biometric measurements could be used to track the PE through a controller. An Xbox [7] 360 controller was altered to include biometric sensors [8]. Heart rate and movements are examples of biometric measurements performed by this altered controller. Sony [9] patented biometric measurements for the PlayStation 5 [10] controllers [11].

In the game industry, biometric measurements are mainly used in research to test game events [12], features [13] or social interactions [14]. The use of biometric measurements to manipulate the game experience in real-time is still in development [15]. Biometric measurements could be used to control characters in Flappy bird [16], Snake [17], World of Warcraft [18], Portal 2 [19] and racing games [20]. It is possible to modify game elements dynamically in a dynamic difficulty system. Here the skill level of the player dictates the difficulty of the game and could be linked to the biometric measurements of the players [21, 22]. Applying biometrics in games can also be done differently by creating a framework [6]. The overall impact of these design changes on the PE has not been assessed. In this framework, Electrocardiogram sensors, electrodermal activity sensors and an accelerometer were used. Four different factors were adjusted based on the measurements. A threshold in the biometric measurements was set for the shooting mechanic, were the player would attack once the threshold was exceeded. The attack of the enemies would become more powerful after the player crosses an arousal level. The emotions of the player impacted the mood of the game [23], creating positive feelings for a bright environment and negative feelings for a dark environment. The difference between the framework [6] and the presented study is that the study focused more on the relationship between the design change and the PE. No research was done on the impact of the framework. The framework is more detailed than the study since the impact of changing one aspect of the game was researched.

In the study, the PE is measured using different indicators. The first indicator is the emotions and feelings of the participants since the PE is often described as the amount of fun of the player [2]. The competence of the participant can also be an indicator for the PE. The enjoyment of the art style impacts the player experience because different types of visual styles are pleasing to different people [24]. Another indicator of the PE is the immersion of the participants which keeps the interests to suspend disbelief. The final indicator used in this study is the experience with virtual reality (VR). To create a pleasant PE, the participant should help with the immersion without motion sickness from VR.

For this study, a VR corn maze was created with two different versions, one (the adapted version) included weather effects that were manipulated when emotional arousal peaks occurred. The other version (the control version) was a set experience without any manipulation of the weather effects. When the arousal levels of the participants were above a set threshold in the adapted version, the weather got worse.

The study focused on improving the PE by applying mood changes based on real-time biometric measurements in a virtual reality corn maze game. The assumption was that manipulating the game world using real-time biometric measurements would impact the PE.

## 2 Method

Two versions of the VR corn maze were developed for the study. The first version of the maze had a constant experience that did not change due to the biometric measurements. The weather and lighting for the second version of the maze were changed due to the biometric measurements.

### 2.1 Research Design

The environment needed to create a visible arousal spike in the biometric measurements of the participant. A questionnaire was made to understand the emotions evoked by different environments using 15 different mood boards. For each mood board, the participant had to rate the pleasantness from one to five, which can be seen in Fig. 1 which shows the emotions evoked by the pictures.

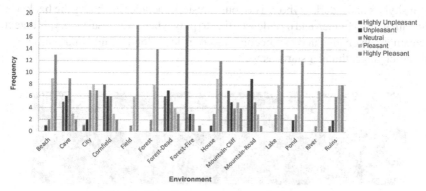

**Fig. 1.** The pleasantness of the mood boards

To trigger the mood changing multiple times, the VR environment should evoke both negative and positive feelings. The cornfield mood board was the only one that seems to evoke a range of different emotions. The horror genre influenced the participants' view on a cornfield, making it chilling when it is dark and soothing when it is light. To make the experience enjoyable, a gameplay element was added by making it a corn maze.

All mazes were completed by two participants who did not participate in the final experiment, which gave an indication of the time it would take to complete the maze. Figure 2 displays the mazes and the completion times of two participants for each maze. The experience was intended to take a couple of minutes, which meant that maze 1, 4, and 6 were too short. With the changing mood and extra decorations, it was expected that the completion time would increase by a couple of minutes. The fifth maze was chosen to keep the experience relatively short. This maze was not the longest, but long enough for the biometric measurements to impact the PE.

A closed area is the start of the VR environment where the maze is the next part of the environment and at the end is another closed-off part. The environment is decorated to resemble a farm. The Empatica E4 [25], the biometric measurement device used for

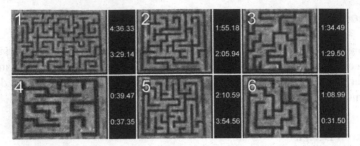

**Fig. 2.** Six different mazes and their completion times (minutes)

the study, needed some time to obtain a baseline for the Galvanic Skin Response (GSR) and the skin temperature of the participant. The gates to the maze would open once the calibration was done.

Three different lighting sets were created (Fig. 3). Two different skyboxes were used, a bright skybox and a dark skybox. The sound system includes changing the background music, rain getting louder, and thunder starting to play when an arousal peak was detected. The weather can change and can become more or less cloudy, rainy and windy. At the last weather stage, thunder starts as well.

**Fig. 3.** The different moods and weather states

Ten zones were created in the VR environment (Fig. 4). In the starting and ending zones and zone 0, calm music played. Halfway between calm and stormy, transitional music would play, when the mood had entirely changed, the stormy scary music would play. Zone 1 works the same as zone 0. As a crow flies past the participant in zone 2, the intensity of the light source placed inside the scarecrows increased, and the transitional music played unless the mood had changed to a full storm. Zone 3 and 4 were almost identical to zone two; the only difference is that there is no crow. In zone 5, light rain started and stayed for all the zones after this and scary music would be playing continuously. A crow crawl sound would play occasionally and the intensity of the light in the scarecrows increased. Zone 6 was almost the same as zone 5; another crow flies past the participant in this zone. Zone 7 was identical to zone 5. Zone 8 and 9 were the same; the music changed back to the transitional music when the mood was not fully stormy. The intensity of the light inside the scarecrow would decrease.

The Empatica E4 [25] did not record the biometric measurements; it was more important for the plug-in to function in Unity [26]. A Python plug-in was used five requirements to discover the presence of an arousal peak [27]. According to rule number

**Fig. 4.** Different zones of the maze

1, the period between the stimulus and response had to be between one and five seconds. Rule number 2 stated that there had to be a drop in the skin temperature after the peak. The latency affected the rising time according to rule number 3. Rule number 4 stated that a steeper slope to the peak indicated a more intense arousal peak. According to the rule 5, the recovery time had to be between one to 10 s. When an arousal peak was determined, the plug-in would send a signal to Unity which could change the weather and lighting in the environment [26]. It took the participants roughly eight minutes to complete the maze.

## 2.2  Materials

The hardware for the biometric measurements was the Empatica E4 wristband [25]. The GSR data and skin temperature were used based on factors that showed an arousal peak [28]. The Python [27] plug-in [29] and the Patterns of Basic Emotions [23] were used as supporting theory.

The Unity Engine [26] was chosen because it was familiar to the participants. The assets for the corn maze were gathered from different places, and two different VR head-mounted displays (HMD) were used.

The assets were selected because they looked like they belonged on a farm. A bright and a dark skybox were used. A couple of different weather particle effects were added in the Unity scene. The sound effects of a crow, rain, thunder, wind and background music were gathered from Quixel Bridge [30], the Unity asset store [31], websites like TurboSquid [32] or a universal sound FX library [33].

There were two HMD, the HTC Vive Pro and HTC Cosmos [34]. Three different VR set-ups were used of which two of them were used for testing the research while the other was for the development. The Experience lab [35], a research group at Breda University of Applied Sciences that works on interactive experiences, was used as the main set-up for the study. A private set-up was used for the participants that could not travel to the campus in Breda (Fig. 5).

**Fig. 5.** Experience lab VR set-up and private VR set-up

## 3  Method

A playtest session was held to discover if the player experience can be enhanced by using real-time biometric data to adapt the mood of a VR game environment. The biometric measurements of the Empatica E4 [2] were used to change the mood in the maze.

Data about the emotions and player experience of the participants before and after the playtest session was gathered from the pre-experience and post-experience questionnaires which gave insights into the feelings of the participants before and after the maze, their experience while playing the maze and their PE. The pre-experience questionnaire included questions about general information such as participant number, time and research group. Participant information such as age, gender, nationality and level of education was gathered if the participant stresses easily, or was a gamer, or had experienced VR before, and their favourite game genre. The last part of this questionnaire measured the arousal, valence and current emotions of the participants [36, 37].

The post-experience questionnaire started with whether or not the participants completed the maze and the time they took. The same questions as in the pre-experience questionnaire were used for the measurement of the arousal, valence and current emotions to compare the participants' emotions before and after the experience. To gather information about the PE, data was gathered on the feelings during the experience, skill of the participant, visuals, engagement and VR. The last part of the questionnaire focused on how recommendable the experience was and the overall grade. A combination of the Game Experience Questionnaire and Player Experience of Need Satisfaction [38, 39] was used. Both questionnaires used the Likert scale from extremely agree to extremely disagree, apart from open questions and emotions. The data analysis was done in SPSS [40].

Thirty-four participants were recruited through convenience sampling. Seventeen participants each were randomly assigned to the control group and the adapted group for the Empatica E4 [25]. The adapted group had real-time biometric measurement mood adaptations, and in the control group, the biometric measurements did not influence the mood. Since the experiment was done in the Netherlands at a university, the majority of the participants were Western European and between the ages of 20 and 30. The experience took place in two locations in the Netherlands, Breda and Zutphen in March 2021.

Fourteen participants were male and 20 were female. The mean age of the participants was 27.5 years, with the youngest being 12 years and the oldest being 69 years old. The 12 year old participant had played with permission from both the parents. One parent participated before the child and the other parent watched the spouse. The study had 28 Dutch participants. Out of the other six participants, four were Bulgarians. The remaining two participants were from Germany and Zimbabwe. Twelve participants had not used any type of VR over the past 12 months. Ten of the remaining participants had used VR once. The last two participants had more experience with VR and had used it 20–30 and 50+ times respectively.

## 4   Results

The control group all had the same experience. The mood was sunny until zone 5, when the rain started. There were five different outcomes for the adapted group (Fig. 6). The biometric measurements of the participant could stay low without fluctuation, implying the participant was calm, due to only sunny weather. With the second outcome, the biometric measurements could stay low with minor fluctuations, implying that the participant was reasonably calm due to the mostly sunny experience. The biometric measurements could continuously stay high, suggesting that the participant was emotionally aroused. The experience quickly went from sunny to stormy. The biometric measurements could stay high and still fluctuate, implying reasonably aroused participants, which lead to a mood that fluctuated between a light storm and a heavy storm. Alternatively, the biometric measurements could fluctuate, insinuating that the participant got emotionally aroused at certain places, which caused an experience where the

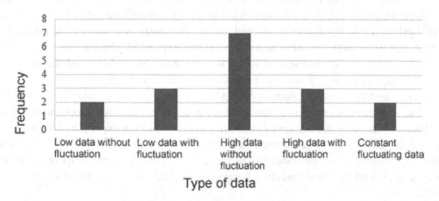

**Fig. 6.** Experience of the adapted group

mood was constantly shifting. The participants were not aware of other participants having a different experience.

The means and standard deviations of six dimensions of the adapted and controlled experiments are shown in Table 1 below.

**Table 1.** Means and standard deviations

| RESEARCH CONDITION | | MEAN | STD. DEVIATION | N |
|---|---|---|---|---|
| ADAPTED EXPERIENCE | EMOTIONS | 4,1397 | ,56403 | 17 |
| | FEELINGS | 4,0368 | ,52434 | 17 |
| | COMPETENCE | 3,6029 | ,55943 | 17 |
| | ART STYLE | 4,1569 | ,56357 | 17 |
| | IMMERSION | 3,6209 | ,54157 | 17 |
| | VR | 4,2843 | ,54571 | 17 |
| CONTROLLED EXPERIENCE | EMOTIONS | 4,5441 | ,41208 | 17 |
| | FEELINGS | 4,2868 | ,49144 | 17 |
| | COMPETENCE | 3,7500 | ,45928 | 17 |
| | ART STYLE | 4,4216 | ,57166 | 17 |
| | IMMERSION | 4,0458 | ,66442 | 17 |
| | VR | 4,3725 | ,49487 | 17 |

## 5   Discussion

Improving the PE by applying real-time biometric mood changes to a game was the intention of the study. Both study groups rated the overall experience pleasant and worth recommending. A minor yet visible dissimilarity could be seen in the data of the control and adapted groups. The participants felt better after the experience than before and the control group felt better than the adapted group. The maze was more difficult for the adapted group due to the worsening weather, which explained why the participants felt less skilled. The visuals, immersion and VR experience were also rated lower by the adapted group. Thus, the PE was not enhanced but rather reduced.

It is possible that arousal changes during the game play do not make for a better PE [41]. The worsening weather may have created a negative feedback loop which would have been enhanced by the negative connotations of rain and storm [42]. It had a negative effect on the feelings of the participants and impacted the sight of the participants. It was taxing for the eyes, the lower-rated visual style, VR experience and competence which could be explained by the connection between real-time biometric mood changes and the PE.

The reduction of PE does not mean that the PE could not be enhanced using real-time biometric data. If a positive feedback loop was created instead, the PE possibly could have been enhanced. The possibility of combining real-time biometric measurements with VR games is relatively new. There has not been much academic research in this field due to which comparing data in the study has proven to be a challenge.

## 5.1  Limitations

Some improvements could be made to the VR corn maze. The resolution and frame rate in VR was sufficient but not optimal. The corn maze walls could have been made denser. Places in the VR environment were not properly lit and some signposts were not readable. Every time the mood changed, the crops reset to their original position. These issues were known but could not be resolved in time due to the scope of the project.

The most important part of the VR environment was the changing of the mood which could have been handled differently. It was used to suit the scope of the project. The lack of an arousal peak could be used as a trigger for the changing of the mood.

The plug-in worked adequately but could have been tweaked more. Arousal peaks were detected occasionally, giving a null or a maximum value. This issue could not be resolved due to the limited time.

Due to the COVID-19 pandemic, gathering participants to play the game was difficult. The extent of their VR experience was therefore limited. The lack of participants resulted in two different game locations.

## 5.2  Future Indications

A continuation of the present study is suggested to inspect the negative relation between the mood changes and the PE. A different implementation of the real-time biometric mood changes could create a positive relationship between the mood changes and the PE, and therefore, further study into this positive relationship is advised. Increasing the number of participants and using a more diverse sample could create a more accurate assessment.

The possible uses for changing a game based on biometrics could be personalization, a dynamic difficulty system and physiological horror elements. A game experience using real-time biometric measurements to customize sound, character or environment design could improve the PE [43]. Real-time biometric measurements could be used for real-time adjustable difficulty settings which could prevent players from getting frustrated due to difficulty of the game and would improve the PE [44].

A different type of implementation could use real-time biometric measurements to increase psychological horror elements in games. If the measurement would pass a set threshold, the actual horror event could happen. If the threshold is not reached, the tension could increase [6, 45].

# References

1. Hagen, U.: Designing for player experience: how professional game developers communicate design visions. J. Gaming Virtual Worlds **3**(3), 259–275 (2011). https://doi.org/10.1386/jgvw.3.3.259_1

2. Hooda, H.: Factors Affecting Gaming Experience, 55 p. (2018)
3. Schell, J.: The Art of Game Design, 2nd edn. Taylor & Francis, Abingdon (2014)
4. Mirza-Babaei, P., Nacke, L. E., Gregory, J., Collins, N., Fitzpatrick, G.: How does it play better? Exploring user testing and Biometric Storyboards in games user research. In: Conference on Human Factors in Computing Systems - Proceedings, pp. 1499–1508 (2013). https://doi. org/10.1145/2470654.2466200
5. El-Nasr, M.S., Drachen, A., Canossa, A.: Game Analytics. Springer London, London (2013). https://doi.org/10.1007/978-1-4471-4769-5
6. Seixas, M.C.B.: A framework for the manipulation of video game elements using the player's biometric data (2016)
7. Xbox. Xbox (n.d.). https://www.xbox.com/nl-NL/?xr=mebarnav. Accessed 27 Oct 2020
8. Stanford University. Stanford University (n.d.). https://www.stanford.edu/. Accessed 15 Oct 2020
9. Sony: Sony (n.d.). https://www.sony.nl/. Accessed 27 Oct 2020
10. PlayStation. Officiële PlayStation®-website: Consoles, games, accessoires en meer (n.d.). https://www.playstation.com/nl-nl/. Accessed 27 May 2021
11. Weiss, E.: Will the PlayStation 5 Have a Biometric Controller? FindBiometrics (2020b). https://findbiometrics.com/will-the-playstation-5-have-a-biometric-controller-902256/
12. Mandryk, R., Inkpen, K.M.: Physiological indicators for the evaluation of co-located collaborative play. In: Proceedings of the CSCW 2004, pp. 102–111. ACM Press (2004)
13. Tafalla, R.J.: Gender differences in cardiovascular reactivity and game performance related to sensory modality in violent video game play. J. Appl. Soc. Psychol. **37**(9), 2008–2023 (2007). https://doi.org/10.1111/j.1559-1816.2007.00248.x
14. Ravaja, N., Saari, T., Turpeinen, M., Laarni, J., Salminen, M., Kivikangas, M.: Spatial presence and emotions during video game playing: does it matter with whom you play? Presence: Teleoperators Virtual Environ. **15**(4), 381–392 (2006). https://doi.org/10.1162/pres.15.4.381
15. Kivikangas, J.M., et al.: A review of the use of psychophysiological methods in game research. J. Gaming Virtual Worlds **3**(3), 181–199 (2011). https://doi.org/10.1386/jgvw.3.3.181_1
16. Desai, K.: How I Played Flappy Bird With My Mind. Towards Data Science (2019). https://towardsdatascience.com/how-i-played-flappy-bird-with-my-mind-e1e5b4da59ce
17. Jain, M.: Playing Games with your Mind: Brain Controlled Snake. Medium (2018). https://medium.com/@mayankj2112/playing-games-with-your-mind-brain-controlled-snake-54a65dca1391
18. BCITugraz. World of Warcraft EEG. Youtube (2010). https://www.youtube.com/watch?v=jXpjRwPQC5Q&t=142s
19. Tugraz. Tugraz video's – Portal 2. Tugraz (n.d.). https://www.tugraz.at/institute/ine/research/videos/. Accessed 12 Oct 2020
20. Green Cave Studio. Mind Controlled Games. Youtube (2015). https://www.youtube.com/watch?v=HUra6i_UCZE
21. Kuikkaniemi, K., Laitinen, T., Turpeinen, M., Saari, T., Kosunen, I., Ravaja, N.: The influence of implicit and explicit biofeedback in first-person shooter games. In: Conference on Human Factors in Computing Systems - Proceedings, vol. 2, pp. 859–868 (2010). https://doi.org/10.1145/1753326.1753453
22. Chanel, G., Rebetez, C., Bétrancourt, M., Pun, T.: Emotion assessment from physiological signals for adaptation of game difficulty. IEEE Trans. Syst. Man Cybern. Part A: Syst. Hum. **41**(6), 1052–1063 (2011). https://doi.org/10.1109/TSMCA.2011.2116000
23. Russell, J.A.: A circumplex model of affect. J. Pers. Soc. Psychol. **39**(6), 1161–1178 (1980). https://doi.org/10.1037/h0077714
24. James, L.: How to Create Atmosphere in Video Games. GameSpew (2019). https://www.gamespew.com/2019/05/create-atmosphere-in-games/

25. Empatica. EmpaticaE4. Empatica (n.d.). https://www.empatica.com/en-eu/research/e4/. Accessed 1 Nov 2020
26. Unity. Unity (n.d.-a). https://unity.com/. Accessed 24 Jan 2021
27. Python. Welcome. Python.Org (2021). https://www.python.org/
28. Kyriakou, K., et al.: Detecting moments of stress from measurements of wearable physiological sensors. Sensors (Switzerland) **19**(17) (2019). https://doi.org/10.3390/s19173805
29. Collet, C., Vernet-Maury, E., Delhomme, G., Dittmar, A.: Autonomic nervous system response patterns specificity to basic emotions. J. Auton. Nerv. Syst. **62**(1–2), 45–57 (1997). https://doi.org/10.1016/S0165-1838(96)00108-7
30. EpicGames. Quixel. Quixel (n.d.). https://quixel.com/. 23 Jan 2021
31. Unity. Asset Store. Unity Asset Store (n.d.-b). https://assetstore.unity.com. Accessed 23 Jan 2021
32. TurboSquid. 3D Models for Professionals (n.d.). https://www.turbosquid.com/. Accessed 4 May 2021
33. Imphenzia. Universal Sound FX—Audio Sound FX. Unity Asset Store (2018). https://assetstore.unity.com/packages/audio/sound-fx/universal-sound-fx-17256#description
34. HTC VIVE. Find the right high-end VR system for you—VIVE United States (n.d.). https://www.vive.com/us/product/. Accessed 4 May 2021
35. Breda University of Applied Sciences. INT Research theme Designing and Managing Experiences (n.d.). https://www.buas.nl/en/research/themes/designing-and-managing-experiences. Accessed 24 Jan 2021
36. Bradley, M.M., Lang, P.J.: Measuring emotion: the self-assessment manikin and the semantic differential. J. Behav. Ther. Exp. Psychiatry **25**(1), 49–59 (1994)
37. Diener, E., et al.: New well-being measures: short scales to assess flourishing and positive and negative feelings. Soc. Indic. Res. **97**(2), 143–156 (2010)
38. IJsselsteijn, W.A., de Kort, Y.A.W., Poels, K.: Game Experience Questionnaire (2013). https://research.tue.nl/. https://eclass.uoa.gr/modules/document/file.php/DI411/PAPERS/Evaluation/Game%20Experience%20Questionnaire%20English.pdf
39. Ryan, R.M., Rigby, C.S., Przybylski, A.: The motivational pull of video games: a self-determination theory approach. Motiv. Emot. **30**, 344–360 (2006). https://doi.org/10.1007/s11031-006-9051-8
40. IBM. SPSS Software (n.d.). Netherlands—IBM. https://www.ibm.com/nl-en/analytics/spss-statistics-software. Accessed 24 Jan 2021
41. Mitas, O., et al.: More is not better: the emotional dynamics of an excellent experience. J. Hosp. Tour. Res. (2020). https://doi.org/10.1177/1096348020957075
42. Denissen, J.J.A., Butalid, L., Penke, L., van Aken, M.A.G.: The effects of weather on daily mood: a multilevel approach. Emotion **8**(5), 662–667 (2008). https://doi.org/10.1037/a0013497
43. Jarrahi, J.: Biometric data for music, game personalization draws controversy, research. Biometric Update (2021). https://www.biometricupdate.com/202104/biometric-data-for-music-game-personalization-draws-controversy-research
44. Baldwin, A., Johnson, D., Wyeth, P.A.: The effect of multiplayer dynamic difficulty adjustment on the player experience of video games. In: CHI 2014 Extended Abstracts on Human Factors in Computing Systems (2014). https://doi.org/10.1145/2559206.2581285
45. Jimenez, M.C., James, A.M.S., Scirea, M., Cermak, D.: Dreadful Virtualities (2017)

# Ordering the Disorder: Preparing Paramedics for Unexpected and Unsafe Mass Casualty Incidents

Pip Lyndon-James[1]([✉]) and Elyssebeth Leigh[2]

[1] Sydney, Australia
[2] University of Technology Sydney, Ultimo, Australia

**Abstract.** Mass Casualty Incidents (MCI) occur when the number of patients in an incident exceed the number of available resources, require a multi-disciplinary approach and are protracted; fortunately, they are rare. When they do occur, first responders –including paramedics, police and fire fighters - must respond instantly and effectively. This article introduces research on use of an MCI simulation as the capstone subject for a degree program preparing student paramedics for the disorder and chaos of their first MCI. The University of Tasmania's (UTAS) Sydney campus ran three iterations of an MCI simulation for students in the Bachelor of Paramedic Practice degree. The MCI required *paramedics* to respond to a *gas explosion involving mass casualties in a public setting* - using 30 moulage enhanced (makeup-based mock injuries) *simulated patients* in varying degrees of distress. The MCI scenario was specifically designed as an immersive experience within which participants could review their current capabilities. This article reflects on the impact of the third iteration, drawing on post event interviews to review experiences occurring during/after such large scale, complex, stress-inducing simulations. Fidelity to conditions in real MCIs was elevated through use of intrusive noise, simulated patients and live radio communications. The impact on participants – both facilitators and students as patients or paramedics – has been long lasting. Future research will consider the extent to which the effect of emotional engagement and skills acquisition persist and re-surface long after the event is over.

**Keywords:** Simulation · Paramedics · Mass casualty incident · Simulated patient · Intrusive noise · Fidelity · Skill acquisition · Experience-based learning

## 1 Introduction

*When I think about that training day, I see how it prepared me to know what I should do, that the scale gets overwhelming but that's part of what happens, crews will go renegade if not included in plans, that clear communication and teamwork is key, and staying calm and following the process helps to keep things running as smooth as possible.* (Graduated participant reflecting on events described here).

© Springer Nature Switzerland AG 2022
U. Dhar et al. (Eds.): ISAGA 2021, LNCS 13219, pp. 182–196, 2022.
https://doi.org/10.1007/978-3-031-09959-5_16

In Australia, paramedics are health care professionals who usually work outside hospital contexts treating medical and trauma emergencies beginning at the site of an incident and continuing during transport to relevant hospital support and/or between such facilities. Formal education programs in Australia provide paramedic students with strong theoretical foundations, practical skill application, and clinical placements.

However, there are indicators that this cannot constitute fully adequate preparation for the disorder of real emergencies, which graduates can expect to encounter in their workplaces. Acquiring skills in isolated sequences does not fully prepare graduates for the confusion created by multiple simultaneous demands being made on their skills and knowledge. Thus, this experience was specifically intended to be messy, noisy, demanding with inherently uncertain outcomes.

## 2 Mass Casualty Incidents

Mass Casualty Incidents (MCI) occur when the location, number, severity, or type of live casualties, requires extraordinary resources (e.g. the number of patients requiring treatment exceeds the number of trained staff available to deal with them). MCIs may have human origins (rail or road accidents) or be the result of natural disasters (earthquakes, bushfires, cyclones, floods, epidemics/pandemics) and include care of evacuated populations.

MCI are unexpected emergencies, involving messy, noisy environments where familiar procedures will be challenged by intensified emotional and physical demands on first responders. To enable practice of formal procedures in volatile and uncertain conditions University of Tasmania's (UTAS) Sydney campus conducted MCI simulations for 2nd year students as a capstone unit in the Bachelor of Paramedic Practice degree. The scenario was created as a *gas explosion involving mass casualties in a public setting* employing 30 *simulated patients* (1st year students) enhanced by moulage (makeup-based mock injuries) with roles indicating their physical condition. Second year students became *paramedic first responders* with functions self-selected from relevant roles including on site, command and control liaison positions.

The scenario, situated in a large relatively secluded open space on university grounds, included distraught patients with minor injuries, who were mobile and distracting for paramedics, as well as patients in various life-threatening conditions with (simulated) complex traumatic injuries. A few patients were designated as *deceased* and some were instructed to *die* during the event. Three patients were depicted as advanced age (>75 years), with grey hair, age-wrinkled faces, and appropriate clothing. Figure 1 shows a moment in the hectic efforts to triage *patients* before deciding medical treatment and evacuation sequences. Triage is a method for determining the severity of illness or injury of patient based on physiological signs and physical activity.

## 3 Rationale

For effective transition from university to unique paramedic workplaces, students need a deep and visceral understanding of what will happen when they encounter such complex, and disordered MCI environments. A limited amount of operational exposure occurs in

**Fig. 1.** 'Mass casualty' – students gaining paramedic practice in a simulated chaotic environment

clinical placements where students, as supernumeraries are able to observe/assist experienced paramedics. Such experiences go some way towards helping students develop important and requisite professional capabilities. Other relevant and specific clinical skills are acquired via use of manikin-based simulations. However, in an MCI, *simulated patients* [1] (real people *in role* as patients) create dynamic learning environments because their emotional engagement produces unpredictable behaviours and continuing levels of intrusive noise hampering essential lifesaving actions. Provision of such an immersive experience is essential for the development of confident and capable paramedics. Notably, such improvements are only achievable if *taught in the undergraduate and early clinical training years* [1].

The design of this MCI simulation deliberately chose to use *simulated patients* (in lieu of manikins) to create a high-fidelity learning event where animated engagement would be essential to establishing an overall environment of disorder. Fidelity is a contested term in simulation given that it may infer such terms as authenticity, degree of realism regarding actual events, and plausibility consistent with real events. This means that simulations must select component/s - from among all that is possible – on which to focus the level of fidelity. Given that the students receive extensive training in sequential management of injuries/patient conditions, the MCI designers chose to replicate the noisy, confusing uncertainty of a sudden emergency where specific skills (inserting a cannula, managing an airway) were subservient to acting effectively in chaotic conditions.

## 4    This MCI Scenario

Events reported here occurred during the third iteration of the MCI. It involved 100 participants, 49 of whom were 2nd year students working *as if* paramedics attempting to bring the chaos to order. Their task was to manage 30 simulated patients (50% female and 50% male, aged 18 and 75) enacted by 1st year students in the Bachelor of Paramedic

Practice. Other participants included academic staff as simulation directors/observers, and relevant qualified professionals supporting the students.

All roles in the simulation were played by student participants, with staff providing educational as well as work, health, and safety support. Student paramedic participants self-selected their role choosing from a management framework representing a formal chain of command. Patients were to be extricated from the scene, as delegated by a site supervisor, to a casualty clearing station for reassessment and hospital allocation.

It is totally impossible to replicate - in the calm sequencing of an academic paper – the noisy chaotic conditions that unfolded on the lawn that morning. Some *patients* spontaneously decided to act-out their *distress* becoming both a nuisance to the *paramedics* and emblematic of how people in real emergency situations may behave. Some *paramedics* were (at least temporarily) confounded by the paradoxical demands of specific health management and general situation control. The impact of this *intrusive noise* created by a multiplicity of micro-events associated with patients, along with the competing demands of patients and management requirements will be the subject of future research. On this occasion it was a surprising and unsettling factor affecting almost every part of the scene.

Figure 2 captures a moment of apparent calm among the chaos of deciding who to extricate and in what order. The boundary between simulation and reality was extended through engagement with the real workings of NSW Ambulance by linking the MCI medical commander's decision process to actual command and control conditions concerning extrication of patients to hospital. This was done via live communication radios, provided by NSW Ambulance - a collaboration with the real world which made the simulation closer to reality.

**Fig. 2.** Managing the chaos - planning the extrication order of patients

Team leaders and paramedics extricated patients to a simulated hospital in a nearby university building, *handing over* to a real Registered Nurse, again paralleling real life. The event lasted four hours, including time for briefing and debriefing.

## 5   Review of the Literature

### 5.1   Increasing Number of Mass Casualty Incidents

The rapid rise in the occurrence of natural disasters and wilful acts of mass destruction resulting in MCIs requires a focused view on preparation of Registered Paramedic [2]. The high number of casualties generated by such incidents often results in medical crises where the 'demand for medical care exceeds the capacity of supplies and staff available' [3] In order to manage this need, timely and effective decision-making processes are indispensable for positive patient outcomes [4] To ensure effective decision making, it is paramount that extensive preplanning and preparedness training is conducted to minimise morbidity and mortality [5].

Interestingly, it has been revealed that perceptions of preparedness are significantly correlated with the volume of training [6]. An inevitable challenge to learning about, and preparing for, such events is their lack of frequency [7]. Furthermore, there are indications that training delivery via *full-scale drills* (such as this MCI Simulation), rather than online learning provides better preparedness [8, 9]. A continuing issue is the limited amount of research into the value and validity of MCI simulations, made difficult by the comparatively low number of actual incidents of appropriate severity [7]. It is also clear that use of manikins for such research and learning purposes is not feasible for MCI learning events due to the large numbers required [10].

### 5.2   Achieving Appropriate Realism

Despite the latest technology in simulation, realism cannot be achieved if the learning environment is not contextualised to professional practice conditions [11]. As MCI exceeds the normal activities of emergency care in the field [12], it warrants a specific approach and requires testing of its durability in a pressurised high-fidelity event [13]. This requires the inclusion of sensory overload, which is imperative to allow realistic practise of skills [7]. Sensory overload, coupled with environmental fidelity [14], suggests that for maximum effect, participants must encounter real difficulties of communicating in noisy situations. Environmental fidelity can be achieved by utilising simulated patients [2] behaving as *people with or without actual disease who have been trained to portray a medical case* [15] Their inclusion in MCI simulations provides an emotional impact, ensuring a disordered environment and adding another dimension to simulated learning events.

### 5.3   Contextualising Experience-Based Learning

The excitement of the technology era, has in many contexts, shifted the learning focus to acquisition of clinical rather than interpersonal or field skills [14]. However, MCI simulations are expressly intended to elevate communication skills, augmenting confidence and providing experience in learning to mitigate the impact of unexpected obstacles [15]. A key point here is that *contextualised* learning is a) acquired from synergistic exchanges between people and environments, b) holistic and c) requires adaptability to the material world [16].

Simulation as *a technique …. to amplify real life experiences* [17] provides exactly such environments when students in health care can gain insights into the vital importance of understanding that *the secret of care of the patient; is in caring for the patient* [18]. Successful acquisition of this unique knowledge requires engagement in environments where participants must learn to choreograph their care of others within disordered situations.

## 6   Method

All participants contributed to an extensive post-event debriefing, and then, for the purposes of collecting data about participant experiences as paramedics the $2^{nd}$ year students were invited to participate in follow up research processes. Information about the study was provided via a *Participant Information Sheet*. All consent forms for their various responses to be used anonymously the research study itself, and all documents were approved by the UTAS Human Research Ethics Committee. Respondents participated in a large-scale debriefing session, followed by post event interviews, which utilised semi structured research questions, presented simultaneously to seven focus groups. Most of the data collected will be analysed and presented in future research reports. In this article some key early observations regarding overall responses, and facilitator observations are introduced to lay the foundation for the research ahead.

An hour was allocated to complete the interviews and 49 of the 50 $2^{nd}$ year students responded, 24 were female. The interviews were electronically recorded to enable transcription of the respondents' responses. An inductive thematic analysis was utilised, to allows for identification, analysis and illustration of emerging patterns within the research data [19]. All focus groups were conducted by different academics at the same time, and all were asked the same set of semi-structured questions.

## 7   Emerging Issues

Several issues emerging from the interview data, are beginning to highlight both the value and limitations of use of MCI learning strategies including the use of simulated patients. What follows are initial impressions arising from the emerging data. Direct quotes are included as indicative descriptions of responses.

### 7.1   Noise is More Than a Distractor

The most surprising initial observation concerns the impact of intrusive noise, which proved to be than just a distractor, moreover it seems possible that mitigation of such distractors can be learned. This event produced a variety of sources of intrusive noise, including the chain of command delegating tasks by radio; paramedics communicating with each other; the screams of patients in pain and patients with minor injuries demanding assistance. Most respondents noted that the presence of intrusive noise enhanced fidelity and allowed for immersion and cultivation of a unique problem-solving environment supporting the findings of Kaplan et al. [13].

Stress resulting from intrusive noise provides insights into the management of disordered environments. The purpose of simulated MCIs is to test participants against numerous stressors that *tax and overwhelm*. This MCI provided an immersive experience providing exposure to and appreciation of the difficulties in communicating during a real MCI. Respondents playing the ambulance control and ambulance command positions were staged separately from the scene of the simulated MCI and provided a commentary of the event from their unique perspective through the radio communications network. Figure 3 shows a rare moment of apparent peace as the Commanders wait for the next wave of patients.

**Fig. 3.** Commander and Deputy Commander engaged in managing the chaos during the simulated MCI

Interviewees specifically noted the elevation of stress among MCI participants, which occurred during extensive periods of noise. Symptoms of elevated stress included alterations in vocal tones, including changes in the *pitch of their voice*. Excessive stress was perceived when chain of command personnel on scene *stopped answering the radio*. These observations are congruent with a study that highlights the importance of *stimulation overload* to imitate stress produced by real MCIs [7].

The limitless array of intrusive noises was a challenging context, which while distracting, provided first-hand experience in learning to mitigate it. The noise was perceived by a team leader as, *a slap in the face initially* and then identified as beneficial for the development of thinking and professional behaviour. It appears that experience-based learning is not always appreciated by educational systems, which rely on classroom learning, literature-based concept acquisition, and teacher's knowledge [20]. However, direct personal experience can be a vital learning element as one respondent noted -

*when they are screaming in your face, you need that experience, that's really what it's about.*

Conversely an absence of noise from patients (shown in Fig. 4) was equally alarming for respondents, who noted that *the ones that were quiet, just lying there, they were the scary ones.* Experiencing a patient's silence was a prompt to seek immediate clinical action and reporting of the patient's severity up the chain of command.

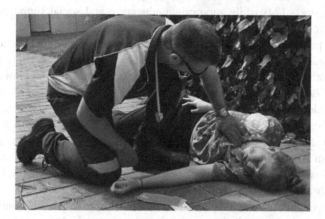

**Fig. 4.** Silence as a scary aspect of chaos

These experiences contextualised the complex communications required in the MCI and contrast with the limited interactions from manikins (usually as moaning or short static statements) [2]. While some manikins allow an operator to speak through them, such interactions fall short of simulating the intrusive noise that real patients generate, nor do they provide ways for learners to develop techniques to mitigate the noise.

Techniques used to combat intrusive noise relied on existing life experiences and ingenuity. Respondents reported that the noise of the event was comparable to playing in a football game with a crowd of fans or coming from a large rowdy family, where *airtime* is at a premium. Yet, it was also rationalised as expected of disordered environments that MCIs present - *you're not walking into a controlled environment!* The experiences led to reframing modes of communication, with non-verbal strategies become the new norm, including the use of direct eye contact and sign language. Learning to adapt practice to the needs of unique contexts is considered a universities responsibility, as graduates must be capable of negotiating workplaces that are constantly evolving [21]. Exposure to a practice MCI has potential to influence actions and reactions of participants in real MCIs making the skills transferable to professional practice.

### 7.2 Emotional Reactions by Simulated Patients as an Added Value

Patient care is a complex process that *requires human empathy and connection* [17]. While simulation using manikins is intended to replicate responses and reactions in a unique learning platform, [22] learners are aware that the manikin will not *die* [23]. For many respondents the possibility of *simulated death* of a real person, was a salient provision of fidelity. One respondent summarised that feeling by saying - *it was great that patients were dropping here and there, because it added more realism.*

Some respondents saw it differently, with one expressing sadness at a patient's death, because the patient was human and the inability to preserve life was emotionally confronting, even during a simulation. This demonstrates the value of incorporating human factors into simulation [17], since exposure to such feelings prepares students for future professional practice; and supports findings that paramedic personnel are at high risk of post-traumatic stress [24] while appropriate education and social support can provide major protective factors [25].

Simulated patients enhanced fidelity by incorporating human expression and non-verbal cues which cannot be accurately reproduced by manikins [23]. There were several mentions of verbal cues as vital for assessing patient pain and even comments such as *you could see his face, he was in pain.* Non-verbal signs of pain and suffering were considered hardest to endure, among them *wincing* and *withdrawing from touch* and such reactions enticed the paramedics to draw on their innate capacity to care, which is reliant on both attitude and emotion [26]. Respondents noticed that their caring extended beyond concern about physical pain and understood that patients' emotional pain was acutely *real.* Some felt this empathic response constrained their efficiency, because they felt *emotionally sucked in* and taxed in terms of both time and energy.

Some respondents used non-technical actions to improve patient comfort and felt that trust and connection with their patients were essential. An example of this was the paramedic who stood blocking the sun from shining on a patient's face. Such non-technical actions showed the coveted benevolence of the healthcare profession [26] brought to the fore by the presence of real people as patients during a simulation-based learning event.

## 7.3 Communication - A Key Capability

Advanced cognitive skills are required when working with simulated patients [22] as demonstrated by a respondent for whom the experience provided opportunities to evaluate their professional approach in the following terms: *Did I treat them with respect? Did I interact? Did I build that rapport?* This self-reflection demonstrates the connection to, and responsibility for, the patient as a human being, and it is one that respondents explained is *just not achievable with a manikin.*

Human interactions and communications are critical for safe patient care and require adherence to specific processes [22]. Figure 5 illustrates some of the technical aspects of the extrication process.

Respondents described how critical aspects of safety, such as seeking consent were more *real* than when practiced with manikin-based simulation, because *we explain things to them, but a manikin doesn't care.* This factor was considered during the design phase when it was decided that providing more complex information to simulated patients could cause unnecessary confusion so 'history taking' (Fig. 6) was limited during the MCI.

One valuable insight came from a respondent who explained they had experienced difficulty in communicating with a simulated patient. The respondent revealed that *I*

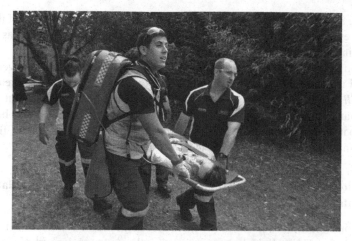

**Fig. 5.** Simulated patients increase difficulty of extrication

**Fig. 6.** History taking of a simulated patient by a paramedic

*was actually stuck for words, and I think that it is because I am used to walking up to a manikin* - and they found the real person intimidating.

## 7.4 Safety with Simulated Patients

Simulated learning experiences must be designed with participant safety as paramount. The literature explains the importance of managing potential risks arising from unpredictable actions and reactions in simulated events [22]. To ensure the safety of the participants, seven UTAS and ten allied personnel provided educational support and work, health and safety compliance. In the three years the event has been run, with over 200 participants, supervising staff have intervened in only a handful of occasions to correct manual handling processes. The safety record is due to extensive manual handling training and a thorough inspection of the simulated MCI scene conducted in the weeks prior to the event. Respondents appreciated the way in which their safety was prepared for, and maintained, throughout the event.

A thorough safety briefing of students and staff ensured expectations were clearly defined and maintained. Within this briefing, the term *No Duff* a phrase meaning *this is not a drill* was introduced as the 'safe word' to be used in the event that an injury was legitimate rather than simulated [27]. An example of this usage could be either a simulated patient or a paramedic saying *No duff, I have pain in my ankle*. To date no injuries from the event have been reported.

### 7.5  Additional Unexpected Outcome – Realising Limitations of Simulated Patients

There are some limitations noted in the literature about use of simulated patients. One of these is that realistic clinical observations to indicate physiological decline are not possible which potentially affects fidelity [10]. Preliminary observations from this UTAS study confirms this limitation. The 1st year students acting as simulated patients had limited knowledge and no clinical experience. Although they were required to memorise their condition and investigate symptoms of their injuries, their clinical presentations remained static. One paramedic identified this as an issue because *if you are giving a certain treatment, and they don't understand that, it might improve their observations*.

An allied concern relates to ineffective suspension of disbelief when the fidelity of an event suffers due to inconsistent portrayal of patient injury. This was identified by a small number of respondents who reported that patients occasionally broke out of character near the end of the event which affected fidelity. However, most respondents tended to disregard such disruptions and encouraged reengagement of the patient by remaining in their paramedic character. It is also noteworthy that the focus on the use of simulated patients is on communication, human engagement, and physical assessment [28]. Several respondents identified this as a central feature of their learning in a disordered untethered environment. In addition, they considered this as of higher importance than diagnostic clinical interventions.

### 7.6  Unforeseen Learning Gains

In this MCI simulation, opportunities to practise on simulated patients resulted in unforeseen learning gains. These included enabling respondents to recall tactics witnessed during clinical placements and test them out in a safe learning environment. Early observations revealed that the simulated patients promoted contractual agreements with their care giver, as one paramedic student reported: *We explained things to them, they knew what was happening, and you have kind of made an agreement*. Figure 7 illustrates difficulties encountered during manual handling.

Another indelible insight involved revelations about challenges with manual handling of real people because manikins are usually of a similar size and do not reflect the weight of a human patient. A team leader explained how: *One patient was a small woman and the next was a 120 kg man, every person you went to had challenges*. Respondents saw that such variation were contributing to their tacit knowledge and

**Fig. 7.** Complex manual handling

expressed appreciation for the opportunity of manually handling patients in a pressurised environment. The respondents also valued having sole responsibility for the management of difficult behaviours and being able to practise negotiation skills, a rare opportunity to develop them. As one respondent noted: during clinical placement the *real paramedics take over when things get messy.* It was also noted that graduates have limited initial ability to apply the knowledge gained in university study, making such events as this MCI vital for practice of key communication and observation skills [29].

The linkage of industry stakeholders to university via MCI events provides opportunities to witness student ability and invites open discussion of learning acquired in such simulations. The NSW Ambulance, as the clinical placement provider for UTAS paramedic students, generously granted time for staff to attend the event. UTAS academics who are not paramedics also attended the event and subsequently were able to further contextualise their classes to paramedic practice. It is noteworthy too, that The Makeup Technicians ™, a vocational education and training provider of moulage (use of special effects makeup – e.g. artificial wounds) incorporated the event into its curriculum. These makeup artist students had the opportunity to transform the 1st year students into bloodied patients under strictly timed conditions, providing them with unique challenges.

Further collaboration across the healthcare system was achieved when paramedic students conducted the handover of patients to real Registered Nurses. These healthcare professionals were also permitted insights into the complex nature of paramedic practice, rarely viewed by hospital staff.

## 8   Limitations

The simulation scenario did not include planned hazards nor require the attendance of allied emergency personnel. Although there could be additional benefits from the use of these components, it was not possible to incorporate them. This was mostly due to the inability of personnel to commit to such an event due to real emergency services operational demands. The authors also acknowledge that learning within this context described may not represent learning across all tertiary paramedic programs.

# 9  Conclusions

The increasing occurrence of Mass Casualty Incidents world-wide highlights the importance of healthcare professional preparedness. Yet, the limited frequency of large-scale
learning events can adversely impact community survival during MCIs. A key aim of
MCI learning events requires exposure to such factors as intrusive noise generated by
emotive patients and continuing uncertainty created by the scope of the incident and
ambiguity about available resources and support. Simulated exposure to such conditions
can help elicit benevolence, promote development of – both personal and agency - con-
tingency plans and flexible responsiveness, vital to graduates entering the workforce.
The opportunity to manage intrusively noisy environments is eliminated by manikin-
based simulation in such a simulated event, due to ill-fitting verbal and absent non-verbal
cues. In addition, the lack of emotional connection between manikins and participants,
demonstrates that not all professional practice aptitudes can be achieved via technical
simulation modalities.

There is a perceived disparity of simulation fidelity within the literature, concerning
the static clinical nature of the simulated patient. However, this study highlighted the
importance to MCI simulation events of appropriate levels of complexity in communication processes, the value of having real people rather than inanimate manikins for
patient assessment, and the adverse impact of high levels of noise on human engagement
in a disordered environment. The literature suggested that safety issues exist for participants; although over the three years this simulation has been conducted, no injuries
have been reported due to detailed planning, clear briefing of expectations and adequate
supervision.

Unforeseen learning gains, such as the experience of contractual agreements with
patients; behavioural management and challenges of patient weight and size during
manual handling, are all part of proposed further exploration. These initial observations
have highlighted the benefits of ordering the disorder in challenging environments, which
may well determine the future survival of a community during a real MCI.

Finally, Fig. 8 shows the entire cohort of simulated patients and staff, demonstrating the scale of the third, and largest of the exercises, and also indicates the sense of
achievement when it was concluded.

**Fig. 8.** MCI, fun, and research – the relief of success is palpable

# References

1. Garling, P.: Special Commission of Inquiry Acute Care Services in NSW Public Hospitals. Final Report of the Special Commission of Inquiry Acute Care Services in NSW Public Hospitals (2008) (2014). ISBN 978-1-921301-83-4. http://www.lawlink.nsw.gov.au/acsinq uiry. Accessed 22 Apr 2014
2. Kobayashi, L., Shapiro, M., Suner, S., Williams, K.: Disaster medicine: the potential role of high fidelity medical simulation for mass casualty incident training. R I Med. J. **86**(7), 196–200 (2003)
3. Admi, H., Eilon, Y., Hyams, G., Utitz, L.: Management of mass casualty events: the Israeli experience. J. Nurs. Scholarsh. **43**(2), 211–219 (2011)
4. Vincent, D.S., Burgess, L., Berg, B., Connolly, K.: Teaching mass casualty triage skills using iterative multi-manikin simulations. Prehosp. Emerg. Care **13**(2), 241–246 (2003)
5. Shover, H.: Understanding the chain of communication during a disaster. Perspect. Psychiatr. Care **43**(1), 4–14 (2007)
6. Fernandez, A.R., Studnek, J.R., Margolis, G.S., Crawford, J.M., Bentley, M.A., Marcozzi, D.: Disaster preparedness of national certified emergency medical services professionals. Acad. Emerg. Med. **18**(4), 403–412 (2011)
7. Wilkinson, W., Avstreih, D., Gruppen, L., Beier, K.P., Woolliscroft, J.: Using immersive simulation for training first responders for mass casualty incidents. Acad. Emerg. Med. **15**(11), 1152–1159 (2008)
8. Chaput, C.J., Deluhery, M.R., Stake, C.E., Martens, K.A., Cichon, M.E.: Disaster training for prehospital providers. Prehosp. Emerg. Care **11**(4), 458–465 (2007)
9. Wetta-Hall, R., Fredrickson, D., Ablah, E., Cook, D., Molgaard, C.: Knowing who your partners are: terrorism preparedness training for nurses. J. Contin. Educ. Nurs. **37**(3), 106–112 (2006)
10. Gillett, B., et al.: Simulation in a disaster drill: comparison of high fidelity simulators verse trained actors. Acad. Emerg. Med. **15**(11), 1144–1151 (2008)
11. Jones, C., Jones, P., Waller, C.: Simulation in prehospital care: teaching, testing and fidelity. J. Paramed. Pract. **3**(8), 430–434 (2011)

12. Spencer, C.: Managing mass casualty events is just the application of normal activity on a grander scale for the emergency health services, or is it? J. Emerg. Prim. Heal. Care **9**(1) (2011)

13. Kaplan, B., Connor, A., Ferranti, E., Holmes, L., Spencer, L.: Use of emergency preparedness disaster simulation with undergraduate nursing students. Public Health Nurs. **29**(1), 44–51 (2011)

14. Power, D., et al.: An evaluation of high fidelity simulation training for paramedics in Ireland. Int. Paramed. Pract. **2**(1), 11–18 (2013)

15. Collins, J.P., Harden, R.M.: The use of real patients, standardised patients and simulators in clinical examinations. AMEE Medical Education Guide No. 13, Association for Medical Education in Europe, UK, pp. 1–6 (2004)

16. Segers, M., Van der Haar, S.: The experiential learning theory. In: Kolb, D., Boud, D., Dochy, F., Gijbels, D., Segers, M., Van den Bossche, P. (eds.) Theories of Learning in the Workplace, pp. 52–65. Routledge, London & New York (2011)

17. Gaba, D.: The future vision of simulation in healthcare. Simul. Healthc. **2**(2), 126–135 (2007)

18. Peabody, F.W.: The care of the patient. JAMA **88**, 877–882 (1927)

19. Braun, V., Clarke, V.: Using thematic analysis in psychology. Qual. Res. Psychol. **3**(2), 77–101 (2006)

20. Kolb, D.: Experiential Learning: Experience as the Source of Learning and Development, pp. 34–36. Prentice-Hall, Englewood Cliffs (1984)

21. Bridgstock, R.: The graduate attributes we've overlooked: enhancing graduate employability through career management skills. High. Educ. Res. Dev. **28**(1), 31–44 (2009)

22. Seropian, M., Brown, K., Gavilanes, J., Driggers, B.: Simulation: not just a manikin. J. Nurs. Educ. **43**(4), 164–169 (2004)

23. Lasater, K.: High-Fidelity simulation and the development of clinical judgement: student experiences. J. Nurs. Educ. **46**(6), 269–276 (2007)

24. Regehr, C., Goldberg, G., Hughes, J.: Exposure to human tragedy, empathy and trauma in ambulance paramedics. Am. J. Orthopsychiatry **72**(4), 505–513 (2002)

25. Hung, K., Chan, E., Graham, C.: Disaster training: lessons learnt from the 2008 Sichuan China earthquake. Int. Paramed. Pract. **1**(4), 133–140 (2012)

26. McLeod, A.: Caring, competence and professional identities in medical education. Adv. Heal. Sci. Educ. **16**, 375–394 (2011)

27. Australian Emergency Management Institute: Australian Emergency Management Handbook 3, 2nd edn. ISBN 978-1-921152-29-0. Commonwealth Government, Commonwealth Attorney-General's Department, 1-100, Australia, Grey Publishing (2012)

28. Ziv, A., Wolpe, P.R., Small, S.D., Glick, S.: Simulation-based medical education: an ethical imperative. Acad. Med. **78**(8), 783–788 (2003)

29. O'Brien, K., Hartley, P., Dawson, D., Quick, J., Moore, A.: Work readiness in paramedic graduates: what are employers looking for? Int. Paramed. Pract. **3**(4), 98–104 (2013)

# Pleasures in Games: Conceptual Analysis of Fun and Its Constructs

Malay Dhamelia$^{(\boxtimes)}$ and Girish Dalvi

IDC School of Design, Indian Institute of Technology Bombay, Mumbai, India
{malay.dhamelia,girish.dalvi}@iitb.ac.in

**Abstract.** Fun is a fundamental driver of games. In serious games, the expectation to fulfil the purpose is oftentimes prioritised over elements of fun. In this paper, we analyse the concept of fun across domains and distinguish it from its allied constructs like flow, enjoyment, amusement, and so forth. We deduce the attributes of fun and elaborate concepts and their relationships. Our approach helps to advance the conceptualisation of fun in games from a design science perspective and suggests possible directions to assess serious games for better player experiences. Implications of the suggested attributes of fun in the domain of serious games are discussed.

**Keywords:** Fun · Conceptual analysis · Player experience · Serious games · Game design

## 1 Introduction

Designers have adopted elements of games to various non-game contexts [1]. Game-based learning, gamification, and serious games are instances of such applications. These efforts aim to improve the efficacy of the task at hand by improving engagement with the content. For example, exergames (a special case of serious games) aim to make players exert physical effort in the most efficient way possible, and game-based learning techniques would focus on better learning outcomes. In this sense, the content to be gamified is designed and evaluated, but player experiences in such games are not designed, they're only evaluated.

Gamifying a context involves applying game elements to non-game contexts [1]. A typical game has anatomical game elements (like goals, rules, mechanics, assets, and so forth) and player experiential elements (like immersion, presence, fun, etc.). Many gamification frameworks focus on anatomical elements of games (like goals, rewards, challenges) [2, 3]. However, player experiential elements are not translated in a non-game context as the focus of most serious game research remains on improving the game's efficacy in achieving the purpose through the game [4, 5]. At times, serious games are defined as "games that do not have entertainment, enjoyment, or fun as their primary purpose" (vide, [4]).

U. Dhar et al. (Eds.): ISAGA 2021, LNCS 13219, pp. 197–210, 2022.
https://doi.org/10.1007/978-3-031-09959-5_17

There are two particular shortcomings to this approach of gamification. First is the shallowness of gamified interactions concerning their content. Researchers of serious games have criticised this type of gamification as "chocolate coated broccoli" [6] and "dry and tedious" [7]. The critique mainly revolves around the shallowness of the game or game-like artifact produced—either the content is retrofitted to the game elements or superficial game elements like points, leaderboards, and game-like graphics are used to call it a gamified experience. This problem of exogenous game designs has been solved by the Endogen framework for purposeful games [8]. It facilitates designers to arrive at game mechanics from within the content in an endogenous manner. However, there is a lack of understanding about the problem of expected player experiences in games [5, 9].

The importance of studying player experiences in serious games has been sufficiently stressed [4, 10]. In the domain of player experiences, there are several concepts that are conflated with fun. Usage of the word fun is so commonplace that any pleasure derived out of games is labelled as fun. This has led to a mix-up of the concept with various other "sorry imposters" like pleasure, delight, amusement, etc. [11] and seemingly similar experiences like flow, engagement, entertainment, leisure, etc. Research on pleasures in games uses "fun" and related constructs like enjoyment, pleasure, motivation interchangeably [12, 13]. To initiate and advance the much-needed work on fun in games, Sharp and Thomas consider fun as a larger (yet, understudied) aesthetic of the game [11]. Other experiences in games such as flow, engagement, immersion, and so forth are considered under the larger gamut of fun. Similarly, Hunicke et al. also intentionally "move away from words like fun" [14] and divide the concept of fun in games into eight aesthetic components. Both these approaches consider fun to be composed of many constructs, highlighting the polymorphic nature of the concept of fun in games.

Given the complexities to understand multi-dimensional, pervasive, and polymorphous concepts like fun, researchers of different domains like education research, health research, nursing sciences, sociology, and sports psychology use Conceptual Analysis as a method [13, 15–17]. We analyse pleasures obtained in games, keeping "fun" in the centre to identify different attributes of fun that can support the construction of a design theory of fun for simulations and serious games.

## 2 Method

The strength of conceptual analysis lies in systematically examining a concept and arriving at its essence without relying on its nominal definitions [18]. It does so by considering the explicated meanings of the concept and synthesising it in a form that can be used by related domains. The method has been primarily used for philosophical analysis of ideas, but several disciplines have used it to establish their core concepts [13, 19–21].

Conceptual analysis is rigorously used in humanities and philosophy of language for the analysis of complex, polymorphous concepts [22]. Of the three types of conceptual analysis suggested by Kosterec, we use Constructive Conceptual Analysis. Constructive Conceptual Analysis aims to build a conceptual meaning by finding new concepts and relations. It does so by preserving existing concepts of the domain. Guidelines to conduct such an analysis is suggested as follows:

1. Specify the initial conceptual background
2. Formulate the conceptual problems
3. State the new conceptual relations
4. Formulate tests of the conceptual relations within the conceptual background
5. Elaborate the new relations by tests respecting the conceptual background
6. If the relations succeed in tests, declare them as a part of conceptual background

Using definitions and existing theories of fun as an initial conceptual background is possible if accepted definitions have few variations. However, in our case, fun has been historically under-theorised [11]. It was considered trivial [11, 20, 23] as compared to other concepts like beauty and truth. Its use is "commonplace"; hence finding attributes through definitions approach would not take us far in conceptualising fun. Hence, we take the distinction approach. We distinguish fun from other concepts, and in the process, we identify attributes and relations of them with fun. Using the above guidelines, we perform the analysis in this paper.

The initial conceptual background is described in Sects. 3 through 5 to arrive at the conceptual problem pertaining to fun. In Sects. 6 through 9, we identify the new concepts and establish relations among them. Those new relations are tested, and the concepts are further elaborated, keeping in mind the formulated conceptual problem (Sect. 10) using constructed cases. Final attributes and their relations are explained in Sect. 11.

## 3 Linguistic Roots of Fun

Fun is often etymologically linked with "fon" and "folly" [11, 24], which depending on the usage, can mean "to fool", "stupidity", or "madness". While folly can be associated with "carelessness" or "uselessness", Sharp and Thomas examine the historical context in which folly was used historically. They argue that "folly", in essence, is delight and pleasure. The futility and pleasure in acts like painting, singing, and enjoying simple things was encapsulated within this medieval word. The futility aspect of the act propagated, leading to multiple interpretations through time, and the pleasure aspect was lost entirely [24].

Bogost digs deeper into the "foolery" aspect of "folly" and "fon". The essay "Fun isn't pleasure, it's novelty" describes the role of a fool in medieval society [24]. A fool is a person who can see and create uncommon things which are oblivious in common settings. As coined by Bogost, this phenomenon is reframing. Reframing reality; seeing the lesser seen and experiencing the lesser experienced is the effort that an individual puts to get the pleasure. Although Bogost, and Sharp and Thomas produce different ways to look at fun, understanding fun through linguistic roots can give us the broadest idea. Such ideas encompass multiple experiences resembling fun but are not fun.

## 4 Distinguishing Fun from Other Pleasures in Games: An Analysis

Enjoyment is a defined and well-studied pleasure in academia, as compared to fun. So much so that fun is considered as a frivolous instance of enjoyment [12]. Kimiecik and Harris argue, most research on enjoyment in psychology focuses on predicting enjoyment through a cause-effect relationship [13]. This approach has some limitations. Primary among them, it does not help in characterising enjoyment or identifying conditions of enjoyment. Kimiecik and Harris, and several others propose enjoyment to be a closer conceptual construct to the concept of flow [12, 13, 25].

Flow is achieved by conditions of "a close match between skill and challenge, clear goals and constant feedback on performance", fun is often considered as a distraction and a trivial experience than the experience of flow [12]. Flow is dependent on the difficulty level of tasks and skills to achieve those tasks. In contrast, fun is not necessarily dependent on skill utilisation. Fun is considered as a short-lived experience, spontaneous and suitable for designing repetitive and routine activities, while enjoyment and flow are progression and absorption based [12]. They consider fun as a spectacle, while enjoyment, flow and psychological absorption as an aesthetic. Fun is considered as a distraction from repetition, while enjoyment and related constructs are considered as a progression.

This view of fun can be contrasted to recent developments in game studies. Lazzaro considers fun as a progression through cycles of emotions [26], so does Järvinen, who considers player experience as a sequence of game events causing emotions [27]. The approach of Bogost partially agrees with Blythe's and Hassenzahl's fun as a distraction in the sense that he considers the act of generating fun as an act of seeing uncommon things in a common setting, a break from the routine and the obvious. Partially because Bogost's reframing is agential and autotelic. The individual reframes the situation, and in the process, they have fun. The goal of individuals reframing is just to reframe, not to be distracted.

Similar contradictions can be presented where fun is seen as a spectacle and enjoyment as an aesthetic. Sharp and Thomas's treatise on fun consider fun as an aesthetic and argue that other experiences such as flow, enjoyment, immersion, and so forth should be looked at as smaller aesthetics under the larger umbrella of fun [11]. In this sense, fun can be a spectacle when looked at from its usage, but we look at it as an aesthetic. The limitation of viewing fun only as a spectacle and distraction is that it does not consider an individual's agency in creating pleasure for herself. It feels that individuals are robbed off of their agencies and then provided entertainment. In his book Amusing Ourselves to Death, Postman imagines a society similar to what Debord imagines as a society of the spectacle [27, 28]. Such spectacles bring users or players into the Magic Circle (as conceptualised by [29]) and supposedly rob off their agency. The primary goal of spectacle and spectacle based fun is to bring users and players into the Magic Circle.

The view of fun as a distraction may be appropriate to consider commuting people stuck with their phones, but players of games have fun while having their agency in the Magic Circle. In the Magic Circle, it is important for a player to have agency and autonomy, as suggested by multiple researchers [30–32]. Players are not distracted or passive while playing a game, but they're active, autonomous, and agential. Designers of serious games consider fun that a game generates inside of the Magic Circle, i.e. while players are playing the game, and in that sense, fun is neither a distraction nor a spectacle in its complete sense. Fun as a spectacle is amusement. When players are already considered passive, distracted consumers of information in a spectacle, interactions among them are not considered.

Fun, on the other hand, is interactional. In leisure studies, it is one of the distinguishing characteristics between fun and enjoyment [21]. While enjoyment is self-referential ([33] vide, [21]) fun has the Other-referential assumption. One cannot have fun with Self; Self needs the Other to have fun. One can enjoy oneself, but, to have fun, one needs the Other. This notion of Other can be manifested in forms of other people (as in playing games with other people), the same person separated by time (playing chess alone), playing against a system (games like solitaire, or single-player computer games). However, the Other has to have autonomy. This deduction can be verified by the presence of player autonomy in several player experience models for video games [30, 32, 34, 35].

Fun is spontaneous, but that does not necessarily make it a distraction, and certainly does not make it trivial and frivolous. When considered inside of the Magic Circle as we are thinking like designers and researchers of serious games, fun needs agency. Agency to perform actions within the Magic Circle. It can be short-lived and spontaneous, as well as it can be a progression and its development, gradual. Here, we subscribe to the approach of Sharp and Thomas—considering fun as a larger aesthetic instantiated to various smaller aesthetics like flow, immersion, enjoyment, absorption, amusement. This type of fun is interactional and needs some manifestation of the Other. This interactional aspect of fun needs more analysis as any interaction that is spontaneous, has the Other, has agential participants, is a positive affect, cannot be called fun. What provides favourable conditions for fun to emerge? How do interactions of individuals with such characteristics bring out fun?

## 5 Emergence of Fun in Interactions

In his essay From Prohibition to Enjoyment, McGowan analyses the role of prohibition in creating enjoyment [36]. The sense of enjoyment used here is different from the Csikszentmihalyian enjoyment (which equates to flow [13]). This enjoyment, as we shall see, is interactional and needs work. The essay does not rely on the motivations of an individual, hence notions of skills or difficulty are not explicitly discussed. However, it looks at the problem of emergence enjoyment among individuals in a society [36]. The essay brings in works of Levi-Strauss, Freud and majorly, Lacan to explain the role of prohibition in enjoyment.

In society, for everyone to be able to enjoy, as the author explains, a shared sacrifice of individual private enjoyment is necessary, which Levi-Strauss calls an "entry fee". An individual cannot enjoy infinitely. This creates a prohibition for everyone to have direct access to enjoyment, at the same time, prohibition promises a form of enjoyment to people who sacrifice their private enjoyment. This kind of collective sacrifice of private enjoyment gives rise to social order. Such an order generated out of prohibition, creates organisation, distributes enjoyment amongst all the subjects. Individuals of this order voluntarily sacrifice enjoyment as the prohibition promises their share of enjoyment. For example, the early capitalist idea of work so that you can enjoy it and religions have the concept of an afterlife where sacrifices in this life ensure unrestricted enjoyment in the afterlife. Although sacrifice is one other feature of collective enjoyment, it does not restrict the reach of the subject to enjoyment completely. This order born out of prohibition is symbolic in nature (vide, [36]). Symbolic order mediates the access to fun and enjoyment of individuals. Without symbolic order, enjoyment does not exist.

With the prohibition on enjoyment, enjoyment now resides in the imaginations and fantasies of individuals. However, this is in the form of desires. McGowan calls such a desire as sustained dissatisfaction. Prohibition takes individuals who have sacrificed their private enjoyments and converts them to dissatisfied desiring individuals who prefer to remain under the secure confines of social order. Thus, symbolic order provides a medium and its norms to interact amongst individuals and access enjoyment within symbolic order (vide, [36]).

### 5.1 Emergence of Equality and Inequality

Prohibition binds individuals of a society by distancing them from enjoyment. This gives birth to social bonds, the basis of which is the collective sacrifice of private enjoyment and shared dissatisfaction. Within symbolic order, every subject is equal. This is similar to what Kelly says about conditions to create fun, fun can happen only amongst equal-human-bonds [20]. Hence, prohibition first creates a sense of equality among the individuals.

Individuals in the realm of Imaginary access are barricaded by the symbolic order. In the imaginary, subjects feel complete power; they forget that access is just temporary and are still in the confines of the symbolic order. In this state where they look at the Other for enjoyment and feel that they have complete power, it gives rise to indifference towards others and hence now the social bonds no longer remain equal, but begin becoming unequal. In such a state, they forget that the Imaginary realm does not embody enjoyment, but it is merely policed. Thus, prohibition creates a possibility of coexistence by making all subjects equal, but also because of the Imaginary, it creates indifference which gives rise to inequality. Hence, it creates distance between subjects and enjoyment, while creating a distance within subjects.

### 5.2 Emergence of Secrets

In addition to distance, equality, indifferences, and imaginations, symbolic order creates secrets. The distance created between subjects and enjoyment and among the subjects mutually is not physical in nature, but symbolic. The symbolic distance makes it possible to conceal something. As an example of symbolic distance in action, consider individuals who go to remote places to ignore the hustle of the city, but still, the hustle is in their reality which cannot be escaped merely by increasing the physical distance. Because physical distance is a property of the Real. Within symbolic order, the nature of distance is not physical. It is possible to access the realm of Imaginary while being in the Real. For example, it is possible to be in the Imaginary created with your loved one, while being in the middle of the city. Games can be looked at in a similar way. While playing the game, the Real is what is seen on the board, but the Imaginary contains the strategies, the concealments, the intentions and possible moves of a player. The players can plot revenge while being present with other players. This resonates with Malone's idea of fun when he says fun lies in unrevealing secrets [37, 38]. In order to conceal things and make someone reveal the concealed things, individuals have to exert effort.

## 5.3  Emergence of Meaningful Work

Understanding enjoyment this way has several implications for researchers and designers of games. Primary being the importance of prohibitions in generating enjoyment. What a player is allowed to do in a game is important as it provides agency, but no player, at any given point in time, should have the ultimate agency. Thus, players should be equally prohibited. Just like in a society operated by symbolic order, equal human bonds are formed, in a game, all the players should be treated equally at the beginning of the game. Inequalities should be generated by the fine balance between prohibition and agency on players. The transgression of the symbolic order allows the reframing in games—the ability to imagine uncommon things in a familiar setting. While Blythe and Hassenzahl consider it fun in transgression, the notion of transgression is not seen in the light of prohibition and the symbolic order that creates it. Transgression within the boundaries of the Magic Circle is fun and pleasurable. In games, because rules prohibit players from achieving the goal directly, players have to take imaginative and analytical leaps. To take leaps is to do work.

The analytical and imaginative leaps under prohibitions need work from players. Each time, a new kind of work has to be done to attain the same kind of fun. There are three concepts associated with work here. First among these is repetition. If the same type of work is to be done, it becomes repetitive to achieve the same transgression in a similar way. The symbolic distance between the Real and the Imaginary decreases. The work done to traverse that symbolic distance reduces with each act of transgression and the meaning that was offered by transgression and prohibition is lost.

In order to create variations in the imagination of individuals and make them do meaningful work, there has to be a method of creating multiple ways to transgress from the Real to the Imaginary. Repetitions, as we saw, cannot make individuals do meaningful work. A game offers variations to players by creating newer gameplays where players have to learn about the system better than the previous game. This learning is quite similar to the learning of patterns as proposed by Koster [39] and Falstein's theory of Natural Funativity [40]. Thus, in the process of working towards the Imaginary and coming back to the Symbolic and learning about the patterns of the system, "meaning" is produced.

Sharp and Thomas propose an important role of ambiguity in creating fun in games and the meaning associated with it [11]. This is the second concept associated with work. Ambiguity produces meaningful work in games. In their triadic model of fun, they believe that meaning is partially generated by the game and partially by players' efforts. Each player has their own meaning subjective to their actions and interpretations. Thus, fun is also grounded in cultural background, age groups, and other subjective determinants of meaning-making processes.

The third one is the reward. Once work is done by individuals, if an external agency, outside of the magic circle validates their work and rewards them with an experience, that would be called reward-based fun. As the experience of fun is dependent on work, the meaning that is acknowledged and verified by a third agency only comes at the end. The work is expected to be done in order to have (or allot) the quota of fun. That fun as a reward is considered capitalistic and makes an individual feel "framed" [2] in absence of fun that is internally motivating-internally rewarding, and an autotelic experience [41, 42].

## 5.4 Summing Up

Thus, fun can be defined as a pleasure that needs prohibitions to emerge. Since it is interactional, the Other, with which an individual is interacting has to be treated as equal. However, the fun lies in bringing inequality through an individual's agency. The equality-inequality flux is fun. To create and maintain the flux, constant reframing by players with an agency is essential. Fun is a spontaneous experience. To maintain the equality-inequality flux, meaningful work needs to be done by individuals. Fun is in the moment, achieved through meaningful work. However, if fun is allotted against the work done, then it ceases being fun as it defeats its autotelic nature. In this sense, fun is work (absorption) and not a break from work (distraction).

# 6  Discussion

In conceptual analysis, the attributes and the relations are tested. Tests are formulated by constructing three types of cases [19]—model case, related case, and a contrary case. The model case depicts a situation or an event or a case where the concept in focus is definitely found. A related case is a boundary case—where a similar concept is discussed, but not the concept in focus. Such an illustration depicts the differentiating attributes. Not all attributes and conditions are varied to produce similar concepts. In the contrary case, a situation or an event or a case is illustrated where the concept in focus is definitely not present.

We discuss the attributes and conditions of fun applied to the players playing a game of Scrabble. Interactions of players in Scrabble are discussed and fun is distinguished and exemplified in this context. Scrabble is not considered here as a serious game, but because it has a learning value and the game is common enough to be known by readers. The situations in the case are fictional and created for illustrating the attributes of fun.

## 6.1  Model Case

Scrabble is fun for adults and children alike. In this case, consider the game is played by three kids of age 10 years—Ankit(m), Sam(m), and Radha(f). The game starts with all the players allotted a random set of letter tiles from a common repository of tiles. The player starting the game has to figure out a starting word from the allotted random set of tiles. Turn by turn, each player has to do the same, except with a constraint that the new word a player makes should contain at least one letter from the existing words on the board. Players can choose to make words in any direction. The goal of the game is to collect the highest number of points by strategically placing long, rare, complex words.

Ankit, Sam, and Radha begin playing the game, in the same order. Ankit being the first player begins the game by placing the word—"GUY" vertically, in the centre. Sam has to choose a word in the constraints of the letters G, U, or Y. He chooses Y and makes "YUM". Radha realises that to maximise her score, she can choose words that cover the premium tiles (double letter, triple letter, double word, and triple word). She executes her strategy and gradually wins the game.

Here, the game begins considering all the players as equal (Equality). Everyone is restricted by the same constraints (Prohibition). Random allotment of tiles makes the players unequal, but the constraints make them imagine newer words (Randomness). These constraints make them do meaningful work. Sam would have to reframe the existing word "GUY" into a new word using some of his tiles "YUM". In the process, not only does he do meaningful work, he interacts with Ankit, indirectly via the game board (Interaction). This process of finding a new word is spontaneous and fun (Temporal aspects). Sam interacts by teasing Ankit and screaming that he got more points than him, that would be fun as it would have a performance and interactional aspect. While all the players have the agency to make words in any direction on the board (Agency), Radha uses it to manifest into finding more meaningful choices—using premium tiles on the board to maximise her points. In other words, she found a new way of meaning-making—premium tiles and used it to achieve the goal.

## 6.2  Contrary Case

Now, if we change the player configuration and make the three kids play with an English professor, the hierarchy is already established. The players are no longer equal, although games try to make them equal through the random distribution of tiles. In such a case, the professor will not have fun as the inequality is already established and no meaningful work is to be done by him to establish the inequality.

Meaning is a subjective property, and work is a cultural and subjective property. For example, Koster takes an example of kids playing tic-tac-toe to talk about how fun ceases to occur when they decipher the pattern [43]. In this sense, once they stop finding meaning associated with the system, they stop working for and hence fun ceases to occur.

## 6.3  Related Cases

While players of Scrabble have fun in their turn by trying to reframe the existing word into a new word, once they place the words and count their points they have enjoyment. Formulating a new word is a fun activity because there is reframing involved and the pleasure is in the task itself. The task derives pleasure from a fine balance between what a player can do (agency and autonomy) and what they cannot do (prohibition). In the process of reframing, meaning is produced. This meaning can be provided by many design elements of games; in the case of scrabble, part of the meaning is provided by the goal to make a word from an English dictionary and part by the ambiguity presented by the board. Once the word is made, points are counted and the score is updated.

In a single turn, collecting points is a self-referential activity, and is not interactional, hence, pleasure from points would be called enjoyment. However, in the larger arc of the game, collecting points becomes interactional as scores are visible by all and the players devise strategies to interact with other players through the system. The goal of the larger arc is then to establish inequality in their favour and subsequently win. In any case, fun is interactional with an autonomous and agential individual.

Scrabble when played online against an AI, the interaction of players with the system can be amusing, it can have learning effects, and it can be an enjoyable experience. However, fun only comes with social interactions; in this case, playing with humans. It is not a matter of autonomy, as the enactivist view of games considers games as autonomous systems interacting with players [34]. They're autonomous in the sense that presents challenges to players and induces randomness through multiple techniques like gameplay mutation, dynamic difficulty adjustments, and so forth. However, playing alone with a system still will not be considered fun, as social aspects of fun are not present in the play [21, 25, 44, 45]. Hence, fun is necessarily produced out of social interactions amongst equals created by prohibition. The work thus produced can then have meaning.

## 7  Critical Attributes

Conceptual analysis brings out the features from the distinctions with allied concepts. These attributes are not definitive or exhaustive, but present an outline of the concept [46]. These attributes are faithful to a domain from which they are derived. In our case, the concept of fun and its attributes are faithful to the domain of games.

1. *Fun is interactional.* Fun needs the presence of the Other to emerge out of the interaction. The Other can take multiple forms—a person, a system. However, the Other should have autonomy against the Self.
2. *Fun as meaningful work.* Fun can be looked at as a meaning producing process. A player works towards something, and the process is engaging and meaningful such that it ceases being effortful and the pleasure is in the effort itself. When looked at fun as an autotelic experience, meaning is found in the work itself.
3. *Fun needs reframing.* Reframing is the act of seeing uncommon things in a common setting. Since fun is interactional, and to reframe reality, one needs to act, creating a reframed reality is also fun. Reframing can be manifested into surprise, secrecy, concealing information. Reframing can be conscious, by an individual or the Other can create situations for reframing. Reframing thus produces meaningful work.
4. *Fun has temporal aspects.* As described by Blythe and Hassenzahl, fun is spontaneous. However, reframing and interactions can also happen over time. Depending on whether fun is spontaneous or gradual, academia has labelled the pleasures. The flow is labelled be gradual, fun would be spontaneous. Enjoyment would be gradual, amusement would be spontaneous.
5. *Fun as a reward.* Fun can be an end. When fun is awarded for work done, fun is treated as a reward. While this will be another manifestation of fun, it is significantly different from fun as meaningful work.
6. *Fun needs equality among individuals.* Since fun is interactional, equality among the Self and the Other has to exist. As Kelly suggests (and Podilchak extends), fun cannot exist in situations of hierarchies and power distance. Individuals, by some means, when treating each other as equals, fun can exist.
7. *Individuals need an agency to experience fun.* In situations of power distance, an individual' agency is a threat. For the equals to interact with each other, an individual must have the agency to make choice, act, object, and interact in such forms.
8. *Fun needs prohibition to emerge.* Just as an individual is allowed to interact with something, they should not have complete freedom. They should be equally prohibited from certain well-defined actions.

9. *Randomness is an essential ingredient of fun.* Randomness (or Uncertainty) can be looked at simultaneous existence of is and is not [11, 47]. It can be individually generated or system generated. Uncertainty should be generated by the Other. As described by Sharp and Thomas, meaningful work is produced by uncertainty.

10. *Fun is social.* An individual cannot have fun in isolation; she needs the Other with the agency. Although enactivist viewpoints suggest viewing systems as autonomous, the pleasure derived out of them cannot be considered fun, it can be considered amusement (as used in amusement machines, [48]) or enjoyment (as used by [21]).

11. *Fun is contextual.* It depends on demographics, culture and other such contextual factors. This is similar to how self-determination theory factors in relatedness. Further probing needs into the contextual aspects of fun, but meaning-making and the notion of work are some constituents.

# 8 Conclusion

Through the process of conceptualising fun, we realise finding meaning and articulating different types of fun is needed for games studies and simulation studies. We acknowledge that consensus will never be reached around notions of fun, enjoyment, and pleasures in games. It would be difficult to claim that the attributes and conditions enumerated here are exhaustive. It is even harder to claim that they encapsulate contemporary or totalistic versions of fun. We also recognise the limitations of conceptual analysis and the paradox of analysis [49]. The aim of a constructive analysis is to be correct and need not always be coherent [22]. Conceptual analysis is considered correct if the relations in the initial conceptual background are intact and is considered coherent if the new relations are made of the same material as the initial conceptual background. This implies that the relations mentioned in our analyses consider existing concepts as their subpart. Hence, we do not claim any modification in the theories of flow, enjoyment, amusement and entertainment, we construct a theory using those concepts which help designers understand the concept of fun in a new light. Another limitation of the conceptual analysis lies in the exceptions explored. While the paper attempts to be as precise and relevant to games, other examples may yield new attributes of fun.

Thinking of pleasures in terms of fun and above listed attributes helps us in understanding related experiences in a richer way. For example, it is indispensable for designers of gamified experiences and serious games to view that fun is interactional and process-based; fun is in the working and not necessarily a reward for the work. We believe such a viewpoint can show an initial direction to keep away from "chocolate-coated broccolis", dull and boring games, and resolve issues of "shallow gamification" and "framification". Our study provides an initial step towards designing and analysing player experience in serious games and simulations, which research and practice have found to be lacking [7–9, 25].

Design research aims to achieve the ultimate particular (vide [9]). The critical attributes and conditions derived in this paper can help designers identify the particulars of a player's experience and attribute them to the design of a serious game. In this sense, our findings have the potential to guide a designer in analysing player experiences in serious games. Since these are the conditions, they can be applied to multiple gamified experiences apart from serious games. Advancement of research in this direction can have sophisticated frameworks to analyse gameplays and troubleshoot game design. Another direction this paper points towards is studying manifestations of the conditions and the attributes. For example, one can analyse how agency manifested through design elements of games? Furthermore, we believe that designers' reflections on these attributes of fun will take the domain further towards designing for aesthetics in simulations and games.

# References

1. Deterding, S., Sicart, M., Nacke, L., O'Hara, K., Dixon, D.: Gamification: using game-design elements in non-gaming contexts. In: Proceedings of the 2011 Annual Conference Extended Abstracts on Human Factors in Computing Systems - CHI EA 2011, p. 2425. ACM Press, Vancouver (2011). https://doi.org/10.1145/1979742.1979575
2. Lieberoth, A.: Shallow gamification. Games Cult. **10**, 229–248 (2015). https://doi.org/10.1177/1555412014559978
3. Bogost, I.: Why gamification is bullshit. In: The Gameful World: Approaches Issues, Applications, pp. 65–79. MIT Press, Cambridge (2014)
4. Alexiou, A., Schippers, M.C., Oshri, I., Angelopoulos, S.: Narrative and aesthetics as antecedents of perceived learning in serious games. Inf. Technol. People (2020). Ahead-of-print https://doi.org/10.1108/ITP-08-2019-0435
5. Cowley, B., et al.: Experience assessment and design in the analysis of gameplay. Simul. Gaming **45**, 41–69 (2014). https://doi.org/10.1177/1046878113513936
6. Hopkins, I., Roberts, D.: 'Chocolate-covered Broccoli'? Games and the teaching of literature. Chang. Engl. Stud. Cult. Educ. **22**, 222–236 (2015). https://doi.org/10.1080/1358684X.2015.1022508
7. Van Eck, R.: Digital Game-Based Learning: It's not just the digital natives who are restless. https://er.educause.edu/articles/2006/1/digital-gamebased-learning-its-not-just-the-digital-natives-who-are-restless. Accessed 18 May 2021
8. Athavale, S., Dalvi, G.: Strategies for endogenous design of educational games. In: DiGRA Conference (2019)
9. William, G., Alexander, M.: Towards Genre as a Game Design Research Approach (2017)
10. van der Spek, E.D., Sidorenkova, T., Porskamp, P., Rauterberg, M.: The effect of familiar and fantasy aesthetics on learning and experience of serious games. In: Pisan, Y., Sgouros, N.M., Marsh, T. (eds.) ICEC 2014. LNCS, vol. 8770, pp. 133–138. Springer, Heidelberg (2014). https://doi.org/10.1007/978-3-662-45212-7_17
11. Sharp, J., Thomas, D.: Fun, Taste & Games: An Aesthetics of the Idle, Unproductive, and Otherwise Playful. MIT Press, Cambridge (2019)
12. Blythe, M., Hassenzahl, M.: The semantics of fun: differentiating enjoyable experiences. In: Blythe, M., Monk, A. (eds.) Funology 2: From Usability to Enjoyment. HIS, pp. 375–387. Springer, Cham (2018). https://doi.org/10.1007/978-3-319-68213-6_24
13. Kimiecik, J., Harris, A.: What is enjoyment? Conceptual/definitional analysis with implications for sport and exercise psychology. J. Sport Exerc. Psychol. **18** (1996). https://doi.org/10.1123/jsep.18.3.247
14. Hunicke, R., Leblanc, M., Zubek, R.: MDA: a formal approach to game design and game research. AAAI Workshop - Technical report WS-04-04, pp. 1–5 (2004)
15. Langford, C.P.H., Bowsher, J., Maloney, J.P., Lillis, P.P.: Social support: a conceptual analysis. J. Adv. Nurs. **25**, 95–100 (1997). https://doi.org/10.1046/j.1365-2648.1997.1997025095.x

16. Kyngäs, H., Duffy, M.E., Kroll, T.: Conceptual analysis of compliance. J. Clin. Nurs. **9**, 5–12 (2000). https://doi.org/10.1046/j.1365-2702.2000.00309.x

17. Wheeler, S., Lord, L.: Denial: a conceptual analysis. Arch. Psychiatr. Nurs. **13**, 311–320 (1999). https://doi.org/10.1016/S0883-9417(99)80063-6

18. Definitions (Stanford Encyclopedia of Philosophy), https://plato.stanford.edu/entries/definitions/#ReaNomDef, Accessed 11 June 2020

19. Hupcey, J.E., Morse, J.M., Lenz, E.R., Tasón, M.C.: Wilsonian methods of concept analysis: a critique. Sch. Inq. Nurs. Pract. **10**, 185–210 (1996)

20. Podilchak, W.: Establishing the fun in leisure. Leis. Sci. **13**, 123–136 (1991). https://doi.org/10.1080/01490409109513131

21. Podilchak, W.: Distinctions of fun, enjoyment and leisure. Leis. Stud. **10**, 133–148 (1991). https://doi.org/10.1080/02614369100390131

22. Kosterec, M.: Methods of Conceptual Analysis, 11

23. Fincham, B.: Theorising fun. In: Fincham, B., (ed.) The Sociology of Fun, pp. 27–46. Palgrave Macmillan, London (2016). https://doi.org/10.1057/978-1-137-31579-3_2

24. Bogost, I.: Play anything: the pleasure of limits, the uses of boredom, and the secret of games (2018). https://doi.org/10.1080/14427591.2018.1455253

25. Reis, H.T., O'Keefe, S.D., Lane, R.D.: Fun is more fun when others are involved. J. Posit. Psychol. **12**, 547–557 (2017). https://doi.org/10.1080/17439760.2016.1221123

26. Lazzaro, N.: Why we play games: four keys to more emotion without story. In: Game Developer Conference (GDC), pp. 1–8 (2004). https://doi.org/10.1111/j.1464-410X.2004.04896.x

27. Debord, G.: Society of the Spectacle. Bread and Circuses Publishing (2012)

28. Postman, N.: Amusing ourselves to death: public discourse in the age of show business. Penguin, New York (2006)

29. Huizinga, J.: Homo Ludens: a Study of the Play Element in Culture. Harper, J.J. (ed.) New York (1970)

30. Deci, E.L., Ryan, R.M.: Self-determination theory. In: Handbook of Theories of Social Psychology, vol. 1, pp. 416–437 (2012). SAGE Publications Inc. https://doi.org/10.4135/9781446249215.n21

31. Ryan, K.M., Kanjorski, J.: The enjoyment of sexist humor, rape attitudes, and relationship aggression in college students. Sex Roles **38**, 743–756 (1998)

32. IJsselsteijn, W., et al.: Measuring the experience of digital game enjoyment. Presented at the (2008)

33. Kelly, J.R.: Freedom to Be: A New Sociology of Leisure. Routledge, Abingdon (2019)

34. Sweetser, P., Wyeth, P.: GameFlow. Comput. Entertain. **3**, 3 (2005). https://doi.org/10.1145/1077246.1077253

35. Vahlo, J.: An enactive account of the autonomy of videogame gameplay. Game Stud. **17** (2017)

36. McGowan, T.: End of Dissatisfaction? The: Jacques Lacan and the Emerging Society of Enjoyment. SUNY Press, Albany (2012)

37. Malone, T.W.: What makes things fun to learn? heuristics for designing instructional computer games. (1980). https://doi.org/10.1145/800088.802839

38. Malone, T.W.: Toward a theory of intrinsically motivating instruction. Cogn. Sci. **5**, 333–369 (1981). https://doi.org/10.1016/S0364-0213(81)80017-1

39. Koster, R.: Theory of Fun for Game Design. O'Reilly Media, Inc., Sebastopol (2013)

40. Gamasutra- Natural Funativity (2019). https://www.gamasutra.com/view/feature/130573/natural_funativity.php

41. Peeren, E.: You must (not) be bored! In: Boredom, Shanzhai, and Digitisation in the Time of Creative China, pp. 101–109. Amsterdam University Press (2019). https://doi.org/10.2307/j.ctvqr1bnw.8

42. What's the Point If We Can't Have Fun? https://thebaffler.com/salvos/whats-the-point-if-we-cant-have-fun. Accessed 28 Apr 2021
43. Fallis, A.G.: A Theory of Fun for Game Design. O'Reilly Media, Inc., Sebastopol (2013)
44. Gajadhar, B.J., de Kort, Y.A.W., IJsselsteijn, W.A.: Shared fun is doubled fun: player enjoyment as a function of social setting. In: Markopoulos, P., de Ruyter, B., IJsselsteijn, W., Rowland, D. (eds.) Fun and Games 2008. LNCS, vol. 5294, pp. 106–117. Springer, Heidelberg (2008). https://doi.org/10.1007/978-3-540-88322-7_11
45. Robertson, S., et al.: More than fun? Towards understanding the impact of socialrecreation programming. Early Interv. Psychiatry **8**, 150 (2014)
46. Wilson, J.: Thinking with Concepts. Cambridge University Press, Cambridge (1963)
47. To, A., Ali, S., Kaufman, G.F., Hammer, J.: integrating curiosity and uncertainty in game design. In: Digra/fdg (2016)
48. Griffiths, M.D.: Amusement machine playing in childhood and adolescence: a comparative analysis of video games and fruit machines. J. Adolesc. **14**, 53–73 (1991). https://doi.org/10.1016/0140-1971(91)90045-S
49. Fumerton, R.A.: The paradox of analysis. Philos. Phenomenol. Res. **43**, 477–497 (1983). https://doi.org/10.2307/2107643

# Virtual Reality Games for Children with ADHD in Formal Education

Meike Belter[✉] and Heide Lukosch

HIT Lab NZ, University of Canterbury, Christchurch 8041, New Zealand
meike.belter@pg.canterbury.ac.nz

**Abstract.** According to national health services, between 5–10% of school-aged children are diagnosed with Attention Deficit Hyperactivity Disorder (ADHD). ADHD can influence the well-being and performance of children in formal education. Children with ADHD can show hyperactivity or impulsiveness and might struggle with their executive functioning, including planning of tasks, remembering instructions or focusing their attention. Virtual reality (VR) games can offer realistic, simplified and safe experiences where children with ADHD could experience learning situations tailored to their unique learning needs. Games are already successful in transmitting learning contents for ADHD diagnosed individuals and VR technology is increasingly incorporated in education. The review of literature explores the use of VR games to support learning of children with ADHD in formal education and shows how certain immersive game elements addressing specific ADHD learning needs could be derived, providing insights into possible game requirements and the first prototype.

**Keywords:** Executive function · Hyperactivity · Impulsiveness · Inattention · Multidisciplinary thinking · Virtual reality · Games

## 1 Introduction

Children who are diagnosed with Attention Deficit Hyperactivity Disorder (ADHD) often face enormous challenges in formal education settings. The classroom, designed for children without learning disabilities, can be overwhelming or distracting. Learning techniques applied in formal education can demonstrate a mismatch for the abilities and needs of ADHD children. The main symptoms of ADHD are hyperactivity, impulsiveness and inattention as well as poor executive functioning [1], which means difficulties in planning and remembering a task as well as keeping the focus on it.

While studies explore ways to address the discrepancy between children with and without ADHD in the classroom, virtual reality (VR) games have not been explored extensively as a tool for learning support yet. VR shows characteristics that are promising in helping children with ADHD to better deal with learning in formal learning settings. It carries the potential to deliver information successfully through visualization and immersion. It provides engaging and attention holding experiences often used for illustrating abstract or inaccessible learning contents [2, 3].

© Springer Nature Switzerland AG 2022
U. Dhar et al. (Eds.): ISAGA 2021, LNCS 13219, pp. 211–220, 2022.
https://doi.org/10.1007/978-3-031-09959-3_18

In this article, the authors discuss the results of review of literature on the use of VR games in formal education for ADHD children leading to an identification of VR game elements related to various aspects of ADHD.

## 2  Challenges Caused by Attention Deficit Hyperactivity Disorder (ADHD) in Formal Education

The authors used multiple search terms such as 'ADHD', 'ADHD symptoms', 'ADHD and school', ADHD and education', 'ADHD intervention', 'ADHD intervention and game', 'ADHD and Intervention and Virtual Reality' to review the databases like Google Scholar, Scopus, SocINDEX, ScienceDirect, ResearchGate and Education Source. The review was undertaken to gather a better understanding of the typical challenges faced by the children with ADHD in formal education.

Scholars have explored the main symptoms of ADHD over the past 50 years. ADHD is characterized by a number of main symptoms, namely hyperactivity, impulsiveness and poor sustained attention [4–6]. It can cause significant negative impact on ones' academic and social engagements [7, 8]. These developmental complications may include poor academic achievements, problems with peer relationships or substance abusive behaviour [9]. Poor executive function (EF) can cause major impairment on neurodevelopment level in ADHD diagnosed individuals [5, 10, 11]. Consequences of this development can negatively affect three key functions of attention, motor planning and working memory [4].

Individuals with ADHD may have poor inference control, causing disruptions of executive functions leading to a lack of self-control and persistence [4]. This may lead to incompletion of tasks with little or no instant reward and eventually, inconsistent, inattentive behaviour. It is clear that inability to be attentive and a weak impulse control can cause difficulties for children in formal learning settings, resulting in a challenging situation for all involved.

Children diagnosed with ADHD attend standard formal education in most cases. Hence, these children follow the same educational curricula and learning plans as children without ADHD diagnosis. The researchers found approximately 5–10% of all children attending formal education affected by ADHD [12]. Schools play a key role in the facilitation of ADHD [13]. Compared to their peers, diagnosed children engage more frequently in off-task behaviour during class [14, 15]. Whilst ADHD affected boys engage more frequently in rule breaking and externalising behaviour, girls seem to be more often involved with verbal aggression in class [14]. Children with ADHD lack basic skill sets, which mark a precondition for academic success [16]. Research indicates that children with a predominately inattentive onset of ADHD show poor academic achievement and difficulties with literacy and numeracy skills [13, 17]. In formal settings such as classrooms, children struggling with a predominant hyperactive ADHD subtype experience day dreaming or engage in creating weird sounds [18].

Weak EF can create impactful difficulties for ADHD children in effective and efficient information retrieval and selection [19]. Children with ADHD experience difficulties with directional execution of tasks grounded in poor working memory, eventually resulting in insufficient in-class task performance [4]. Poor executive functioning of working memory influences several basic school subjects such as reading, writing, language and mathematics negatively [13]. An association between weak EF and physical aggression for mainly hyperactive children has been reported [20].

In literature, a link between impaired executive functioning and academic success is often discussed. Thus, when accommodating ADHD children in the classroom, the right stimulation of EF would play a key role. Accommodating these challenges with successful interventions requires a holistic approach and an interdisciplinary view. Successful interventions may be best applied in school settings directly [19]. Involvement of teachers and parents in the accommodation process is essential for academic success of the affected children [16]. The adoption of successful interventions in learning challenges of ADHD children requires considerate administration and curricula [19].

## 3 Virtual Reality Games for Learning in Formal Education

Multiple search terms such as 'Immersive Virtual Reality', 'Immersive Virtual Reality and School', 'ADHD and game based learning', ADHD and games', 'ADHD and learning and school', 'ADHD intervention and game', 'Applied Immersive Games and ADHD and school' where used to review the databases like Google Scholar, Scopus, SocINDEX, ScienceDirect, ResearchGate, and Education Source.

In the past, games have drawn increased attention in education. Educational games seem to support many skills such as planning, strategic thinking, communication and group decision-making [21]. Video games are an effective tool for acquiring knowledge in several domains such as language or history [22]. Besides the positive results of applying games in educational contexts, literature maps out several complications in regards to the usage of games in formal education. Games seem to be hard to integrate in traditional learning routines due to time and space restrictions present [21, 23]. Games not tailor-made per curricula often fail to match the required learning content [21].

The potential of games in educational settings is often accompanied by scepticism from teachers, parents and students [23]. Technology and technological skills of humans are fast progressing and new opportunities for games in education are emerging rapidly. Educational designers, parents and teachers must explore to which extent educational games may be useful for learning to exhaust its full potential for education [22]. Incorporating pedagogy and educational design in digital games is essential for future development and success of serious games [24].

Recent technological advancement made VR games accessible to the broad consumer market and therefore, also feasible for implementation in formal education [25]. VR has gained increasing attention in literature due to its promising effects on learning. Research has mapped out the potential of VR to enhance learning through visualization of information eventually allowing for effective information retention [2, 26]. VR tools hold the capability to enhance classroom instructed learning by adding engaging and immersive experiences that would motivate learners [2, 25]. VR is often used for scenarios or environments which cannot be experienced in reality or for experiencing physically inaccessible objects such as the solar system [3]. The gamification aspect of VR in education appears to be of great importance. Students preferred game-based VR software to a non-game-based application [25].

The implementation of VR in education represents an underexplored field in its usability and user acceptance, as most VR applications tend to host complex user interfaces. Students trained in VR displayed greater levels of interest, engagement and motivation. VR holds great potential for engaging and attention sustaining education which is interesting for children with ADHD but needs to be equally effective when it comes to learning.

Only limited literature can be found on how VR may be of advantage in knowledge transmission and retrieval for ADHD children. Most studies investigate the usage of VR tools for ADHD assessment rather than for knowledge transfer [27–29]. VR holds great potential for controlled assessment of ADHD children in education [30]. The researchers created a virtual classroom and were able to conclude that ADHD diagnosed children are impacted by distractions, making more errors of commission and omission than peers.

VR is effective for attention enhancement and improved task focus, marking a promising result for VR usage in ADHD accommodation [16] and improves time perception of ADHD individuals [31]. Time perception belongs to a category of executive functioning and therefore encourages the usage of VR for ADHD in education. ADHD severity and core symptomatic differ per affected individual and therefore, needs customizable VR for effective learning. Immersive VR classified as an effective tool for enabling the required flexibility and immediate response to accommodate ADHD patients [5]. The flexibility provided by VR is beneficial not only in ADHD rehabilitation but also in formal learning settings when children with ADHD are involved. VR allows for active movement and therefore, allows for the effectiveness of exercise in ADHD accommodation [32]. A virtual world may also be used for knowledge transmission without further negative implications of VR on individuals with ADHD. Effective VR learning applications for children with ADHD could support difficulties with inattention, EF and hyperactivity.

## 4   VR Game Design Requirements for the Learning of Children with ADHD

The authors could not find any design guidelines defined for VR game that supports children with ADHD in formal education. To close this gap, the authors aim at matching characteristics of ADHD as defined in literature with VR game elements, and look closer into the main characteristics of ADHD. Three major models of ADHD were defined over the past two decades; the cognitive interaction model [10], the behavioural inhibition model [4] and the transactional neurodevelopmental model [44]. The characteristics of ADHD such as hyperactivity, inattention and inhibitory difficulties lead to impairment in executive functioning.

Inhibitory difficulties show as an individual with ADHD's problems with planning and control [1, 4, 10]. Similarly, inattention and hyperactivity demonstrate a generic high-level concept of ADHD with all models attributing deficits in self-regulation and arousal modulation to the appearance of hyperactivity. Children with ADHD need specific support, meaning learning requirements have to be adjusted to develop skills and strategies to cope with the ADHD related challenges. In a formal education setting, a VR game needs to help the children with planning and controlling, focusing their attention, and coping with hyperactivity.

The possible factors causing ADHD in the first place range from genetic disposition to exposure to environmental toxins and premature birth [1, 4]. It often remains unclear what is causing this neuro-diversity in individuals. While VR cannot reverse the onset of ADHD, it may address other influencing factors. Environmental factors like home and school context, or social factors influence the severity and development of ADHD in children [33]. Since authors are aiming at developing VR games for children in a school context, environmental factors are considered, where ADHD characteristics are matched with VR game elements and requirements.

For an applied immersive game to be effective, the application context must be understood and translated into technological features. The authors match major impairments of children with ADHD experience with principles or guidelines that have proven to be effective for their special needs. The mitigations are derived from a variety of interventional backgrounds and have been selected upon translatability into an immersive VR context. Environmental factors are contemplated and factors from a school context are selected to be of importance for creating effective immersive VR games for children with ADHD in formal education.

VR games are an emerging field of research and seem to be promising for supporting children with ADHD in a school context. A study of related work to define mitigation strategies marks an important starting point for establishing guidelines and requirements for such an application in the future.

### 4.1 Addressing Inattention Challenge

Inattention as a characteristic of ADHD includes difficulties to complete two tasks at once (divide attention), to stay on-task, to disregard distractions effectively and to sustain attention [33]. Design requirements for VR games to address this include:

- visual features identifiable for producing correct attention patterns in immersive scenes [34]
- avoidance of visually or semantically similar objects as they may cause distraction and interrupt attention [34]
- allowing enough time to observe visual cues for greater attention and correct intake of information provided, e.g. by fixating crucial visual cues [34]
- avoiding scenes that depend on exact timing of attention as that can cause misinformation [34]
- creation of consistent player feedback and clear goals for higher task engagement [35]

### 4.2 Dealing with Self-regulation and Arousal Modulation

Individuals affected by this ADHD symptom are unable to self-regulate, e.g. control emotions and arousal levels [33]. This leads to following design requirements:

- No imposition of time limits as they may affect arousal negatively [36]
- Immersive VR can increase physiological arousal levels and must be designed avoiding over-stimuli for children with ADHD [36]

### 4.3 Improving Working Memory

One of the main ADHD characteristics children struggle with in formal educational settings is the affected working memory. Diagnosed children can have difficulties with short-term memory and holding information temporarily, making it difficult to memorize information important to carrying out learn-related tasks [1, 4]. The VR game should include elements such as:

- Display of few information at a time to avoid information overload [37]
- Allow enough time for extended practice [38, 39]
- Balanced game challenges and defined goals that match player performance [35, 40]

### 4.4 Helping with the Internalization of Speech

Subjects can have deficits in internalizing speech that in turn guides behavior and actions [1, 4]. Children with ADHD can hear what a teacher says but may find it difficult to understand it and to translate it into concrete action. Game elements that need to be considered to help children are:

- Incorporation of clear verbal cues for supporting task-switching situations and guiding actions [41]
- Inclusion of reminder questions into the game play for training inner speech [42], such as 'What is the task that you have to complete?', 'How are you supposed to execute the task?'

### 4.5 Dealing with a Demanding School Environment

The school environment can be very demanding for children with ADHD. Some elements that work well for such children should be incorporated into VR games for their learning such as:

- Using a pedagogical agent displayed as virtual character in computer mediated learning environment with an instructional goal [43]
- Creating and welcoming aesthetic and safe learning environment for accommodating ADHD children [44]
- Making use of the name of students frequently, with calm and stern voice as well as short instructions for attention and engagement [44].

## 5 First Low-Fidelity Game Prototype

Based on the comprehensive review of literature and game design requirements, this early prototype provides an immersive and non-distracting environment for children with ADHD. One game design expert and a subject matter expert have been consulted to support and shape the creation of the first design idea. A math game was created for children aged 7–12 years which is the age range for ADHD to show in an unmasked way and further, mathematics often presents as a weak subject for children with EF and inhibitory difficulties [1, 4].

The overarching structure of the game refers to a series of mini-games that all lead to earning coins of rewards and are centred on the principle of helping people to conduct a certain task. The reward coin system has been included based on the need of children with ADHD for immediate reward as motivational and attention keeping measure. Helping people within the mini-games has been included to provide the children with a sense of responsibility leading to greater task engagement. No time limitations are imposed to avoid cognitive stress and to allow enough time for extended practice at individual pace [38, 39].

For the VR environment, a tropical coastline and beach scenario can be pictured. The player goes on a ride on a sea turtle to travel between several islands each marking one mini-game. This design choice has been made based on its friendly and adventurous look and feel [44]. While prototyping the environment, attention was paid to keeping it clean and with little cognitive distractors, with the idea of focussing attention on the actual task [36]. The player is at all times accompanied by a guiding figure named Maia. This character functions as reassuring and harmonious support but also as an entity that is supposed to draw attention of the child back onto the actual task through questions and feedback [42, 44]. This supports the children's needs of engagement, close instructional support and verbal cues especially in task switching situations [35, 41, 43].

The game user interface provides the option for the player to access a so-called task sheet at all times. This sheet summarizes in easy language the next steps to be taken for the player to progress in the game and reminds the player of the overarching game goal [35]. The player can also access their personal game achievements directly through the user interface. This function remains present during all times and provides the player with the option of retrieving immediate reward and motivation through a feeling of mastery and success [35].

The overall aim of the game is to allow for math practice and does not intend to be a teaching tool. The prototype has been designed with the unique challenges faced by children with ADHD. Next to its strong applied focus in the area of learner needs, this game is also designed with the future application context in mind in an educational environment. Unity has been chosen to develop a first fully functional digital prototype as it is a cross-platform game engine. This development platform is selected due to its wide range of assets, its extensive game development community and due to its availability free for the anticipated development scale of this project.

## 6    Discussion and Conclusion

ADHD diagnosis in children often correlates with weak academic performance leading to unequal opportunities for those affected. Inattention, hyperactivity, impulsivity and poor EF can cause major difficulties with knowledge acquisition, retrieval and repro-duction for ADHD children in formal education. Educational institutions play a major role in accommodating and facilitating the special learning needs. Rapid technological advancement allows for new and feasible ways of digital learning and testing in schools. VR games seem to hold great potential for aiding distinct learning difficulties associated with ADHD.

Literature from across several disciplines offers principles and factors which are well suited for being translated into a VR game design. The flexible and customizable nature of VR offers the possibility to create a learning environment with only essential visual cues and features for minimal distraction. Utilizing the full potential of VR games in formal education requires more in-depth multidisciplinary thinking and research. Research findings from different disciplines could be combined for implementing these new ways of learning into formal curricula with the goal to change learning for children with ADHD in formal education.

Future research will be focused on a deeper analysis of the ADHD aspects and their impact on performance and behaviour of children in formal learning settings. By matching ADHD characteristics with VR game elements, concrete design decisions can be made, leading to case studies by the teachers and caregivers of children diagnosed with ADHD. This study offers a design framework for VR games in formal education to support children in facing learning challenges and to provide customized education to enable equal learning opportunities for ADHD diagnosed and undiagnosed children.

**Acknowledgements.** This study received funding from the Tertiary Education Commission (TEC), New Zealand under the Entrepreneurial Universities Scheme, Edumis no: 7005, and the University of Canterbury as part of the Applied Immersive Gaming Initiative. No conflicts of interest result from this funding.

# References

1. Barkley, R.A.: Behavioral inhibition, sustained attention, and executive functions: constructing a unifying theory of ADHD. Psychol. Bull. **121**(1), 65 (1997)
2. Pilgrim, J.M., Pilgrim, J.: The use of virtual reality tools in the reading-language arts classroom. Texas J. Literacy Educ. **4**(2), 90–97 (2016)
3. Freina, L., Ott, M.: A literature review on immersive virtual reality in education: state of the art and perspectives. In: The International Scientific Conference E-Learning and Software for Education, vol. 1, no. 133 (2015)
4. Barkley, R.A.: Impaired delayed responding. In: Routh, D.K. (eds.) Disruptive Behavior Disorders in Childhood, pp. 11–57. Springer, Boston (1994). https://doi.org/10.1007/978-1-4899-1501-6_2
5. Bashiri, A., Ghazisaeedi, M., Shahmoradi, L.: The opportunities of virtual reality in the rehabilitation of children with attention deficit hyperactivity disorder: a literature review. Korean J. Pediatr. **60**(11), 337 (2017)
6. Hinshaw, S.P., et al.: Prospective follow-up of girls with attention-deficit/hyperactivity disorder into early adulthood: continuing impairment includes elevated risk for suicide attempts and self-injury. J. Consult. Clin. Psychol. **80**(6), 1041 (2012)
7. American Psychiatric Association: Diagnostic and statistical manual of mental disorders (DSM-5®). American Psychiatric Publishing (2013)
8. Booster, G.D., et al.: Functional impairments in children with ADHD: Unique effects of age and comorbid status. J. Attent. Disord. **16**(3), 179–189 (2012)
9. Teichner, G.: Attention-Deficit/Hyperactivity Disorder in Children and Adolescents: A DSM-5 Handbook for Medical and Mental Health Professionals. Momentum Press (2017)
10. Douglas, V.I.: Higher mental processes in hyperactive children: implications for training. In: Treatment of Hyperactive and Learning Disordered Children, pp. 65–92 (1980)

11. Silverstein, M.J., et al.: The relationship between executive function deficits and DSM-5-defined ADHD symptoms. J. Attent. Disord. **24**(1), 41–51 (2020)
12. Faraone, S.V., et al.: The worldwide prevalence of ADHD: is it an American condition? World Psychiatry **2**(2), 104 (2003)
13. Martinussen, R.L., et al.: Increasing awareness and understanding of attention deficit hyperactivity disorder (ADHD) in education to promote better academic outcomes for students with ADHD. Except. Educ. Canada **16**(2/3), 107 (2006). https://www.researchgate.net/profile/Alison_Mcinnes/publication/234774396_Increasing_Awareness_and_Understanding_of_Attention_Deficit_Hyperactivity_Disorder_ADHD_in_Education_to_Promote_Better_Academic_Outcomes_for_Students_with_ADHD/links/55c63b4608aeca747d6335d1.pdf
14. Abikoff, H.B., et al.: Observed classroom behavior of children with ADHD: relationship to gender and comorbidity. J. Abnorm. Child Psychol. **30**(4), 349–359 (2002)
15. Atkins, M.S., Pelham, W.E.: School-based assessment of attention deficit-hyperactivity disorder. J. Learn. Disabil. **24**(4), 197–204 (1991)
16. Climie, E.A., Mastoras, S.M.: ADHD in schools: Adopting a strengths-based perspective. Can. Psychol. **56**(3), 295 (2015)
17. Fuchs, L.S., et al.: The prevention, identification, and cognitive determinants of math difficulty. J. Educ. Psychol. **97**(3), 493 (2005)
18. Jacob, R.G., O'Leary, K.D., Rosenblad, C.: Formal and informal classroom settings: effects on hyperactivity. J. Abnorm. Child Psychol. **6**(1), 47–59 (1978)
19. Pfiffner, L.: Psychosocial treatment for ADHD-inattentive type. ADHD Rep. **11**(5), 1–8 (2003). https://guilfordjournals.com/doi/pdfplus/10.1521/adhd.11.5.1.23504
20. Diamantopoulou, S., et al.: Impact of executive functioning and symptoms of attention deficit hyperactivity disorder on children's peer relations and school performance. Dev. Neuropsychol. **32**(1), 521–542 (2007)
21. Kirriemuir, J., McFarlane, A.: Literature review in games and learning (2004)
22. Young, M.F., et al.: Our princess is in another castle: a review of trends in serious gaming for education. Rev. Educ. Res. **82**(1), 61–89 (2012)
23. Egenfeldt-Nielsen, S.: Overview of research on the educational use of video games. Nordic J. Digit. Literacy **1**(03), 184–214 (2006). https://www.idunn.no/file/pdf/33191508/overview_of_research_on_the_educationaluseof_video_games.pdf
24. De Gloria, A., Bellotti, F., Berta, R.: Serious Games for education and training. Int. J. Serious Games **1**(1) (2014)
25. Virvou, M., Katsionis, G.: On the usability and likeability of virtual reality games for education: the case of VR-ENGAGE. Comput. Educ. **50**(1), 154–178 (2008)
26. Wohlgenannt, I., et al.: Virtual reality in higher education: preliminary results from a design-science research project (2019). https://aisel.aisnet.org/isd2014/proceedings2019/NewMedia/5/
27. Nolin, P., et al.: ClinicaVR: classroom-CPT: a virtual reality tool for assessing attention and inhibition in children and adolescents. Comput. Hum. Behav. **59**, 327–333 (2016)
28. Parsons, T.D., Duffield, T., Asbee, J.: A comparison of virtual reality classroom continuous performance tests to traditional continuous performance tests in delineating ADHD: a meta-analysis. Neuropsychol. Rev. 1–19 (2019)
29. Rizzo, A.A., et al.: A Virtual Reality Environment for the Assessment of ADHD. ADHD Rep. **9**(2), 9–13 (2001). https://guilfordjournals.com/doi/pdf/10.1521/adhd.9.2.9.19077
30. Parsons, T.D., et al.: A controlled clinical comparison of attention performance in children with ADHD in a virtual reality classroom compared to standard neuropsychological methods. Child Neuropsychol. **13**(4), 363–381 (2007)

31. Gongsook, P., et al.: A virtual reality based time simulator game for children with ADHD. In: 2nd International Conference on Applied and Theoretical Information Systems Research (ATISR), Taipei, Taiwan (2012)

32. Mulrine, C.F., Prater, M.A., Jenkins, A.: The active classroom: supporting students with attention deficit hyperactivity disorder through exercise. Teach. Except. Child. **40**(5), 16–22 (2008)

33. Teeter, P.A., Semrud-Clikeman, M.: Integrating neurobiological, psychosocial, and behavioral paradigms: a transactional model for the study of ADHD. Archiv. Clin. Neuropsychol. **10**(5), 433–461 (1995)

34. Jiang, M., et al.: Fantastic answers and where to find them: immersive question-directed visual attention. In: Proceedings of the IEEE/CVF Conference on Computer Vision and Pattern Recognition (2020)

35. Adams, R., et al.: Distractibility in attention/deficit/hyperactivity disorder (ADHD): the virtual reality classroom. Child Neuropsychol. **15**(2), 120–135 (2009)

36. Chittaro, L., Buttussi, F.: Assessing knowledge retention of an immersive serious game vs. a traditional education method in aviation safety. IEEE Trans. Vis. Comput. Graph. **21**(4), 529–538 (2015)

37. Kalyuga, S., Plass, J.L.: Evaluating and managing cognitive load in games. In: Handbook of Research on Effective Electronic Gaming in Education, pp. 719–737. IGI Global (2009)

38. Klingberg, T., et al.: Computerized training of working memory in children with ADHD-a randomized, controlled trial. J. Am. Acad. Child Adolesc. Psychiatry **44**(2), 177–186 (2005)

39. Klingberg, T., Forssberg, H., Westerberg, H.: Training of working memory in children with ADHD. J. Clin. Exp. Neuropsychol. **24**(6), 781–791 (2002)

40. Tekinbas, K.S., Zimmerman, E.: Rules of Play: Game Design Fundamentals. MIT Press, Cambridge (2004)

41. Kray, J., Kipp, K.H., Karbach, J.: The development of selective inhibitory control: the influence of verbal labeling. Acta Physiol. (Oxf.) **130**(1), 48–57 (2009)

42. Healy, J.M.: Your Child's Growing Mind: Brain Development and Learning from Birth to Adolescence. Broadway (2004)

43. Mohammadhasani, N., Fardanesh, H., Hatami, J., Mozayani, N., Fabio, R.A.: The pedagogical agent enhances mathematics learning in ADHD students. Educ. Inf. Technol. **23**(6), 2299–2308 (2018). https://doi.org/10.1007/s10639-018-9710-x

44. Geng, G.: Investigation of teachers' verbal and non-verbal strategies for managing attention deficit hyperactivity disorder (ADHD) students' behaviors within a classroom environment. Aust. J. Teach. Educ. **36**(7), 2 (2011)

# Policy Formulation and Serious Games

# Between Urban Resilience and Serious Gaming: Applying Games for Policy Implementation

Weronika Szatkowska(✉) ⓘ and Marcin Wardaszko ⓘ

Kozminski University, Jagiellońska 57/59, 03-301 Warsaw, Poland
{wszatkowska,wardaszko}@kozminski.edu.pl

**Abstract.** The use of serious games in training and policy development has the potential to enhance communication and creativity, simplifying complex environments and consensus building. This article explores examples of existing games in urban resilience policy implementation on the basis of a systematic literature review. It delves into the theory on urban resilience and stresses the role of policymaking within it as well as the application of serious games in complex environments like cities. The findings reveal the core urban resilience areas addressed by games. The article defines the goals, the participants and the characteristics of games that reinforce the implementation of urban resilience policies. The research offers a differentiation between the approaches to distinct stakeholders including their roles in urban resilience. It shows the existing shortcomings in measuring the long-term effects of serious games on the implementation of urban resilience policies.

**Keywords:** Serious games · Urban resilience · Policy · Complexity · Meta-analysis

## 1 Introduction

This article is an attempt to explore examples of existing games dealing with urban resilience policy implementation. The use of serious games in training and policy development has the potential to enhance communication and creativity, simplifying complex environments and consensus building [1]. Games appear to be a promising tool in the challenging areas of urban resilience [2–4]. To analyze the current state of research and practical implementation, the authors have conducted a systematic literature review in the aforementioned thematic area. The article also defines the core focus areas, goals, participants and characteristics of games that address the problem of implementing urban resilience policies.

### 1.1 Urban Resilience

In 2018, over 55% of the world's population inhabited cities. In 2050, the number is expected to exceed 68%. The unsustainable growth of urban areas is followed by

© Springer Nature Switzerland AG 2022
U. Dhar et al. (Eds.): ISAGA 2021, LNCS 13219, pp. 223–238, 2022.
https://doi.org/10.1007/978-3-031-09959-5_19

an increasing vulnerability to acute problems including air pollution, floods, droughts, overpopulation and natural disasters [5–7].

Dealing with such issues is problematic because cities are complex systems composed of multidimensional structures. Yet, defining what is urban raises concerns; while some agree on the commonly adopted administrative or geographic boundaries, others point to identity, population density or the infrastructure and services available as core urban indicators [8]. In this research project, urban boundaries are considered administrative borders because policies affect certain administrative areas. Nevertheless, it is generally agreed that urban systems are composed of some ecological, technical and social elements. Depending on literature, the emphasis is put on distinct aspects and connections, leading to the perspective of cities as socio-ecological systems [9] or cities as socio-technical networks [10]. Such networks have a dynamic nature because of the constant interactions between the actors and the socio-economic and biophysical forces involved. Like natural ecosystems, urban systems adapt to changing environments to survive [11].

As a concept, urban resilience has been introduced to describe the complexity of vulnerability, risks and adaptation of cities [12]. As a term, resilience is rooted deeply in the natural sciences of ecology and physics. It implies the ability of a material or an ecosystem to absorb a disturbance without changing its permanent structure [13], deal with external shocks efficiently and bounce back to the state of equilibrium [14]. Urban resilience links the definition of resilience with cities. Its underlying idea is that a city is able to survive, adapt and develop despite the problems arising from the advanced level of industrialization, growing urbanization, decaying infrastructures or natural disasters [15].

However, academic sources are not consistent in terms of what makes a city resilient and how this resilience is manifested. Urban resilience is the degree to which cities tolerate alteration before reorganizing around a new set of structures and processes [9]. It referred mostly to the urban environment, agriculture, and biology [16], underlined the aspect of sustainability of human communities and physical systems. The core characteristic of a resilient city is its ability to adjust [17], while a resilient city quickly created a new, improved equilibrium after facing a disaster or a problem [18]. Therefore, it can be summarized that a resilient city displays some skills to adapt rather than a specific state.

The set of adaptive skills was described as the transformative capacity to face uncertainty and change [18]. Others have followed this idea, distinguishing the ability to respond, recover and adapt quickly to new circumstances [19, 20], involving an innovative approach to foster transformation [21] and the establishment of the necessary functionality to prevent catastrophic failure at a minimum and the ability to thrive at best [22]. Urban resilience has been explored further in social sciences, equated for instance with the general quality of the city's social, economic and natural systems to be sufficiently future-proof [23]. Urban resilience was a task and a shared responsibility for all societal actors of the system, which demanded an inclusive approach [24]. Therefore, urban resilience requires new forms and ways of collaboration between stakeholders, going beyond the already existing networks [25, 26].

The lack of collective understanding of urban resilience has resulted in distinct operationalization strategies and subdomains derived from the same backbone of resilience such as disaster or community resilience. Disaster resilience focuses on risk preparedness and post-disaster recovery. Community resilience refers to the adaptive capacities of vulnerable groups [27]. Nevertheless, all concepts concentrate on resisting stress, recovering from disasters, adapting to changing conditions and transforming to maintain and ensure fair and livable conditions for all citizens [6].

## 1.2 Policy Implementation

Urban resilience assumes that cities have the capacity to self-organize and adapt to change [28, 29]. However, at an ontological level, urban resilience derives from Lefebvre's right to the city (1968) viz., voting citizens have a right to safe, fair and sustainable life within urban boundaries, regardless of their ethnicity, origin or identity. It implies necessary changes in policymaking and governance. Thus, suitable policies play a vital role in the practical implementation of urban resilience. However, establishing them is challenging in the complex urban reality.

Firstly, urban authorities face the need to measure, benchmark and plan for resilience. It requires a certain level of knowledge of decision-makers as well as collaboration to achieve the set goals [6]. It involves the application of measurement tools, constant data tracking, and a comprehensive analysis of risks by decision-makers and citizens. Operationalizing urban resilience is another challenging aspect where cities must develop a context-specific understanding of urban resilience with core dimensions that may evolve.

Secondly, urban resilience tackles policies with various backgrounds including climate change, urban planning, urban communities, energy and various types of disaster preparedness [17]. Integrating those policies is essential as social, environmental and economic dimensions of urban resilience are interdependent. Nevertheless, infrequently siloed from reality, political mechanisms are not cross-sectoral or interdisciplinary. The reasons behind this situation are disputable due to the lack of mutual understanding between individual actors, high complexity of urban systems, fragmentation of executive bodies or different interests or values represented by different policies [5, 27].

Thirdly, policymaking requires active engagement of citizens. It is especially problematic as the awareness of urban resilience and the concepts related thereto is insufficient. The processes related to resilience are complex and have sources in wicked problems. Citizens need appropriate means to absorb knowledge and understand the impact of urban resilience on their lives. Situational awareness is critical in terms of risk preparedness, viable solutions, and developing scenarios for a resilient future [30].

Lastly, urban resilience involves cross-sectoral collaboration and a transdisciplinary approach which is determined by the complex nature of the stress factors and responses of urban systems. Such collaboration provides opportunities for interdisciplinary solutions to wicked problems and synergic outcomes beneficial for various groups of interests [19]. Nevertheless, it requires an inclusive approach and communication based on consensus. Therefore, authorities need to provide means for consensus-building and collaboration between various stakeholders to foster the development of future-proof cities.

## 2  Serious Games

Games are believed to be significantly effective in teaching complex problems and explaining how systems work [31]. They facilitate discussion about possible futures without setting a trap resulting from knowledge limitations [32]. It is especially important in the case of urban resilience where an inclusive discussion on adaptation to future challenges is essential. Specifically, serious games represent a variant of games designed for non-entertainment purposes and could support the implementation of urban resilience-related policies. They may be defined as experimental, experiential, rule-based, interactive environments where players learn by actions and self-assessing their efforts through feedback mechanisms. There have been attempts to systematize serious games made, for instance, by [33] who proposed a simple G/P/S model modified and developed further by [34]. It consisted of gameplay (game-based or play-based), Purpose (message broadcasting, training or data exchange), and Scope (market or public). [35] came up with classification into application area (sector), activity (physical/physiological/mental), modality (visual, auditory, haptic, smell, other), interaction style, and environment (online or offline).

Games were classified according to their application domain, distinguishing health, public policy, strategy and communication, education, and training & simulation [36]. [37] applied a perspective of skills, dividing them into soft skills (team building, communication, interpersonal, negotiation, creativity, collaboration or learning) and hard skills (product or service knowledge, sales, discipline-based training, project management, innovation, health and safety, risk management, legal or regulatory compliance) while [38] proposed a division into the environment of application, design elements of user interface, target groups, goals, objectives and feedback, user relation/community and model. These are only a few examples showing that despite the collective understanding of what a game is, there is no clear way to classify and define the game.

Serious games embedded in urban systems must deal with urban complexity, an issue that invariably emerges in heated discussions. Complexity refers to interconnected parts of a system characterized by an overly complicated arrangement [39]. The outcome of interactions results in more than just the sum of its elements [40, 41]. Complexity is a relative term, depending on the eye of the beholder. In an urban context, complexity derives from the intersection of governmental, environmental, economic and social factors and their physical manifestation [5]. It is evident even in the earliest attempts to deal with urban complexity which took place in 1950 in urban planning games [42, 43]. With time, serious games have also gained recognition in relevant urban sectors like governance, education, corporate, healthcare and crisis response in cities [44].

Gaming provides a safe, interactive and cooperative environment based on simplified reality in which participants can experiment with decisions and negotiations [31, 45]. The simplified representation of real stakeholders and actual problems makes games perfectly capable of inspiring discoveries of unexpected solutions through social interactions. Games are effective in representing interactions between participants, flows of resources, urban space, roles and dependencies between city actors or infrastructure and the systems around them [46]. The outcomes of such games have three kinds of impact: they enable their participants to learn and comprehend a system through hands-on experience, they provide data and information for researchers about the interactions between participants and elements of the model, and they create a safe environment to design and test new decision-making and policymaking concepts [47]. [48] underlined the explorative potential of simulation games for investigating urban complexity and different policy outcomes. On the other hand, a positive impact on urban participatory planning and design is indisputable.

Games are related to policymaking in several ways. Firstly, they help to foresee the possible future which is crucial to appropriate policy design and the anticipation of negative consequences. Secondly, gaming makes it possible to test various versions of new or existing policies and determine which one is most effective in a particular context. An experimental environment enables thinking outside the box, beyond the existing patterns or knowledge boundaries and offers a new perspective on the existing status quo. Thirdly, gaming facilitates and initiates a dialogue between stakeholders, creating a universal language [49] to discuss policies and their outcomes, thus supporting urban governance and inclusive dialogue. Lastly, it is a source of knowledge for actors to comprehend, interpret and navigate within the complex systems of understanding of what is crucial for urban policymaking.

## 3 Method

The research was based on a systematic review of literature [50]. Firstly, three key phrases were selected: urban resilience, policy and serious games. They were searched for in the most recognized databases including Science Direct, JSTOR, Web of Science and Google Scholar in the time frame of 2005–2021. The initial search revealed 786 articles. After the initial title and abstract screening, 61 articles were selected for further investigation. Articles were chosen based on exclusion criteria – lack of relevance for urban areas (e.g. rural areas, unspecified areas), games designed before 2005, lack of keywords, metaphorical application of keyword or repeated material.

The next phase consisted of full screening and selection based on the perspective of resilience in the urban context (different aspects of urban resilience such as community resilience or social resilience), application of a game to improve resilience or its elements, and sufficient information about the game to assess it.

### 3.1 Exclusion Criteria

The first exclusion criterion was the lack of one of the adopted keywords (urban resilience, serious games or policy) because it pointed to the lack of relevance for the subject and indicated other areas of research (e.g. policy games, policymaking for urban resilience or games loosely related to resilience). The metaphorical (or random) use of keywords was excluded such as rules of the game, game changers and game theory. Articles were excluded if published before 2005 because the concept of urban resilience in policy discourse started to emerge at that time. Articles in which game cases were repeated excluded. The last exclusion criterion was unspecified or non-urban embeddedness of the game. Resilience in regions or geographical areas does not consider urban complexity and policymaking. It was important as the aim of this research was to focus specifically on cities.

## 3.2   Inclusion Criteria

Only the articles that indirectly referred to resilience policies in the urban context were taken into consideration. It was important to find cases explicitly addressing urban stakeholders and considering their characteristics, which were verified by checking the goals of the games. Only the cases that contributed to urban resilience or its derivatives were considered. Finally, if there was not sufficient information about game design, games were not included in the research.

The review resulted in a total number of 20 articles. By applying the snowball method, two new articles were discovered in references and added to the list during the full screening stage. Finally, 22 articles were selected as case studies (Fig. 1). Seven articles provided an evaluation of games and debriefing.

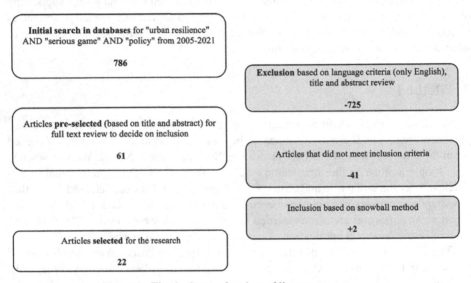

**Fig. 1.**  Steps of review of literature.

## 3.3   Research Process

Based on the chosen elements of game taxonomy, the authors decided to research the following elements: application area, goals, target groups, main design elements and feedback. The qualified articles were classified according to keywords relevant for each element. Then, the keywords were standardized by proximity criterion to create clusters. In terms of the area, the initial research revealed four main thematic groups referring to relevant urban policies: (general) urban resilience, disaster resilience, community resilience, climate change adaptation and one non-specific category. The investigated games originated from 17 countries and were from 2010–21. Three cases focused on developed countries, while 19 cases on developing countries. Six referred to one specific city, seven to a region or country. Others were abstract and did not refer to any specific location. Seven of the games were game-interventions to solve existing problems, and 15 were educational games.

## 4   Discussion

Among the topics covered by serious games for urban resilience policies, disaster resilience was the most common one (8 games) that dealt with preparation for natural hazards, teaching the origin of risk, raising awareness of the process, building resilience, and testing policy responses (Table 1). The popularity of games for disaster resilience is understandable as the link between risk management and virtual simulations is clear. The second group was games related to community resilience (5 games) that included intending to strengthen community bonds, empower citizen engagement, improve situational awareness, communication, collaboration and coordination. The third group consisted of games focusing on urban resilience (4 games), its improvement and supporting the decision-making process. It also included one game addressing the field of planning for urban resilience. The fourth group included games addressing climate change adaptation (3 games) which explained the complexity of the problem and knowledge co-creation. Two games were not classified; one dealt with sustainable tourism and the other with sustainable energy management for urban resilience.

**Table 1.** Goals of serious games related to urban resilience areas.

| Community resilience | Climate change adaptation | Urban resilience | Disaster resilience | Others |
|---|---|---|---|---|
| Understand the complexity and the concept | Understand the complexity and the concept | Understand the complexity and the concept | Situational awareness | Test future scenarios |
| Knowledge transfer | Knowledge transfer | Multi-stakeholder inclusion in planning & co-design | Knowledge transfer | Support decision-driven approach |
| Increase situational awareness | Increase situational awareness | Improve collaboration | Assessment of the current situation | |
| Building consensus among stakeholders | Introduce solutions | | Risk preparedness | |
| Support decision-making | Knowledge co-creation and information exchange | | Inclusion of stakeholders | |
| Communication | Improve collaboration | | Crisis management | |

*(continued)*

**Table 1.** (*continued*)

| Community resilience | Climate change adaptation | Urban resilience | Disaster resilience | Others |
|---|---|---|---|---|
| Identify risks | | | Build adaptive capacity | |

Another classification emerged while the content was analyzed. It divided games into context-specific and universal. The first group consisted of games designed to solve a context-specific problem, applied real data and referred to a location recognized by the participants. The second group applied to a wider public, not addressing any specific problems, but raising awareness or introducing a problem. Some universal games dealt with specific problems, for instance, with sustainable tourism for urban resilience. Nevertheless, the proposed solutions and the framework were applicable in distinct locations.

Games reinforcing urban resilience policies were most common in Europe (17 cases), namely in the Netherlands (3), Germany (3), Sweden (2), Spain (2), Great Britain, Hungary, Serbia, France, Switzerland, Norway and Italy. One of the games was designed as a joint Dutch-Serbian-German-Swedish-Norwegian-Spanish undertaking. Such popularity may be justified by the relative popularity of urban resilience in the EU policy discourse. There were six identified cases from North America – one from Canada and five from the USA (including three different games designed within the framework of one project). Only two cases were identified in Asia and South America. In South America, games were designed collaboratively with Switzerland and the Netherlands (Table 2).

**Table 2.** Countries included in the research. *Some cases are overlapping in one game.

| Region | No. of cases* | Countries |
|---|---|---|
| Europe | 17 | Netherlands (3), Germany (3), Sweden (2), Spain (2), Great Britain, Hungary, Serbia, France, Switzerland, Norway, Italy |
| North America | 7 | USA, Canada |
| South America | 2 | Mexico (collaboration), Peru (collaboration) |
| Asia | 2 | Thailand, India |

## 4.1 Disaster Resilience

Disaster resilience urban games turned out to be the most common type of games encountered. Policies that addressed this subject concerned mostly urban infrastructure, risk management and preparedness. Therefore, most games have been designed for citizens and/or students. However, there were exceptions: one case was designed for city decision-makers, one for multiple urban stakeholders, and one for emergency response personnel.

Games for urban disaster resilience educated homeowners and residents in the area of the impacts of natural hazards and extreme weather conditions, including building individual adaptive capacity [4, 51] and taught territorial risk management as well as new concepts related to urban resilience [2, 52–54]. They helped to reinforce (specifically) flood urban resilience and explore vulnerability as well as test responses of different actors to policy innovations [2, 55]. One game was designed to assess resilience-related competencies and improve them by translating general knowledge into procedural knowledge. It was the case of emergency response personnel who took part in an immersive simulation of disaster to improve their preparedness [2, 56].

Games for urban disaster resilience represented two types of mechanics: mobile-based and board-based. Mobile-based games strove mostly to create an immersive experience, often achieved by first-person narratives and enabling learning by doing [2, 52, 57]. Interestingly, mobile games were merely context-specific and deployed real data. On the other hand, board games involved more interactions between the participants, for instance, through role-play or practicing different risk reduction strategies by taking various protective actions [4, 55].

Regardless of the design, every game presented real dangers and problems, for instance, regional characteristics of socio-economic factors [4], housing and land use [51], environment and health [2, 53] and flood management [54]. Among the most crucial elements, the authors have stressed immediate feedback [2], convincing visual representations and discussions on hazards [2, 54, 57], spatial exposure, vulnerability, disaster risk reduction and mitigation strategies [2, 52].

## 4.2 Community Resilience

Community resilience games tackled areas of infrastructure/built environment, disaster mitigation (flood and drought) and planning. Most games were based on disaster scenarios [58, 59] while one addressed social problems and social resilience [60]. The participants were either citizens, or in two cases, representatives of the most vulnerable groups.

There was a gap between awareness-focused and skills-focused goals. The first group covered familiarizing and educating citizens [60], empowering their engagement in building urban resilience [2, 61] and education on sustainable living [62]. The second group of goals referred to increasing situational awareness and orientation in a post-disaster environment [58, 59]. Every game focused to some extent on consensus-building, communication and cooperation. It was exposed in various aspects such as urban planning, mapping community assets and risk mitigation.

The formats used to deliver games were diverse such as board games [62], mobile app [58], a digital program based on GIS [2, 61] and role-playing game (RPG) [59]. In this case, RPG and board games were applied to transfer general knowledge on resilience, whereas mobile app and programs focused on issues such as to prepare communities for disastrous situations or to plan a road in a specific location. In the case of the GIS application, the participants were expected to use critical thinking and GIS-based tools to analyze and overcome both topographic and economic obstacles for constructing a road which represented a specific problem faced by citizens. Nevertheless, the emphasis was on collaboration, negotiation and consensus-building [2, 61]. The core elements of the app included a realistic environment that provided players with an immersive experience of a post-disaster setting, an option to self-evaluate and utilize the abilities required for improved community resilience and effective game design balancing realism with resource use [58].

### 4.3  Urban Resilience

Games on urban resilience were dedicated mainly to citizens who were familiarized with the concepts [63] and core competencies [64]. In one case, the participants were relevant city decision-makers [3]. The game operationalized the concept of urban resilience and supported decision-making within the process. Other games focused on multi-stakeholder inclusion, co-design, planning and examining crisis dynamics [65].

Despite similar goals, the applied mechanics differed significantly, including rule-based emergent planning supported through mobile augmented reality [64], RPG [65] boardgame [63] and simulation of policies implementation based on existing scenarios [4]. The last example was designed for city decision-makers to experiment with future policies. There were two groups of core elements: immersive and abstract. Immersive games offered a convincing simulation of the built environment [64], applied existing data and information (crowd-sourced data, maps, realistic representation of existing policies and resources) [64]. On the other hand, abstract games provided unrealistic (future-based) narratives and focused on collaboration, resources exchange, time pressure and stimulating knowledge flows. It was achieved through a metaphorical approach to urban resilience as communicating vessels [65].

### 4.4  Climate Change Adaptation

Climate change adaptation was another important theme incorporated in the games supporting urban resilience policies. All the games were designed for citizens to raise awareness of the problem [66] and to underline the dilemmas involved in climate-proof construction/restructuring and spatial developments inside and outside the city [67]. One of the games supported knowledge exchange between experts and citizens [68].

Realistic representation was underlined in all games as it pertained to urban conditions, the complexity of adaptation to climate change and conflicting values. Nevertheless, every game showed appropriate solutions to deal with climate change using different media as in RPG [68] Minecraft software [66] and simulation program of the city [67]. Each game resembled a part of reality in a specific way (flooding/heat island effect, decision-making process or conflicting values within risk management), depending on its goals. Immersion was also considered an essential element and was offered, for instance, through first-person experience [66] of exploring urban spaces [67] and role-play design [68]. There was no experience required to play those games which made them inclusive, of which one game became an integral element of official urban resilience strategy implementation.

## 4.5 Others

Some games supported specific policies related to urban resilience, addressing very specific areas such as sustainable urban tourism [69] and energy management [70] in Northern Europe. The games were designed for relevant stakeholders such as city decision-makers, entrepreneurs and NGO representatives. They investigated specific problems such as in the first case, price-effects, experimenting with different scenarios, and anticipating the problem; in the second case, it was destination design-driven approach to tourism governance [69]. Energy management was explored through scenario-based decisions in response to rising energy prices according to the participants' actual roles and responsibilities in local government. The simulation was realistic and applied existing data reflecting real conditions in which policymaking actually occurred and occurs [70].

Sustainable tourist management was improved through flexible modeling, storyboarding and quantitative simulation. The participants were stimulated and supported to collaboratively reflect on the current situation, its true complexity, and the intended/unintended implications of a range of possible interventions.

## 5  Evaluation

None of the articles measured the outcomes reaching beyond the game sessions. They focused on elements related to policy dissemination and future improvements. Nevertheless, debriefing game results were very promising. Debriefing consisted either of generic surveys [58–60, 69], an informal session [58, 60] or an open discussion [52]. In two cases, participants took tests immediately after the game [52, 60]. Nonetheless, in terms of the evaluation of long-term learning outcomes and impact on policies, there was a lack of systematic feedback.

Debriefing sessions revealed an improved situational awareness [58], a better understanding of problems [52], successful acquisition of specific knowledge (drought resilience, risk management and planning) [52, 59] improved decision-making [59, 60] and an in-depth reflection on existing and future policies [60]. The players admitted that they had a stronger motivation to focus on urban resilience-related initiatives in the future [52, 59] using new approaches and new ideas [4]. They reflected upon the differences in policy goals [69] policymaking styles and real-life issues [4]. The sessions enhanced collaboration and communication and showed different points of view, engaging the players in a search for satisfying solutions [69].

The investigated games contributed to policy implementation in several ways. They led to the creation of strategic documents [60], enhanced the skills and attitudes necessary for the process of policy implementation [64, 65, 68] revealed the possible outcomes of policy implementation [3] pointed to the shortcomings and future challenges [4] and contributed to policy awareness [63]. They were designed mostly as supplements to the policy implementation process and therefore, their long-term effects were not measured. On the other hand, urban resilience policies are implemented in complex environments, which means that assessing only the impact of the considered games could be problematic. As for the achievement of short-term goals, most of the cases appeared to be successful.

# 6 Conclusion

Diversified forms of application of serious games prove that their use is highly context-specific. It can be seen in the featured themes (community resilience, disaster resilience, climate change adaptation and general urban resilience), goals (knowledge exchange and transfer, hard and soft skills development and future projections), media (boards, RPG, virtual simulations and apps) and areas (water management, spatial planning, risk management, power balance and roles within city) or the stakeholders (citizens, decision-makers, business representatives, NGOs and academics). This is a group of games with an abstract, metaphorical message, though it is still in line with urban resilience implementation through education.

Regardless of the theme, immersion was named as a crucial gameplay element. There were different ways to offer and achieve it through augmented reality application and first-person perspective, convincing representations of built infrastructure or urban elements, and application of existing data. Every game contained elements of knowledge transfer or/and exchange. Engaging relevant stakeholders, in general, was limited, especially in the games addressing climate change adaptation and community resilience, which makes games a tool for education rather than a driving force of real change. However, in several cases, games were treated as interventions, solving real problems of communities or supporting the policymaking process and evaluation.

The featured narratives were based mostly on a natural disaster (natural forces) story to understand the phenomenon's complexity and connection with various urban elements to prepare and act after a disaster. Most of the games were models of simplified reality. Yet, in several cases, abstract narratives were used to focus on a certain real problem (e.g. power imbalance). Although developing countries are more vulnerable to acute problems, serious gaming in the urban resilience context was a domain of developed states.

The goals of the games concerned implicitly urban resilience policies. They promoted the concept of resilience, explored its different aspects, helped to operationalize it and developed inclusive tools to implement it in cities. What raises concerns is that none of the games investigated the long-term effects of applying serious games to support the implementation or development of urban resilience policies. It could be reasonable to focus on games addressing the matter of stakeholders and cross-sectoral collaboration in the future as this area was underrepresented among the games analyzed in this project.

The article suffers from a lot of limitations. The article sample was limited to both period and online availability, the search engines, and language (English). The authors are aware that there are significantly more articles and papers published in the area of concern, and that the selection is limited due to the methods applied and other constraints. Their future efforts will broaden and study the underlying design methods, implementation taxonomies, narratives for serious game design and fostering urban resilience in more detail. The aims of the future are to extend the classifications of serious games usage and look for similarities to create a meta-model of serious games design and implementation for improving urban resilience.

# References

1. Geurts, J., Duke, R.D., Vermeulen, P.: Policy gaming for strategy and change. Long Range Plan. **40**, 535–558 (2007)
2. Tomaszewski, B., et al.: Geo-Information Supporting Disaster Resilience Spatial Thinking with Serious GeoGames: Project Lily Pad (2020)
3. Iturriza, M., Hernantes, J., Labaka, L.: Coming to Action: Operationalizing City Resilience (2019)
4. Marome, W., Pholcharoen, T., Wongpeng, N.: Developing and using a board game as a tool for urban and social resilience and flood management planning in the Bangkok Metropolitan Region. Urbanisation **2**(1), 28–37 (2017)
5. Healey, P.: Urban Complexity and Spatial Strategies: Towards a Relational Planning for Our Times (2007)
6. Meerow, S., Pajouhesh, P., Miller, T.: Social Equity in Urban Resilience Planning (2019)
7. United Nations Development Program (UNDP): Goal 11: Sustainable Cities and Communities (2018)
8. Brenner, N., Schmid, C.: The 'urban age' in question. Int. J. Urban Reg. Res. (2014)
9. Alberti, J.M., Marzluff, E., Shulenberger, G., Bradley, C., Ryan, C., Zumbrunnen, C.: Integrating humans into ecology: opportunities and challenges for studying urban ecosystems. Bioscience **53**(12), 1169–1179 (2003)
10. Graham, S., Marvin, S.: Splintering Urbanism: Networked Infrastructures Technological Mobilities and the Urban Condition. Routledge, London (2001)
11. Simme, J., Martin, R.: The economic resilience of regions: towards an evolutionary approach. Camb. J. Reg. Econ. Soc. 1–17 (2009)
12. Norris, F., Stevens, S., Pfefferbaum, B., Wyche, K., Pfefferbaum, R.: Community resilience as a metaphor, theory, set of capacities, and strategy for disaster readiness. Am. J. Commun. Psychol. **41**, 127–150 (2008)
13. Holling, C.S.: Engineering resilience versus ecological resilience. In: Schulze, P.E. (ed.) Engineering within Ecological Constraints, pp. 31–43. National Academy Press, Washington DC (1996)
14. Davoudi, S., et al.: Resilience: a bridging concept or a dead end? "Reframing" resilience: challenges for planning theory and practice interacting traps: resilience assessment of a pasture management system in Northern Afghanistan urban resilience: what does it mean in planning practice? Resilience as a useful concept for climate change adaptation? The politics of resilience for planning: a cautionary note. Plan. Theory Pract. **13**, 299–333 (2012)
15. ARUP/The Rockefeller Foundation: City Resilience Framework (2015)
16. Godschalk, D.R.: Urban hazard mitigation: creating resilient cities. Nat. Hazards Rev. **4**(3), 136–143 (2003)
17. Pickett, S.T.A., Cadenasso, M.L., McGrath, B.: Resilience in Ecology and Urban Design: Linking Theory and Practice for Sustainable Cities. Springer, Dordrecht (2013). https://doi.org/10.1007/978-94-007-5341-9
18. Ernstson, H., van der Leeuw, S.E., Redman, C.L., Meffert, D.J., Davis, G., Alfsen, C.: Urban transitions: on urban resilience and human-dominated ecosystems. Ambio **39**(8), 531–545 (2010)
19. Wardekker, J.A., de Jong, A., Knoop, J.M., van der Sluijs, J.P.: Operationalising a resilience approach to adapting an urban delta to uncertain climate changes. Technol. Forecast. Soc. Change **77**(6), 987–998 (2010)
20. Ahern, J.: From fail-safe to safe-to-fail: sustainability and resilience in the new urban world. Landsc. Urban Plan. **100**(4), 341–343 (2011)

21. Tyler, S., Moench, M.: A framework for urban climate resilience. Climate Dev. 4(4), 311–326 (2012)
22. Brown, K.: The global environmental change I: a social turn for resilience? Prog. Hum. Geogr. 38(1), 107–117 (2013)
23. Thornbush, M., Golubchikov, O., Bouzarovski, S.: Sustainable cities targeted by combined mitigation–adaptation efforts for future-proofing. Sustain. Cities Soc. 9, 1–9 (2013)
24. Spaans, M., Waterhout, B.: Building up resilience in cities worldwide – Rotterdam as participant in the 100 Resilient Cities programme. Cities 61, 109–116 (2017)
25. Restemeyer, B., Woltjer, J., van den Brink, M.: A strategy-based framework for assessing the flood resilience of cities-a Hamburg case study. Plan. Theory Pract. 16(1), 45–62 (2015)
26. Hutter, G.: Collaborative governance and rare floods in urban regions – dealing with uncertainty and surprise. Environ. Sci. Policy 55(P2), 302–308 (2016)
27. Meerow, S., Newell, J.: Urban resilience for whom, what, when, where, and why? Urban Geography (2016)
28. Levin, S.: Fragile Dominion: Complexity and the Commons. Perseus Books, Reading (1999)
29. Holling, C.S.: Understanding the complexity of economic, ecological, and social systems. Ecosystems 4, 390–405 (2001)
30. Leichenko, R., Mcdermott, M., Bezborodko, E.: Barriers, limits and limitations to resilience. J. Extreme Events 2 (2015)
31. Duke, R.D.: Gaming: The Future's Language. SAGE, London (1974)
32. Kikkawa, T.: Gaming as the future's language: case studies and development. In: Duke, R.D., Kriz, W.C. (eds.) Back to the Future of Gaming, pp. 93–99 (2014)
33. Djaouti, D., Alvarez, J., Jessel, J.-P.: Classifying serious games: the G/P/S model. In: Felicia, P. (ed.) Handbook of Research on Improving Learning and Motivation Through Educational Games: Multidisciplinary Approaches, pp. 118–136. IGI Global (2011)
34. Uskov, A., Sekar, B.: Serious games, gamification, and game engines to support framework activities in engineering: case studies, analysis, classifications, and outcomes. In: IEEE International Conference on Electro/Information Technology, pp. 618–623 (2014)
35. Laamarti, F., Eid, M., Saddik, A.E.: An overview of serious games. Int. J. Comput. Games Technol. 11 (2014)
36. Zyda, M.: From visual simulation to virtual reality to games. Computer 38(9), 25–32 (2005)
37. Hauge, J.B.: State of the art of serious games for business and industry. In: 2011 17th International Conference on Concurrent Enterprising (ICE), pp. 1–8 (2011)
38. Greco, M., Baldissin, N., Nonino, F.: An exploratory taxonomy of business games. Simul. Gaming 44(5), 645–682 (2013)
39. Webster's: Ninth New Collegiate Dictionary. Merriam-Webster, Springfield (1989)
40. Simon, H.A.: The Sciences of Artificial. MIT Press, Cambridge and London (1969)
41. Wardaszko, M.: Interdisciplinary approach to complexity in simulation game design and implementation. Simul. Gaming 49(3), 263–278 (2018)
42. Brewer, G.: Methods for synthesis: policy exercises. In: Sustainable Development of the Biosphere (1986)
43. Toth, F.: Policy exercises, the first ten years. In: Crookall, D., Arai, K. (eds.) Simulation and Gaming Across Disciplines and Cultures, pp. 257–264. Sage, Beverly Hills (1995)
44. Michael, D.R., Chen, S.L.: Serious Games: Games that Educate, Train, and Inform. Muska & Lipman/Premier-Trade (2005)
45. Geurts, J., Joldersma, C., Roelofs, E.: Gaming/Simulation for Policy Development and Organizational Change. Tilburg University Press, Tilburg (1998)
46. Hanzl, M.: Information technology as a tool for public participation in urban planning: a review of experiments and potentials. Des. Stud. 28(3), 289–307 (2007)

47. Mayer, I., Veeneman, W.: Games in a World of Infrastructures: Simulation-Games for Research, Learning and Intervention. Eburon, Delft (2002)
48. Cecchini, A., Rizzi, P.: Is urban gaming simulation useful? Simul. Gaming 32(4), 507–521 (2001)
49. Duke, R.D., Geurts, J.: Policy Games for Strategic Management: Pathways into the Unknown. Dutch University Press, Amsterdam (2004)
50. Okoli, C., Schabram, K.: A guide to conducting a systematic literature review of information systems research. SSRN Electron. J. (2010)
51. ICLEI: Resilient Cities, Thriving Cities: the Evolution of Urban Resilience (2019)
52. Taillandier, F., Adam, C.: Games ready to use: a serious game for teaching natural risk management. Simul. Gaming 49(4), 441–470 (2018)
53. Mossoux, S., Delcamp, A., Poppe, S., Michellier, C., Canters, F., Kervyn, M.: Hazagora: will you survive the next disaster? A serious game to raise awareness about geohazards and disaster risk reduction. Nat. Hazards Earth Syst. Sci. 16(1), 135–147 (2016)
54. Vamvakeridou-Lyroudia, L.S., et al.: Assessing and visualising hazard impacts to enhance the resilience of Critical Infrastructures to urban flooding. Sci. Total Environ. 707, 136078 (2020)
55. Mechler, R., McQuistan, C., McCallum, I., Liu, W., Keating, A., Magnuszewski, P., Schinko, T., Laurien, F., Hochrainer-Stigler, S.: Supporting climate risk management at scale. insights from the Zurich flood resilience alliance partnership model applied in Peru & Nepal. In: Mechler, R., Bouwer, L.M., Schinko, T., Surminski, S., Linnerooth-Bayer, JoAnne (eds.) Loss and Damage from Climate Change. CRMPG, pp. 393–424. Springer, Cham (2019). https://doi.org/10.1007/978-3-319-72026-5_17
56. Jainer, S., Anand, A.: Code Red for Humanity: Sinking Indian Cities (2021)
57. https://www.origamirisk.com
58. Meesters, K., Olthof, L., Van de Walle, B.: Disaster in my Backyard: a serious game to improve community disaster resilience. In: Proceedings of the European Conference on Games-Based Learning, vol. 2, no. January, pp. 714–722 (2014)
59. Poděbradská, M., Noel, M., Bathke, D.J., Haigh, T.R., Hayes, M.J.: Ready for Drought? A Community Resilience Role-Playing Game (2020)
60. Marome, W., Natakun, B., Archer, D.: Examining the Use of Serious Games for Enhancing Community Resilience to Climate Risks in Thailand (2021)
61. Poplin, A., Vemuri, K.: Spatial game for negotiations and consensus building in urban planning: YouPlaceIt! In: Book: Geogames and Geoplay, pp. 63–90 (2018)
62. Watson-Puskás, N.: A case study on Budapest: lessons on urban resilience. In: Proceedings of 33rd PLEA International Conference: Design to Thrive, PLEA 2017, vol. 3, no. July, pp. 4538–4545 (2017)
63. Ilgen, S.: Knowledge transfer and policy learning in the context of urban resilience: a case study of water management in Mexico City and Rotterdam, pp. 1–50 (2016)
64. Imottesjo, H., Kain, J.H.: The Urban CoBuilder – a mobile augmented reality tool for crowd-sourced simulation of emergent urban development patterns: Requirements, prototyping and assessment. Comput. Environ. Urban Syst. 71(May), 120–130 (2018)
65. Shearer, A.W.: Roleplaying to improve resilience. Architecture_MPS 18(1), 1–14 (2021)
66. Neset, T.S., Andersson, L., Uhrqvist, O., Navarra, C.: Serious gaming for climate adaptation—assessing the potential and challenges of a digital serious game for urban climate adaptation. Sustainability (Switzerland) 12(5), 1–18 (2020)
67. National League of Cities: Climate Adaptation and Resilience, October, pp. 1–3 (2013). http://www.sustainablecitiesinstitute.org/topics/climate-adaptation-and-resilience

68. Sakonnakron, S.P.N., Huyakorn, P., Rizzi, P.: Urban gaming simulation for enhancing disaster resilience. a social learning tool for modern disaster risk management. TeMA J. Land Use Mob. Environ. 841–851 (2014)
69. Koens, K., et al.: Serious gaming to stimulate participatory urban tourism planning. J. Sustain. Tour. 1–20 (2020)
70. Maaß, J.: Serious Games in Sustainable Land Management, pp. 185–205 (2021)

# Designing Business Game by Student-Teacher Collaboration

Ryoju Hamada[1](✉), Tomomi Kaneko[2], and Masahiro Hiji[3]

[1] National Institute of Technology, Asahikawa College, Asahikawa, Japan
hamada@edu.asahikawa-nct.ac.jp
[2] National Institute of Technology, Tomakomai College, Tomakomai, Japan
t_kaneko@tomakomai.kosen-ac.jp
[3] Graduate School of Economics and Management, Tohoku University, Sendai, Japan
hiji@tohoku.ac.jp

**Abstract.** Designing simulation game is a difficult task, although demands for such learning methods are increasing. Currently, many games are created by an original author and are improved independently. If one can include young students who have just finished playing a game to enhance games, then one might be able to solve human resource shortage. Student-teacher collaboration is rare and such experience is limited. At Tohoku University in Japan, and at Thammasat University in Thailand, a business game designing project was conducted during 2003–2019 that included students and teachers under the management policy called The Great Charter. The authors assigned the most appropriate roles to individual students who were stimulated through collaboration. Some students were awakened, later harnessing and sharing their young energy as great game designers and global players and through businesses as entrepreneurs.

**Keywords:** Awakening · Business game camp · Close communication · Entrepreneurship · Mindset

## 1 Introduction

Demand for simulation and gaming (S/G) for education is increasing and many teachers are developing S/G alone. Opportunities to acquire, share and exchange ideas remain limited. Many developers do not know how to gain such opportunities. Developing new S/G with colleagues in a university is generally difficult. It is necessary to secure human resources for sustainable S/G development.

Business and Accounting School for Entrepreneurs (BASE) Project is a rare example by which students collaborate with a teacher to produce a new business game. The Project was sustained for 16 years (2003–2019) over 15 generations and included 110 students. In the BASE Project, students with intense enthusiasm and talent persistently surrounded paths of developing analogue business games. They designed and created new games rapidly, thereby delivering joy to later generations. The BASE Project includes various related works such as sales, technology transfer to foreign institutions, internal management and funding. They dressed in business suits and worked globally. They were no

© Springer Nature Switzerland AG 2022
U. Dhar et al. (Eds.): ISAGA 2021, LNCS 13219, pp. 239–253, 2022.
https://doi.org/10.1007/978-3-031-09959-3_20

longer mere students but acted as entrepreneurs. The authors believe that students can be reliable partners for a teacher with appropriate management style. Sometimes, they contribute more than their teachers in terms of social achievements.

Using the BASE experience, the authors discuss new possibilities for student–teacher collaboration in new gaming to contribute to society. In so doing, they determine a standard approach to let students participate in game development and to extend their interests to globalization and entrepreneurship.

## 2 Review of Literature

There has been wide consensus on the importance of abandoning one-way lectures. The most famous idea is active learning. Student–teacher collaboration and similar approaches have been discussed since the 1970s in three methods. One is to let students participate in lectures. A second is to induce students to teach together in a lecture. A third is to allow students to teach instead of a teacher.

### 2.1 Letting Students Participate in the Lecture

Some approaches involve students in one-way lectures whose major idea is active learning. In 1970s to 80s, to replace teacher-centered to student-centered become common in higher education, educators argued that students must work as a team to find the problems of history and the present [1]. The importance of collaborative work of students was found in role-play, debate, case study and other activities [2].

With respect to language education, the collaborative learning in foreign language education had become a tradition and learners are fundamental resources for collaborative learning [3]. Collaboration helps learners to extend their knowledge and language learning for bilingual students. Teaching was categorized in three ways: traditional pedagogy, progressive pedagogy and transformative pedagogy [4]. Progressive pedagogy posits the student as an excellent learner. It is a process that lets students study positively and experientially using collaborative inquiry and construction of meanings by a teacher and students. The study showed that teacher-student/student-student collaboration is important on foreign language training [5].

### 2.2 Letting Students Study Together

Computer-Supported Collaborative Learning (CSCL) has been explored with information and communications technology (ICT) education. It has created a stream of research using ICT to support student learning. For the efficiency of mathematics education, student group work was introduced in middle schools [6]. In music education, the effectiveness of student teaching became a standard mode of music teaching in the 1980s but it was criticized for its over-reliance on student–teacher effectiveness [7, 8]. In medical education, teaching effectiveness in clinical training is recognized as a type of Program Based Learning (PBL) that is still commonly used [9, 10].

## 2.3  Letting Students Teach as Student Teachers

Students teach in the classroom as Teaching Assistants (TA). TA covers various academic disciplines and has excellent opportunities to apply their pedagogical skills in a classroom [11]. Comparable research has covered the status and skills of graduate student TA at universities in the United Kingdom and North America [12].

In career development education, Mie University in Japan certifies senior students as Student Assistants (SAs) and lets SAs teach junior students [13]. The SA system connects faculty members, academic affairs division and student support affairs which supervise SA activity.

# 3  BASE Project

To keep human resources focused on game development, the authors invited students to act as game developers to develop and maintain more effective games. They have been practicing Student–Teacher collaboration in the BASE Project.

**Outline.** BASE is the brand name of the tabletop business game series. The BASE Project represents actual activities to develop business games. The original meaning of BASE was 'Business and Accounting School of Entrepreneurs'. Skill or knowledge is obtained by playing the games as a BASE skill of any business person.

Nineteen games were developed in eight categories under the BASE brand at Tohoku University, Japan (2003–2014) and at Sirindhorn International Institute of Technology (SIIT), Thammasat University, Thailand (2014–2019). Table 1 shows major achievements of the project and an approximate portion of efforts from students and teachers through student–teacher collaboration for the details of individual games [14–22].

**Table 1.**  Major BASE business games

| Year | Name | Approximate efforts on original idea (%, total 100) | | Approximate efforts for development (%, total 100) | | Approximate accumulated number of participants |
|------|------|---------|---------|---------|---------|---------|
| | | Student | Teacher | Student | Teacher | |
| 2007 | Hospital | 50 | 50 | 80 | 20 | 50 |
| 2008 | Manufacturer *1 | 50 | 50 | 50 | 50 | 2000 |
| 2009 | Software *2 | 90 | 10 | 80 | 20 | 1000 |
| 2011 | Supply Chain *3 | 0 | 100 | 0 | 100 | 500 |
| 2011 | Large Classroom Version | 20 | 80 | 50 | 50 | 1600 |
| 2013 | Medical Device | 30 | 70 | 90 | 10 | 50 |

*(continued)*

**Table 1.** (*continued*)

| Year | Name | Approximate efforts on original idea (%, total 100) | | Approximate efforts for development (%, total 100) | | Approximate accumulated number of participants |
|------|------|------|------|------|------|------|
| | | Student | Teacher | Student | Teacher | |
| 2016 | Manufacture in Thai *4 | 50 | 50 | 100 | 0 | 80 |
| 2017 | Agriculture *5 | 80 | 20 | 90 | 10 | 40 |
| 2018 | Construction *6 | 50 | 50 | 90 | 10 | 60 |

**Tangibility.** The most notable feature that distinguishes BASE games from others is their analogue style (Fig. 1). They are mostly designed to play in a real stage, not on a computer screen or the internet. Students form a company, receive share capital, purchase machines and materials, hire engineers and salespersons, and sell. They record those processes in a couple of paper tables using a pencil, eraser and calculator. It is a rare opportunity to use hand-writing to learn the business. Due to excessive digitalization in recent days, such experience has a fresh impact on learners. As players calculate all numbers by themselves, they understand the value of numbers better than computer-generated numbers and acquire respect for the rules of business.

**Fig. 1.** BASE Software Manufacture Game (Left), BASE Software Kaihatsu (Development) Game Company Board (Right)

**Close Communication.** In BASE games, two or three students of diverse profiles form a firm, considering the students' academic grade, major and gender. In most cases, a game workshop is the first opportunity to work and learn together through conversation to carry out their tasks.

There are three to four rivals on the same table. They closely talk and learn a lot within close communications. Since players are human beings, not machines, they often become excited, delighted, disappointed and make mistakes. Failure is the mother of success. They recognize important ideas to manage a company through tough communication and experience.

### 3.1 BASE Project in Its Early Days

The authors took a long time to develop a framework. At this moment, the authors can relate the BASE project history from a human-related perspective.

**Origin: Step-in students at Tohoku University.** The authors hosted a large event called a Business Game Camp to provide opportunities for engineers to learn businesses within a limited duration. The first Business Game Camp was held for three days at a lodge during a weekend in December 2004. About 30 students participated from various faculties, grades, gender, nationalities, and from many departments and schools of Tohoku University.

Within a week thereafter, three students stated their opinions related to their experiences in the business game. One had failed at the game and wished to have another chance at playing it. One had a complaint about the rules of the game and urged that it must be improved. The authors were receptive to their enthusiasm. After some discussion, a gaming group of interested people was launched which became the origin of the business game-related work for student.

**Increased Personal Communications.** The author respected the opinions of those students because they came to continue the Business Game Camp during the next year on their own time despite their other responsibilities at their primary laboratories or seminars. After the authors had many lively discussions, in November 2005, they hosted the second camp. The first batch of students had to leave the project. However, the next batch of students participated in the games of their own accord. By holding high awareness of their duties and continuing such a project cycle, the team maintained an intergenerational chain of human resources. The team repeated ten such changes during 11 years at Tohoku University, and during four years at SIIT.

**Game Development Through Student–Teacher Collaboration.** Around 2006, the authors recognized that the game methods and practices were correct. Creating an original business game had become a common interest. Corresponding to the many demands to play the game was important. Under tightened student–teacher collaboration, the team released the first game (BASE Hospital) in 2007. In 2008, the team created a fundamental engineering business game called Base Manufacture Game. Original games made the BASE Project possible to host an event at any request at any time.

### 3.2 The Great Charter: Rule of Student-Teacher Collaborative Projects

In 2009, the authors reviewed the situation and directions for future management. The members implicitly shared the idea that they could develop new games. They might feel anxious whether their work is correct. To satisfy such demands, the team tried to present ideas in sentences. In 2010, the team compiled The Great Charter, consisting of seven articles representing the BASE project's fundamental principles as the basic framework of Student–teacher collaboration, university–industry collaboration and entrepreneurship.

**Articles.** BASE develops world-class analogue business games.

1. BASE contributes to society by spreading our business games to encourage industry.
2. BASE members must be ambitious, active, innovative, and global.
3. BASE provides equal opportunities to members despite their affiliation.
4. BASE sustains its own sales revenue and does not overly rely on subsidies.
5. BASE merges social science and engineering to cultivate an interdisciplinary community.
6. BASE recognizes its high appreciation and responsibility in the world and behaves as an example to game developers.

**Explanations.** The charter expresses the BASE project features clearly. Article 1 presents the vision. Throughout the experiences, the authors know that the digital game market is highly competitive and challenging for beginners. The authors recognized BASE analogue games as having sufficient characteristics to appeal to people worldwide. Article 2 explains the mission briefly. Business games are useful not only in academia but also in industry. The business game must describe characteristics of the market principles. Therefore, it must be a useful tool in society. Article 3 states that BASE members must have definite views. To see the new horizon of analogue games for themselves, they work with high performance while recognizing that the work will spread worldwide. To achieve this purpose, the author selected students carefully.

Article 4 declares that all people involved in the BASE project have the same rights and an equal and fair relation that includes teachers. BASE becomes an activity that is fulfilling with delight and joy, as proved later. Article 5 addresses the spirit of our origin, Business and Accounting School of Entrepreneurs. The business game is not supported by government or university subsidies, presenting an awkward relation to real business. It was a real business resembling that of an entrepreneur. Article 6 describes a core value, diversity. To ensure a member's new trial, being interdisciplinary is fundamentally necessary. The BASE Project includes students from various fields of study from fine arts to agriculture, gender and nationalities. Those commitments from different disciplines and aspects make the Project more fun. The business game bonds them with stronger friendships. Article 7 represents our responsibility to society by developing new business games and behaving as business entrepreneurs.

**Student Attitudes About the Great Charter.** Before the enactment of the rules, the BASE Project seemed to lack long-term strategies, only to repeat game-events. The Great Charter assured members as global challengers to seek worldwide research without the need for a finance perspective. Members welcomed the use of explicit knowledge and are proud to be members of the most entrepreneurial group at traditional, conventional universities. They are motivated to work as the number one analogue business game developer. The fixed policy confirmed and supported their efforts. As a result, students came to enjoy a relaxed atmosphere and to concentrate their efforts in the games.

**Students at Thammasat University.** As other faculty members do, the first author took care of 3–4 teams (total 8–15 students/year) as a senior project advisor. Most students were fourth-year students of the undergraduate program. Selecting the author's topic was their choice. If a group did not prefer to do gaming, the author provided topics of other kinds. If they selected gaming, it was the same story as that at Tohoku University.

## 4  BASE Human Resource Management Protocol

Most members were students before they participated in a BASE event or applied for the senior project. They had no experience at developing games. An innovative atmosphere was fulfilled through joy, producing outstanding human resources not only in terms of developing a game, but also in terms of globalization and business. To promote such diverse career development opportunities, following the earlier case and the Great Charter, the authors completed the BASE Human Resource Management Protocol in six stages, as presented in Fig. 2.

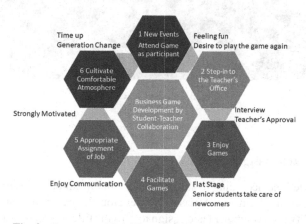

**Fig. 2.** Structure of BASE to encourage member's growth.

### 4.1  Origin: Decision by Student

By playing the game and listening to the debriefing, some players were deeply impressed. That is true because any impression decreased as time passed. The author never called a student. A person's own will is necessary to keep further motivation. Because it was their decision first, no one expressed regret later.

### 4.2  Students Learn Games

In the BASE Project, the teacher does not speak much and should take care of students. The first step is to introduce oneself to other members. The second step is to replay the game. Game lovers can learn by themselves.

## 4.3  Students Teach Games

The authors have lecture duties using games apart from the project. The authors invited the team to participate in the lecture but from the teacher's perspective. To facilitate the game lecture, they must learn the game deeply and should be able to answer questions in front of their juniors (Fig. 3). They raised motivations and increased teaching experience, and finally got some confidence in their talents. They developed close communications with colleagues. When they read the Great Charter in this period again, they recognize the meaning of their work, understand senior generation students' achievements and encourage themselves based on past efforts.

**Fig. 3.** Student teachers

## 4.4  Adequate Role Assignment

The roles were defined according to skill at games, and as human relationships become established. For example, if Mr. A wishes to develop the game, the authors carefully evaluate his ability at development and assign to him the title of Developer. Ms. D is proficient at English and wishes to communicate with international students using business games. In this case, the person's title is International Officer. The student's duty is taking care of exchange students during events that are ongoing or upcoming. By exploiting appropriate roles for individuals, they respect other members and recognize the importance of teams. That is a moment to form a strong team similarly to an entrepreneur developing an enterprise.

## 4.5  Business Game-Centered Atmosphere

In the teacher-only project, the teacher must take care of all game-associated activities of the human network in BASE Project (Fig. 4). Work is separated into three segments: academic, international and social. Students who are proficient in English come into the green circle, pure game lovers are assigned to the red circle, and students who wish to learn entrepreneurship join the blue circle. They plan to export the work to the university from which foreign graduate students came from within the green circle. They design,

**Fig. 4.** Human resource management system in BASE project.

manage and choose the international conference to proceed. In the red circle, they play a game every day and polish new ideas. In the blue circle, they wear a business suit, prepare business cards and find sales opportunities to host seminars or events. Sometimes, they drive to the client company.

There is a business game-centered atmosphere of engage members, shared interests, innovative atmosphere and a strong desire for success. The teacher's role resembles that of an ambulance. The teacher prepares for cases that students cannot resolve and if some difficulty arises, can devote efforts to other works while overseeing the circles. Being free from a teacher's unnecessary commitment motivates students. They feel that it is great fun and proceed to learn autonomously.

### 4.6  Generational Limitations

Students have time limitations and when their primary duties in the laboratory such as master thesis, job hunting or graduation become pressing, they must return to them. They know that from the beginning and therefore, work hard during their period. To carve their names and achievements in the history of BASE is an important value for them. They met their seniors who worked hard and leave their actual results as a legacy. After a year, they wish to overtake their seniors. To compete with the seniors' legend in their minds, they plan an annual event as a Business Game Camp to leave a strong impression on their juniors as a last duty.

## 5  Students' Rapid Growth

Approximately 3–6 months after an orchestra starts to play a symphony, some students in the group show amazing progress. The phenomenon, which is called Awakening, is not universal for all members but appears regularly in the group. The student is free from being nervous as a beginner, works as a leader and acts with full confidence.

## 5.1  Are You a Faculty Member?

The reader of the book may have met the authors and a group of young undergraduate students at Simulation/Gaming (S/G) conferences. Students were often asked similar questions over the years such as 'Are you faculty member?' Collaboration with the teacher is flexible and adequate. After disclosing that a person is a fourth-year student of SIIT, most people have been strongly shocked.

## 5.2  Examples of Awakening

Here the authors present three examples of awakening from three dimensions: development, international and entrepreneurship.

**Development.** During the development of the Software Development Game (Table 1, Column. 3), Kota Toma, a Graduate Student of Information Sciences at Tohoku University, was inspired by games and wished to develop an ICT-related game. One day, the BASE project got a request to train ICT company employees to understand ICT business activities from a broad perspective. The first author and Toma interviewed some companies across three months to make a game scenario that is available to most software development firms in Sendai city. Toma introduced ideas from a computer-based role playing game and drafted a new game proposal. The members testified to the prototype and confirmed its effectiveness and developed the new game. His idea is still alive in 2020 with its original features except for three minor changes to improve operations.

**International Activities.** Yuta Morimoto was a graduate student of Information Sciences at Tohoku University. He promoted the BASE Business Game at U.S. universities and was granted appointments for meetings not only at UC Berkeley but at Stanford and MIT. The first author and four students visited those business schools and discussed future collaboration. They could not make further use of the business game with them but acquired many fruitful comments from the top authorities of American business education. After finishing the U.S. stay, Morimoto came to Thailand to teach Thai students without remuneration as he regarded it as an investment in himself.

**Entrepreneurship.** Shigeru Ikeda and Mizuki Shimada, first-year students at the School of Economics of Tohoku University, joined BASE camp 2013 as members. They launched a small business called 'BASELABO.com' and registered it at the Legal Affairs Office in Sendai in April 2014. Although the teachers were no longer in Japan, they developed customized business games for employee education. They attended business game lectures and made presentations at Thaisim International Conference as undergraduate students.

## 5.3 Awakening

According to the Great Charter article 3, BASE members are ambitious and innovative and its awakening students are an active example of mindsets. No one in the group expressed jealousy against successors. Other members welcomed those colleagues' achievements and worked diligently to make a good impression. Over the generations, BASE produced many marvelous games in development and produced well-talented entrepreneurs.

## 5.4 Limitations

Some ideas are widely recognized as useful methods to encourage students to participate in lectures. There are limitations to student involvement in education. Teachers decided earlier on the teaching framework. Then students followed the policy. Both teachers and students are wedded unconsciously to the idea of 'Teachers are of higher status than students'. Even in the Mie University case, SAs are under the supervision of the student support division. The authors doubt such prejudice because students are likely to be more familiar with game culture than people of the teacher's generation. Developing and updating the game are difficult to achieve, especially for busy instructors.

# 6   Reason of Success in the BASE Project

The BASE project has student–teacher collaboration, a well-structured group and outstanding growth which is not an accidental success. The reasons may be found in the nature of S/G, another in the effectiveness of management like a company, and finally another in students' mindsets.

## 6.1   Characteristics of Simulation/Gaming (S/G)

The most important reason for the student–teacher collaboration in the BASE Project is the characteristic and standpoint of S/G. In a traditional discipline, a teacher knows the target work much better than the students and must follow the state-of-the-art as well. By contrast, S/G is an experiential and practical discipline. S/G stands between teaching and research. Therefore, the distance between research and a lecture is shorter than that of conventional studies. S/G accompanies great fun and teaching effectiveness to learners and can cover most topics. Emotional factors affect the game quality. Therefore, S/G has a characteristic that is familiar to beginners, easy to master and easy to develop. It is possible to overtake mature people depending on the talent.

## 6.2   Entrepreneurship

Many readers were surprised at the Great Charter Article 5. The project was managed as if it was a small company. The business principle learning method (game) or such personnel (team) must not rely on the government's deep pockets or university. Company seminars were proposed to gain the financial resources. BASE was not a company, students are not employees, and the teacher is not a president. However, it existed on the university campus. Doing the same trial at an active company is too risky for students. An interface such as a university laboratory makes students feel safe. The members understood that the team must earn funds independently of its academic success. Such beliefs forced the team and the students to be entrepreneurial.

## 6.3   Mindsets of Students for the Awakening

The authors conducted interviews with many students to understand their actual image of the BASE Project. To understand many reasons individually, the following mindsets might be reported (Mindset A).

Mindset A (BASE)

1. I love this environment.
2. I love my friends and my teachers.
3. I love a game. I do not mind even there is no remuneration or credit.
4. I love to act socially. I want to spread our game.
5. I want to take over my senior's contribution to delivering to the next generation.

The authors conducted many formal lectures with credits using a business game where the student mindset was characterized as shown below (Mindset B).

Mindset B (Lecture using Game)

1. I am neutral on this game. I have to play a game because the teacher checks attendance.
2. I want to get a better score than my rivals get.
3. I like this game. However, it remains on the level of 'better than a one-way lecture'.
4. It is an obstacle to be forced to communicate with other students in the game.
5. After this semester, I will be free from the game, also from the teacher.

The Mindsets A and B differed for many reasons. A traditional lecture does not provide close communication among students. Students are isolated but are compelled to participate in active learning. Merely playing the game is insufficient to arrive at an Awakening from the descriptions above. Some factors other than those of games are necessary.

If BASE is a real company selling a business game or proposing a seminar to other companies, what is a mindset of an employee of a company (Mindset C)?

Mindset C (Company)

1. I am neutral on this game, but demonstrating, promoting, and selling it is my duty.
2. I must work harder to receive a salary and to gain a promotion.
3. I associate with my colleagues only to stay in this company comfortably.
4. If I resign from this company, I have no relation to the game and colleagues anymore.

Compared with mindset B, mindset C recognizes the target more positively because it is necessary to live. Communication takes place between a customer and colleagues because it is necessary to remain in the company. Those skills and behaviors are derived from a sincere motivation. It might be readily apparent that working in mindset C is not fun, just as a gaming lecture in mindset B is not attractive. In mindsets B and C, they are forced to attend, participate passively and gain something other than a game, feeling obstacles to committing to others. The differences between mindsets A, B and C are summarized (Table 2).

**Table 2.** Mindsets in BASE

|  | Do they love their activity? | Do they form a group and communicate? | What do they acquire as remuneration? | Motivation |
|---|---|---|---|---|
| Mindset A (BASE) | Strongly Yes | Private, tighten, and hot network | Happiness Friendship Satisfaction | Remarkably High |
| Mindset B (Lecture using game) | Better than one-way lecture, but less interested | Least group and least communication; Temporally | Credit | Neutral or Low |
| Mindset C (Company) | Neutral | Least group and least communication; Official and dry network | Salary and position | Neutral or Low |

The key factors of project success are ambitious mindsets shared with the following features: 1) students love games; 2) they feel a bond with other members; and 3) they see no relation to money, duty or academic credits.

To achieve student-teacher collaboration as a tool to develop a great game with the possibility of extension to wider society, students who have no experiences with game-play can be admitted to create a group with common interests. Then, the game development experience would let students stimulate their curiosity, awaken, extend their talents without limitations and deliver new generations' impression. The primary factor of student–teacher collaboration led to strong loyalty, friendship, awakening and sustained an incredible business games network.

# 7 Conclusion

This study explored the possibility of generalizing the BASE project characteristics. BASE developed new student-teacher collaboration style that was more practical and durable than similar trials based on the recognition of a teacher as higher than students. BASE included youth power in a digital age as important potential partners, while optimizing rules, arranging a stage on which to work comfortably and ensuring student growth in the right direction without limitation. Awakening produced an ambitious mindset, a global spirit, and entrepreneurship. Such practices derived from student-teacher collaboration have proven its effectiveness throughout BASE history.

Across 16 years since the beginning of the project, the team obtained ideas to sustain its own experiences. Individual readers should design a unique solution to comply with each demand and limitation. The BASE project introduces many tips delivered from student-teacher collaboration on S/G development that are ready to use in a project. Student-teacher collaboration is useful to seek a dream and provide the project sustainability.

# References

1. Freire, P.: Pedagogy of the Oppressed. Continium, New York (2007)
2. Bonwell, C.C., Eison, J.A.: Active Learning: Creating Excitement in the Classroom. 1991 ASHE-ERIC Higher Education Reports. ERIC Clearinghouse on Higher Education, The George Washington University, Washington, DC (1991)
3. Nunan, D. (ed.): Collaborative Language Learning and Teaching. Cambridge University Press, Cambridge (1992)
4. Cummins, J.: Language, Power, and Pedagogy: Bilingual Children in the Crossfire, vol. 23. Multilingual Matters (2000)
5. Zalyaeva, E.O., Solodkova, I.M.: Teacher-student collaboration: institute of economics and finance Kazan federal university approach. Proc. Soc. Behav. Sci. **152**, 1039–1044 (2014)
6. Webb, N.M., Farivar, S.: Promoting helping behavior in cooperative small groups in middle school mathematics. Am. Educ. Res. J. **31**(2), 369–395 (1994)
7. Wink, R.L.: The relationship of self-concept and selected personality variables to achievement in music student teaching. J. Res. Music Educ. **18**(3), 234–241 (1970)
8. Bergee, M.J.: A scale assessing music student teachers' rehearsal effectiveness. J. Res. Music Educ. **40**(1), 5–13 (1992)
9. Irby, D.M.: Clinical teacher effectiveness in medicine. Acad. Med. **53**(10), 808–815 (1978)
10. Bulte, C., Betts, A., Garner, K., Durning, S.: Student teaching: views of student near-peer teachers and learners. Med. Teach. **29**(6), 583–590 (2007)
11. Shannon, D.M., Twale, D.J., Moore, M.S.: TA teaching effectiveness: the impact of training and teaching experience. J. High. Educ. **69**(4), 440–466 (1998)
12. Park, C.: The graduate teaching assistant (GTA): lessons from North American experience. Teach. High. Educ. **9**(3), 349–361 (2004)
13. Nakagawa, T.: Development of curriculum including student support: trial to quality assurance of higher education in Mie University. Nagoya J. High. Educ. **15**, 23–38 (2015)
14. Hamada, R., Kaneko, T., Hiji, M.: Development of BASE manufacturing business board game. In: Lukosch, H.K., Bekebrede, G., Kortmann, R. (eds.) ISAGA 2017. LNCS, vol. 10825, pp. 34–40. Springer, Cham (2018). https://doi.org/10.1007/978-3-319-91902-7_4
15. Hamada, R., Hiji, M., Kaneko, T.: Development of software engineering business board game. Dev. Bus. Simul. Exp. Learn. **41**, 292–299 (2014)
16. Kaneko, T., Hamada, R., Hiji, M.: Development of BASE supply chain collaboration game. Dev. Bus. Simul. Exp. Learn. **43**, 8–16 (2016)
17. Hamada, R., Kaneko, T., Hiji, M.: Development of supply chain collaboration game by using tangible blocks. Dev. Bus. Simul. Exp. Learn. **45**, 280–294 (2018)
18. Kaneko, T., Hamada, R., Hiji, M.: Business game promoting supply chain collaboration education at universities. In: Hamada, R., Soranastaporn, S., Kanegae, H., Dumrongrojwatthana,

P., Chaisanit, S., Rizzi, P., Dumblekar, V. (eds.) Neo-Simulation and Gaming Toward Active Learning. TSS, vol. 18, pp. 137–146. Springer, Singapore (2019). https://doi.org/10.1007/978-981-13-8039-6_13

19. Hamada, R., Hiji, M., Kaneko, T.: Development of BASE manufacture game in Thai. Thaisim J.: Learn. Dev. (TSJLD) 1(1), 1–17 (2016)
20. Chairungroj, N., et al.: Development of BASE mass manufacturing production game. Thaisim J.: Learn. Dev. (TSJLD) 2(2), 37–52 (2017)
21. Engpraphunkorn, V., et al.: Development of BASE agriculture game. J. Liberal Arts 1(2), 29–43 (2018)
22. Hamada, R., Panuwatwanich, K., Kaneko, T., Hiji, M., Burunchai, K., Choompolanomakhun, G., Sri-on, C.: How to describe a large business on a business board game: an Illustration of construction company. In: Hamada, R., Soranastaporn, S., Kanegae, H., Dumrongrojwatthana, P., Chaisanit, S., Rizzi, P., Dumblekar, V. (eds.) Neo-Simulation and Gaming Toward Active Learning. TSS, vol. 18, pp. 485–504. Springer, Singapore (2019). https://doi.org/10.1007/978-981-13-8039-6_46

# Gamifying Serious Games: Modding Modern Board Games to Teach Game Potentials

Micael Sousa(⊠) (iD)

Department of Civil Engineering, CITTA, University of Coimbra, Coimbra, Portugal
micaelssousa@gmail.com

**Abstract.** The growing interest in game-based approaches is evident. But establishing Gamification and Serious Game processes are challenging, especially when there are few available resources and game design knowledge. Low-tech and low-budget games can be the solution to learn and foster game-based approaches. We propose a method where modern board games were successfully adapted, through a modding process, to deliver a game-based experience to adult students, allowing them to learn about serious games and gamification as tools to train skills. Ice-breaking exercises and an expositive lecture introduced game-based approaches. Selected modern board games to play with students were adapted previously through interactive playtest with hobby gamers. The final play session was done during a one-day session, playing seven different modified board games followed by debriefing stages, discussion, and evaluation of each experience. Students were able to identify the skills defined for each game and differentiate between gamification and serious game approaches.

**Keywords:** Analog games · Board games · Gamification · Modding · Serious games

## 1 Introduction

Game-based approaches have been increasing in the last years [1, 2]. Despite some failures, many new projects explore the benefits of gamification and Serious Games (SG) [3]. Games fascinate innovators that want to improve performances while providing enjoyable experiences. But profiting from these game usages is challenging to do in practice due to insufficient knowledge and resources [4].

Gamification and SG can motivate and engage players to learn, develop skills and produce valuable outcomes to many different activities [5]. But authors like Deterding et al. [6] argue that in gamification, players are prone to focus on secondary traits of the experiences, like too much focus on winning and getting prizes without being connected to the serious purposes of the activities. Authors like Werbach et al. [7, 8] and Chou [9] give some solutions to go beyond the simple patching and pasting of "Points, Badges, Leaderboards and Prizes" to generate a gamification approach. In a successful gamification approach, game mechanisms must relate to goals beyond the game system. Deterding et al. [6] argue that SG can surpass this problem because the intrinsic motivation of play dismisses the need for extrinsic prizes. Despite these problems, there have

© Springer Nature Switzerland AG 2022
U. Dhar et al. (Eds.): ISAGA 2021, LNCS 13219, pp. 254–272, 2022.
https://doi.org/10.1007/978-3-031-09959-5_21

been many successful uses of gamification and SG [5, 10]. We argue that the quality of the game design is the core ingredient for success for gamelike approaches, even when the product is not complete games [11, 12].

But how can we explore and use successful game design traits to improve game-based approaches for specific purposes? Are there ways to prepare users and institutions to profit from gamification and SG without being experts in game design? Can this be done progressively and using low-budget and low-tech solutions to learn and test prototypes?

We believe that modern board games can play a role as a support tool for gamification and SG development. Learning from modern board game design innovation [13] can be valuable. The innovation in the components and the fascination with the materiality of these games [14] and their social engagement potential [15] can teach us about game design and user engagement.

Several experiences of modding modern board games to became SG exist [16–20]. These entertainment board games became serious games when played to address specific purposes beyond playing for fun. For example, we can invite players to play a storytelling game and transform it into a serious game by defining the theme and later debriefing the game outcomes. Tweaking the rules also can work. Modding are inexpensive approaches that deliver fast results. Diving into their game systems and mechanisms to design new games is another promising possibility. In these analogue game, the lack of automation empowers the players [21] and establish inevitable collaborations [22–25], which demand players to interact directly with each other and the game mechanisms [26, 27]. This way players can reflect on what is common regarding systems of entertainment games, gamification, and serious games. Players can see how the game mechanisms can deliver experiences (aesthetics) and relate these experiences to the goals of serious games. Simultaneously, players can testify how to go beyond points, badges, leaderboards, and extrinsic rewards, focusing on the effects of the mechanisms to build intrinsic gamification.

The main objective of this experience is to propose a method that allows introducing newcomers to gamification and SG. By playing modified modern board games and debriefing out the experiences, players will train skills and develop a new consciousness about game usage. In this experiment, adult students played several modified modern board games to practise skills and reflect on the implemented SG and gamification approaches. Modding in this context is a softer and simpler way of redesigning game-based approaches. The success of the proposed method depends on the ability to engage students during the games and verify if they related the game experiences with the skills. We present a method to select, modify and conduct game sessions to teach about SG and gamification while training soft skills. Other skills, issues and objectives can be addressed by the prosed method.

## 2    Method

Before the game session, the game session facilitator selected and modified (modding) seven modern board games to deliver specific experiences to students. The game session had a duration of 8 h, attended by mini-MBA adult students. After a brief presentation about modern board games and game-based approaches (30 min), the facilitator conducted the game session to train generic skills valuable professional activities. We will use the terms "students" and "players" as synonyms to describe the experiment subjects.

We started by defining what skills to explore in the sequence of games. These skills were the main goals of playing the games. The concept of Soft skills delivers a base of essential skills all professionals must have [28, 29]. We defined "communication, creativity, problem-solving and collaboration" as the basic skills to approach during the experiment. We combined "communication and creativity" as two related concepts to match the Engagement Design Model (EDM) [30] and establish relationships to what engages player profiles (Fig. 1). We acknowledge that the player typified profiles by Zagalo [30] are guides. Players tend to relate in different percentages of the several typified player profiles (Abstracters, Tinkerers and Dramatists). Absolute matching is unlikely to happen. Communication between players is a transversal skill because it is necessary to play multiplayer games.

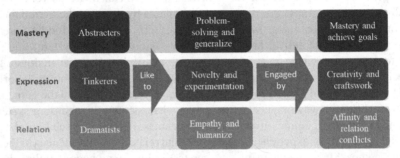

**Fig. 1.** Simplified Engagement design [30] model to support game selection.

Figure 2 presents the implemented method. First, we recorded players' experiences in a questionnaire, gathering data from their previous game experiences and preferences (Step 1). The same questionnaire recorded feelings and players' perceptions after each game (Step 4) and at the end of the session (Step 6).

Although we will propose games playable within the available time because we can estimate how much time they require to play according to *Board Game Geek* (BGG) (www.boardgamegeek.com) databases, games may take longer to play. BGG is the biggest database for modern board games and the one the industry and hobby community uses to analyse, critic and rank games [13, 15, 31]. The game durations can vary because players might need extra explanation [17, 32, 33]. On the other hand, engagement during play and debriefing might go beyond expectations. Stopping these dynamics might frustrate players and reduce learning [34].

The questionnaire followed Mayer et al. [35] framework, evaluating players' game experiences, enjoyment during play, and final perceptions. It was a simple form with multiple-choice questions through a Likert scale (1 to 7), allowing to gather data fast and without downtime or breaking the flow of games. Additionally, players could write words to describe the skills they experienced.

During Step 4, players filled out the questionnaire recording feelings (Table 1) and perceptions before and after the session (Tables 5, 6, 7, 8 and 9). These predefined feelings resulted from *The Big Five Personality traits* [28] and related skills with the preferences of the EMD [30] player profiles, as tested before in the *Light Collaborative Process for Ideation* [19]. The continuous questionnaire filling allowed the record players' engagement in every played game of the session. After playing each game, players directly classified their feelings through a Likert scale (1 to 7), as presented in Table 1. After the session, players classified how the overall game session trained the skills (S) defined in Table 1, again through a multiple-choice Likert scale (1 to 7). The general perceptions of the game experiences, like fun, potential using games as tools for serious purposes, the compatibility of addressing seriousness issues through fun, and the potential of analogue games over digital games were classified by the participants following the same method.

**Table 1.** Feelings after each game and relationships to the EDM profiles preferences.

| Feelings | Profile typology | Value by the profile | Related skills (S) |
| --- | --- | --- | --- |
| Efficiency/competence | Abstracters | Progression and challenge | Problem-solving and decision-making (S1) |
| Imagination/creativity | Tinkerers | Expression and creativity | Communication and creativity (S2) |
| Empathy/altruism | Dramatists | Narrative and interaction | Communication and collaboration (S3) |
| Confusion/complexity | All | General | General |
| Sadness/tedious | | | |
| Excitement/motivation | | | |

After each game, players wrote words related to the skills they thought each game trained. These words were analysed through the grounded theory [36] to cross with other data from the questionnaires.

We selected seven different modern board games that could explore the predefined skills and engage the three typified player profiles during Step 5. In Step 2, for the "Ice-breaking" dynamic, we used *Dixit* [37] cards as support. We displayed 100 cards on a table and allowed students to choose a card and use it to present themselves (self-presentation).

Step 3 consisted of a presentation to introduce the game systems, modern board games, gamification and SG principles and usages (30 min).

For the seven games played in Step 4, we defined a weighting classification for each game, according to the skills each game was supposed to deliver, balancing the skills (S#) and the player profiles (S1: Problem-solving; S2: Communication and Creativity; S3: Collaboration). We selected games with complexity below 2.0 (considered medium according to BGG ranking from 1 to 5) playable in less than 30 min. *Sheriff of Nottingham* [38] and *Detective Club* [39] games were adapted to reduce playtime (modding).

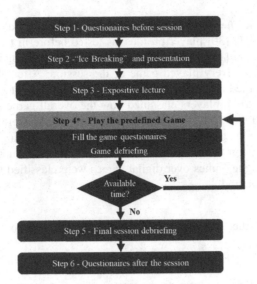

**Fig. 2.** Train session with modern board games scheme.

Tables 2 and 3 describe the selected games for the session. They also refer to the level of modification done in each game (modding). These game adaptations were how these entertainment games were transformed into serious games, addressing the skills to train as objectives for the session. Building these tables (2 and 3) are necessary to plan the session. Selected games must be easy to understand (low complexity) and be played in the available time of the session, leaving time to fill out questionnaires, do the discussions and debrief. Each game is presented with its expected impact (percentage height) regarding the silks (S#) players explore when playing them). These relationships are how the game relates to the goals of the serious games.

After Step 4 (Fig. 2), we introduced a decision box to evaluate available time because time could not be enough to do the final debriefing (Step 5) and finish filling out the questionnaires (Step 6).

Final scoring is the sum of the scores of each game. After each played game, the leaderboard changes according to accumulated scores. The defined gamification badges correspond to the three general skills (S1, S2, and S3). Badge scoring results from the multiplication of the weight factor of the contribution of each game to the specific skill (S#). The sum of the percentages of all the game's contributions to each skill equals one. It means that all games approached all the skills but in different intensities. In short, the scoring value of each badge was the sum of the contribution of all games. The calibration of these weights for each game occurred previously as a subprocess. Playtesting before with experienced gamers helped define these values (subprocess of Step 4). Playtesting, evaluating, and changing values demanded to define a specific subprocess for Fig. 2. This subprocess of Fig. 3 may require multiple iterations until the final selection of games are selected because games should deliver SG goals and an equilibrium between the different skills to address during gameplay (Fig. 3).

**Table 2.** Selected games, related skills, and weighting values to final scoring. Morning.

| Game | Brief description | Modification Level (Modding) | Complexity (1–5) (BGG) | Time (min.) (BGG) | Skills (S) to train (Weights) | | |
|------|-------------------|------------------------------|------------------------|-------------------|-----|-----|-----|
| | | | | | S1 | S2 | S3 |
| Happy Salmon [40] | Players do different forms of actions and greetings related to cards they have to get rid of them. Players need to find other players with a matching card to do the actions. When players get rid of all the cards they win. Real-time play | Low: mixing several copies of the game to allow more players playing the game simultaneously | 1.10 | 2 | 0.05 | 0.10 | 0.10 |
| Magic Maze [41] | Players collaborate to explore a maze, moving pawns to objectives and then escape the maze. Players cannot talk. Each player can only make a specific move. Real-time. Limited time | Low: reducing complexity without traps, doble time to pause, and only one exit | 1,75 | 15 | 0.3 | 0.05 | 0.35 |
| Rail Pass [42] | Players collaborate to deliver cargo cubes to stations by manoeuvring trains. Trains must be passed hand to hand, through tunnels and bridges. Penalties for losing cargo, dropping trains and resigned train drivers. Real-time. Limited time | Low: running two games simultaneously to introduce competition between tables | 2,00 | 10 | 0.3 | 0.05 | 0.35 |

**Table 3.** Selected games, related skills and weighing values to final scoring. Afternoon.

| Game | Brief description | Modification level (Modding) | Complexity (1–5) (BGG) | Time (min.) (BGG) | Skills (S) to train (Weights) | | |
|------|------------------|------------------------------|------------------------|-------------------|------|------|------|
| | | | | | S1 | S2 | S3 |
| Sheriff of Nottingham [38] | Players negotiate and try to have the most goods and money. Players play the role of traders and the sheriff to collect, negotiate and bribe. Turn-based game. Limit of turns | Low: reduce the number of turns to play faster | 1.65 | 30 | 0.2 | 0.2 | 0.05 |
| Telestrations [43] | Players do sequences of words and drawings in notebooks. Each turn, players pass the notebooks in a chain, seeing only the last page. If a player gets a word, they must draw it. If they get a drawing, they must write a word. Turn-based game with simultaneous play. Limit of turns | Medium: players choose the word to start drawing related to the theme the facilitator provided | 1.08 | 30 | 0.05 | 0.20 | 0.05 |

*(continued)*

**Table 3.** (*continued*)

| Game | Brief description | Modification level (Modding) | Complexity (1–5) (BGG) | Time (min.) (BGG) | Skills (S) to train (Weights) | | |
|------|-------------------|------------------------------|------------------------|-------------------|------|------|------|
| | | | | | S1 | S2 | S3 |
| Detective Club [39] | Players play illustrated cards to match the narrator selected word. One player ignores the word. After the card play the narrator revealed the word to all players. They do storytelling to justify their card play. Players vote to find which one ignored the word. Turn-based. A limited number of turns | Medium: players choose the word to start drawing related to the theme the facilitator provided | 1.19 | 30 | 0.05 | 0.20 | 0.05 |
| Ikonikus [44] | Players play cards to try to guess the beast answer the active player would take or feel. The active player chooses a card /response that better suits its preferences | High: the storytelling was about a project or idea | 1.19 | 15 | 0.05 | 0.20 | 0.05 |

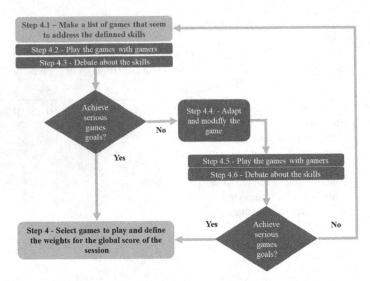

**Fig. 3.** Sub process of Step 4 scheme.

Table 4 highlight the type of adaptations done to each game (modding), adding the scoring systems to implement the point system of the gamification approach. Each score range is also associated with the skill at stake (S#).

**Table 4.** Game adaptations and modification to achieve the session serious goals.

| Feelings | Profile typology and modding | Value by the profile | Related skills (S) |
|---|---|---|---|
| Happy Salmon | Played with 2 copies of the game to allow playing altogether | 1st & 2nd place: 6VP<br>3rd & 4th place: 3VP<br>Other others: 1VP | S1: 0.05<br>S2: 0.10<br>S3: 0.10 |
| Magic Maze | Low adaptation<br>Two tables playing at the same time competing to be the fastest | 1st team to finish: 6VP<br>2nd team to finish: 3VP | S1: 0.30<br>S2: 0.05<br>S3: 0.35 |
| Rail Pass | Low adaptation<br>Two tables playing at the same time competing to be the fastest | 1st team to finish: 6VP<br>2nd team to finish: 3VP | S1: 0.30<br>S2: 0.05<br>S3: 0.35 |
| Sheriff of Nottingham | Low adaptation<br>Two tables playing at the same time, with each player competing to have the most money | 1st & 2nd place: 6VP<br>3rd & 4th place: 3VP<br>Other others: 1VP | S1: 0.20<br>S2: 0.20<br>S3: 0.05 |

*(continued)*

**Table 4.** (*continued*)

| Feelings | Profile typology and modding | Value by the profile | Related skills (S) |
|---|---|---|---|
| Telestrations | Each player could pick the initial word. Words should be related to the final work of the mini-MBA course<br>Two tables playing at the same time, with each player competing to have the most votes | 1st and 2nd players: 6VP<br>3rd and 4th players: 3VP<br>Other players: 1VP | S1: 0.05<br>S2: 0.20<br>S3: 0.05 |
| Detective Club | The narrator should pick a word related to an idea related to the final work of the mini-MBA course<br>Two tables play at the same time, with each player competing to win the most rounds | 1st & 2nd place: 6VP<br>3rd & 4th place: 3VP<br>Other others: 1VP | S1: 0.05<br>S2: 0.20<br>S3: 0.05 |
| Ikonikus | The narrator picks a concrete situation related to the mini-MBA final work and asks for feedback. Other players critically analyse the proposed situation and choose a card to support their argument. The narrator chose the best feedback<br>Two tables playing at the same time, each player competing to win the most votes | 1st & 2nd place: 6VP<br>3rd & 4th place: 3VP<br>Other others: 1VP | S1: 0.05<br>S2: 0.20<br>S3: 0.05 |

We followed the "points, badges, leaderboards and prizes" for the gamification approach. This gamification approach did not require do modify the game mechanisms. The winning conditions of each game were converted into points (Table 4) to define the leaderboard, the badges, and the prizes. The facilitator attributed scores to the players after each game, according to Table 4. Players accumulated points for every played game for motivational purposes. Game points resulted from the multiplication of the weight of the game and the player score in each played game. The accumulated game points generated the leaderboards of players. The top-score players got badges according to the typology of skills (S1, S2, S3). A spreadsheet supported the overall gamification approach. These options were addressed during the final debriefing session (Step 5) as an example of "pasted" gamification. At this stage, players could suggest modifications. It was expected that students suggested integrating game mechanisms with the gamification system.

We established four badges and associated prizes: Global Winer; Winer for "Problem-solving" (S1: Abstracters); Winer for "Communication and Creativity skills" (S2: Tinkerers); Winer for "Collaboration skills" (S3: Tinkerers). Each winner receives a scratch card.

Final debriefing should reinforce learning and promote discussion to improve gamification mechanisms and relate them to the session's goals. In the final questionnaire, students also classified the impact and usefulness of the "points, badges, leaderboards, and prizes" for the game session. They did this following the same Likert scale as implemented for the other session dimensions. Additionally, players could freely write loose words to describe the generic skills experimented during the session. This data was analysed through grounded theory [36, 45] clustering of clustering of similar words to express quantitative results.

## 3 Results

Ten participants (n = 10) attended the session, eight male and two female. Only one participant was familiar with modern board games. 30% of the participants had previous experiences with SG. Attendants had 42.5 years old on average (Av), with a Standard Deviations (SD) of 8.70 years. Participants revealed a moderate interest in sports games (4.60) but low, below 4 (Likert scale 1 to 7) in analogue games (2.60) and digital games (3.10).

**Table 5.** Students' preferences per type of game.

| Type of games | Preferences (Likert scale results 1 to 7) | |
|---|---|---|
| | Average (Av) | Standard Deviation (SD) |
| Sports | 4.60 | 1.02 |
| Analog | 2.60 | 1.62 |
| Digital | 3.10 | 1.97 |

During Step 4, players filled out the questionnaires to record their feelings (implementing the relationship expressed in Table 1). Table 6 and Fig. 4 express the changes in players' feelings from game to game. "Efficiency/competence", "Imagination/creativity", and "Empathy/altruism" varied continuously but ended higher than before the games. "Stress/Anxiety" and "Sadness/tedious" decreased as expected. The unfamiliarity with modern board games and SG could make attendants uncomfortable at the start of the session. "Excitement/motivation" also changed, ending lower than before the session. The enjoyment of each game was always equal to or above 5.20, which can be considered positive.

**Table 6.** Session attendants' feelings after playing each game (Average)

| Feelings | Before | Happy Salmon | Magic Maze | Rail Pass | Sheriff of Nottingham | Telestrations | Detective Club |
|---|---|---|---|---|---|---|---|
| Efficiency/competence | 4.80 | 4.90 | 5.80 | 5.70 | 5.10 | 5.00 | 5.50 |
| Imagination/creativity | 4.50 | 4.40 | 5.20 | 5.40 | 5.10 | 6.30 | 6.60 |
| Empathy/altruism | 4.90 | 6.00 | 5.40 | 5.60 | 5.00 | 4.70 | 5.90 |
| Confusion/complexity | 3.80 | 3.70 | 5.00 | 4.80 | 4.50 | 3.40 | 4.30 |
| Stress/anxiety | 4.30 | 3.20 | 5.20 | 4.50 | 3.80 | 2.70 | 4.10 |
| Sadness/tedious | 2.10 | 1.50 | 1.40 | 1.50 | 1.40 | 1.20 | 1.20 |
| Excitement/motivation | 5.20 | 5.20 | 5.40 | 6.00 | 5.90 | 5.30 | 5.80 |
| Enjoyment of the game | - | 6.10 | 6.60 | 6.80 | 6.50 | 6.10 | 6.50 |

Figure 4 highlights tendencies along with the game session. It is notorious for some tendencies. Start playing the games reduced tedious/sadness at the beginning of the session while increasing again at the end due to tiredness. Stress was high in games with time pressure (*Magic Maze, Rail pass*) and creativity busted in games specifically chosen to foster imagination (*Telestrations, Detective Club*).

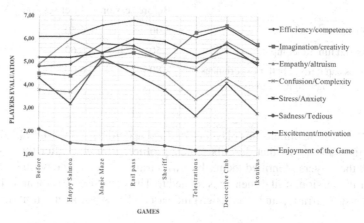

**Fig. 4.** Graphical evolution of feelings during the game session

After playing the games, players classified the potential of the session to train skills (related to soft skills) [28, 29], as defined previously in Table 1. All the evaluations were above 5.50 (Table 7). "Communicative expression", "Idea generation", "Teamwork" and "Meet other attendants/players" skills had evaluations equal to or over 6.00.

According to Mayer et al. [35], it is necessary to consider the background of each player and if the games delivered a pleasant. Table 8 compares the change of players'

**Table 7.** Players' evaluation of the session potential to train skills (Av)

| Skills | Players' perceptions (Av) |
|---|---|
| Communicative expression | 6.20 |
| Idea generation | 6.40 |
| Teamwork | 6.00 |
| Problem-solving | 5.90 |
| Negotiation | 5.60 |
| Time management | 5.50 |
| Strategic planning | 5.50 |
| Meet other attendants/players | 6.70 |

perceptions of fun, the relationship between seriousness and fun, and the potential of analogue games to deliver meaningful experiences (+1.20). The relationship of seriousness and fun increased slightly (+0.10).

**Table 8.** Players' perceptions about fun and seriousness of games

| Affirmations | Players' level of agreement (Av) | | |
|---|---|---|---|
| | Before session | After session | Variation |
| Games are fun | 6.00 | 6.50 | +0.50 |
| Seriousness and fun are compatible | 6.50 | 6.60 | +0.10 |
| Analog games can deliver better experiences for serious purposes than digital games | 4.80 | 6.00 | +1.20 |

Table 9 shows the dimensions players identified according to the EDM [30]. Players classified the dimensions that described their profile before and after the sessions of games. All the players identified themselves with traits related to the typified three profiles. After the session, trait dimensions related to Tinkerers (expression and challenge) and Dramatists (narrative and interaction) increased. The Abstracters' trait dimensions

| Valued by players in a game (color code of the EDM) | Players' level of agreement | | |
|---|---|---|---|
| | Before session | After session | Variation |
| Progression and challenge (Abstracters) | 5.90 | 5.80 | -0.10 |
| Expression and creativity (Tinkerers) | 5.30 | 6.20 | +0.90 |
| Narrative and interaction (Dramatists) | 4.90 | 5.60 | +0.70 |

**Fig. 5.** What players value in games and the relationship to the EDM player profiles. (Color figure online)

(progression and challenge) decreased slightly (see Fig. 5). Figure 5 relates to Table 1 skills and feeling identification.

Table 9 provides an overall evaluation of the session's final remarks. Players considered the games to be above medium complexity (4.50). When comparing to gameplay data (Table 6 and Fig. 4), *Magic Maze* was the most complex game (5.00), followed by *Rail Pass* (4.80), which is coherent with BGG complexity (Table 1). Evaluations were all considered good, above, or equal to 5.70.

According to player perceptions, games related to the objectives of the session (5.90) and the gameplay contributed to achieving it (6.60). Attendants' perception of their ability to use the games as SG and their willingness to play these games just for fun was lower but still positive (5.70 each).

**Table 9.** Final evaluation of the session and the relationship to the SG goals.

| Session classification | Player's perception |
| --- | --- |
| Complexity of games | 4.50 |
| Game relationship to the serious goals | 5.90 |
| The games achieved their serious goals | 6.60 |
| Application of the games in the attendants' professional activities | 5.70 |
| Willingness to play the games just for fun | 5.70 |
| Complexity of games | 4.50 |

Participants did not express relevant difficulty to understand some games (4.50). If the modding did not simplify games, the complexity value could be higher. There was no record of any game failure during gameplay, which means the modding did not affect the game's playability.

Players wrote in the questionnaire's words related to skills they think they trained while playing. These words were analysed through the grounded theory [36, 46], gradually defining clusters that relate to the skills. Several iterations lead to five skills (Fig. 6). Because students wrote isolated words, they were directly associated with the defined skills of Table 1 and EDM three player profiles (Fig. 1).

The player reactions to the gamification approach were varied (Fig. 7). The competition trait had the most spread votes. One person disliked the competition while four loved it. Badges had a similar distribution in preferences, but fewer players loved it. The points, leaderboards, and prizes were enjoyed by eight participants, while two loved it.

In the end, one of the players won three prizes and respective badges (Global Prize, "Communication and Creativity", and Problem-solving). This result allowed the game facilitator to approach gamification issues during debriefing [6]. Players considered that the leaderboard motivated the players with the most score and demotivated those at the bottom. Attendants considered it unfair that a single player could win three prizes. Players decided that the Global winner could only win this prize. The other prizes should go to the second-place players. This solution demonstrated the importance of design flexibility. It motivated players by introducing the feeling of justice. It highlighted the

| Games | Skills (color code of the EDM) | | | | |
|---|---|---|---|---|---|
| | Communicatio n S2 & S3) | Creativity (S2) | Empathy (S3) | Decision-making (S1) | Collaboration (S3) |
| Happy Salmon S1:0.05 S2:0.10 S3:0.10 | 4 | 0 | 6 | 0 | 2 |
| Magic Maze S1:0.30 S2:0.05 S3:0.35 | 4 | 0 | 0 | 6 | 6 |
| Rail Pass S1:0.30 S2:0.05 S3:0.35 | 4 | 0 | 0 | 5 | 5 |
| Sheriff of Nottingham S1:0.20 S2:0.20 S3:0.05 | 6 | 0 | 6 | 6 | 0 |
| Telestrations S1:0.05 S2:0.20 S3:0.05 | 7 | 5 | 5 | 0 | 0 |
| Detective club S1:0.05 S2:0.20 S3:0.05 | 7 | 6 | 0 | 0 | 0 |
| Ikonikus S1:0.05 S2:0.20 S3:0.05 | 6 | 8 | 0 | 0 | 0 |

**Fig. 6.** Players' evaluation of the skills trained in each game.

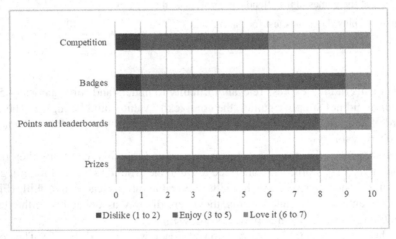

**Fig. 7.** Players' evaluation of gamification traits.

importance of debriefing in learn-based processes [34]. The collective decision changed the scoring mechanism of the gamification dimension to improve the process. Although a simple modification, this example showed that changing the system affect results and motivation. Players acknowledge the objectives of the session (training skills of communication, decision-making, and collaboration).

# 4 Discussion

We argue that the method provided results and achieved intended objectives. Welcoming students with "ice-breaking" game exercises and delivering a simple expositive lecture worked. It helped players to understand that they were playing with purposes. It prepared them to approach the games beyond entertainment. The debriefing stages and reflections after each gameplay (Step 4 of Fig. 2) reinforced the awareness of the serious side of games.

Players enjoyed the games and considered them able to address other objectives beyond entertainment (Table 6 and Fig. 4). Each player was able to relate with the trait dimensions of the player EDM typified profiles. No Single player matched totally with just a type of profile. Selecting a group of games that can provide experiences all player profiles can enjoy can have a higher potential of global engagement. The player appreciation of the games and ability to identify the skills each game should approach proved that the selection and modifying process (Fig. 3) was successful. Searching for games, gathering information and playtesting the games with hobby gamers before building a game session is valuable.

Having players engaged helps to achieve SG goals. During the session, the levels of Stress/Anxiety and Sadness/Tedious were low. Players considered that selected games achieved the serious game objectives of using games to explore relevant skills for professional activities. Players' perceptions match the words they wrote when analysing what skills each game could foster (Fig. 6). Players recognized they would play the games just for fun (5.70), and the perception that games are fun activities increased after play (from 6.00 to 6.50), which is relevant because students' interest in games at the beginning of the session was low (Table 5). The perception of what to value in a game also changed. The valorisation of expression, creativity, empathy, and relation increased significantly (Fig. 5). This growth might also explain the increasing notion that games are fun.

In general, we can argue that the games accomplished their serious goals. Table 7 reveal high values in all skills. These player perceptions accompany the feelings expressed during play (Table 6 and Fig. 4) and the summary of words (Fig. 6). Modding the games was able to control complexity and focus the gameplay experience into the intended skills to explore.

From Fig. 6, we recognize that weight adjustments could improve the scoring system. In the game *Sheriff of Nottingham*, the weight should be higher. Negotiation experiences demand communication and empathy, which relate to Tinkerers (S2) and Dramatists (S3) profiles. This example shows that the weights must be constantly tested, also considering the duration of each game. If a game takes 5 min (i.e., *Happy Salmon*) to play and another 30 min (i.e., *Sheriff of Nottingham*), the impact on players can be different. Players might not have enough time to acknowledge the SG dimensions. In games like *Magic Maze* and *Rail Pass*, the match between the weights and players' perception was more accurate (Table 6, Fig. 4 and 6) for collaboration skills. These variations suggest that playtesting this SG process is constantly necessary. But gamers' previous feedback avoided even higher gaps and mismatches. Constant playtest and adapt to the public and available resources (e.g., time, space) can improve these experiences and interactions.

Although the gamification approach was simple and a "pasting" of the "points, leaderboards, badges and prizes", players realized its potential to maintain ongoing engagement. However, the debriefing stage was essential to establish the collaborative decision-making process that corrected the gamification approach. It proved that attendants understood the potentials and challenges of gamification while being introduced to SG approaches. The game session demonstrated that a one-day training session impact attends and deliver experiences to learn about basic gamification and SG. Inexperienced players played modern board games during several hours, maintaining focus and energy. The games proved to be adaptable for specific goals beyond entertainment. In the case of this experiment, game trained essential skills for professional use (soft skills). As expected, the collaboration and communication skills were high due to the nature of these analogue games.

## 5 Gaps and Future Research

Future research should consider an evaluation per individual player and establish statistical significance between data information. Video recording and biometric data collection could lead to clear conclusions.

Testing the weights and the scoring system for different values and groups of players could lead to the emergence of meaningful patterns to support game-based approaches.

Future experiments could profit more from codesign to adjust and correct the game-based process. Testing if the students could apply what they learned about serious games and gamification to their projects will be recommended. This new learning process requires more time and sessions. But it would allow evaluating the session impact better and with more detail. We could realize the exact duration of a future course and what kind of supervision would be adequate to teaching gamification and SG with modern board games in a way students could deliver ready-to-use solutions.

## References

1. Connolly, T.M., Boyle, E.A., MacArthur, E., et al.: A systematic literature review of empirical evidence on computer games and serious games. Comput. Educ. **59**, 661–686 (2012)
2. Boyle, E.A., Hainey, T., Connolly, T.M., et al.: An update to the systematic literature review of empirical evidence of the impacts and outcomes of computer games and serious games. Comput. Educ. **94**, 178–192 (2016)
3. Larson, K.: Serious games and gamification in the corporate training environment: a literature review. TechTrends **64**, 319–328 (2020)
4. Laamarti, F., Eid, M., El Saddik, A.: An overview of serious games. Int. J. Comput. Games Technol. **2014**, 1–15 (2014)
5. Subhash, S., Cudney, E.A.: Gamified learning in higher education: a systematic review of the literature. Comput. Hum. Behav. **87**, 192–206 (2018). https://doi.org/10.1016/j.chb.2018.05.028
6. Deterding, S., Dixon, D., Khaled, R., Nacke, L.: From game design elements to gamefulness: defining "gamification". In: Proceedings of the 15th International Academic MindTrek Conference: Envisioning Future Media Environments, pp 9–15 (2011)
7. Werbach, K., Hunter, D.: For the Win: How Game Thinking Can Revolutionize Your Business. Wharton Digital Press, Upper Saddle River (2012)
8. Werbach, K., Hunter, D.: The Gamification Toolkit: Dynamics, Mechanics, and Components for the Win. Wharton School Press, Upper Saddle River (2015)

9. Chou, Y.: Actionable Gamification: Beyond Points, Badges, and Leaderboards. Packt Publishing Ltd., Birmingham (2019)
10. Trinidad, M., Ruiz, M., Calderón, A.: A bibliometric analysis of gamification research. IEEE Access **9**, 46505–46544 (2021)
11. Fuchs, M., Fizek, S., Ruffino, P., Schrape, N.: Rethinking Gamification. Meson Press, Luneberg (2014)
12. Hamari, J.: Gamification. In: The Blackwell Encyclopedia of Sociology, pp. 1–3 (2019). https://doi.org/10.1002/9781405165518.wbeos1321
13. Sousa, M., Bernardo, E.: Back in the game: modern board games. In: Zagalo, N., Veloso, A.I., Costa, L., Mealha, Ó. (eds.) Videogame Sciences and Arts, pp. 72–85. Springer International Publishing, Cham (2019). https://doi.org/10.1007/978-3-030-37983-4_6
14. Rogerson, M.J., Gibbs, M., Smith, W.: "I love all the bits": the materiality of boardgames. In: Proceedings of the 2016 CHI Conference on Human Factors in Computing Systems, pp. 3956–3969. Association for Computing Machinery, New York (2016)
15. Rogerson, M.J., Gibbs, M.: Finding time for tabletop: board game play and parenting. Games Cult. **13**, 280–300 (2018). https://doi.org/10.1177/1555412016656324
16. Castronova, E., Knowles, I.: Modding board games into serious games: the case of climate policy. Int. J. Serious Games **2**, 41–62 (2015). https://doi.org/10.17083/ijsg.v2i3.77
17. Sousa, M., Dias, J.: From learning mechanics to tabletop mechanisms: modding steam board game to be a serious game. In: 21st Annual European GAMEON® Conference, GAME-ON® 2020. Eurosis (2020)
18. Abbott, D.: Modding tabletop games for education. In: Gentile, M., Allegra, M., Söbke, H. (eds.) GALA 2018. LNCS, vol. 11385, pp 318–329 (2018). https://doi.org/10.1007/978-3-030-11548-7_30
19. Sousa, M.: Serious board games: modding existing games for collaborative ideation processes. Int. J. Serious Games **8**, 129–147 (2021). https://doi.org/10.17083/ijsg.v8i2.405
20. Sousa, M.: A planning game over a map: playing cards and moving bits to collaboratively plan a city. Front Comput. Sci. **2**, 37 (2020). https://doi.org/10.3389/fcomp.2020.00037
21. Booth, P.: Playing for time. In: Douglas, B., MacCallum-Stewart, E. (eds.) Rerolling Boardgames: Essays on Themes, Systems, Experiences and Ideologies. McFarland & Co Inc., Jefferson (2020)
22. Zagal, J.P., Rick, J., Hsi, I.: Collaborative games: lessons learned from board games. Simul. Gaming **37**, 24–40 (2006). https://doi.org/10.1177/1046878105282279
23. Rogerson, M.J., Gibbs, M.R., Smith, W.: Cooperating to compete: the mutuality of cooperation and competition in boardgame play. In: Proceedings of the 2018 CHI Conference on Human Factors in Computing Systems, pp. 1–13 (2018)
24. Duarte, L.C.S., Battaiola, A.L., Silva, A.H.P.: Cooperation in Board Games. An do XIV Simpósio Bras Jogos e Entretenimento Digit Soc Bras Comput (2015)
25. Zhang, T., Liu, J., Shi, Y.: Enhancing collaboration in tabletop board game. In: Proceedings of the 10th Asia Pacific Conference on Computer Human Interaction, pp. 7–10 (2012)
26. Duarte, L.C.S., Battaiola, A.L.: Distinctive features and game design. Entertain. Comput. **21**, 83–93 (2017). https://doi.org/10.1016/j.entcom.2017.03.002
27. Engelstein, G., Shalev, I.: Building Blocks of Tabletop Game Design: An Encyclopedia of Mechanisms. CRC Press LLC, Boca Raton (2019)
28. Heckman, J.J., Kautz, T.: Hard evidence on soft skills. Labour Econ. **19**, 451–464 (2012). https://doi.org/10.1016/j.labeco.2012.05.014
29. Schulz, B.: The importance of soft skills: education beyond academic knowledge (2008)
30. Zagalo, N.: Engagement Design : Designing for Interaction Motivations. Springer Nature, Cham (2020). https://doi.org/10.1007/978-3-030-37085-5

31. Kritz, J., Mangeli, E., Xexéo, G.: Building an ontology of boardgame mechanics based on the BoardGameGeek database and the MDA framework. In: XVI Brazilian Symposium on Computer Games and Digital Entertainment, Curitiba, pp. 182–191 (2017)

32. Sato, A., de Haan, J.: Applying an experiential learning model to the teaching of gateway strategy board games. Int. J. Instr. **9**, 3–16 (2016)

33. Sousa, M.: Modern serious board games: modding games to teach and train civil engineering students. In: 2020 IEEE Global Engineering Education Conference (EDUCON), pp. 197–201 (2020)

34. Crookall, D.: Serious games, debriefing, and simulation/gaming as a discipline. Simul. Gaming **41**, 898–920 (2010). https://doi.org/10.1177/1046878110390784

35. Mayer, I., Bekebrede, G., Harteveld, C., et al.: The research and evaluation of serious games: toward a comprehensive methodology. Br. J. Educ. Technol. **45**, 502–527 (2014). https://doi.org/10.1111/bjet.12067

36. Charmaz, K.: Constructing Grounded Theory: A Practical Guide through Qualitative Analysis. Sage, London (2014)

37. Roubira, L.: Dixit. Libellud (2008)

38. Halaban, S., Zatz, A.: Sheriff of Nottingham. Arcane Wonders (2014)

39. Nevskiy, O.: Detective Club. IGAMES (2018)

40. Gruhl, K., Weir, Q.: Happy Salmon. North Star Games (2016)

41. Lapp, K.: Magic Maze. Sit Down! (2017)

42. Green, R.T.: Rail Pass. Mercury Games (2019)

43. Användbart Litet Företag: Telestrations. Användbart Litet Företag (2009)

44. Palau, M.: Ikonikus. Brain Picnic (2013)

45. Farkas, T., Wiseman, S., Cairns, P., Fiebrink, R.: A grounded analysis of player-described board game immersion. In: CHI Play 2020 - Proceedings of the Annual Symposium on Computer-Human Interaction in Play, pp. 427–437 (2020). https://doi.org/10.1145/3410404.3414224

46. Sousa, M., Antunes, A.P., Pinto, N.: Fast serious analogue games in planning: the role of non-player participants. Simul. Gaming, 1–19 (2022). https://doi.org/10.1177/10468781211073645. (in press)

# Knowledge Sharing Game for Sales Recovery and Food Waste Reduction at Restaurants

Mizuho Sato[1]([⊠]) [iD] and Hajime Mizuyama[2] [iD]

[1] Department of Food Environment Economics, Tokyo University of Agriculture, 1-1-1, Sakuragaoka, Setagaya-ku, Tokyo 156-0054, Japan
ms207184@nodai.ac.jp
[2] Department of Industrial and Systems Engineering, Aoyama Gakuin University, 5-10-1 Fuchinobe, Chuo-ku, Sagamihara-shi, Kanagawa 252-5258, Japan

**Abstract.** The coronavirus disease (COVID-19) has affected global economies including food industry. The food service industry is unable to operate normally and faces issues such as frequent leave requests, shortened business hours and reduction in the number of seats in restaurants to prevent the spread of COVID-19. As a result, several restaurants have been forced to close. Therefore, this study proposes a game system that applies the mechanism of the prediction market to solicit ideas from employees for recovery of sales in small restaurants and effective use of ingredients (including reduction of food waste) under the business scenario in COVID-19. In such a game, routine restaurant operations can be understood, current issues can be analyzed and the deductions from these can be used as a reference for subsequent business opportunities. The game will improve communication between owners and employees. Understanding the contents of food waste will be beneficial to employees and consumers.

**Keywords:** Foodservice studies · Interview survey · Prediction market · Purchase behaviour · Reduction method

## 1 Introduction

Coronavirus disease (COVID-19) which spread around the world in 2020 affected the food industry. Restaurants continue to be unable to operate normally and face issues such as frequent leave requests, shortened business hours and reduction in the number of seats to prevent the spread of COVID-19. As a result, restaurant management has been severely compromised and many restaurants have been forced to close. According to a report by the Japan Society of Foodservice Studies, restaurants' sales in 2020 decreased 15.1% from 2019 [1]. However, such a sharp decline is because the data includes those of fast-food restaurants which were relatively dominant in the foodservice industry. The loss of sales of small restaurants is expected to be quite large. Moreover, such an impact on the restaurants is occurring not only in Japan but also overseas. According to the National Restaurant Association, American restaurant businesses lost approximately $24 billion in 2020 under the influence of COVID-19 [2].

© Springer Nature Switzerland AG 2022
U. Dhar et al. (Eds.): ISAGA 2021, LNCS 13219, pp. 273–279, 2022.
https://doi.org/10.1007/978-3-031-09959-5_22

Although the business situation of restaurants is deteriorating, new systems responding to COVID-19 have been introduced both in Japan and overseas such as online ordering and takeout systems. These systems had been introduced in some restaurants before COVID-19 but they are expanding now due to the influence of COVID-19. In delivery systems such as Uber Eats, the delivery cost is added to the unit price of the dish and the price per dish increases. Therefore, in a With-COVID-19 scenario, the content promotes purchase behavior when consumers use online orders [3]. When ordering online, the visual quality of the food and its delivery method reduce the risk of COVID-19 infection and promote purchase behavior.

It is important to make good use of online orders, especially in small restaurants. Large-scale restaurants such as large-chain restaurants have begun to reduce the number of unprofitable restaurants. For small restaurants such as private restaurants, reducing the number of restaurants often means closing the business. Innovations such as online ordering to promote consumers' willingness to purchase and improve sales are indispensable for business continuity. As more detailed services are required, it is necessary to share the knowledge of employees. COVID-19 implications have reduced the number of visitors and made it difficult to forecast the number of visitors, thus reducing the feasibility of purchasing ingredients and adjusting the menu. Therefore, the ingredients need to be used efficiently or else, they would be wasted.

The waste from the food industry in 2016 was 27.59 million tons contributed by 16.17 million tons from the food manufacturing industry, 270,000 tons from the food wholesale industry, 1.27 million tons from the food retail industry, 1.99 million tons from the food service industry (including restaurants) and 7.89 million tons from consumers [4]. Among them, the amount of edible food discarded (known as food loss) is 6.43 million tons [5]. In the food service industry, approximately 10% of the food is wasted and 23% of this waste is recycled [4].

Before COVID-19 impacted the food service industry (including restaurants), the causes of food waste were leftover food and over-preparation. From interviews on food waste efforts at 15 restaurants in Setagaya-ku, Tokyo, it was found that employees are interested in understanding food waste at most restaurants [6]. In addition, the most common type of food waste was found to be leftover food. To reduce leftover food, efforts should be made such as not to order for more food than can be eaten at each restaurant and using the surplus ingredients for meals. It is difficult to reduce food waste at restaurants. In university cafeterias, more over-prepared food (cooked food that has not been eaten) is wasted than leftover food. Unsold dishes are put together in a lunch box and sold cheaply. These measures are implemented independently by each restaurant and are rarely discussed. Thus, employees are making efforts to reduce food waste under Before-COVID-19 but their efforts are not effective. With-COVID-19 emphasizes the recovery of the business situation to the Before COVID-19 scenario. Therefore, the awareness and role of employees are significant, and it is necessary to make good use of that knowledge.

The purpose of this research is to develop a game system that applies the mechanism of the prediction market to solicit ideas from employees for the recovery of sales in small restaurants and the effective use of ingredients (including reduction of food waste) in the With-COVID-19 scenario. The prediction market is a future trading market where many users can buy and sell securities in a virtual market. Based on the changes in securities prices, it is possible to obtain dynamic predictions about the future state of the forecast target. This prediction market model will be used as a communication tool between employees and customers. The base prediction market model uses the model of product proposals at companies [7].

## 2 Review of Literature

Most workers in Japanese restaurants are part-time employees such as students and housewives whose turnover rate is high. The deterioration of human relations, dissatisfaction with the guidance system and dissatisfaction with work and growth were found to be factors of job turnover of part-time college students [8]. To decrease the turnover rate, job satisfaction and communication between employees are important. In high-class restaurants in India, employees who share knowledge such as new menu development have a positive impact on restaurant management [9]. Communication with employees and utilisation of their knowledge contributes to restaurant management. If the menu developed by the employees is adopted in the restaurant, it will motivate the employees to work and reduce the turnover rate. The role of employees is greater due to the effects of COVID-19.

The food waste of restaurants (taverns and fast-food joints) could be understood in terms of food loss, cooking waste, cooking loss and leftover food. A considerable amount of leftover food is generated in all restaurants and it is difficult to reduce it by company efforts alone [10]. From the food waste in student cafeterias in Japan, 16% was leftover food and 84% was unsold food, i.e., there was more unsold food than leftover food. Approximately 97% (7,122 g/day) of unsold rice was utilized by storing white rice in the refrigerator and using it the next day and selling the unsold food to employees [11]. A large-scale study of school meals in 78 schools in Italy showed that the food waste is related to the ingredients (such as bread), amount of food, location of cooking, meals provided during the morning break, menu structure and geographical location of the school [12].

A survey of Portuguese restaurant managers and owners during COVID-19 led to a grounded theory analysis that identified issues and 18 themes. The owners introduced takeout as a new business so as to attend to employee payments [13]. Takeout at restaurants helped to continue the restaurant business. When restaurant management and takeout management did not perform well, restaurant performance may deteriorate. From a survey in food waste among consumers in the USA and Italy between Before-COVID-19 and With-COVID-19 scenarios, it was found that food waste was less during COVID-19 for reasons such as increased cooking at home [14]. Since the number of consumers who cook at home is increasing, it is necessary to devise a takeout menu that meets the needs of consumers. For this reason, it is important to use the knowledge of employees.

Using games is one of the effective methods of sharing the knowledge of employees. Overseas studies have been reported that showing the amount of reduction in food waste in terms of monetary amount and environmental load leads to incentive effects [15, 16]. Games can be used to analyze restaurant pricing [17]. In an educational game about restaurant management, each group (each restaurant) competes in purchasing ingredients at an auction for the purpose of maximizing profits, although, it is not actually implemented in restaurants [18].

The mechanism of the prediction market can be used as a gamified approach for sharing knowledge among employees [7, 19]. This approach aims at collecting effective knowledge from employees to achieve a goal or solve a problem in an organization. It was successfully use for refining the strategy of a sales negotiation with shared knowledge among several salespersons [7]. It is composed of a few prediction market sessions in each of which the participants can forecast the success or failure of sales negotiation. When buying or selling prediction securities in the session, they must explain their buying or selling decisions and review other participants' comments. These comments contain valuable knowledge to refine the decisions of the sales negotiation and collected and evaluated throughout the sessions. This paper extends the approach for collecting employees' knowledge on how to enhance sales and reduce food waste in a restaurant.

## 3   Overview of the Proposed Game

### 3.1   Knowledge Sharing Game for Sales Recovery

First, an interview survey is conducted on purchasing, cooking, eating, and preservation at restaurants in Tokyo (Fig. 1: Step 1). The results focus on issues and aspects that have not been visualized until now (e.g., supplier, ordering method, food delivery method,

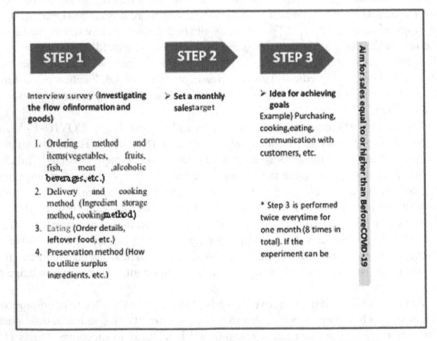

**Fig. 1.** Knowledge sharing game for sales recovery at restaurant

cooking method, order contents, leftover food and storage method of surplus food) Then, a sales target is set (Fig. 1: Step 2). Subsequently, employees, owners and consumers (university students and working people) use the prediction market model to buy and sell securities for ideas that can contribute to the recovery of restaurant sales as well as improvement of sales for each restaurant (Fig. 1: Step 3). Step 3 is performed twice every time for one month (eight times in total).

If the experiment can be longer, it may be extended for approximately 3 months. In this prediction market, restaurant employees can become owners of their proposals by offering new ideas. Other participants (employees, students and adults) evaluate proposals, provide improvement comments, predict the effect of each idea (buy and sell forecast securities) and suggest methods to implement these ideas. The opinions of the participants are assessed and disclosed to other participants so that they are evaluated for their quality according to the subsequent price fluctuations of the forecast securities. By repeating the trading of these securities for a certain period, it will be possible to devise and evaluate ideas that are more suitable for each restaurant.

## 3.2 Knowledge Sharing Game for Reducing Food Waste

First, an interview survey is conducted on purchasing, cooking, eating and preservation at restaurants in Tokyo and regarding food waste at each stage (Fig. 2: Step 1). Then, goals are set such as aiming for food waste "0" (Fig. 2: Step 2). Subsequently,

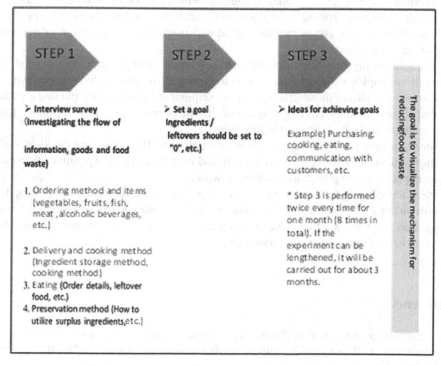

**Fig. 2.** Knowledge sharing game for reducing food waste

employees, owners and consumers (university students and working people) use the prediction market model to buy and sell securities for ideas for reducing food waste and to find a food waste reduction method that suits each restaurant (Fig. 2: Step 3). Step 3 is performed twice every time for one month (eight times in total). If the experiment is longer, it is performed for approximately three months. In this prediction market, restaurant employees can become owners of their proposals by offering new ideas. Other participants (employees, students and adults) evaluate proposals, provide improvement comments, predict the effect of each idea (buy and sell forecast securities) and suggest methods to implement these ideas. The opinions of the participants are assessed and disclosed to other participants so that their opinions are gathered according to the subsequent price fluctuations of the forecast securities. By repeating the trading of these securities for a certain period, each restaurant can devise and evaluate food waste.

### 3.3  Fusion of Shared Knowledge for Sales Recovery and Food Waste Reduction

Reducing food waste mitigates waste generation and leads to recovery in sales at restaurants. The results from the knowledge sharing games for sales recovery and reducing food waste can be compared, integrated and studied for their relationship.

## 4  Conclusions

1.  There are various types of small restaurants which are run by a limited number of people. Therefore, routine operations are difficult to visualize. By visualizing such operations, current issues can be studied and used as a reference for subsequent business opportunities.
2.  The relationship between employees and restaurant owners is not always good. In addition, employees may find it difficult to express their opinions to the owner which results in employee dissatisfaction and subsequent resignations. By playing a game that shares the knowledge of employees, it will be easier to express opinions that cannot normally be expressed to the owner.
3.  Ideas for sales recovery are also given by employees. By combining the ideas with the opinions of various people to improve and implement them, a positive effect can be expected on employee motivation for work.
4.  Ideas for reducing food waste have not been proposed. Therefore, understanding the current situation and its cause of occurrence and proposing ideas for waste reduction methods will be helpful. Understanding the contents of food waste will lead to awareness of employees and consumers.

## References

1.  Japan Society of Foodservice Studies: Food service industry market trend survey, annual result report of Reiwa 2 (2020). http://www.jfnet.or.jp/files/nenkandata-2020.pdf. Accessed 28 Apr 2021

2. National Restaurant Association: Industry Research. https://restaurant.org/manage-my-restaurant/business-operations/covid19/research/industry-research. Accessed 28 Apr 2021
3. Brewer, P., Sebby, A.G.: The effect of online restaurant menus on consumers' purchase intentions during the COVID-19 pandemic. Int. J. Hosp. Manag. **94**, 102777 (2021)
4. Ministry of Agriculture, Forestry and Fisheries, 2016 fiscal year food waste and recycling, https://www.maff.go.jp/j/tokei/kekka_gaiyou/loss/jyunkan_h29/index.html. Accessed 30 Mar 2021
5. Ministry of the Environment: Usage status of food waste, etc. (2016 estimate) Conceptual diagram. http://www.env.go.jp/press/106665.html. Accessed 30 Mar 2021
6. Sato, M., Hatta, K., Higuchi, W., Hayashida, T., Hotta, K., Wunderlich, S.M.: Efforts to reduce food loss in restaurants and to assess consumer awareness in Japan. In: Environmental Impact 2020, Proceedings, vol. 245, pp. 21–30 (2020)
7. Mizuyama, H., Yamaguchi, S., Sato, M.: A prediction market-based gamified approach to enhance knowledge sharing in organizations. Simul. Gaming **50**(5), 572–597 (2019)
8. Hattori, K., Kawaki, T., Kusuno, K., Nakano, K., Ito, K.: In the food service industry securing human resources and improving retention rate. J. Japan Soc. Foodserv. Stud. **20**, 24–34 (2015)
9. Chowdhury, M., Prayag, G.: The impact of social capital and knowledge sharing intention on restaurants' new product development. Int. J. Contemp. Hosp. Manag. **32**(10), 3271–3293 (2020)
10. Kobayashi, T., Ishii, N., Miyazaki, K.: Analysis of food loss management in the food service industry- positioning as a marketing strategy and direction of development-. J. Japan Soc. Foodserv. Stud. **18**, 24–25 (2013)
11. Takahashi, J., Saito, T., Yamakawa, H.: Evaluation of food loss reduction efforts in university cafeterias and user acceptance. In: Proceedings of the 28th, Annual Conference of Japan Society of Material Cycles and Waste Management, pp. 115–116 (2017)
12. Boschini, M., Falasconi, L., Cicatiello, C., Franco, S.: Why the waste? A large scale study on the causes of food waste at school canteens. J. Clean. Prod. **246**, 118994 (2020)
13. Madeira, A., Palrão, T., Mendes, A.S.: The impact of pandemic crisis on the restaurant business. Sustainability **13**(1), 40 (2021). https://doi.org/10.3390/su13010040. Accessed 13 May 2021
14. Rodgers, R.F., et al.: "Waste not and stay at home" evidence of decreased food waste during the COVID-19 pandemic from the U.S. and Italy. Appetite **160**, 105110 (2021)
15. Comber, R., Thieme, A.: Designing beyond habit: opening space for improved recycling and food waste behaviors through processes of persuasion, social influence and aversive affect. Pers. Ubiquit. Comput. **17**, 1197–1210 (2013)
16. Werfl, P., Seabrook, J.A., Gilliland, J.A.: "Reduce food waste, save money": testing a novel intervention to reduce household food waste. Environ. Behav. 1–33 (2019)
17. Guo, X., Zheng, X.: Examination of restaurants online pricing strategies: a game analytical approach. J. Hosp. Market. Manag. **26**(6), 659–673 (2017)
18. Brozik, D., Zapaska, A.: The restaurant game. Simul. Gaming **31**(3), 407–416 (2000)
19. Plott, C.R.: Markets as information gathering tools. South. Econ. J. **67**, 1–15 (2000)

# Natural Security Games in the Regenerative Economy: A Review

Vaisakh Yesodharan[1]($\boxtimes$), Feng Weiyu[1], Zaid A. Almuala[1],
Eric G. Heckenauer Barrón[1], Shoeib Faraji Abdolmaleki[1],
J. Julio Fernández Rodríguez[2], and Pastora M. Bello Bugallo[1]($\boxtimes$) (iD)

[1] TECH-NASE Research Group, School of Engineering, Universidade de Santiago de
Compostela, Av. Lope Gómez de Marzoa, s/n, 15782 Santiago de Compostela, Spain
vaikash.yesodharan@rai.usc.es, pastora.bello.bugallo@usc.es
[2] CESEG, Faculty of Law, Universidade de
Santiago de Compostela, Santiago de Compostela, Spain

**Abstract.** Natural security refers to all aspects of security related to a reliable,
sufficient, affordable and sustainable supply of natural resources, and energy to
meet the needs of society by protecting the environment, human health, and living
things. Effects derived from climate change are one of the biggest challenges
encountered in terms of natural security. Simulation games play a vital role in
building a sustainable world. This study investigates the games for topics like
natural security, energy security, carbon capture and storage, renewable energy
and waste. A review of the literature showed forty-three studies which focused on
the objective of the study. Most of the games were used in education and used to
transfer knowledge in the field of waste. The paper points out the importance of
natural security and the need to develop more games in natural security and its
related fields to build a regenerative economy.

**Keywords:** Simulation game · Serious game · Carbon capture and storage ·
Energy security · Renewable energy

## 1 Introduction

Natural security refers to all aspects of security relating to a reliable, sufficient, affordable and sustainable supply of natural resources and energy to meet the needs of society
by protecting the environment, human health, and living things [1]. According to the
proposal for the VIII Environmental program of the EU, the long-term priority objective
for 2050 states that 'citizens live well, within the planetary boundaries in a regenerative economy where no waste is generated, no net emissions of greenhouse gases are
produced, and economic growth is decoupled from resource use and environmental
degradation, and natural capital is protected, restored and valued in ways that enhance
resilience to climate change and other environmental risks' [2].

Natural capital refers to the world's stocks of natural resources which include geol-
ogy, soil, air, water, and all living things [3]. From minerals for manufacturing goods,

© Springer Nature Switzerland AG 2022
U. Dhar et al. (Eds.): ISAGA 2021, LNCS 13219, pp. 280–287, 2022.
https://doi.org/10.1007/978-3-031-09959-5_23

water for drinking, and land for agriculture to produce food, humans rely on natural resources beyond limits. Excessive use of natural resources has resulted in resource depletion and improper waste treatments have increased landfills affecting biodiversity and climatic change [4, 5]. To fuel vehicles, light and heat homes and businesses and to run industry and agriculture, energy dependence has increased drastically and become an essential part of all dimensions of human life. This has created a huge demand for fossil fuels which has resulted in the depletion of non-renewable resources and global warming affecting biodiversity [6]. In this context, it is essential to ensure the natural security related to energy and natural resources. Some of the essential factors with which natural security can be achieved are using renewable energy resources [7], attaining energy security [8], implementing carbon capture techniques [9], and reducing waste [10].

Gaming/simulation was defined as 'a gestalt communication mode which contains a game-specific language, appropriate communication technologies and multilogue interaction pattern'. Gaming and simulation give importance to a heuristic under-standing of complex reality [11]. Scientific results can be translated into a language easily understood by the public with the application of games [12]. Simulation games are best suited for dealing with complex and interrelated problems and could be used beneficially in the field related to environmental problems and sustainable development [13]. They have the potential to embrace time, approach a large audience, and generate a real impact to contribute to sustainability [14]. Serious games were first recognized as 'games which have an explicit and carefully thought-out educational purpose and are not intended primarily for amusement' [15]. They are 'digital games, simulations, virtual environments and mixed reality/media that provide opportunities to engage in activities through responsive narrative/story, gameplay or encounters to inform, influence, for wellbeing, and experience to convey meanings' [16].

This paper will present an overview of the games related to natural security along with energy security, renewable energy, carbon capture and storage, and waste. It presents a complete review of the games related to the fields related to natural security and analyses certain specific characteristics such as year, type of games, and area of application.

## 2  Method

A survey of the literature was carried out using the Web of Science (WoS) and Scopus comprehensive database platform from the year 1950 to 2021 [17]. The keywords used for the global search were 'natural security', 'carbon capture and storage', 'renewable energy', 'waste', 'energy security', 'game', 'simulation game', and 'serious game'. The resultant articles were screened after reading the abstracts.

Despite their lexical similarities, game theory and gaming simulations are employed to define two seemingly distinct topics. The study of mathematical models of conflict and cooperation between intelligent rational players which leads to 'game concepts' is known as 'game theory' [18]. The articles on game theory were not included in this review.

## 3  Development

Based on critical keywords, 17 articles in the field of renewable energy were found. The sources of more than 50% of the articles were proceedings of international conferences

(Fig. 1(a)). Since 1993, twenty articles are found in the field related to waste and most of them are simulation and serious games (Fig. 1(b)). Six articles on carbon capture and storage from 2013 to 2020 are obtained (Fig. 1(c)) which consist of simulation games, video games, and online games, of which the most widely used type of game is the simulation game.

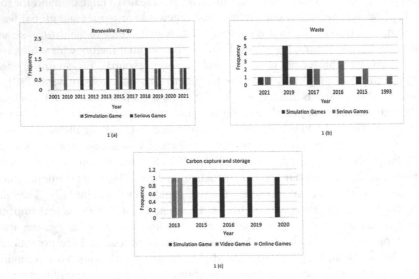

**Fig. 1.** Game type assessment over years

## 4   Results

Serious games and simulation games are the most important types of games in renewable energy, with increasing research interest in the serious games (Table 1).

The objective of these games is to increase the understanding of the players and their familiarity with the engineering process (Fig. 2(a)). The scope of the games in renewable energy is for education and understanding the processes in renewables. The interaction of games and renewables requires more comprehensive study (18%). Generally, most articles have referred to energy transition and considered renewable energy as a sustainable alternative ([19, 20], and [21]). Although games have dealt more with the use of renewables (such as energy supply [22], increase awareness of renewable energy [19], energy system [23], and complex energy system functions [20]), a few games have partially addressed the deeper concepts of natural security [7, 21, 24]. Some games focused on both definitions (12%).

Simulation games and serious games have been widely used for a long time for creating awareness about waste and its prevention, recycling, and reduction effectively. They were mostly used (60%) to educate school children, university graduates, and workers in industries (Fig. 2(b)). Most serious games used robots [31], board games [32], role-play [38], 3D virtual environment [39] and tangible user interface [40]. Recent

**Table 1.** Description of games related to waste

| Type of game | Scope of the game | Building blocks of the game | Reference |
|---|---|---|---|
| Serious games | Academic, training university graduates | Software development kit (Microsoft Kinetic software), virtual interface, waste sorting algorithm | [30] |
| | Academic, children's attitude | Social robot (PeppeRecycle), convolutional neural network | [31] |
| | Academic, construction management students | Board game, tower of infinity, LEGO bricks | [32] |
| | Academic, environmental education | Android video game consisting of characters | [33] |
| | Academic, high school students | Gagne's learning model (pedagogical aspects) | [34] |
| Simulation game | Academic, process management students | Assembly of the toy house, simulation of real process | [35] |
| | Public administration, citizen training | GarbMAS, multi agent system | [36] |
| | Academic, higher education students | Electriver board game | [37] |

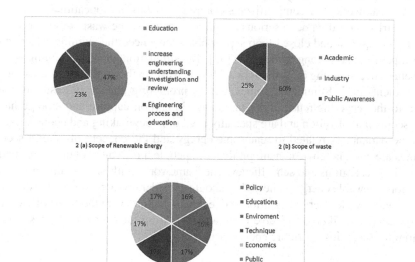

2 (a) Scope of Renewable Energy

2 (b) Scope of waste

2 (c) Scope of Carbon Capture and Storage

**Fig. 2.** Scope of various games

advances in the field of waste are the use of simulation games for improving the skills of engineering graduates and training industrial workers in lean manufacturing [41]. The use of simulation games creates a behavioural change in its players, helping them to understand the impacts created by waste on the environment and to act accordingly.

The articles on carbon capture and storage address areas of applications such as environment, policy, economics, education, public, and technique (Fig. 2(c)). Several simulation games relate to carbon capture and storage [25–28]. An evolutionary game model can analyze the stability of and discuss the systematic dynamic processes to cover the conflict of interests on carbon capture and storage adoption between governments and coal-fired power plants in China [25]. There are other types of games such as video games [26] and online games [29]. While searching for games related to energy security, it was found that a major share of the results was related to the game theory which was out of the scope of this study as mentioned in the methodology and there were no simulation or serious games related to energy security. Another interesting search result was related to natural security as there were no games developed in this field.

## 5   Discussion

This study has shown an overview of games related to natural security and its associated building blocks such as renewable energy, carbon capture and storage, energy security, and waste. Forty-three studies on games were found and used in the study.

Most games are applied in education. A simulation game on the sustainability of plastic waste improved the knowledge acquisition and behavioural changes of University students [42]. Games not only help in enhancing technical knowledge and skill but also improved teamwork and competitiveness among scholars in educational institutions [43]. Electriver board game, a serious simulation game on the waste of electronic and electrical equipment and closed-loop supply chain, enhanced the learning effectiveness and competitiveness among participants [37]. The simulation games in training workers for a better understanding of methods in analyzing waste in the assembly process showed improvements [41]. Simulation games help in promoting change in customer habits related to the recycling/reuse of waste. Games in carbon capture and storage have a larger scope of application and are specially used in policymaking and economics.

Some parameters related to renewable energy and the concept of natural security in games are cost and environment, production, people, profit and balance information, technical issue, regions and self-efficacy. The frameworks with more details are needed to develop renewable energy games. They should consider social factors and institutional points of view while energy transition and technical factors were the focus of the game. Energy security is likely to receive more attention from the theme of games with the potential for scenarios for future energy issues.

## 6   Conclusion

Natural security is a novel idea that has a major role in achieving sustainable development goals. This article provides a review of simulation and serious games in natural security, energy security, carbon capture and storage, renewable energy and zero waste. It gives a strong analysis of the areas of applications of simulation and serious games. The huge gap in games for natural security and energy security requires an adequate amount of development to enhance the knowledge for a heuristic understanding of complex reality.

# References

1. Lema Martínez, A.M.: Visión prospectiva de la seguridad natural en un sistema global sostenible. Universidade de Santiago de Compostela (2020)
2. E.-L.-52020PC0652-E.- EUR-Lex: Proposal for VIII Environmental Program EU (2020). https://eur-lex.europa.eu/legal-content/EN/TXT/?uri=CELEX%3A52020PC0652. Accessed 29 May 2021
3. United Nations: Glossary of Environment Statistics, Studies in Methods (1997). https://stats.oecd.org/glossary/detail.asp?ID=1730. Accessed 29 May 2021
4. Tonini, D., Albizzati, P.F., Astrup, T.F.: Environmental impacts of food waste: learnings and challenges from a case study on UK. Waste Manag. **76**, 744–766 (2018). https://doi.org/10.1016/j.wasman.2018.03.032
5. Bugallo, P.M.B., Andrade, L.C., De la Torre, M.A., López, R.T.: Analysis of the slaughterhouses in Galicia (NW Spain). Sci. Total Environ. **481**(1), 656–661 (2014). https://doi.org/10.1016/j.scitotenv.2013.11.079
6. Burke, S.: Natural security. Nat. Secur. (june) (2012). https://doi.org/10.1525/california/9780520253476.001.0001
7. Dresner, M.: Changing energy end-use patterns as a means of reducing global-warming trends. J. Environ. Educ. **21**(2), 41–46 (1990). https://doi.org/10.1080/00958964.1990.9941930
8. Universidade de Santiago de Compostela: Centro de Estudos De Seguridade (CESEG), Energy Security. Universidade de Santiago de Compostela (2017)
9. Kelsall, G.: Carbon capture utilisation and storage - status barriers and potential, CCC/304|IEA Clean Coal Centre. https://www.iea-coal.org/report/carbon-capture-utilisation-and-storage-status-barriers-and-potential-ccc-304/. Accessed 28 May 2021
10. Bello Bugallo, P.M., Cristóbal Andrade, L., Magán Iglesias, A., Torres López, R.: Integrated environmental permit through best available techniques: evaluation of the fish and seafood canning industry. J. Clean. Prod. **47**, 253–264 (2013). https://doi.org/10.1016/j.jclepro.2012.12.022
11. Duke, R.D.: Gaming: The Future's Language. Sage (1974)
12. Reckien, D., Eisenack, K.: Climate change gaming on board and screen: a review. In: Simulation and Gaming, vol. 44, no. 2–3, pp. 253–271. SAGE Publications, Los Angeles, 13 April 2013 (2013). https://doi.org/10.1177/1046878113480867
13. Ulrich, M.: Gaming/Simulation for Policy Development and Organizational Change Games/Simulations About Environmental Issues Existing Tools and Underlying Concepts (1997). www.ucs.ch. Accessed 29 May 2021
14. Ulrich, M.: Gaming, the language to shape a sustainable future. A journey from 1974 to 2054. In: Back to the Future of Gaming (2014)
15. Abt, C.C.: Serious Games. University Press of America, New York (1970)
16. Marsh, T.: Serious games continuum: between games for purpose and experiential environments for purpose. Entertain. Comput. **2**(2), 61–68 (2011). https://doi.org/10.1016/J.ENTCOM.2010.12.004
17. Gerber, A., Ulrich, M., Wäger, P.: Review of haptic and computerized (simulation) games on climate change. In: Wardaszko, M., Meijer, S., Lukosch, H., Kanegae, H., Kriz, W.C., Grzybowska-Brzezińska, M. (eds.) ISAGA 2019. LNCS, vol. 11988, pp. 275–289. Springer, Cham (2021). https://doi.org/10.1007/978-3-030-72132-9_24

18. Roungas, B., Bekius, F., Meijer, S.: The game between game theory and gaming simulations: design choices. Simul. Gaming **50**(2), 180–201 (2019). https://doi.org/10.1177/104687811 9827625

19. Khatib, T., et al.: Development of DAYSAM: an educational smart phone game for preschoolers to increase awareness of renewable energy. Sustainability **13**(1), 433 (2021). https://doi.org/10.3390/su13010433

20. Li, H., Chabay, I., Renn, O., Weber, A., Mbungu, G.: Exploring smart grids with simulations in a mobile science exhibition. Energy Sustain. Soc. **5**(1), 1–8 (2015). https://doi.org/10.1186/s13705-015-0066-4

21. Ouariachi, T., Elving, W.: Accelerating the energy transition through serious gaming: testing effects on awareness, knowledge and efficacy beliefs. Electron. J. e-Learn. **18**(5) (2020). https://doi.org/10.34190/JEL.18.5.004

22. Prilenska, V.: Serious game for modelling neighbourhood energy supply scenarios. IOP Conf. Ser. Earth Environ. Sci. **410**, 012091 (2020). https://doi.org/10.1088/1755-1315/410/1/012091

23. Veeningen, J.W., Szirbik, N.B.: Using serious gaming to discover and understand distributed ledger technology in distributed energy systems. In: Moon, I., Lee, G.M., Park, J., Kiritsis, D., von Cieminski, G. (eds.) APMS 2018. IAICT, vol. 535, pp. 549–556. Springer, Cham (2018). https://doi.org/10.1007/978-3-319-99704-9_67

24. Ouariachi, T., Elving, W., Pierie, F.: Playing for a sustainable future: the case of we energy game as an educational practice. Sustainability **10**(10), 3639 (2018). https://doi.org/10.3390/su10103639

25. Forouzandehmehr, N., Han, Z., Zheng, R.: Stochastic dynamic game between hydropower plant and thermal power plant in smart grid networks. IEEE Syst. J. **10**(1), 88–96 (2016). https://doi.org/10.1109/JSYST.2014.2317555

26. O'Byrne, M., Endres, D., Feldpausch-Parker, A.M.: The Adventures of Carbon Bond: using a melodramatic game to explain CCS as a mitigation strategy for climate change. Greenh. Gases Sci. Technol. **3** (2012). 10.1002

27. Babonneau, F., Bahn, O., Haurie, A., Vielle, M.: An oligopoly game of CDR strategy deployment in a steady-state net-zero emission climate regime. Environ. Model. Assess. **26**(6), 969–984 (2020). https://doi.org/10.1007/s10666-020-09734-6

28. Zhao, T., Liu, Z.: A novel analysis of carbon capture and storage (CCS) technology adoption: an evolutionary game model between stakeholders. Energy **189**, 116352 (2019). https://doi.org/10.1016/j.energy.2019.116352

29. Dowd, A.-M., et al.: Developing an interactive survey game for informing opinions about CCS. Energy Proc. **37**, 7428–7435 (2013). https://doi.org/10.1016/j.egypro.2013.06.685

30. Menon, B.M., Unnikrishnan, R., Muir, A., Bhavani, R.R.: Serious game on recognizing categories of waste, to support a zero waste recycling program, June 2017. https://doi.org/10.1109/SeGAH.2017.7939292

31. Castellano, G., De Carolis, B., D'Errico, F., Macchiarulo, N., Rossano, V.: PeppeRecycle: improving children's attitude toward recycling by playing with a social robot. Int. J. Soc. Robot. **13**(1), 97–111 (2021). https://doi.org/10.1007/s12369-021-00754-0

32. van den Berg, M., Voordijk, H., Adriaanse, A., Hartmann, T.: Experiencing supply chain optimizations: a serious gaming approach. J. Constr. Eng. Manag. **143**(11), 04017082 (2017). https://doi.org/10.1061/(asce)co.1943-7862.0001388

33. Lee, Y.-S., Kim, S.-N.: Design of "TRASH TREASURE", a characters-based serious game for environmental education. In: de De Gloria, A., Veltkamp, R. (eds.) GALA 2015. LNCS, vol. 9599, pp. 471–479. Springer, Cham (2016). https://doi.org/10.1007/978-3-319-40216-1_52

34. Sreelakshmi, R., McLain, M.L., Rajeshwaran, A.: Gamification to Enhance Learning Using Gagne's Learning Model (2015)

35. Terelak-Tymczyna, A., Biniek, A., Nowak, M.: The Use of simulation games in teaching lean manufacturing. In: Hamrol, A., Kujawińska, A., Barraza, M. (eds.) MANUFACTURING 2019. LNME, pp. 358–369. Springer, Cham (2019). https://doi.org/10.1007/978-3-030-18789-7_30

36. González-Briones, A., et al.: GarbMAS: simulation of the application of gamification techniques to increase the amount of recycled waste through a multi-agent system. In: De La Prieta, F., Omatu, S., Fernández-Caballero, A. (eds.) DCAI 2018. AISC, vol. 800, pp. 332–343. Springer, Cham (2019). https://doi.org/10.1007/978-3-319-94649-8_40

37. Destyanto, A.R., Fajar, N.F., Ardi, R.: Serious simulation game design to support extensive understanding of closed-loop supply chain concept in e-waste management context. In: ACM International Conference Proceeding Series, September 2019, pp. 101–105. https://doi.org/10.1145/3364335.3364347

38. Bevilacqua, M., Ciarapica, F.E., Mazzuto, G., Paciarotti, C.: 'Cook & teach': learning by playing. J. Clean. Prod. **106**, 259–271 (2015). https://doi.org/10.1016/j.jclepro.2014.11.085

39. Nunes, E.P., Luz, A.R.: Mobile Serious Game Proposal for Environmental Awareness of Children (2016)

40. Havrez, C., Lepreux, S., Lebrun, Y., Haudegond, S., Ethuin, P., Kolski, C.: A design model for tangible interaction: case study in waste sorting. IFAC-PapersOnLine **49**(19), 373–378 (2016). https://doi.org/10.1016/j.ifacol.2016.10.594

41. Terpend, R., Shannon, P.: Teaching lean principles in nonmanufacturing settings using a computer equipment order quotation administrative process. Decis. Sci. J. Innov. Educ. **19**(1), 63–89 (2021). https://doi.org/10.1111/dsji.12227

42. Yeung, S.K., So, W.M.W., Cheng, N.Y.I., Cheung, T.Y., Chow, C.F.: Comparing pedagogies for plastic waste management at university level. Int. J. Sustain. High. Educ. **18**(7), 1039–1059 (2017). https://doi.org/10.1108/IJSHE-04-2016-0073

43. Vieira, E.L.: Signatures factory: a dynamic alternative for teaching - learning layout concepts and waste disposal. Production **27**(Special issue) (2017). https://doi.org/10.1590/0103-6513.221716

# Participatory Simulation Framework for Agent-Based Model Validation in Air Traffic Management

Bill Roungas[1](✉), Lucía Herrero Álvarez[2], and Sebastiaan Meijer[1]

[1] KTH Royal Institute of Technology, Stockholm, Sweden
{vasroung,smeijer}@kth.se
[2] Universidad Politécnica de Madrid, Madrid, Spain

**Abstract.** The EU Air Traffic Management (ATM) system is responsible for the safe and timely transportation of more than a billion passengers annually. It is a system that depends heavily on technology and is expected to stay on top of the technological advancements and be an early adopter of technologies. Technological change in ATM has historically developed at a slow pace. An agent-based model (ABM) of the ATM technology deployment cycle has been developed. This ABM is part of a larger project, which intends to recommend new policy measures for overcoming any barriers associated with technology adoption in ATM. In this paper, a participatory simulation framework validating this ABM is proposed. The aim of the framework is to be able to provide evidence for validation both in an agent level as well as in a system level.

**Keywords:** Belief-Desire-Intent architecture · Knowledge validation · Modeling assumptions · Technological upgrade · Tweaking

## 1 Introduction

Air Traffic Management (ATM) is an umbrella term used in aviation for describing all systems that enable an aircraft to depart from an airport, transit the airspace and eventually land at the destination airport. Particularly in EU, ATM as a system was responsible for the safe and timely transportation of more than one billion passengers in 2019. Despite the major disruption due to COVID-19 crisis, this is a figure that is expected to grow and consequently the demands for ATM will also grow. Despite depending heavily on technology, ATM is still required and expected to stay on top of the technological advancements and be an early adopter of technologies.

Nevertheless, technological change in ATM has historically developed at a slow pace. The demanding safety requirements, the coordination effort required to harmonise standards around the world, the interdependencies between ground and airborne technologies, the monopolistic nature of air navigation service provision and the relatively small size of the global ATM market compared to other technology markets are among

© Springer Nature Switzerland AG 2022
U. Dhar et al. (Eds.): ISAGA 2021, LNCS 13219, pp. 288–296, 2022.
https://doi.org/10.1007/978-3-031-09959-5_24

the reasons that explain why ATM technological modernisation has traditionally followed a slow, evolutionary path. In recent years, the need to accelerate ATM technological change has become more and more evident. The growing traffic demand and new market entrants, such as commercial drone applications, are rapidly pushing the ATM system to its limits, calling for disruptive solutions to boost the performance of ATM operations.

Emerging technologies, especially digitisation and automation, have the potential to facilitate this urgently needed technological upgrade. Technology evolution is a necessary but not sufficient condition; innovation is a complex phenomenon, which depends not only on the development of new technologies but also on the existence of regulation and institutions to facilitate and foster the implementation of such technologies. Therefore, decisions that affect ATM as a whole are not just influenced by the technical and economic factors but also by political, legal and social aspects [1].

To identify the factors that hinder technology adoption in ATM and to tackle them, an agent-based model (ABM) of the ATM technology deployment cycle has been developed [2]. As a modelling method, ABM offers several features that make it particularly interesting for the study of innovation processes such as the possibility to model agents' heterogeneity, the explicit representation of the agents' interactions, the possibility to endow the agents with non-rational behaviours and behavioural biases (such as loss aversion) and the ability to model learning processes, evolutionary behaviour and path dependence [3]. The novelty of the model stems from the fact that scarcely any references, and hence relevant work, were identified in the field of ABM in ATM technology diffusion. The organisational point of view at the stakeholders' level, the focus on policy testing and the inclusion of behavioural economics aspects separately do not represent a new contribution. It is the first time that such comprehensive approach is applied to the study of technology adoption by combining all these three aspects.

The ABM is focused on reproducing the mechanisms that drive the adoption and implementation of new ATM technologies. It includes a representation of all stakeholders identified as relevant for technology adoption in ATM such as air navigation service providers (ANSPs), airports, airlines, the network manager, aircraft manufacturers and ATM technology providers, labour unions and policy makers. The model represents the long-term evolution of the system (such as up to 2050), paying special attention to the coupling between slow and fast dynamics (to explain how the cumulative effect of the system performance on short timescales ends up triggering long-term decisions such as the decision to invest in new technologies) and building on and extending approaches [4]. As with all models, development is just one phase towards having a model that can effectively be used in real-world decision making. Validation is the next phase that gives credibility to the model's results.

The aim of this paper is to propose an ABM validation framework which includes a behavioural analysis of agents and a participatory simulation experiment. The analysis will examine the behaviour of actors in past and future scenarios. The participatory simulations will validate the model in an aggregated/system level and in an individual/agent level.

## 2 Background

ABM validation consists of 3 steps as following (Fig. 1):

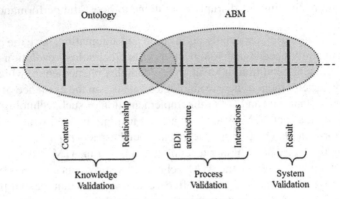

**Fig. 1.** Stages of ABM validation

1. Knowledge validation: Ontology is the first step for developing an ABM [5] with the agents, their attributes and relationships. Therefore, the validation of ABM starts with the validation of the ontology [6].
2. Process validation: The existing relationships between agents are not enough to define the interactions. Therefore, the attributes and interactions of agent behaviour must be modelled separately. At this stage, ABM agents mainly represent two components: behavioural attributes and interaction protocols.
3. System validation: The third stage of the validation follows traditional procedure. The performance indicators of models are validated with hypothesis (in case of synthetic data) or real world measurements of those indicators (in case of real data) [7].

ABM validation could benefit greatly from participatory methods where various quantitative methods can be and have been used with success as well.

### 2.1 Quantitative Methods

In a quantitative validation, the results of the ABM are analysed with empirical data where four aspects are considered: i. the nature of the object under study (qualitative or quantitative), ii. the goal of the analysis (such as descriptive, forecasting and policy analysis), iii. the modeling assumptions (such as size of the space of representation and time considerations), and iv. the sensitivity of the results to different criteria (such as initial conditions and micro/macro parameters) [8].

In ABM validation, traditional quantitative validation methods can be used such as the Temporal Variant - Invariant Analysis (TVIA) [9], the Analytical Hierarchy Process

[10], the Mean Square Error and Kappa Index of Agreement [11] and traditional statistical techniques [12]. On the other hand, validation frameworks specifically targeted at ABM have been proposed to provide an intuitive and comprehensive validation analysis like VOMAS [13] and VALFRAM [14].

## 2.2 Participatory Methods

Participatory simulations are an effective alternative to the more traditional methods [15] for gathering information about stakeholders, their interlocking behaviour, and their tacit knowledge [16]. Participants are placed in the dynamic environment of the ABM so that their decision making is intertwined with each other. By joining an agent-based simulation model with human participants, an environment is created using formal methods [17] where they make decisions based on underlying rules that are consistent and coherent [18]. Results from the application of participatory simulations in ABM validation have shown qualitative and quantitative agreement between the decision-making of agents and the players [19, 20].

In order to validate the behaviour of agents using participatory simulations, information about the representative participants' behavioural attributes is collected. An agent's decision-making mechanism follows the Belief-Desire-Intent architecture. An agent's belief is defined as the information it perceives about the state of the model's environment and represents the agent's perception of the current state of the system. The agent's desire is then represented as a desirable motivational state where desires are priorities for the agent's goals in different situations. Finally, the agent's intention is described as the final act that the agent performs based on the beliefs and desires at the particular stage of the system [21].

The schema for ABM validation using a participatory simulation is shown below (Fig. 2). The left side represents the typical process for developing the agent's behaviour in the ABM. The right side shows the process for collecting decision-making attributes from participants using the participatory simulation [20].

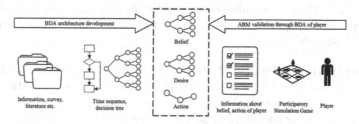

**Fig. 2.** ABM validation using participatory simulations

## 3 ABM Validation Framework

The framework consists of a behavioural analysis which covers the knowledge validation and partially the process validation and participatory simulations which complement the behavioural analysis by covering the remaining part of the process validation and the system validation. The validation of an ABM model occurs at two levels which coincide with the two parts of the framework, i.e. the behavioural analysis and the participatory simulations. The first level is behavioural analysis which validates the conceptual model. The second level is the participatory simulations which validates the operational model.

### 3.1 Behavioural Analysis

The aim of the behavioural analysis is to validate the conceptual model of the assumptions made by the modellers while building the ABM and the behavioural aspects embedded in the ABM. To gather data for conducting the behavioural analysis, interviews with experts in the field of ATM will be conducted. The questionnaire in the interview has four different stages:

1. Experts check the list of assumptions and in a semi-structured short discussion, they clarify whether they agree or not with them and why. Then, they are informed on the proposals with the new potential technologies to adopt in the ATM system.
2. Experts indicate their role and the agent they represent. Then, through a series of questions, they answer whether they would adopt each of the technologies proposed as well as questions related to the behavioural aspects of the ABM.
3. Experts are asked to rank the new technologies based on their probability to be accepted by other agents. Their objective is to capture the perspective of the agents of the other agents and the assumptions of considerations about the vision of the people involved in ATM.
4. Experts are asked whether they would change their answers knowing the answers of the rest of stakeholders, aiming to get greater insight into the social dimension.

### 3.2 Participatory Simulations

The participatory simulations will be used to validate the operational model which is the executable ABM. The aim of participatory simulations is to enable the validation of the ABM in an individual/agent level and in an aggregated/system level using both formal and informal methods.

**Formal and Informal Validation Methods.** The combination of formal and informal validation methods allows for a more holistic approach to validation since the shortcomings of the former can be mitigated by the advantages of the latter and vice versa. Formal methods have the major advantage of data-driven results from hard evidence and two significant disadvantages. Informal methods are human-driven, rely almost exclusively on experts' opinion and are considered equally powerful as formal methods.

The first disadvantage of formal methods is that validation can only be performed synchronously. To validate the model or a component of the model, the model or the component should first be built and later, all the necessary data should be gathered in order to run all the tests. This sequential process is time and resource intense and could cause unforeseen delays and expenses. This is where informal methods complement formal ones by using both synchronous and asynchronous validation. An informal method can be applied before, during and after the design and implementation of the model or the component of the model, enabling an iterative process where improvements can be identified and implemented in a timely efficient manner.

The second disadvantage is that formal methods can only validate what is already known. The application of a formal method for validation requires specific criteria that need to be defined beforehand which in turn means that if certain aspects of the model are not known during the design of the validation study, a formal method would fail. Informal methods can be very handy because of their human-driven nature which enables them to capture relationships that had not been identified and account for, them almost immediately. Therefore, informal methods enable the validation of models beyond the defined KPIs.

**Levels of Validation.** The participatory simulation is implemented in such a way as to allow for the validation to occur in two different levels, in an individual/agent level and in an aggregated/system level. To accomplish that, participants are able to play in two different ways:

- *Playing in the model:* Participants assume the role of agents in the model. This gameplay enables participants to actually play the role of an agent who is relevant to their experience, thus allowing for the validation of the agents' behaviour (individual/agent level).
- *Playing with the model:* Participants tweak the parameters of the model. This gameplay enables participants to play around with the model changing parameters not necessarily directly related to their expertise, thus allowing for the validation of the model as a whole (aggregated/system level).

In both gameplays, it is important for designers and decision makers to have two questions in mind:

1. What are the questions we need to answer now?
2. What are the decisions that need to be made?

Keeping track of these questions would enable to always know what is needed from any game session.

**Modes of Play.** The participatory simulation which is in the form of a game is developed online with the capability of interacting with the ABM. The game has two modes of play both of which can accommodate the validation of the ABM in both levels, i.e. agent and system as described above. The two modes of play are single-player and multi-player.

*Playing in the model* in the single-player mode allows one participant to take over an agent while the remaining agents are run by the model itself. Playing with the model in the single-player mode allows the participant to tweak the parameters of the model in order to see the model reaction. In the multi-player mode, many participants take over several or even all agents.

*Playing with the model* in the multi-player mode allows many participants to tweak parameters in the model at the same time, although this is very challenging. While it seems more realistic and intuitive to have only a multi-player mode for the many agents of the ABM, it comes with certain challenges that the single-player mode can overcome. The challenges of having all agents or even several of them played by human participants at the same time are the following:

1. It is a logistical nightmare to coordinate 10+ very busy professionals to participate at the same time. The single-player mode allows them to play at their own time when it is convenient for them.
2. Given that it is very difficult to coordinate many participants at the same time, the best case scenario would be to conduct two or three game sessions with each having five or six variations. This would result in a maximum of 20 distinct exercises, which although not entirely bad, is still weak with regards to establishing statistical significance.
3. *Playing with the model* with many players tweaking more than a few parameters at the same time would most probably yield results very difficult to analyse. It would be very challenging to interpret the effects of tweaking a certain parameter for 10 or even more parameters. The concept of tweaking a single parameter in order to observe its effects to the whole is known in economics as ceteris paribus and the single-player mode could in several occasions accomplish it.
4. From the design and implementation point of view, it is much more complicated and time consuming to build an interface for a multi-player game. When a player tweaks one parameter or takes any action within the game, the change of state should be immediately communicated to the other players, which is one of the most challenging tasks in to software development.

## 4 Conclusion and Future Work

In this paper, a participatory simulation framework was defined for the validation of an agent-based model (ABM) in air traffic management (ATM). The framework consists of two parts; the first part is the behavioural analysis of agents and the second part is a participatory simulation experiment. The behavioural analysis examines the behaviour of actors in past and future scenarios, whereas the participatory simulations validate the ABM in an individual/agent level and an aggregated/system level. The participatory simulations are in the form of a game and are played with two options, playing in the model and playing with the model. The game can be played in both single and multi-player mode, with an emphasis on the former due to its several advantages. The work presented in this paper is just the first step towards a comprehensive participatory simulation framework for ABM validation, not just in ATM but in various other fields as well.

# References

1. Zeki, E.: Assessing technology adoption in the European Air Traffic Management: the cases of virtual centre and flight-centric operations. Ph.D. École Polytechnique F´ed´erale de Lausanne (2020)
2. Roungas, B., Baena, M., Ros, O.G.C., Alcolea, R., Herranz, R., Raghothama, J.: Technology adoption in air traffic management: a combination of agent-based modeling with behavioral economics. In: Kim, S., et al. (eds.) 2021 Winter Simulation Conference. Phoenix, AZ, USA (2021)
3. Zhang, H., Vorobeychik, Y.: Empirically grounded agent-based models of innovation diffusion: a critical review. Artif. Intell. Rev. **52**(1), 707–741 (2017). https://doi.org/10.1007/s10 462-017-9577-z
4. Torres, J., Toribio, D., Marcos, R., Cantú Ros, O.G., Herranz, R.: An agent-based auction model for the analysis of the introduction of competition in ATM. In: Schaefer, D. (ed.) Proceedings of the 7th SESAR Innovation Days 2015. Belgrade, Serbia (2017)
5. van Dam, K.H., Lukszo, Z.: Modelling energy and transport infrastructures as a multi-agent system using a generic ontology. In: 2006 IEEE International Conference on Systems, Man and Cybernetics, vol. 1, pp. 890–895. IEEE (2006)
6. Banks, J.: Handbook of Simulation: Principles, Methodology, Advances, Applications, and Practice. John Wiley & Sons, Hoboken (1998)
7. Sargent, R.G.: Verification and validation of simulation models. In: Proceedings of the 2010 Winter Simulation Conference, pp. 166–183. IEEE (2010)
8. Windrum, P., Fagiolo, G., Moneta, A.: Empirical validation of agent-based models: alternatives and prospects. J. Artif. Soc. Soc. Simul. **10**(2), 8 (2007)
9. Bone, C., Johnson, B., Nielsen-Pincus, M., Sproles, E., Bolte, J.: A temporal variant-invariant validation approach for agent-based models of landscape dynamics. Trans. GIS **18**(2), 161–182 (2014). https://doi.org/10.1111/tgis.12016
10. Saaty, T.: How to make a decision: the analytic hierarchy process. Eur. J. Oper. Res. **48**(1), 9–26 (1990)
11. Krebs, F.: An empirically grounded model of green electricity adoption in Germany: calibration, validation and insights into patterns of diffusion. J. Artif. Soc. Soc. Simul. **20**(2) (2017)
12. Roungas, B., Meijer, S.A., Verbraeck, A.: A framework for optimizing simulation model validation & verification. Int. J. Adv. Syst. Measur. **11**(1 & 2), 137–152 (2018)
13. Niazi, M.A., Hussain, A., Kolberg, M.: Verification & validation of agent based simulations using the VOMAS (virtual overlay multi-agent system) approach. arXiv preprint arXiv:1708. 02361 (2017)
14. Drchal, J., Čertickỳ, M., Jakob, M.: VALFRAM: validation framework for activity-based models. J. Artif. Soc. Soc. Simul. **19**(3) (2016)
15. Roungas, B., Meijer, S.A., Verbraeck, A.: The future of contextual knowledge in gaming simulations: A research agenda. In: Rabe, M., Juan, A.A., Mustafee, N., Skoogh, A., Jain, S., Johansson, B. (eds.) Proceedings of the 2018 Winter Simulation Conference, pp. 2435–2446. IEEE, Gothenburg (2018). https://doi.org/10.1109/WSC.2018.8632377
16. Roungas, B., Lo, J.C., Angeletti, R., Meijer, S., Verbraeck, A.: Eliciting requirements of a knowledge management system for gaming in an organization: the role of tacit knowledge. In: Hamada, R., et al. (eds.) Neo-Simulation and Gaming Toward Active Learning. Translational Systems Sciences, vol. 18, pp. 347–354. Springer, Singapore (2019). https://doi.org/10.1007/ 978-981-13-8039-6_32
17. Roungas, B., Bekius, F., Meijer, S., Verbraeck, A.: Improving the decision-making qualities of gaming simulations. J. Simul. 1–14 (2020). https://doi.org/10.1080/17477778.2020.172 6218

18. Colella, V.: Participatory simulations: building collaborative understanding through immersive dynamic modeling. J. Learn. Sci. **9**(4), 471–500 (2000)
19. Nguyen-Duc, M., Drogoul, A.: Using computational agents to design participatory social simulations. J. Artif. Soc. Soc. Simul. **10**(4), 5 (2007)
20. Anand, N., Meijer, D., Van Duin, J.H.R., Tavasszy, L., Meijer, S.: Validation of an agent based model using a participatory simulation gaming approach: the case of city logistics. Transp. Res. Part C: Emerg. Technol. **71**, 489–499 (2016)
21. Rao, A.S., Georgeff, M.P.: BDI agents: from theory to practice. In: ICMAS, vol. 95, pp. 312–319 (1995)

# Author Index

Printed in the United States
by Baker & Taylor Publisher Services